THE STRAIGHT LINE

THE STRAIGHT LINE

How the Fringe Science of
Ex-Gay Therapy Reoriented Sexuality

TOM WAIDZUNAS

University of Minnesota Press
Minneapolis | London

Portions of the Introduction were previously published as Tom J. Waidzunas, "Intellectual Opportunity Structures and Science-Targeted Activism: Influence of the Ex-Gay Movement on the Science of Sexual Orientation," *Mobilization: An International Journal* 18, no. 1 (2013): 1–18; reprinted with permission of *Mobilization: An International Journal.*

Published by the University of Minnesota Press
111 Third Avenue South, Suite 290
Minneapolis, MN 55401-2520
http://www.upress.umn.edu

Library of Congress Cataloging-in-Publication Data
Waidzunas, Tom, author.
    The straight line : how the fringe science of ex-gay therapy reoriented sexuality / Tom Waidzunas.
    Includes bibliographical references and index.
    ISBN 978-0-8166-9614-7 (hc)—ISBN 978-0-8166-9615-4 (pb)
    1. Sexual reorientation programs—United States—History. 2. Ex-gay movement—United States—History. 3. Homosexuality—United States—History. 4. Gays—United States—History. I. Title.
    HQ76.3.U5W35 2015
    306.76'60973—dc23   2015026526

Printed on acid-free paper

The University of Minnesota is an equal-opportunity educator and employer.

*For all people who have ever struggled
with conflict over sexual orientation*

CONTENTS

introduction

THE SHIFTING STRAIGHT LINE

The waiting room of the Thomas Aquinas Psychological Clinic seems like that of many other mental health facilities in the United States. The decor is calming, and magazines and comfortable seating are provided. A cordial receptionist sits at a window where clients sign in. Despite the rather ordinary and professional character of the office, the therapeutic work done at this facility has attracted much heated protest and scientific condemnation. Here in Encino, California, Dr. Joseph Nicolosi and his colleagues perform "reparative therapy" with men seeking to rid themselves of "unwanted same-sex attractions" and unleash their "heterosexual potential." Nicolosi, author of books on the treatment and prevention of homosexuality, is white, heterosexual, of middle age and Catholic faith, and has an animated speaking style.[1] A leader in the reorientation world, he exudes confidence despite fervent opposition by all mainstream mental health organizations in the United States, which have discredited sexual orientation change attempts as ineffective and potentially harmful. Back in 1992, Nicolosi helped found the organization NARTH, the National Association for Research and Therapy of Homosexuality, which acts as the leading science-engaged organization within the predominantly religious ex-gay movement in the United States. Despite the professional marginalization of reorientation practices, Nicolosi's website notes his many public media appearances, including The *Oprah Winfrey Show*, *Dr. Phil*, Dr. James Dobson's *Focus on the Family* radio show, the "Dr. Drew" show, and BBC News, signifying his continuing influence in U.S. culture.[2]

In 2009 I visited the Aquinas Clinic to learn more about this particular facet of the ex-gay world. Reparative therapy at this treatment center primarily consists of talk therapy, in addition to group sessions. I had

1

met Nicolosi at a NARTH conference in Dallas a couple of years prior. He declined a personal interview with me but referred me instead to his protégé, David Pickup, also a licensed professional mental health counselor. Unlike Nicolosi, Pickup had once been gay, but claims a personal transformation to heterosexuality, which he attributes to successful reparative therapy.[3] Because Pickup's own life story stands as testimony to the efficacy of the therapy practiced at the Aquinas Clinic, this is a likely reason why Nicolosi wanted me to talk with him.

Mainstream science has discredited reorientation therapies, yet many ex-gay activists like Pickup have personally testified that they have been changed from gay to straight as a result of such treatments. On what basis could mainstream mental health organizations dismiss these therapies, when so many efficacy studies in mental health, including research on pharmacological and talk therapies, are based on clients' reports of transformation? Why are reorientation therapies rejected when treatment professionals uphold values of client autonomy and self-determination in their ethics codes? This book takes up such questions, examining how struggles over reorientation therapies for homosexuality have, over the years, been redirected into technical disputes over how to measure sexual orientation and other outcomes in scientific research. These struggles have been deeply interwoven with ethical concerns, as the very existence of reorientation therapies and ex-gay ministries are taken by many to devalue gay and lesbian identities and ways of life. Given these stakes, debates about reorientation have been entangled with gay rights policy concerns. Discussions of reparative therapies and conversion programs may seem divided in the public arena, but within science, these practices have been firmly relegated to the fringe, cast alongside astrology, ufology, and paranormal psychology. But if personal testimony of change is insufficient proof that a formerly gay person has become "straight" through therapeutic alteration, then what kinds of evidence could ex-gay therapists and their clients provide to meet the necessary criteria? In *The Straight Line*, I explore how scientists in the mainstream have approached these challenging questions. I also examine the effects that the ex-gay movement's science-targeted activism has had for shaping scientific understandings of what human sexualities are at their core.

To learn more about techniques at the Aquinas Clinic, I sat down in the reparative therapy clients' chair. While Pickup sat in his therapist's chair, I noticed that next to him under a small end table, a video camera was pointed toward me and connected to a monitor. This equipment was turned off, but as I heard at the NARTH conference, men in therapy ordinarily view themselves on-screen as a form of biofeedback when they talk about their lives and their same-sex attractions. If a client begins to slouch, it is understood that he is feeling "gender shame"—a sense of insufficient masculinity prompted by something that has happened in his past or in the course of the discussion. During such moments, he is believed to be in danger of slipping into a "homosexual enactment" phase, a state of vulnerability for seeking out gay sex. As he and his therapist identify these postures on the monitor, he becomes aware of the feelings of shame, sits up straight again, and reenters an "assertion" phase as part of ushering in his heterosexuality. Through discovering triggers of emasculation from family problems and other social issues, Pickup believes these techniques have become increasingly effective. He stated in the interview:

> Reparative therapy has gotten so laser-like and pinpointed on the issues that it's become much more successful, we've noticed in the last five years. . . . We noticed that men, when we're going deep enough to address their wounding, gender identity shame, and male emotional needs, when they go through that kind of process of reparative therapy in which there is grief felt, then a natural state of assertion, and a greater sense of masculinity comes up within them—that process ultimately lets the homosexual need dissipate.[4]

The "male emotional needs" to which Pickup refers include nonsexual same-sex bonding that men allegedly naturally require—needs that become sexualized due to alienation from other men. Once these needs are addressed, therapists in this organization strongly believe sexual orientation can be changed at a deep level. They also believe that heterosexual desires exist deep in the nature of every gay and lesbian person, but they are occluded. Above all, NARTH has promoted the idea that homosexuality is not an inborn trait but a problem that can be overcome through addressing doubts about gender. These doubts are allegedly caused by a range of factors, including sexual abuse, overbearing mothers and distant fathers, shaming by peers, and negative experiences pursuing heterosexuality.

Despite Pickup's confidence, the years following this interview were particularly devastating for the ex-gay movement in the United States. NARTH is still operational, but its leading religious counterpart and the most visible organization for ex-gays, Exodus International, folded in 2013. The relationship between these two organizations had been one of a division of labor for many years, as Exodus utilized spiritual approaches to leaving homosexuality while NARTH attended to more secular ones. Yet over time, Exodus president Alan Chambers and other religious leaders became skeptical of the prioritization and the possibility of changing same-sex attractions, emphasizing salvation instead.[5] The rift became sizable, and Exodus closed its doors.[6] Furthermore, in the wake of a 2009 American Psychological Association report declaring reorientation attempts potentially harmful, two states, New Jersey and California, have banned reorientation therapy for minors, and other states are considering similar legislation. Yet, the remnants of the ex-gay movement, including NARTH, have regrouped into the "Restored Hope Network."

At the same time as reparative therapists were being further marginalized in science and policy arenas, a new compromise was negotiated in the American Psychological Association that accommodated some moderate forms of conversion. The widely publicized report published in 2009 by the APA, *Appropriate Therapeutic Responses to Sexual Orientation,* included a therapeutic guideline called "sexual orientation identity exploration." According to this principle, when a client struggles with conflict between same-sex attractions and religious beliefs, a therapist should defer to a client's chosen identity, whether it be straight, bisexual, gay, nonidentifying, or something else, as long as the client and therapist acknowledge that sexual orientation, defined as attractions, is unlikely ever to change. This compromise came about with the realization that religious identity and connection to one's religious community may be more important to an individual than his or her sexual orientation. In those cases, the client and therapist must not be guided by anti-gay stereotypes, understanding that being gay does not mean one cannot have a family or play other social roles. Instead, a client might choose to live with a heterosexual identity in alignment with religious views, and a therapist might guide the client in this process, both realizing that attraction patterns will not change. Although some religious ex-gay groups welcomed this compromise, NARTH rejected it, and the organization continued to promote the possibility of full sexual reorientation even at the level of attractions. Behavior and identity might be malleable, but the newly established scientific truth of sexual orientation, existing at the deep level of physiology, was understood to be fixed.

The notion frequently espoused by NARTH members that homosexuality is caused by a deficit in gender identification is an old idea that was actually once scientific orthodoxy, but has been discredited in mainstream science. International health organizations including the World Health Organization, and national mental health associations in the United States now describe gay, lesbian, and bisexual orientations as "normal variants" of human sexuality, definitely not in need of any kind

Reparative therapist David Pickup testifies before members of the California legislature in 2012 to prevent passage of the bill that banned reorientation therapy for minors. AP Images/Rich Pedroncelli.

of therapeutic cure and generally unrelated to forms of gender variance. The idea that psychological deviation from traditional gender roles is associated with same-sex sexuality can be traced to ideas about "inversion" that emerged in the late nineteenth century, when scientists in the new field of sexology described homosexuality as characteristic of a "third" sex.[7] Many sexual reorientation therapies, which became popular in the 1950s and 1960s in the United States, draw on these concepts. Moreover, it has long been a common trope of anti-gay stereotypes to assume that gay men are excessively feminine, and lesbians are excessively masculine, effectively conflating gender and sexuality. Today, within sexual reorientation therapy groups and ex-gay religious ministries, such notions continue to form a large component of the underlying ideology given that homosexuality and gender variance are often considered to be part of the same pathology. While this movement may conflate these issues, in this book I primarily examine conflicts over the treatment of same-sex attraction; other scholars have examined struggles over medical knowledge in relation to transgender and intersex persons.[8]

Even though reorientation has been cast to the scientific fringe, many gay affirmative perspectives in mainstream science today can be understood as responses to reorientation's long legacy and perceived contemporary threat. Although people experiencing same-sex attractions may choose to undergo such therapies, there is a remembered history of legally coerced and often physically and psychologically invasive and painful treatments, especially occurring prior to the removal of "Homosexuality" from the list of mental disorders in 1973. Many gay and lesbian people recall stories of electric shock aversion therapies and even lobotomies. Mainstream scientific ideas about the nature of sexual orientation are, in part, responses to this oppressive past, and continue to be developed in a context in which the idea that gays and lesbians can be reoriented has tremendous real and potential consequences for individual lives and for public policy. In the United States, there is an alignment between opposition to gay rights and the view that homosexuality is a chosen behavior that can be unchosen. Conversely, those who believe homosexuality is innate and unchangeable tend to support gay rights policy.[9] NARTH members, representing themselves as experts on the science of homosexuality, have testified along with religious ex-gay leaders at judicial hearings and legislatures in opposition to gay rights measures. Meanwhile, the American Psychological Association and other mainstream mental health professional groups have supported gays in policy arenas, declaring that homosexuality is a "normal variant" of human sexuality, and that depriving gay people of rights can have deleterious mental health consequences. Thus, in the United States, debates about gay rights are simultaneously debates about the nature of human sexuality itself.

Within this context, the American Psychological Association, American Psychiatric Association, American Academy of Pediatrics, National Association of Social Workers, American Counseling Association, and American Psychoanalytic Association have all taken firm stands against programs claiming that sexual orientation can be therapeutically altered, and especially against programs and camps to which youth may be taken against their will.[10] The report published by the American Psychological Association in 2009 definitively stated that that there is "no evidence for the efficacy" of sexual orientation change efforts, and such attempts are "potentially harmful."[11] Professional opponents of reorientation have observed that the assumptions built into these therapies devalue homosexuality and reify stereotypical notions of what it means to be a man or woman. According to this critique, the work of the Thomas Aquinas Psychological Clinic, which equates same-sex desire with gender inadequacy, threatens to render unthinkable any notion that homosexual identity, behavior, or attractions might be sources of dignity for men. Defining male heterosexuality as a form of assertion and an expression of healthy masculinity continues to rely on the trope of the feminized gay man, dominated by the good, dignified, and masculine heterosexual male. It also relies on patriarchal ideas of gender, in which weakness and vulnerability are relegated to the domain of the feminine.

Alongside the criticisms launched by mainstream professionals, former reorientation clients have also come forward to claim that reorientation interventions not only often fail but also have deeply harmful consequences. For example, Daniel Gonzales, a former client of Nicolosi and an outspoken anti-reorientation activist, describes how reparative therapy did not change his sexual orientation, and because insurance would not pay for the therapy, he lost thousands of dollars in addition to losing his religious faith during his change attempts.[12] Gonzales is not alone. Beyond Ex-Gay was founded in 2007 as a national ex-gay survivors' organization. This group is made up of people who attempted reorientation through secular therapies and/or religious ministries, say that the attempt to change sexual orientation failed, and often claim they experienced some kind of harm. Personal damages might include excessive shame, emotional harm, depression, suicide attempts, and reinforced self-hate.[13] Peterson Toscano, cofounder of Beyond Ex-Gay, explained in an interview that recovery from reorientation treatment may require a complicated process of disentangling a false causal chain: because traumatic events in one's past may have been falsely named in reorientation treatments as causes of homosexuality, healing from these therapies requires accepting homosexuality while dealing with traumatic events directly, learning to comprehend their actual effects.[14]

Given the high stakes of these debates from national politics all the way down to individual lives, the concept of "sexual orientation" in the United States research community has been more than just an issue of scientific curiosity. Many consequences hang in the balance regarding who does and does not get to be considered a full citizen with all the benefits of social inclusion and the dangers of exclusion. Within science, the definition of "sexual orientation," how to measure this entity, and what exactly constitutes good "evidence" of a person's sexual orientation have all become matters of concern. With the phrase "the shifting straight line" in the title of this introduction, I am referring to the ways in which mainstream science has set the standards of proof that are required to truly accept reorientation clients as "straight," and how this line has changed over time.[15] When reorientation was in its prime, this "straight line" was once seen as crossable, but now, the line has been placed out of reach, and this has been a key means for relegating reorientation to the scientific fringe. Despite being marginalized in science, the professional therapists and researchers in the ex-gay movement have still engaged in performances of scientific expertise, providing expert testimony in court cases, producing a journal, holding conferences, and highlighting their professional credentials. Ambiguous declarations of the possibility of "change" effectively blur boundaries between "straight" and "gay." In contrast, gay-affirmative scientists have worked hard to shore up the boundaries of "straight." Thus, as a by-product of these struggles, the encounter between the ex-gay movement and mainstream science has effectively consolidated particular scientific understandings of what it means to be a sexual person.

The philosopher Ian Hacking has used the phrase "making up people" to describe the ways that science can define and deploy categories and associated measurements to constitute different ways of being human, in this case, "gay," "straight," or "ex-gay."[16] Rather than simply describing the realities of human life, science provides authoritative cultural material that we may use for developing our own definitions of selfhood. While science may compete with other ways of knowing, such as theology, it has gained immense authority in a wide range of domains of human life in the United States. Sociologist Anthony Giddens has asserted that in late modernity, science plays a crucial role in the construction of our sexual selves in the West, including notions of what it means to be sexually fulfilled, leading us to draw on scientific information to develop more satisfying relationships.[17]

The relegation of reorientation practices to the scientific fringe was not an inevitable process; moving these ideas from the mainstream to the margins of science has required a tremendous amount of work. A key first step was removing the diagnosis "Homosexuality" from the official list of mental disorders in the early 1970s. The ex-gay movement formed soon afterward, but keeping the movement out of the mainstream has required limiting opportunities for reorientation proponents to advance their ideas. In this book, I use the concept "intellectual opportunity structure" to describe those features of scientific and other knowledge-producing institutions that enable and constrain social movements in their intellectual endeavors. Such institutional features include ethics codes and official position statements that block and at times enable movements trying to shape scientific knowledge. Looking at scientific knowledge of the nature of "sexual orientation" as the outcome of struggles for scientific credibility, I highlight the ways in which historical context, different professionals seeking to define the issue, and opposing social movements have all shaped scientific understandings of this concept. And measurement practices have been key. Whether scientists take the authority of the psychoanalyst's assessment, the physiological measurement instrument, or the self-report of the reorientation client to be definitive evidence of sexual orientation change has mattered in terms of whether these practices of sexual orientation change attempts have been considered "efficacious." I argue that definitions and measurements of "sexual orientation" emanating from these debates are not simply transparent representations of nature, but rather, they constitute socially negotiated sexual subjectivities that have emerged historically.

In struggles over reorientation therapy in the United States, the story of the definition and redefinition of sexual orientation has been a process in which a scientific concept rooted in sexual behavior has been supplanted by one based on attraction, and these sexual attractions are thought by many to be best known through physiological testing. But as the "straight line" has been set by scientists in ways that may benefit gay rights policy in recent years, it has ironic consequences that limit forms of sexual expression. While reorientation therapists may promote the correction of fluid sexual desire that they believe has gone astray, the response from mainstream science has been to promote a view of fixed and immutable sexual orientations, especially for men, and this idea shores up a widespread gay/straight dichotomy. However, as the case of Uganda illustrates in the last chapter of this book, the attraction-based definition is vulnerable to being replaced by one based primarily on behavior, with dangerous consequences for LGBT-identified persons. Thus, scientific decisions in this area can shape how we understand the very nature of human sexuality and have cultural impacts beyond the lives of people attempting reorientation treatments.

To date, sociological literature that examines the ex-gay movement treats it primarily as a religious phenomenon.[18] However, we need to take seriously the ways in which the ex-gay movement, in addition to the gay rights movement, has engaged with scientific institutions, and the effects of this activism on scientific knowledge. This includes considering not only NARTH members but also researchers working with the more religious wing of the movement, who have produced research based on the self-reports of ex-gays undergoing religiously mediated change efforts. Moreover, as the ex-gay movement has become part of a transnational network, it is important to understand its prominence in some places around the world where gay rights are not taken seriously. In the final chapter of this book, I explore these transnational connections with a focus on Uganda and that nation's passage in 2014 of the Anti-Homosexuality Act, assessing the role of reorientation groups and ideas in the events that led up to that law.

Opposing Social Movements Targeting Science

In many ways, ex-gay activists, like their gay rights counterparts, comprise a social movement in a classic sociological sense. Social movements can be defined as "collective challenges, based on common purposes and social solidarities, in sustained interaction with elites, opponents, and authorities."[19] Ex-gay groups have indeed cohered as a collective, sustained movement, united in their purpose of leading people out of homosexuality, and, over time, they have been engaged with science and the state. It is noteworthy that a social movement must be sustained over time—a single protest event is insufficient. Cohesion necessitates the development of a collective identity—a sense of "we" as opposed to "them"—that creates an insider/outsider boundary.[20] In advocating for opposition to gay marriage and opposing other gay rights policies on the grounds that gays can be changed, ex-gay activists and the broader religious right certainly have targeted authorities in the state. Yet scholars have pointed out that the state, while a classic target for social movements, is not the only locus of societal power that interests activists. A "multi-institutional framework" is needed to see that movements are engaged with other institutions beyond the state, including science.[21]

At the same time, ex-gay groups have taken on a much more diffuse form. Movements engaged with what sociologist Nancy Whittier calls "therapeutic politics" can have a more hybrid organization beyond the traditional network of social movement organizations.[22] Certainly the ex-gay movement has engaged in organized protest, but more frequently its interventions have been at the level of therapist and client, or ministry leader and follower, shaping the inner feelings of its members and encouraging the wider public to have a different view of what kinds of changes in feeling and identity are possible. Beyond the individual working with a therapist, therapeutic politics in this case takes forms of religious youth camps designed for reorienting sexual orientations, live-in reorientation camps for adults, weekend retreats in the woods designed for ex-gay men to help each other "heal" from gender wounding, and conferences held by religious ministries in which attendees break into sex-segregated sessions for group sharing and mentoring. Advertisements for these interventions not only recruit participants but also attempt to educate the public that homosexuality is not necessarily a basis for identity, nor is it necessarily a basis for rights. Researchers have worked with participants in these groups to build evidence that sexual orientations can change, in efforts to shape public opinion as well as scientific facts. In this sense, the ex-gay movement exhibits hybridity in its tactics and approaches, from interventions designed to affect science and the state to efforts to change individuals and cultural understandings.

In the United States, the demographics of the ex-gay movement have been predominantly white, male, and Christian. There have been more women involved, especially over the past decade, but reorientation therapy theories and practices have tended to focus on changing men, with most consumers being male. While there is a Jewish organization, Jews Offering New Alternatives to Homosexuality (JONAH), and Catholic groups, such as Courage International, the evangelical Christian version has been largest. Some activists have called NARTH merely a "scientific front" for religion.[23] However, I take seriously the ways in which the ex-gay movement, along with the gay rights movement, has been seriously engaged with scientific institutions, and I examine the palpable impact these movements have had on scientific knowledge about "sexual orientation." NARTH comprises a large segment of what I call the ex-gay movement's "science-oriented wing." Organizations like the former Exodus International and many within the newly formed Restored Hope Network promote a religious approach to reorientation, with an emphasis placed on salvation. The religion- and science-oriented wings of the movement have often worked with a peaceful division of labor, as

NARTH therapists addressed sexual feelings and religious leaders addressed spiritual needs. Although tension between these wings has been acute at times, culminating in the folding of Exodus International, the remaining religious groups in the Restored Hope Network now appear to work harmoniously with NARTH.

Social movements targeting science, and especially the medical sciences, often fall into the category of "patient groups and health movements."[24] The concerns of these groups vary along many dimensions. Some health movements may be interested in getting health care for a particular constituency, such as women or the poor. Others may be concerned with obtaining resources for a particular illness. Alternately, such movements are often concerned with the very definitions of health and illness. Some health movements may be seeking demedicalization, or the removal of a diagnosis from an official list of disorders, such as the gay liberation movement in the 1970s. Other groups concerned with definitions may seek medicalization, such as the ex-gay movement of the 1980s and early 1990s, which fought to redefine homosexuality as a medical condition.[25] Patient movements may also seek medicalization for legitimation. For example, in the early years of the establishment of the homosexuality diagnosis, some homosexual activists actually welcomed this as an alternative to criminalization.[26] In this book, I treat both the ex-gay and gay rights movements as health movements insofar as they target mental health institutions and are concerned with shaping treatments and definitions of health and pathology.

Rather than being composed of actors with the same backgrounds, many health movements bring professionals together with laypeople, leading to an exchange and coordination of experience and skills. In the case of the ex-gay movement, ex-gays who make claims about their own changed sexuality have worked with researchers with the technical expertise to transform personal stories into data that can be statistically analyzed and presented as research findings. Bringing these forms of expertise together has advanced the movement's cause through the publication of a few large self-report research studies, sometimes with hundreds of participants, thereby purportedly demonstrating the efficacy of reorientation. As such, the movement exhibits a hybrid "partnership" in terms of expertise.[27]

In addition to treating the ex-gay movement as seriously engaged with science, I also take into account the complex back-and-forth dynamics of the ex-gay and gay rights groups acting as "opposing social movements." When opposing movements share a common target, they work not only to shape particular outcomes but also to undermine each other's efforts.

Sociologists have shown that when opposing social movements both target the state, such situations can produce complicated dynamics.[28] I extend this research to examine how such dynamics unfold when both movements simultaneously target knowledge-producing institutions. Sociologists have documented a range of these kinds of dynamics in cases of state-targeted activism. The broader political conditions may sustain or exacerbate such conflict. For example, a divided governmental authority can encourage opposing groups to fight one another. It is important in the reorientation debate to consider that when the mass media seek coverage of "both sides" of an issue to depict it as controversial, even if that issue is settled among mainstream scientists or public officials, it can provide fertile ground to sustain opposing movements in conflict. Also, when it is challenging a stronger movement, a weaker movement often will seize upon a "critical event"—some kind of monumental, often unexpected, event that is created by the government, chance, or the movement itself.

In this model, if one movement experiences a defeat in some respect, it may shift venues and attempt another strategy. Once a movement has shifted to another venue, then its opponent must respond, often requiring the diversion of precious resources. For example, when religious right groups funded advertisements promoting the ex-gay movement in the late 1990s in an effort to undermine gay identity, gay rights organizations were forced to shift venues to these kinds of media campaigns and respond in turn. Because of such frequent venue shifting, activists with opponents must often be nimble in their tactical decisions.[29]

Cultural theories are also important for understanding opposing social movement dynamics. The way in which activists define reality through rhetoric has been described in terms of "frames," definitions of the situation, which emphasize some aspects of reality rather than others.[30] Movements deploy "collective action frames," making meaning in ways that enroll supporters and influence targets.[31] When there is an opposing social movement, which is deploying alternative rhetoric, dynamics of framing and counterframing can take various forms. For example, the gay rights and religious right movements, when trying to influence sex education programs in schools, often talked past each other because their messages were articulated in different registers. Spokespersons for gay rights framed sex education as a civil rights issue, whereas conservative Christians talked in terms of societal morality.[32] In an alternate case, the pro-life and pro-choice movements converged on the concept of "partial birth abortion," a term that did not exist prior to the dynamic of "dialogical framing." While opposing movements attached different meanings to this term, the concept itself emerged out of these back-and-forth processes.[33] Finally, a shift in one movement's framing can shape the messaging and tone of the other. When Anita Bryant's "Save Our Children" campaign alleged that gays were recruiting minors in the 1970s, the gay rights movement shifted from a tone of inclusiveness to one of angry "us versus them" rhetoric, framing gays as an oppressed minority.[34]

While opposing movements engage in these framing challenges, it is not uncommon for there to be "frame disputes" within a social movement itself.[35] Activists fighting for the same cause may still have differences in the definition of a situation with different versions of reality, different diagnoses of social problems, and different proposed solutions to these problems. A frame dispute may benefit a movement if it can be managed, but it can also have disastrous results. On the one hand, if a frame dispute can exist without being disruptive to the operations of the movement, it might enable different factions to work together, attracting a broader range of members with different understandings. During the 1990s and early 2000s, the ex-gay movement seemed to function this way, as secular reorientation therapists, who understood the need for sexual orientation change as the ultimate goal for ex-gays, worked in a peaceful division of labor with leaders of religious ex-gay ministries, who saw salvation as the most important goal. On the other hand, a frame dispute can become a serious rift if something exacerbates that conflict, or in times of high pressure. In the case of the ex-gay movement, increased pressure to define the meaning of "change" made this dispute devastating for the movement, causing a major rift and the folding of Exodus International and other religious ministries.

Social movement theorists have also developed a number of tools to describe the various tactics and strategies that movements undertake. The term "repertoires of contention" has been used to describe the tactics of protest that become expected from activists.[36] The ex-gay movement has typically utilized public personal testimony. Such repertoires may be derived from previous social movements in what has been called "social movement spillover," or the borrowing of other movements' approaches.[37] This term has often been used to describe politically related movements, as AIDS activists borrowed concepts and strategies from the feminist health movement. But with opposing social movements, this spillover may happen in unlikely ways that cross political lines. For example, ex-gays borrowed tactics from gay liberationists of the 1970s by directly protesting the American Psychiatric Association and enrolling the expertise of sympathetic psychiatrists.

Standing in opposition to ex-gays, gay rights activism in the United States has also had an important relationship with science, with mainstream researchers increasingly working in this movement's favor. Often overstating the certainty of scientific findings, gay rights activists increasingly invoke biological determinist rhetoric, framing sexual orientation in terms of innateness and immutability. By contrast, the gay liberation movement, which was active in the early 1970s and saw the removal of homosexuality from psychiatry's *Diagnostic and Statistical Manual of Mental Disorders (DSM)* as a major cause, viewed sexuality as largely fluid, and saw the opportunity to express a range of sexual behaviors as a form of liberation for all human beings. The gay rights movement, which grew through the late 1970s and into the 1980s up to the present, has turned to treating sexual orientation as a form of fixed difference, advancing legal notions of "immutability" that have been useful for the civil rights movement. This idea of sexual orientation as an innate and immutable property of gay persons is also known as "essentialism." This way of understanding sexual orientation is particularly prominent in the United States, and found its most explicit expression in the early 1990s, when the research of scientists such as Simon LeVay, Dean Hamer, and Michael Bailey was widely interpreted by activists as evidence for a "gay gene" or a "gay brain." More recently the anti-reorientation organization Truth Wins Out has published the website LGBTscience.org, intended to bring biologically based sexual orientation research to a global online audience.

Today's gay rights movement might seem incomprehensible to gay liberationists of the past, but these changes have happened gradually over time. Promoting essentialist and distinct sexual orientations in the mainstream gay rights movement in the United States is not only a response to ex-gays but also is connected to struggles over the issue of gay marriage. This development emerged in response to the religious right, which used defense of marriage as a rallying issue in the 1990s. As a response to this venue shifting, gay rights activists' interests turned to marriage rights, whereas hate crimes and employment discrimination had been more central.[38] Many within a larger LGBT rights community have criticized this emphasis because marriage does not address the concerns of unmarried persons, and transgender rights often take a backseat to rights of gender-conforming and upper-class gay men and women.[39] Transgender persons have frequently been marginalized within the broader LGBT movement, as gender variance, once part of the category "gay," has increasingly been eschewed within gay politics. "White normativity" is also a problem within LGBT organizations, in which white cultural norms marginalize people of color, despite attempts at increasing diversity.[40] To achieve a status of normality, the gay rights movement has increasingly conceptualized people in fixed sexual orientation boxes, shoring up a heterosexual/homosexual binary, and the movement has succeeded on this basis in many policy arenas.[41] As a result, it has ceded notions of sexual fluidity to the ex-gay movement.

As the ex-gay movement has experienced marginalization in the United States, its focus has become increasingly transnational. In a sense, some within the movement have shifted political venues to global politics as a result of the successes of gay rights supporters. The transnational ex-gay movement can be seen as a loose coalition of affiliated groups, or a "transnational advocacy network." Such networks exchange information and possibly resources, but activism takes different shapes depending on the local context. For example, ex-gay ministries have formed in postapartheid South Africa during a period when religious institutions have stepped in to fill gaps in health care.[42] By contrast, in Ecuador, drug and alcohol rehabilitation centers have imported ex-gay ideas and have implemented reorientation clinics, even resorting to kidnap, torture, and rape to force women to give up lesbian lives.[43] In Uganda, where there is no widespread acceptance of talk therapy more broadly, being ex-gay means being paraded by religious activists to demonstrate that homosexuality is a learned behavior that can be unlearned. Individual ex-gays often tell stories of being recruited into homosexuality with financial rewards. In these different cases, there has been an exchange of information in the advocacy network about reorientation, but the groups touting these ideas have somewhat different goals in mind. In Uganda, for example, anti-homosexuality activism is strongly tied to a project of promoting Ugandan state sovereignty in a postcolonial era, and is important for shoring up President Yoweri Museveni's regime, which is under criticism for other human rights abuses.

Simultaneously, the transnational focus of the gay rights movement has also grown immensely over the past two decades. Through the 1990s, as the United Nations became seen as a means to solve problems in the post–Cold War era, gay rights became part of a larger human rights agenda in many circles. Many mainstream Western gay rights advocates argue for rescuing a "gay population" that is assumed to exist in every country around the world. Critics of this approach point to the need to examine the complexities of different sexual systems, as not all cultures divide human beings into typological categories like "gay" and "straight." Large organizations that address global gay rights include the

International Lesbian, Gay, Bisexual, Trans, and Intersex Association and the International Gay and Lesbian Human Rights Commission, both of which lobby the UN and have offices around the world. These umbrella groups work in coalitions with LGBT rights organizations in different countries and with smaller transnational organizations to help protect people from abuse and discrimination on the basis of sexual and gender minority status. The success of this movement is uneven across global regions. In the final chapter, I will discuss the relationship between the local advocacy group Sexual Minorities Uganda and the broader human rights community as part of this transnational social network.

A Queer Constructionist Theoretical Perspective

To examine the consolidation of sexualities through struggles over re-orientation treatments, I bring together queer and social constructionist theories, rather than basing my work on presumed essentialist ideas of sexual orientation used by gay rights activists. In some circles, the term *queer* has been reclaimed from its historically derogatory connotation and deprived of its ability to wound. Instead, queer broadly refers to an intellectual and political orientation that challenges many assumptions of both mainstream contemporary gay and lesbian politics as well as the assertion of heterosexual norms found in social conservatism. Queer challenges the denigration of consensual sexual expressions, and it includes maintaining a broad commitment to social justice along numerous social dimensions, including race, class, and gender. As gay marriage becomes legal, many queer theorists have been particularly critical of an assimilationist mode of gay and lesbian life, especially conformity with consumerist lifestyles. Thus, queer theory offers a perspective advocating for inclusion of a broader range of genders and sexualities;[44] it offers a "third way" of approaching a polarized social situation—the societal fracture often referred to as a "culture war." Queer theory is a useful perspective from which to analyze, critique, and report, moving toward a future beyond polarization.[45]

The roots of queer theory are often traced to Michel Foucault, the French philosopher, and the first volume of his *History of Sexuality*. In that book, Foucault unearths the origins of the idea that human beings have something called a "sexuality," and he traces this development to the late nineteenth century, when sexologists in the West developed a *scientia sexualis*, or "sexual science." Before this time, people were not classified on the basis of something like a sexual orientation. Instead, non-normative sexual behaviors were considered crimes worthy of punishment, not defining characteristics warranting a lifetime label. Summarizing this intellectual shift, Foucault famously states, "The sodomite had been an aberration; the homosexual was now a species."[46]

Foucault argues that the categorization of the "homosexual" as a separate type of person came about through specific practices employed by scientific experts with their research subjects. To discover what they thought were the hidden truths of sexuality, scientists extracted confessions from subjects, utilizing techniques derived from Christianity. Confession had become such a normalized practice within religious traditions that it seemed unnatural *not* to speak about one's inner self, as though something were being held back. Sexologists transformed confession into scientific "discourse." Contrary to the idea that sexuality had simply become a taboo subject that had been silenced or repressed, discourses about a litany of different kinds of sexualities proliferated.[47] Yet this new science was not merely an appeal to fanciful intellectual curiosity. It involved cataloging a "pornography of the morbid" that shored up the social status of turn-of-the-century elites promoting their own moral purity. As society became increasingly secularized, morality was enforced under the guise of medical treatment. The sexual science then grounded the purportedly superior status of "normal" people in the truths of authoritative science.[48] This work also functioned to alarm, since "strange pleasures, it warned, would eventually result in nothing short of death: that of individuals, generations, the species itself."[49] Foucault argues that through the development of treatments like psychoanalysis, confession became the basis of therapy in addition to being an apparatus for the production of scientific knowledge about sexuality.[50] Extending this analysis has shown that "heterosexuality" was also an invention that came into being around this same time, with the term initially describing a form of deviance involving sex between a man and woman for pleasure rather than reproduction. This version of heterosexuality soon became the established norm.[51]

Building on these insights into the expert production of a heterosexual/homosexual dichotomy, Eve Kosofsky Sedgwick has argued that an "endemic crisis of homo/heterosexual definition, indicatively male" has structured much of Western thought since the latter nineteenth century.[52] Using a queer theory approach to the study of the scientific production of sexualities can unearth widely held assumptions about the fixity and boundaries of sexual orientation categories encoded in accepted knowledge conventions that are part of this crisis, allowing us to imagine a much more complicated world of human sexualities for all

sexes.[53] Sedgwick calls for understandings of sexuality that extend beyond those based on gender of object choice alone. By no means is the
homosexual/heterosexual binary the inevitable system for categorization. Rather, it is one cultural convention particular to the West. A queer
theory lens highlights those historically contingent practices, including
those within science, that shore up the division of human sexualities
into a fixed homo-/heterosexual binary, using a fixed sex binary of male/
female. Queer theory also allows us to examine how the dominance of
that categorization system overshadows and precludes other possible
sexual subjectivities, genders, and social arrangements.

Queer theorist Sara Ahmed has further examined and questioned
what it means to be sexually "oriented" in the first place.[54] Considering
this in terms of a spatial metaphor, being oriented for Ahmed means
having a body that occupies a space associated with a direction from a
desiring subject toward a desired object. The "straightness" of heterosexual sexual orientation implies that other paths are bent or deviant. In
this book, I describe the standards of achieving straightness in a similar
sense, but I also am interested in the "straight line" as a divider. To draw
"the straight line" is to set the criterion of proof that delineates people as
either straight or gay. The project by pro-gay scientists to draw this line
is also an attempt to make innate and immutable "gay" people part of the
norm. In this case, the normalizing goal consolidates subjects who desire
either the same sex *or* the other sex; in effect, paths other than these two
become deviant.

While queer theory's roots are often traced to Foucault, much of queer
theory today, especially in sociology, would not have been possible were
it not for the prior work of sociologists of sexuality.[55] John Gagnon and
William Simon developed a theory of sexual scripts that responded to
many biological theories of sexuality that they found dissatisfying. For
these sociologists, a person's sexual desire, behavior, and attraction are
all drawn from the broader cultural fabric, as people become sexual beings much like they become anything else. Children whose experiences
of their own bodies are initially diffuse and unlabeled quickly learn rules
of what are inappropriate behaviors, such as rules against public nudity,
even though they might not initially understand any of these rules in
terms of sexuality. Whether through the family, peer networks, or other
sources, people obtain a language for understanding sexual experience
and how sexual encounters unfold, all of which influence the possibilities for sexual identification and expression. Systems of meaning are
central in this theory, as all of the physical ingredients for a sexual encounter might be present, but arousal and orgasm are not possible if

participants do not recognize the encounter as sexual.[56] Gagnon and Simon built on a symbolic interactionist perspective, in which meaning is understood to be collectively produced. Thus, meaning is central to sexuality, and what is understood as "sexual" varies from culture to culture. Furthermore, sexual behavior is understood as being coordinated through a process of sexual scripting; "cultural scenarios" are general cultural depictions of how sexuality is supposed to unfold, representations that become internalized as we learn to become sexual. Culture does not determine sexuality, since people apply these scripts to their own unique situations through improvisation, and they can creatively rewrite these scripts if needed, but they do so working with the cultural fabric available to them.[57]

Insights from queer theory and social constructionism can be brought together in an analysis of knowledge production about sexuality, where science can be understood as a location in which meanings of "sexuality," and the homosexual/heterosexual binary in particular, have been produced and remain a locus of struggle over sexual meaning. Science is the authoritative way of knowing in the United States and is sometimes considered the "fifth branch" of government, providing knowledge of human beings in tandem with public policy.[58] Yet there are many issues such as homosexuality in which religion competes strongly with science as policy adviser. Nonetheless, mainstream scientific organizations, including the American Psychological Association and the American Psychiatric Association, routinely submit amicus briefs and policy statements on a range of issues including those related to sexual orientation. NARTH, representing itself as a group of scientific experts, has also submitted a range of policy documents in court cases and legislative hearings.

When we consider these deployments of knowledge and how they shape our lived arrangements, we can see that science not only describes but also has generative effects. From a Foucauldian perspective, the kind of power that is embedded in scientific knowledge is productive, as opposed to a form of power based only on repression and restriction. Power and knowledge are fused together in what Foucault calls "discourse," ways of speaking about truth, and these discourses become embedded in institutional practices and policies. Although power does emanate through the discourses of experts, it does not only work in a top–down fashion. Indeed, for Foucault, wherever there is power, there is also the potential for resistance. He characterized power relations as a "microphysics," as power, flowing through discourse in a capillary form, could be challenged at a multitude of points. For example, a "reverse discourse" can take the terms of knowledge and turn them around. Gay activists deployed a reverse discourse when they challenged the homosexuality diagnosis and declared that being gay was a normal variant of human sexuality. In this case, homosexuality spoke "on its own behalf," as gay men and lesbians created a new identity with different meanings. This reverse discourse retained elements of the original, however—the terms *gay* and *lesbian* still denoted a different kind of person, even if these human kinds were no longer to be pathologized. Within science, the idea that gay and lesbian sexuality is a normal variant of human sexuality has now become the dominant discourse, and scientists have developed theories to explain homosexuality's existence, ironically placing reorientation advocates in the position to now challenge dominant discourse through resistance. Thus, while some discourses may be more dominant than others at any given time, they exist in a complex interplay.

Through locating the genesis of scientific discourses about sexuality, research based on queer and constructionist theories offers a critique of the "natural." It is commonplace in sexual reorientation therapy debates, and in sexual politics more broadly, for experts to make claims about the "nature" of human sexuality, whether it be fixed and rooted in biology or fluid and malleable with a heterosexual evolutionary imperative. By suspending assumptions about what nature entails, an analyst can explore how nature comes to be known and framed, and subsequently internalized by individuals. Thus, queer constructionism offers both a critique of essentialist notions of sexuality and a means to trace the effects of and relationships between different essentialisms. While people may experience their sexual desires as fixed or fluid, that does not mean they have a "nature" that is independent of "culture," as all aspects of human experience are mediated by cultural understandings.

Turning this queer constructionist lens on the reorientation debate allows an analysis of how these struggles have produced ways of being human, including the creation of the line between "straight" and "gay." Dominant scripts assert that sexual identity, behavior, and attraction should naturally align within a person, but unearthing such an assumption as essentialist allows us more easily to comprehend that these dimensions of sexuality might not align for an individual. For instance, one ethnographic study of an ex-gay ministry discovered "queer conversions," as the participants in the ministry went through phases of "sexual falls" with members of the same sex, only to repent, and all the while maintaining a heterosexual identity. Such forms of sexual expression involving mismatch between identity and behavior become analytically comprehensible through a queer constructionist lens, whereby we may understand the meanings people apply to their own lives without necessarily imposing an assertion that they are truly "gay" or "straight."[59]

By tracing the construction of sexual subjectivities in reorientation debates with a focus on scientific measurement, my study contributes to queer theory by rendering unstable notions of "evidence," "credibility," and "knowledge" utilized in the construction of sexual subjectivities. Rather than taking them as merely given representations of truth, I interrogate taken-for-granted assumptions about how science comes to represent the sexual human. By tracing shifts in the kinds of scientific evidence used to consolidate sexual subjectivities, changes in "credibility hierarchies" of evidence are presented as outcomes of struggle rather than taken-for-granted truisms. Knowledge of what constitutes sexual orientation, whether that orientation is based on attraction, behavior, and/or identity, and whether it is produced by scientific authorities or social movements, is always embedded within historical contexts and always involves the assertion of values. Therefore, the "truth" of sexual orientation cannot be taken for granted as simply revealed by science but rather is under negotiation, stabilizing at some moments and becoming less stable at others. This does not mean there is only relativism; knowledge, evidence, and credibility must be understood as outcomes of struggle rather than given realities, and through social negotiations and interactions with entities in the world, scientists come to realize collectively that some facts and some measurements are better constructed than others.

When I turn to transnational flows of knowledge of sexuality beyond the West in the final chapter, the study of sexual subjectivities presents particular challenges because of the varied meanings of terms like *LGBT, gay,* and *queer.* In the postcolonial Global South, the circulation of these terms may be an affront to local cultures, not necessarily because of the sexual and relationship practices they are associated with in the West, but because they involve individualized and white racialized notions of selfhood. In a rapidly changing world of global communications, taking rigid Western notions of identity for granted is problematic, but so is presuming that local notions of gender and sexuality are somehow "pristine." While I use the activist term *LGBTI* in discussions pertaining to Uganda (including *I* for intersex), it is unsafe to presume that this acronym carries the same meaning in that nation as it would for activists in the Global North. Rather, its genesis and application are objects of inquiry.[60]

Because, in chapter 5, this book looks to the global stage to follow the ex-gay and gay rights movements as transnational phenomena, it is necessary to consider the relationship between queer theory and scholarship around the globe. Queer theory is sometimes considered to have a West-centered bias, one that has not been taken up by scholars in many regions of the world, including Africa.[61] Yet a number of authors have used queer analysis to examine a wide range of sexualities across that continent.[62] Broadening the queer theory analysis, it is still important to incorporate local dialects and concepts.[63] For this reason, especially as chapter 5 focuses on the role of reorientation knowledge in the context of the Uganda debate over the Anti-Homosexuality Bill, I draw on the work of Ugandan legal scholar and sociologist Sylvia Tamale in addition to including her as an interview participant. I also discuss local terminology such as *kuchu* and local understandings of *homosexual*. Beyond terminology, I also look to transnational flows of scientific knowledge as resources for constructing sexual subjectivities around the globe. Sexual subjectivities have varying relationships with science and other knowledge systems, depending on the dominant discourses where they are located. To add more depth to an analysis of the *scientia sexualis*, and the forms of sexual subjectivity that science has produced, it is necessary to turn to the field of science studies.

Drawing Scientific Boundaries

When considering struggles over knowledge production, science studies provides a number of conceptual tools for analyzing the contingency of scientific knowledge and technological production, and to examine the broader cultural effects of knowledge production.[64] With an intellectual move that sociologists of scientific knowledge call a principle of "symmetry," science studies perspectives tend to bracket the "truth" and "falsity" of facts under investigation, and instead explore the social and historical processes by which facts come into being as truths, or become rejected as nontruths.[65] Rather than asserting whether or not sexual reorientation therapy "works," I investigate how it is that reorientation has been rejected in the United States, and what social conditions underlie these attributions. When looking at the case of Uganda, I will further explore the conditions that have led to reception of ex-gay ideas in that country, even though reorientation is rejected by international professional organizations such as the World Health Organization and International Federation of Social Workers. An important concept in examining these dynamics is "boundary work," the practices used by scientists to shore up the cultural boundaries of what is considered to be scientific and what is not.[66] As reorientation has been relegated to the scientific fringe through the position statements of various professional associations, we can consider these position statements to be a form of boundary work.

Ufology, paranormal psychology, astrology, and phrenology are but a few of the practices that populate the scientific fringe in the United States, and today, sexual reorientation therapies sit alongside these as discredited and baseless in the eyes of mainstream scientific organizations. While ufology enjoyed a heyday of major scientific interest in the late 1960s, an influential government report concluded that the study of UFOs was no longer warranted, as UFO sightings always turned out to be conventional phenomena.[67] Cold fusion is a more recent example of relegation to the fringe. In 1989 there was a great deal of excitement among scientists that nuclear fusion reactions might be created at room temperature, but the government soon declared that this was not a scientifically valid concept. In the case of reorientation, the removal of "Homosexuality" from the American Psychiatric Association's *DSM* in 1973 set up a series of events that have likewise pushed reorientation to the margins. Nonetheless, in the cases of ufology, cold fusion, and reorientation, each fringe practice maintains a public following that accuses mainstream science of biases leading to unfair assessments of pioneering work.

Within science, establishing the boundaries between science and the fringe involves the social attribution of credibility to both claims and claimants. In turn, the attribution of credibility can be shaped by a potentially infinite number of cultural factors.[68] Subsequently, the production of facts involves "credibility struggles," as claimants attempt to convince people that they and their scientific work can be trusted.[69] Through such struggles, some discourses emerge victorious, producing credibility hierarchies of claims.[70] While the concept of credibility hierarchies can be applied to people and expertise, here I extend this idea to the formation of "hierarchies of evidence," in which some forms of evidence become seen as more credible than others for the purposes of representing some entity, like sexual orientation. In scientific controversies, dissenters frequently question the relationship between a form of evidence and the entity it is supposed to represent. It is when a fact is no longer contested that it becomes "black boxed"—people no longer care how the fact was determined or what kind of evidence was used to establish it, and they treat it as common sense.[71] Although one hierarchy of evidence may prevail at a given time, scientific communities and various public constituencies exist within "social worlds," groups with shared goals, practices, and systems of meaning, and thus, different hierarchies of evidence may exist within these various groups.[72]

To conceptualize the arena of struggle in which actors from different social worlds struggle to shape the production of knowledge, I utilize a concept of "field." Pierre Bourdieu has theorized a "scientific field" as "a locus of a competitive struggle, in which the specific issue at stake is the monopoly of scientific authority" as well as a "monopoly of scientific competence, in the sense of a particular agent's socially recognised capacity to speak and act legitimately . . . in scientific matters."[73] Although this is a useful definition to conceptualize credibility struggles within science, disputes over knowledge of sexual reorientation have occurred within a much broader swath of professional domains, including theology and health-care professions, each of which has a complex relationship with science. Indeed, professions such as "religious counseling" draw on a blend of scientific and theological precepts, so confining the locus of analysis to science alone would preclude understanding the breadth of processes involved. Therefore, I theorize a "field of therapeutics" as an arena in which experts struggle over knowledge and practice addressing various mental, emotional, and spiritual health issues, including those related to homosexuality. This field cuts across the institutions of medicine, mental health (including psychiatry, psychology, and social work), and theology (especially the profession of religious counseling).[74] Given this conceptualization of the arena of struggle, it is possible to consider that someone on the fringe of science may still find credibility within religious institutions.

Moreover, I theorize that the multiple institutions that produce knowledge within the field of therapeutics are characterized by an "intellectual opportunity structure."[75] This concept was originally theorized to examine how groups of professional academics are enabled or constrained by academic institutions in the production of knowledge.[76] I extend this concept to apply to social movements more broadly, and to a larger field of knowledge production beyond the academy. In my conceptualization of "intellectual opportunity structure," social movements encounter factors that enable or constrain their efforts when trying to shape knowledge production. "Political opportunity structure" has been an important concept in theorizing social movements that target the state.[77] However, power is exercised at multiple loci within society beyond the state, and institutional practices that are both material and symbolic have been the target of social movements in various domains.[78] As such, the ex-gay and gay rights movements have targeted science over the past several decades, and have sought to shape knowledge production within theology, yet each has encountered particular opportunities and constraints in these endeavors. The intellectual opportunity structure contains both material and symbolic elements, since it sets the boundaries for who can be considered a scientific expert. As this story will show, the relationship between an intellectual opportunity structure and a social movement is more complex than a structure/agency dichotomy. This is because part of what is at stake in these struggles is the very existence of conceptualizations of the human agent: Is it considered scientifically possible to even be an "ex-gay"? What does it actually mean to be "gay" or "straight"? Thus, an intellectual opportunity structure contains both material and cultural elements, and is by no means a rigid structure external to systems of human meaning.

I theorize the "intellectual opportunity structure" as being composed of five primary components. First, this structure includes both *formal* and *informal credibility boundary markers:* aspects of institutions that delimit the boundaries of valid knowledge production practices and distinguish credible actors from those who are discredited. For example, professional ethics codes and their enforcement are important formal institutional policies which set limits on what kinds of practices practitioners can perform while maintaining legitimacy. If an organization like the American Psychological Association formally passes a position statement declaring that professional members must respect the sexual orientation of clients, this can hinder knowledge production formed on the basis of anti-gay ideals. Position statements, such as the one published by the American Psychological Association in 2009 that renounced reorientation, have further limited intellectual opportunities for the ex-gay movement, although they have enabled those opportunities in other ways. In addition to such formal documents, informal boundaries such as professional norms can set limits on the possibilities for social movements, and these may be considered part of an "epistemic culture," the characteristic modes of thought and practice that shape the organization of inquiry in a field.[79]

A second facet of knowledge-producing institutions that can hinder or facilitate social movement efficacy is the kinds of *organizational forms found in institutions.* For example, an organization's governance structure can shape its vulnerability to movement activity. Heightened vulnerability can exist especially when organizations are fragmented in their structure, or when they are going through periods of growth.[80] The governance structure of the American Psychological Association, which includes a board of directors elected by members of the various divisions within the association, has come under fire from reorientation groups, especially through the efforts of former APA president and reorientation proponent Nicholas Cummings. According to Cummings, several of the divisions within the APA are devoted to what he calls "politically correct" concerns, such as promoting LGBT psychology or the psychological well-being of minorities.[81] Regardless of his analysis, this particular governance structure has bearing on the outcomes of organizational policy.

Third, the *relationships between institutions within a larger institutional field* are a key element of an intellectual opportunity structure. This is particularly significant in the field of mental health, where the American Psychiatric Association sets the definitions of health and pathology with the standardized *DSM*, and other mental health fields generally follow suit. This is a relationship of professional subordination, although other arrangements are possible, such as strict divisions of labor.[82] Such a split of jurisdiction may occur across science and theology because religion often addresses existential concerns that science tends to bracket.

Another crucial relationship across institutions exists between the state and the professions. States often regulate professions, including licensing and targeted funding, and certain forms of research may be mandated or prohibited by law. In the case of reorientation, the states of California and New Jersey have banned sexual reorientation therapies for minors at the time of this writing, and other states are considering such bans, largely due to harms listed in position statements of professional organizations. Thus, ex-gay therapists and researchers in those states, including those at the Thomas Aquinas Psychological Clinic in California, are unable to legally produce research on minors undergoing reorientation.

The broader political culture of a state can play a significant role in shaping professional intellectual behavior as well. In the United States, where there is a propensity to trust numerical evidence over other forms of knowledge in policy deliberations, statistical researchers' credibility is often bolstered. The United States has a history of societal fragmentation, and numbers can appear to speak from an adjudicating "view from nowhere."[83] In addition, granting rights in democratic states frequently requires the delineation of fixed groups of people. Responding to challenges to the idea of identity from queer theory, Joshua Gamson has pointed out that in order to protect a gay population from discrimination, gay identities are necessary.[84] Gay rights groups in the United States have built their identity politics strategies on the civil rights movement, which often obtained rights based on the claim that states should not discriminate on the basis of an immutable characteristic. Because pro-gay claims in the United States are often based on the idea that sexual orientations are fixed and distinct parts of selfhood, there is an incentive to create knowledge regarding the immutability of sexual orientation for use in political and legal contexts. Thus, in addition to producing research, mainstream professionals and ex-gay groups have been active in deploying such research findings in various state arenas.

Fourth, if a social movement wishes to influence a knowledge-producing institution, a crucial feature of the intellectual opportunity structure is the *relationship between that institution and the public.* If a scientific organization, for instance, is secretive and conducts proceedings with extremely inaccessible jargon and communication pathways, a social movement will have a much more difficult time having an impact. However, if organizations are more transparent and have public liaisons such as the American Psychological Association's Office of Lesbian, Gay, Bisexual and Transgender Concerns, and if they have an open relationship with the press, social movements may have more influence. Beyond these communication channels, some knowledge-producing organizations may be more or less beholden to public credibility concerns. Mental health professionals, who compete with experts from other knowledge systems for patients, must establish the credibility of their knowledge base for public audiences. Psychology is especially vulnerable to this concern, and through its public campaigns the ex-gay movement has been successful in pressing mainstream psychology in the United States to clarify its position on homosexuality. Social movements on the fringe have the capacity to create public influence that "feeds back" into mainstream knowledge production, either through the incorporation of fringe views, or in the case of the ex-gay movement, by leading scientists to clarify or modify their positions in order to keep an undesired perspective outside the boundaries of science.[85]

Fifth and finally, *an opposing social movement* may be part of the intellectual opportunity structure. If a countermovement, such as gay rights, is fighting to shape the same knowledge-producing institution, a range of different kinds of movement–countermovement dynamics can emerge. In the case of the ex-gay movement, not only has it had to contend with gay rights activists in struggles to shape scientific knowledge, it also has encountered the newly formed "ex-ex-gay movement," also known as "ex-gay survivors." The organization Beyond Ex-Gay, formed in 2007 as the first national ex-ex-gay group in the United States, publishes narratives about how sexual reorientation attempts have harmed them.

While these features of knowledge-producing institutions play a role in the story of forming knowledge about sexual orientation, this analysis will also take into account the broader culture of the United States surrounding these institutions. This larger cultural fabric, or "toolkit" as sociologist Ann Swidler has described, serves as a resource for the development of ideas within social movements and among professionals.[86] Thus, when "homosexuality" was removed from the *DSM* in 1973, those interested in sexual reorientation could turn to the flourishing institutions of religion as a cultural source for an alternative epistemological base. While science commands immense credibility in the United States, it competes with religion on certain topics in ways not seen in other Western countries. The presence of evangelical Christianity and the U.S. culture of rugged self-determination have helped support reception of ex-gay movement messages in the broader culture. While some have theorized the broader set of ideas that movements have to draw from as "cultural opportunities,"[87] others have utilized a similar idea of "discursive opportunities"[88] to outline the broader possibilities that can be articulated in discourse during a cultural moment. While these concepts are related to intellectual opportunity structures, they are not the same, as the latter is meant to refer to properties of knowledge-producing institutions and the relationships among them.

These conceptual tools from science studies and queer theory enable the understanding of knowledge production as a complex process of struggle involving a range of actors. As professionals struggle for credibility within the field of therapeutics, the boundaries of science have taken shape. While opposing social movements and professionals jockeying for jurisdiction and authority have all shaped knowledge with their own vision, research subjects themselves have also played a key role. Although the theoretical formulations outlined so far help to explain the consolidation of cultural understandings of sexuality, they do not sufficiently address the ways in which the materiality of bodies plays a role in the creation of these notions of sexuality. Matter, including the matter of research subjects' bodies, shapes the construction of knowledge with its own forms of unfolding agency.[89] However, the utilization of different measurement techniques in research plays a central role in what forms of matter signify in knowledge construction. If the body is scrutinized in research, it becomes "materialized" as an actor in knowledge construction, but if it is ignored, it may become "dematerialized." Thus, scientific research involves the deployment of "regimes of perceptibility and imperceptibility" depending on the technique used to acquire evidence.[90] While social constructionist and queer theory perspectives tend to treat human sexuality as widely malleable and fluid, such ideas about the agency of matter are useful to draw attention to the ways in which bodies are present in scientific experiments—they are not infinitely malleable, and they have agency in ways that researchers and research subjects may not expect.[91] Taking this material agency into account, the construction of knowledge can then be understood as a complex process of interaction among experts, materialized bodies, opposing social movements, and their historical context.

The Straight Line

To summarize, *The Straight Line* is a study of how notions of sexual orientation have come into being through struggles over scientific knowledge, with a focus on sexual reorientation therapy debates. Sexuality studies provides tools to understand that sexual subjectivity is not a natural given, but is something that is culturally shaped. In this historical moment, science plays a crucial role in that process. Science studies provides additional theoretical tools for understanding these dynamics, including a symmetrical analytical strategy for examining fact construction, and for exploring ways in which social movements have influenced the production of knowledge. Finally, social movement theories provide ways of looking at the strategies, challenges, and dynamics of movements and their relationships with opponents, as these groups have struggled to shape knowledge production.

Methodologically, my book draws from approaches developed by Steven Epstein, building on the work of Foucault, to examine knowledge production as it is influenced by social movements.[92] This involves writing a narrative history that traces the minute negotiations of credibility as actors from different social worlds clash. Using methods that are "archaeological," I examine the conditions that facilitate some ways of thinking but that make some things unthinkable. Epstein states, "Such an analysis concerns itself with a recovery of the immanent rules of what is sayable and unsayable, thinkable and unthinkable." Also, as a study that is "genealogical," this history identifies crucial moments of rupture and discontinuity, rather than assuming a smooth teleological account of the production of knowledge.[93]

To trace the consolidation of claims and the crystallization of hierarchies of evidence within the field of therapeutics, I attended relevant conferences as a participant observer, performed content analysis on scientific, theological, and activist literature, and conducted thirty-five interviews with relevant claimants, within both the United States and Uganda. Tracing news stories required searching databases for stories concerned with major events, such as the publication of the Spitzer study, and for general terms such as *reorientation, reparative therapy, ex-gay, ex-ex-gay, ex-gay survivor,* and *homosexuality.* To make these searches more manageable, I limited them to the *New York Times* and the *Los Angeles Times* in the United States and the *Daily Monitor* and *New Vision* in Uganda, unless I was alerted to other important news stories in the course of conducting research. This approach required reading and indexing approximately 250 news articles over the course of the study, and approximately 200 research and scientific articles from mainstream science and from activists.

Determining the most influential claimants to interview required reading literature to identify the most cited, and also listening at conferences to identify the most frequently referenced. These determinations were triangulated in early interviews to make sure I was talking to the most important people in the field, whenever possible. My data include two interviews with prominent psychiatrist Dr. Robert Spitzer, a central figure in this story. He was an influential member of the Nomenclature Committee for the American Psychiatric Association in 1973 during the removal of "Homosexuality" from the *DSM*. However, he later conducted a study published in 2003 that purportedly showed gay men and lesbians could be changed through reorientation. I conducted my first interview with Spitzer in 2008, before he publicly apologized for his study; our second interview took place in 2013, following the apology.

My interviewees include three members of the American Psychological Association Task Force that published a review in 2009 declaring that there is no evidence for the efficacy of reorientation attempts and that it is potentially harmful. I also interviewed leaders of Beyond Ex-Gay and Exodus International and members of NARTH. I attended conferences organized by NARTH, Exodus International, the American Psychological Association, and Beyond Ex-Gay. In Uganda, I interviewed a number of mental health professionals and activists, including Sexual Minorities Uganda director Frank Mugisha. I also interviewed Member of Parliament David Bahati, sponsor of the Anti-Homosexuality Bill, and two mental health professionals who later became members of the Ugandan Ministry of Health panel that developed a scientific statement on homosexuality to advise President Museveni. Transcribed interviews and field notes were then coded for relevant themes and consolidated, along with the analysis of relevant scientific and activist literature, into a narrative history that is recounted in the chapters that follow, tracing the movement of reorientation from the mainstream of science to the fringe.

Beginning at a moment when reorientation therapies became scientific orthodoxy in the United States, chapter 1 opens with the years following the Kinsey studies and then describes the rise of the reorientation regime. While Alfred Kinsey's research normalized homosexuality to a large extent, psychoanalysts and behavior therapists took advantage of national anxieties about this issue and advanced the regime of reorientation treatment. At this time, homosexuality was listed as a paraphilia in the *DSM*, but this diagnosis would soon come under attack from the burgeoning gay liberation movement. Chapter 1 examines the hierarchy of evidence prior to the removal of homosexuality from the *DSM*, when the straight line was considered crossable, and follows the creation of new ideas about healthy homosexuals in the working relationship between psychologist Evelyn Hooker and the homophile movement.

Chapter 2 traces key shifts in the definition of sexual orientation from the 1970s to the early 2000s, highlighting the role of psychiatrist Dr. Robert Spitzer. Spitzer was an influential member of the American Psychiatric Association Nomenclature Committee, which allowed gay liberation activist and psychologist Charles Silverstein to present evidence to the committee to support demedicalization. Gay-affirming mental health professionals worked to entrench the view that homosexuality is a normal variant of sexuality that should be affirmed with gay identity. Without a scientific basis for the treatment of homosexuality, the religious ex-gay movement flourished as many turned to this alternative venue. Yet, by 2001, Spitzer unexpectedly decided to conduct a study demonstrating the efficacy of reorientation therapies and religious ministries. His credibility established in the 1970s increased the influence of this research, especially in the press and in the public. While many have portrayed Spitzer as changing his point of view, I argue that all the while he has maintained a constant position that homosexuality does not qualify as a mental illness but rather is a "suboptimal" condition.

In the wake of the Spitzer study, a new ex-gay survivor countermovement emerged. While these activists provided testimony to the inefficacy and harms of reorientation treatments, they maintained some ties to ex-gays, influencing the development of a more moderate "middle path." At this time, gay-affirmative therapists and religious ex-gay leaders and researchers began to converge on intermediary approaches offering therapeutic alternatives to clients beyond the extremes of gay-affirmative and sexual reorientation therapies. Chapter 3 explores the consolidation of these middle path approaches as the beginning of a process of standardization of definitions of "sexual orientation," defined in relation to attractions, and "sexual orientation identity," defined as the willingness or ability to acknowledge sexual orientation. Convergence toward a middle path required members of social movements on both sides of the debate to part ways with more hard-line activists, and I examine these dynamics and their outcomes.

The American Psychological Association Task Force on Appropriate Therapeutic Responses to Sexual Orientation, which convened in 2007, published its report in 2009. This report cemented the idea in mainstream science in the United States that sexual orientation is a physiological phenomenon based in sexual attraction, declared that there is no evidence for the efficacy of reorientation treatments, and argued that such treatments are potentially harmful. Chapter 4 first examines the process by which the task force was formed and the reasoning behind excluding NARTH nominees. It also recounts the formation of the compromise concept of "sexual orientation identity exploration," as it emerged out of the work of psychologists influenced by moderate factions of fragmented opposing movements. In this chapter, psychologist A. Lee Beckstead stands out as a key figure central to the development of the report and compromise. As an ex-ex-gay himself, he was a primary advocate for attending to religious concerns, and considering the force of religious identities in the development of selves.

Finally, Chapter 5 examines ex-gay and anti-homosexuality movements on the global stage, as reorientation has been increasingly blocked within the United States. While this chapter surveys the complex work of organizing these movements across national borders, it takes the case of the controversy over the Ugandan Anti-Homosexuality Bill as a major flashpoint. This bill, which proposed the death penalty for "aggravated homosexuality," was filed in 2009, just months after the Family Life Network hosted a conference in Kampala. Members of prominent ex-gay groups from the United States attended the meeting. This chapter looks into transnational flows of knowledge and discusses how, despite a growing consensus in the international mental health community that it is a normal variant of human sexuality, many Ugandan professionals maintain that homosexuality is an unwanted "learned behavior that can be unlearned."

Finally, in the conclusion, I further analyze how it is that fringe advocacy has had an effect on mainstream science, and how this process has consolidated a range of gendered sexual subjectivities, both within the mainstream and within the ex-gay movement. The conclusion juxtaposes these developments within other cases of fringe–mainstream relationships, as the ex-gay case exemplifies a "dialectical" shaping of mainstream definitions and concepts. Drawing on insights from queer theory, it also considers how establishing sexual orientation as a fixed entity rooted in binary gender and separate from sexual orientation identity precludes a range of human sexual expressions, even as it resists forms of oppression.

one

THE REORIENTATION REGIME
Therapeutic Techniques in an Anti-Homosexual Era, 1948–1972

In the decade following World War II, a reassertion of gender norms and a grand sense of nationalism accompanied ideals about heterosexual family life and work in mainstream U.S. culture.[1] In the midst of this constrained atmosphere, Dr. Alfred Kinsey and his research team at Indiana University dramatically changed the ways in which issues of sexuality, including homosexuality, could be discussed in the United States. The widely read *Sexual Behavior in the Human Male* (1948) and *Sexual Behavior in the Human Female* (1953) transformed the landscape of culture and sex by forcing people to consider discrepancies between moral prohibitions of various sexual behaviors and surprisingly high reported prevalence rates. The two books ignited a media firestorm. In the first, Kinsey and his team made an astounding claim: "The data in the present study indicate that at least 37 per cent of the male population has some homosexual experience between the beginning of adolescence and old age. This is more than one male in three of the persons that one may meet as he passes along a city street."[2] If these statistics were not staggering enough at the time, the authors made a call for nothing less than the acceptance of homosexual behaviors as natural variations:

> In view of the data which we now have on the incidence and frequency of the homosexual, and in particular on its co-existence with the heterosexual in the lives of a considerable portion of the male population, it is difficult to maintain the view that psychosexual reactions between individuals of the same sex are rare and therefore abnormal or unnatural, or that they constitute within themselves evidence of neuroses or even psychoses.[3]

For those experiencing same-sex attractions in this conservative era, such claims evoked tremendous hope. For those opposed to homosexuality, they evoked outrage and even panic.

Today, it is widely accepted that Kinsey's numbers overstated the rates of homosexual and other allegedly "deviant" behaviors in the population at that time. His methods, derived from his background in the field of zoology, sought the full extent of natural variation of behavior in a species, and were thus skewed to find overrepresentation of variations. By taking an extraordinarily large number of personal sexual case histories, Kinsey and his team believed that they were objectively collecting the range of diversity of human sexual behavior. However, by emphasizing prisons, mental hospitals, and other marginalized locations, and by asking questions in suggestive ways, they likely found higher rates of nonnormative sexual expressions.[4] Regarding homosexuality, Kinsey was adamant that all people had a basic mammalian capacity for same-sex erotic behavior. What is often forgotten is that he also disliked sexual identity labels, stating that human beings should not be sorted into "sheep" and "goats." He famously created what has come to be known as the "Kinsey scale," a measure of behavior and attraction (not identity), rating people from 0 (100 percent heterosexual) to 6 (100 percent homosexual) with five shades in between, and an X value for no sexual activity or behavior, as a representation of the complexity of human sexual behavior and desire along this dimension.

By asserting that homosexual attractions and behaviors were more prevalent than commonly thought, the Kinsey studies had various contradictory effects.[5] On the one hand, they reversed a sense of isolation felt by many homosexual people throughout the United States. While World War II had created conditions for the growth of gay subcultures in U.S. cities, the studies provided an important morale boost for these communities. Ultimately the studies would even provide a scientific basis for legal rights claims.[6] On the other hand, the studies became resources for those warning of a vast "homosexual menace" permeating the fabric of society. During the Red Scare, incited, in part, by Senator Joseph McCarthy of Wisconsin, homosexuality and communism were grouped together as threats to national security. Homosexuals were purged from state employment and were subject to other forms of legal prosecution. The large incidence numbers in the Kinsey report were used to argue that the threatening problem was immense.[7] Psychiatrists, whose profession had grown in prominence during World War II for the treatment of "war neuroses" with psychoanalytic techniques, stepped in to address the problem. They developed reorientation treatments based on theories descended but significantly departing from the work of Sigmund Freud. By the late 1960s, behavior therapists, guided by the idea that human behavior can be molded through systems of reward and punishment, joined in the treatment of homosexuality in the United States. While many clients sought treatment on their own in order to escape oppressive circumstances and to conform, in many of these cases, reorientation was court mandated in response to violations of laws prohibiting homosexual acts. The relationship between the schools of psychoanalysis and behaviorism was complex, united by many shared assumptions and even converging theories, but divided over philosophy of the mind in addition to therapeutic and measurement practices. While Kinsey rejected the idea of sexual "types," his data were used to reinforce these types by both sides of the debate, as homophiles and reorientation therapists alike classified sexualities.

The story of the rise of reorientation therapies in mainstream mental health professions in the mid-twentieth-century United States has been told quite well many times before.[8] However, the story warrants a retelling for what it can reveal about how notions of "sexual orientation" came to be constituted, not only in the theories of reorientation experts, but also through the measurement practices they used. In this chapter, I review the key reorientation therapy texts from the time period and situate them in their historical context. In terms of the intellectual opportunity structure, this was a time in which criminalization of homosexuality by the state and medicalization by the mental health professions reinforced one another, in turn favoring reorientation practitioners. State prohibitions of homosexuality could result in mandatory treatment for offenders, leading to increased interest in the treatment of homosexuality, not only from those who were caught, but also from people with same-sex attractions seeking to avoid societal marginalization. Furthermore, when homosexuality was considered a mental illness, it could be a career risk for a mental health professional to reveal his or her own support for the demedicalization of homosexuality, let alone that he or she was gay or lesbian. In this context, credibility boundaries in science favored heterosexual mental health professionals seeking to treat homosexuality as a pathology, and the measurement techniques used by professionals predominantly defined sexual orientations in terms of behavior. Those challenging the diagnosis in the 1950s and 1960s found an intellectual opportunity in one sympathetic professional in particular, psychologist Evelyn Hooker, but it would be years before evidence for the demedicalization of homosexuality could accumulate and the gay liberation movement strengthened, culminating in the removal in 1973 of "Homosexuality" from the *DSM*.

This review of the reorientation regime provides important background for understanding contemporary struggles over sexual reorientation therapies and scientific ideas about sexual orientation. I begin with a discussion of the emergence of the concepts of a treatable and psychogenic form of homosexuality in the United States, as it emerged out of white middle-class cultural anxieties over race and class near the turn of the twentieth century, before Kinsey entered the conversation. I then turn to a discussion of the development of psychoanalytic and behaviorist interventions and early challenges to the reorientation regime within the homophile movement.

Pre-Kinsey Notions of Homosexuality

Homosexuality was a rare topic of scientific discussion in the United States prior to the explosive Kinsey studies. Relegated to the shadows and fringes of society, it was taboo for most scientists and medical doctors, and even subject to censorship.[9] During the late nineteenth and early twentieth centuries, scientists in Europe developed many causal theories, some of which were imported to the United States and modified. These early years were, according to philosopher Michel Foucault, the time when homosexuality was invented to define a kind of person, or a "species." Prior to this, sodomy had been described an illegal behavior indulged in by all manner of social "degenerates."[10] As the nascent medical professions grew in power in both Europe and the United States, the regulation of homosexuality became an issue of contention within them. The history of medical treatments for homosexuality, while often grisly, must be understood as being on par with early treatments for mental illnesses more broadly.

In Europe, medical scientists developed three major models in their attempts to understand the causes of this newly invented pathology. The first was the theory of "degeneration," advanced by Richard von Krafft-Ebing. Krafft-Ebing viewed homosexuality as part of an overall tendency toward vice, manifested as a form of "sexual inversion," with the sex of the body not corresponding to the sex of the mind. This theory stood in contrast to the "naturalist" view, advanced by Magnus Hirschfeld and Karl Ulrichs, that homosexuality was a natural variation, or an inborn anomaly, and it was not a disease. Theirs was also a theory of inversion; they believed homosexuals had androgynous body types and cross-sex psychological characteristics. The third theory, developed by Sigmund

Freud, was "psychogenic": homosexuality was a form of arrested development due to early childhood experiences. Freud did not believe that
homosexuality could be "cured," and he was not troubled by its presence.[11]
In all these European models, the body played some role as a location for
drives. Even Freud's theory, which relied most on environmental conditions, rooted homosexual desires in the body, as naturally polymorphous
libidinal drives became focused on particular objects through repression
of alternate options and through the existence of unresolved conflicts.[12]

While various forms of same-sex eroticism have existed throughout
recorded history, gay male communities began forming in cities in in-
dustrializing nations, including the United States, in the early twentieth
century. U.S. experts, confounded by these developments, considered
homosexuals to be both sick *and* morally deficient.[13] The earliest medical
ideas about homosexuality imported into the United States by medical
experts were rooted in Krafft-Ebing's degeneracy school. While Krafft-
Ebing had maintained a sympathetic moral view of homosexuality, the
U.S. version mixed that view with moral opprobrium, especially when
found within racial minority groups. Writing in the *Journal of Nervous
and Mental Disease* in 1892, Dr. Irving C. Rosse of Georgetown University cataloged various sexual aberrations, and in doing so, he described
an innate degenerative illness that afflicted some African American men
in Washington, D.C.:

> Among other genital idiosyncrasies of negroes coming to the knowl-
> edge of the Washington police, is the old Scythian malady spoken of by
> Hippocrates and Herodotus, and observed by contemporary travelers
> in the Caucasus. A band of negro men, with all the androgynous char-
> acteristics of the malady, was sometime since raided by the police. The
> same race a few years ago had one or more gangs that practiced a kind
> of phallic worship. An informant, who has made a study of skatological
> rites among lower races, described to me how a big buck, with turges-
> cent penis, decorated with gaily-colored ribbons, stood and allowed his
> comrades to caress and even osculate the member. Performances of
> the same nature are known to the rites of vadouxism.[14]

The "old Scythian malady" Rosse described was not just homosexuality
but an affliction of effeminacy. Such depictions expressed and fed the
fears of white middle-class men in the United States, including medical
professionals, who perceived threats to their social position due to major
transformations in society, as mass migration to cities brought people
together from different races and class positions. White middle-class
males' fears of changing social order translated into attempts to shore up

class divisions with scientific notions of difference.[15] Early medical ideas
about homosexuality in the United States were thus forged in this context; this "malady" with all its "androgynous" symptoms was seen to be
characteristic of "lower races" and "degenerate" peoples.[16] As Ann Stoler
has argued in the case of the construction of European notions of sexuality, notions of white sexual elitism were also constructed in juxtaposition
with characterizations of the deviant sexualities of so-called savage races
as partial justification for U.S. colonialism.[17]

Such ideas were expressed within the eugenics movement, which was
widespread in the United States by the early twentieth century. Eugenics sought to rid the human race of unwanted genetic material, either
through encouraging breeding of those with favored traits, or by ster-
ilizing the unfit. Two tracks of treatment of "sexual perversion" developed under eugenics. For the "lower" classes and races, sterilization was
often implemented to prevent corruption of the species.[18] For the middle
classes, however, rehabilitative treatment was needed. To preserve the genetic basis for class superiority, rehabilitation required that homosexuality not be considered part of the inherent "constitution" of the afflicted
among the middle class. Rather, it had to be understood as learned and
therefore able to be unlearned.[19] In this context, the fear that homosexuality could be acquired via seduction by an afflicted member of a lower
class reinforced race and class divisions.

Couched in a language of scientific objectivity and social engineering, the treatment of psychogenic homosexuality in the United States
became a project of psychiatrists influenced by the Progressive Era project of "social ameliorationism" within the mental hygiene movement.
These theories posited homosexuality as more likely to develop among
the lower classes due to their morally contaminated social circumstances.
Psychiatrist Adolf Meyer was instrumental in developing therapies, aimed
at reforming those who were not dismissed as "hopeless cases" of entrenched degeneracy. Meyer understood the personality to be the product
of the interaction of the body and the environment. The ego, structured
through a process of interaction between mind and body, could overcome
mental disorder with the appropriate reconfiguration of an individual's
immediate environmental circumstances—the creation of a healthy "social adjustment." The approach appealed to an American "can-do" spirit.
By changing the environment to ameliorate those stressful conditions of
modernity that he thought gave rise to the sexual disorder, some achieved
abstinence from homosexual practices, which was Meyer's minimal goal
of success.[20]

In the 1930s in New York City, a team of researchers formed the Com-

mittee for the Study of Sex Variance to better understand the kinds of
social conditions that produced homosexuality. Supervised by psychiatrist George Henry, the committee, following the inversion model, interviewed several "sex variants." "Jan Gay," a pseudonymous lesbian
journalist, recruited subjects for the research, and many subjects voluntarily participated. The interdisciplinary team examined the physical and mental attributes of research participants to learn how to treat
patients with "sexual maladjustment." The exams included psychiatric
evaluations, tests of masculinity and femininity, X-rays, and measurements of physique, metabolism, and hormone levels. Genitals were also
examined and measured. The team concluded that homosexuality was
likely caused by the inability to adjust to the rigors of modern society
and was a form of arrested development. The study had the effect of reinforcing gender norms, especially as those norms informed education
programs for youth.[21]

Although this social ameliorationist view gained ground in the United
States, some medical experts approached the issue of homosexuality by
prescribing hormonal treatments. In the late nineteenth and early twentieth centuries in the United States, hormones and glandular secretions
were another means of explaining racial superiority and shoring up racial hierarchy. While some theories of degeneracy explained behavior
differences in terms of the quality of the nervous system, other theories
explained them in terms of hormonal concentrations.[22] Beginning in the
1890s, "organotherapies" involved the injection of small quantities of
animal hormones to cure various illnesses.

The treatment of homosexuality using endocrinology was first pursued in early twentieth-century Europe. Austrian physiologist Eugen
Steinach devised a theory of sex gland antagonism by removing ova-
ries from female guinea pigs and replacing them with testicles, which
caused the animal to develop a masculinized body. Magnus Hirschfeld
was particularly enthused about this work. Theorizing that homosexuality was caused by a lack of sex differentiation in the gonads, Steinach
worked with surgeon Robert Lichtenstern to experiment on humans,
taking testicles from cadavers of heterosexual men and grafting them
into the bodies of homosexual men. Although the first patient reported
increased heterosexual behavior, the surgery was ultimately deemed ineffective and by the 1920s had ceased. Nonetheless, this work helped
establish a theory of sex-differentiated hormones that would be a basis
for later research.[23]

The availability of mass-produced hormones in the United States beginning in the 1930s created renewed interest in chemical treatments

for a panoply of human needs and ailments.[24] Studying the effects of hormone treatment on "homosexual psychotics" in Kings Park State Hospital in New York, Dr. Hyman Barahal wrote:

> We have undoubtedly, in testosterone, a potent product which either resembles or represents the hormonal secretion of the male gonad. Its activity is manifested by the stimulation of secondary sex characteristics. . . . There generally results also an increase in the size of the external genitalia, with a concomitant stimulation of the libido. It is interesting to note, however, that in homosexuals this libido does not change its direction following treatment with testosterone; on the other hand, there results an increase in homosexual activity.[25]

Testosterone came to be seen as generally ineffective in reorienting homosexuals.[26] The use of androgens in women had similar effects—masculinized bodies and increased sex drive—but testosterone did not redirect sexual orientation.[27] Synthetic estrogen treatments were applied in men, but researchers found only a decrease in libido, and with high doses, chemical castration.[28] With these treatment failures and the growing prominence of psychoanalysis in the United States, organotherapies for homosexuality waned.[29]

Several intellectuals migrating from Europe to the United States during the interwar period brought psychoanalytic theories and techniques with them. Some established a new American psychoanalysis that departed greatly from the ideas of Freud and his circle. Throughout his career, Freud attempted to find a middle path between those who claimed homosexuality was "acquired" and those who said it was "inherited," proposing theories that involved an interaction of both. All people were born "polymorphously perverse," meaning they had the potential to be attracted to all sorts of objects. Human beings were also born bisexual, according to Freud, meaning that they possessed features of both masculinity and femininity within them. His view of masculinity corresponded to activity while femininity corresponded to passivity. His understanding of homosexuality also involved inversion: for men, homoerotic desire was a form of femininity and lesbian desire was a form of masculinity.[30]

Although Freud believed homosexuality was abnormal, he was pessimistic regarding the possibility of reorientation. In a famous letter to the mother of a homosexual man, he stated:

> By asking me if I can help, you mean, I suppose, if I can abolish homosexuality and make normal heterosexuality take its place. The answer is, in a general way, we cannot promise to achieve it. In a certain num-

ber of cases we succeed in developing the blighted germs of heterosexual tendencies which are present in every homosexual, in the majority of cases it is no more possible. It is a question of the quality and the age of the individual. The result of the treatment cannot be predicted.

What analysis can do for your son runs in a different line. If he is unhappy, neurotic, torn by conflicts, inhibited in his social life, analysis may bring him harmony, peace of mind, full efficiency, whether he remains a homosexual or gets changed.[31]

In this letter, Freud expressed pessimism regarding, but not outright opposition to, the practice of reorientation. In 1920 he had published one account, "The Psychogenesis of a Case of Homosexuality in a Woman," in which he described a request from the parents of a young teenage girl to reorient their daughter. In this case, Freud studied the conditions that formed her homosexuality but claimed it was not the place of psychoanalysis to try to "cure" it.[32] The idea of treating homosexuals would require departing from these classical Freudian views. Many of the new psychoanalysts faulted Freud's neglect of theorizing the active capacities of the ego, arguing that this led him to be unduly pessimistic about the possibility for cure.[33]

A key figure in the early development of what came to be known as the "adaptational school" of psychoanalysis in the United States was Hungarian émigré Sandor Rado of Columbia University. Rado had been Freud's pupil, and he was a key organizer of the Berlin Psychoanalytic Institute. He left for the United States in the 1930s. Rado blended psychoanalysis with ideas of mental hygienist Adolf Meyer, who was his close personal friend. Rado also followed the ideas of Herbert Spencer, the social theorist and philosopher who coined the term "survival of the fittest," applying a version of Charles Darwin's theory of evolution to human beings and societies. Adaptational psychoanalysis provided a psychological framework that characterized humans as striving for survival, and described human behavior in terms of adaptations developed within an environment understood to be hostile and competitive.[34]

Following Freud's death in 1938, Rado orchestrated a key departure from Freud, publishing "A Critical Examination of the Concept of Bisexuality" in 1940.[35] Rado's philosophy of the sexes began with reproduction as the primary goal of all human sexuality, a human need required for the preservation of the species. Refuting notions of "fluid sexes" based on reductionist hormonal or psychological research, Rado claimed that sex differentiation can be understood only when science takes into account that each person is part of a larger system:

> It is not permissible to single out any one element no matter how conspicuous, such as the gonad, and make it the sole criterion of sex. To attempt to determine "maleness" or "femaleness" by the relative percentage of male and female hormones in blood or urine is obviously to carry this error to an extreme. Sex can be determined only by the character of the reproductive action system *as a whole.* The human being is not a bundle of cells or tissues but a complex biological system, in which new system properties appear on every hierarchic level of integration.[36]

Within this reproductive action system, Rado believed homosexuality emerged because individuals became fearful and resentful of the opposite sex through traumatic experiences in early childhood. These might include shaming by parents about sexuality, catching parents engaged in the "marital act," and learning to associate intercourse with violence and "genital degradation." As an expression of fear, male homosexuality is based on the reassuring presence of the penis during sexual behaviors; female homosexuality is based on the reassuring absence of the penis.

Another part of Rado's psychoanalytic perspective that would be important for later theorizing involved ego psychology, in which the ego produced "emergency behaviors" whenever overwhelmed with fear. "Emergency behaviors" were directed by the ego to avoid a threat. To avoid the fear of the opposite sex, for example, the homosexual engaged in the emergency behavioral pattern of same-sex sexual activity, as a "reparative adjustment." Such a pattern of behavior was "reparative" in that it allowed for sexual gratification, even in a diseased form. In a sense, Rado's theory provided a canvas upon which psychoanalysts could paint many speculations about different sources of fear.

Early psychoanalytic concepts in the United States were sometimes used to justify other treatment methods, even those that were physically invasive. In one notorious case in 1940, psychiatrist Newdigate Owensby, working in the state of Georgia, used the chemical Metrazol to induce grand mal seizures in six homosexual subjects, creating in some cases up to fifteen seizures during the course of treatment. Owensby explained the basis of the therapy:

> Our investigations were based on the assumption that homosexuality and lesbianism are symptoms of an under developed schizophrenia which was arrested at the particular phase in its psychosexual development where the libido became fixated and that metrazol liberates this

previous fixation of the libido and the psychosexual energy becomes free once more to flow through regular physiological channels.[37]

In all six cases, subjects became heterosexual in terms of behavior. The case briefs described clients who sought therapy either because of court mandate or to escape some form of social pressure:

Case 2.—A white male aged thirty-four years. Had been a homosexual since his fifteenth year. He was frank enough to admit that the only reason for seeking treatment was fear of exposure and subsequent disgrace. All homosexual desires disappeared after seven grand mal attacks were induced by metrazol. He was married four months later. At the expiration of ten months he stated there had been no recurrence of homosexual desires or practices.[38]

Apparently, Owensby blended psychoanalytic concepts with other psychiatric treatments to produce the effect of overcoming arrested development, measurable in this case through heterosexual marriage and cessation of homosexual behaviors. While treatments such as Metrazol are indeed grisly from a contemporary perspective, it should be noted that such invasive treatments were applied to a range of mental conditions.[39]

This brief history of the rise of treatable versions of homosexuality highlights their origins in relation to social cleavages of race and class. While many early treatments and diagnoses located homosexuality in the "degenerate" body, especially for the lower classes, a psychogenic regime that conceptualized homosexuality as a learned behavior, brought about by contaminating effects of contact with "degenerates" and later from abnormal family dynamics, would come to prevail in psychiatry. Conceptualizing the condition as a learned behavior rather than an inherent part of a person made "rescue" possible for those deemed worthy. Prior to the Kinsey studies, the theory and treatment of psychogenic homosexuality was a relatively obscure enterprise, addressing an aberration that existed in the shadows of society. Most therapists maintained Freud's therapeutic pessimism. Once the Kinsey studies emerged, the urgency with which medical experts attended to homosexuality increased dramatically, because it appeared that this condition was widespread. Suddenly homosexuality existed within every third man walking by on the street. Psychoanalytic psychiatry, which had been seen as successful in the treatment of war neuroses in World War II, was poised to dominate the mental health fields in the postwar era and to promote the treatment of homosexuality, among other maladies.

The Psychoanalyst and the Case Study

In psychiatry's ascent to professional power, the *Diagnostic and Statistical Manual of Mental Disorders* was established in 1952 to help carve out and clarify the jurisdiction of the profession from the rest of medicine. In the *DSM,* "Homosexuality" was officially classified as a personality disorder. The cultural condemnation of homosexuality during this period strongly supported the idea of pathology upon which reorientation therapy rested. Given state, cultural, and now official psychiatric sanction of such treatments, reorientation therapists enjoyed the intellectual opportunities to flourish within science. Although these psychoanalysts can be classified as "neo-Freudian" and departed from Freud in many ways, one component of classical analysis was maintained in particular—the case study—which came to be the favored form of evidence in sexual reorientation work through the 1950s and early 1960s.

In addition to Sandor Rado's innovations, one crucial strain of thought that shaped the new psychoanalytic treatment of homosexuality in the United States was an emphasis on the "oral period" of psychosexual development. This phase of psychosexual development, in which infants learn to identify the mouth as an erotogenic zone, became emphasized as a source of neuroses and perversions, including homosexuality. This trend looked to the relationship between the infant and mother as crucial for shaping the outcome of psychosexual development.[40] Edmund Bergler was a key figure in developing an oral stage theory of the etiology of male homosexuality in the United States. He asked:

> What is the unconscious situation of a man suffering from the disease-entity "perversion homosexuality"? He has regressed to the earliest level of psychic development, the "oral stage." Every child has to cope with the fact of weaning from bottle or breast. The normal solution is in itself fantastic: The male child overcomes the trauma of weaning by denying its dependence on the mother and by consoling himself that he has on his own body an organ similar to the withdrawn breast or bottle, that is, the penis. Anatomic differences do not bother the child. His problem is to rescue vestiges of childish megalomania. Hence the ridiculous over valuation of the "breast substitute," hence the well-marked "penis pride" of the boy.[41]

For Bergler and other U.S. psychoanalysts, the equation "penis = breast" was used to explain many male same-sex sexual behaviors, especially fellatio. This formula often also included the equation "sperm = milk." Bergler argued that the futile search for the breast substitute and its inability to meet true human needs explained why homosexual men are "psychic masochists" and "injustice collectors," purposely setting up situations in which they are rejected, dominated, or disappointed, and repeatedly complaining about it.[42]

Another key departure from Freud was the rejection of "instincts" and "drives." Rather than being driven by psychic energy and libido, any human behavior or mental state could be explained without recourse to such concepts. The adaptational school rejected instincts as nonfalsifiable and scientifically useless, preferring instead discussions of "motivation," especially survival and the satisfaction of basic needs.[43] To satisfy these needs (food, shelter, sex, etc.), humans form attachments to objects through learned associations that facilitate the meeting of those needs. Resonant with Rado, this school viewed homosexuality as adaptive because, when normal heterosexual development is somehow impeded, a person seeks out members of the same sex as a pathological solution to the need for sex. "Ego psychology" therapists aimed to harness and redirect the ego to control this and other aberrant behaviors. Because homosexuality was a learned adaptation, it could be unlearned and overcome through the power of the ego.[44]

In addition to these theoretical departures from Freud, adaptational psychoanalysts deviated somewhat in terms of technique. Freud's therapeutic method was based on bringing elements of the client's unconscious into consciousness to better understand underlying conflicts. Ego psychology in the adaptational school, however, deliberately reeducated the ego to achieve goals deemed to be healthy. At times, this could even involve direct confrontation by the therapist. In one exchange from a case study, Bergler confronts "Mr. P." whom he describes as an effeminate man:

> "In addition to smelling your expensive perfume, I also smell a rat. Your story, as presented by you, simply does not add up. You don't give the impression of wanting to change. What is the 'hidden motive' and where do I fit in? Are you in any legal trouble? Are you being blackmailed?"
>
> "Absolutely no!"
>
> "Then what is it?"
>
> "Nothing. Just simple outside pressure."
>
> "You will have to be less evasive than that."
>
> "You will have to trust me."
>
> "I see no reason to do so."[45]

Such therapeutic practices, considered in the context of widespread legal and social ostracism of homosexuals, both reflected and constituted the power imbalance that existed between the psychiatrist and the client.

After 1948 adaptational psychoanalysts had to contend with the threat posed by the Kinsey studies. Perhaps no psychoanalyst expressed more scathing criticism of Kinsey than Bergler. Writing in the journal *Psychiatric Quarterly,* he provided a multipronged critique of *Sexual Behavior in the Human Male.* Emphasizing that Kinsey was a "zoologist," Bergler highlighted Kinsey's lack of medical expertise, which, he argued, explained the failure to account for unconscious motivations underlying the pathology of homosexuality.[46] Additionally, Kinsey neglected to account for the motivations of his research subjects, all of whom likely exaggerated their reports of sexual deviance in order to feel less guilty. If a research study published statistics showing high rates of deviant behavior, then subjects would feel more normal. Bergler criticized grouping together all forms of homosexual behavior, an approach, he maintained, that glossed over the many reasons why men engaged in homosexual activities. Furthermore, Bergler predicted that the study would bring nothing less than the deterioration of society, because homosexuals now had a "scientific" justification to maintain and spread their disease. Pathology would spread among "borderline cases," and men suffering from impotence would now see themselves as homosexual.[47] Appealing to a sense of nationalism, Bergler issued a warning:

> Last but not least, Kinsey's erroneous psychological conclusions pertaining to homosexuality will be politically and propagandistically used against the United States abroad, stigmatizing the nation as a whole in a whisper campaign, especially since there are no comparative statistics available for other countries.[48]

At that time, Bergler's views resonated with broader cultural sentiments within the public and the state, viewing homosexuality as a threat to the social fabric and even the nation as a whole.

Within psychoanalysis, the purpose of the case method was to make visible the universal structures of the mind through the dynamic narrative of the single case. Reading the published case, one became aware of the structures of ego, id, and superego, and gained insight into the stages of development of the psyche. In U.S. case studies of homosexual patients, demonstrating a "cure" usually involved showing that the subject undergoing analysis had not only changed sexual behavior but had also internalized the analyst's worldview—the theory of the underlying cause. Indeed, the case study functioned not only to demonstrate cure but also to show that the analyst's approach was worthy of followers. This usually involved acknowledgment from the client that what was learned in the analysis actually led to heterosexuality. The evidence of "cure" was not only a patient's changed sexual behavior but also a newly internalized system of meaning. During this period, therapists and clients were almost exclusively men. Female homosexuality remained undertheorized, with "homosexual" often being a term used to refer to men only in psychoanalytic texts. Women did participate in psychoanalytic therapies but were usually not showcased in case reports during this time.

Among the earliest reports of the "successful" psychoanalytic treatment of a homosexual in the United States was one conducted by New York psychoanalyst John S. Poe in 1950 and published posthumously in 1952. Poe treated a forty-year-old "passive" homosexual man who tended to be the receptive partner in anal sex. In line with Rado's view of etiology, Poe described the patient's homosexuality as deriving from a fear of the penisless woman. The patient's father (either in reality or in fantasy, it is unknown) climbed into bed with him as a child and threatened to cut off his penis with a folding knife if he did not stop masturbating. According to Poe, the patient, "Mr. B.," being exclusively interested in anal sex, is, in Rado's terms, an "eidolic she-male," exhibiting femininity in his passive sexual role, as well as his appearance. Poe states, "His clothes and accessories are too extreme. He sways his hips as he walks and gestures delicately with his hands."[49] Poe described his client's problem as deriving from childhood fears stemming from his father's threats and from sleeping with his parents and later his mother alone, making the "standard coital pattern" seem like violence to the female. His sexual submissiveness became an extension of fear as a "reparative pattern." By the end of therapy, after learning to interpret his life through the lens of the adaptational school, Mr. B. changed. Poe reported on Mr. B.'s interpretation of a dream he had about his fiancée:

> On January 11, 1949 the patient reported the following dream of the night before:
>
> > "I was wandering around in E.'s apartment. I stumbled over a kitten that had a bleeding forepaw. I put some antiseptic on it but it continued to bleed. I picked the kitten up and examined the bleeding paw carefully. (I felt as though E. were around, in the kitchen or somewhere close.) I then noticed that there was a sharp wooden peg stuck into the paw. I gently withdrew it, being conscious that E. was watching me, and having a feeling of tenderness for her and the kitten. The bleeding then stopped and the kitten seemed comfortable."
>
> The patient related this dream to the fact that he had had intercourse with E. the night before and that she had been menstruating. He felt

that this made the dream interpretation obvious. He felt this indicated that he had no fear for the integrity of his penis but rather looked on it now as an aggressive organ which could inflict injury on the female genital but which he could control without permanent damage to her. It was felt that this dream indicated that a basic dynamic change had occurred.

Mr. B. was married to E. in February 1949 and has been very happy to this date (October 1, 1949).[50]

In this excerpt, not only did Mr. B. become heterosexual and happily married to E., he was also able to interpret his own experiences, including dreams, in line with the adaptational theory that male homosexuality is caused by fear of the female genitals.

If clients participated in heterosexual activity in the course of analysis but did not internalize the therapists' theory, this condition was not sufficient for "cure." This principle was evident in a case reported by Lionel Ovesey, another psychoanalyst who followed Rado but who developed his own theory of "pseudohomosexuality" that extended Rado's adaptational perspective. Ovesey believed homosexuality was motivated by more than just homosexual urges themselves. Rather, pseudohomosexuality involved a form of sought-out dependency, in which homosexuals deliberately set up situations in which they would be powerless. It also manifested as excessive aggression—a compensation for the feeling of dependence. Consequently, homosexuals tended to create relationships with power imbalances, even with a therapist:

> After six months of treatment, he felt he was cured: He was ready to marry the girl, his problem on the job had disappeared, and he was free of anxiety. He said, "I look back on my homosexual life as something of the past. I guess I was just sowing my wild oats and now I'm ready to settle down."
>
> The patient's rapid improvement had all the earmarks of a transference "cure." In his opening dream he had already indicated his magical expectations from therapy. Apparently, he had acted on them and, in the transference, had supplanted the original weak father with a stronger one represented by the therapist. Thus, magically armed with the latter's strength, he sufficiently overcame his fear of women to embark on his heterosexual adventures, but the fear was hardly resolved, nor were its unconscious origins understood.[51]

It was only after the client learned to understand the underpinnings of his fear of female genitals—deriving from his conflicts with his parents based in the Oedipus complex—that he could experience real change. He became less dependent on his therapist, less competitive and more successful at work, dated less "hysterically," learned to frame his life experiences within Ovesey's framework, and developed a stable relationship with his female partner, "L."

By the 1950s psychoanalysis began to face a major intellectual challenge from experimental psychology, including a school of behavior therapy that challenged the effectiveness of psychoanalysis as "insight-based."[52] In 1952 British behaviorist Hans Eysenck published a landmark study in the *Journal of Consulting Psychology* in which he claimed that psychoanalysis and other talk therapies were no better than "spontaneous recovery." To estimate a baseline spontaneous recovery rate, Eysenck looked at the annual percentage of neurotics who were discharged from mental hospitals where there was little, if any, psychotherapy. He estimated that two-thirds of neurotics recovered on their own. Compiling various case studies of psychoanalysts and other eclectic talk therapists, he found that the recovery rate for clients of psychoanalysts was 44 percent and for clients of eclectic therapists, 64 percent. Eysenck stopped short of saying psychoanalytic therapies were ineffective, but he claimed there was insufficient evidence to show they worked. He provocatively concluded:

> In the absence of agreement between fact and belief, there is urgent need for a decrease in the strength of belief, and for an increase in the number of facts available. Until such facts as may be discovered in process of rigorous analysis support the prevalent belief in therapeutic effectiveness of psychological treatment, it seems premature to insist on the inclusion of training in such treatment in the curriculum of the clinical psychologist.[53]

The Eysenck study was the first of many challenges to psychoanalysis. By contrast, demonstrations of the efficacy of behavior therapies were based on experimental methods, using control groups and physiological measures in the tradition of experimental psychology.

Partially in response to such challenges to the scientific basis of psychoanalysis, the Society of Medical Psychoanalysts in New York began a large study that would become the most influential of the early 1960s. Led by psychoanalyst Irving Bieber and published in 1962, a decade after the research began, *Homosexuality: A Psychoanalytic Study* aggregated data on the psychoanalytic treatment of 106 homosexual men and 100 heterosexual male controls, with an emphasis on understanding underlying causes. Each of the seventy-seven psychoanalysts participating in the study was given a questionnaire divided into questions about their patients' relationships in a set of subsystems, including the mother–son relationship, father–son relationship, and sibling relationships, to uncover which explanation of the cause of homosexuality had the most force among a series of possible theories.[54]

On the basis of their results, the authors claimed the study supported Rado's adaptational theory in which homosexuality is caused by overwhelming fears of the opposite sex. In the "typical" pattern, boys developed fears of women through interactions with the "close binding intimate" (CBI) mother and the detached, hostile, or absent father. As a boy, the future homosexual man was typically placed at the center of a triangular marital conflict, in which the mother conspired to turn the son against the father and sought to fulfill her own unmet romantic needs with her son. In turn, father turned against both mother and boy. The mother seduced her son, catering to his unconscious incestuous wishes, while simultaneously undermining his masculinity, ensuring that he would not leave her for another woman. The father, who would typically challenge the influence of a CBI mother, was instead distant, detached, and even hostile, further compounding the mother's domination of the boy. As a boy, the typical homosexual was sexually overstimulated by the "romantic but not sexual" relationship with his mother. This overstimulation, combined with the fact that the mother continually undermined the boy's masculinity, induced a general fear of the female sexual organ and forced the son to eventually meet sexual needs with other men. Homosexuality is a "reparative pattern" because it is a means of trying to restore heterosexuality. Men seek other men with masculine characteristics, such as large penises, in order to symbolically incorporate the other man's masculinity, usually through oral sexual practices.

While the Bieber study primarily investigated causes of homosexuality, it also included a chapter on treatment. A heterosexual behavioral outcome was the most important concern for the research team. In a typical example, case no. 166 became exclusively heterosexual despite his close binding mother and distant and hostile father: "At last follow-up, three years after completion of psychoanalysis, the patient reported that he was happily married, had a son in whom he took great pride, and that he has continued to do exceedingly well in his work."[55]

Thus, psychoanalytic treatments of homosexuality brought together ideas about pathological adaptations, sources of fear, oral stage regression, and the power of the ego to overcome mental illness. During a period when traditional gender norms were strongly enforced, it is perhaps not surprising that psychoanalysts would find a pattern of doting mothers and preoccupied fathers in their client narratives, which they could theorize as the cause of homosexuality. In these cases, a proper psychoanalytic "cure" of homosexuality required that two conditions be fulfilled: the client behaved heterosexually, and he incorporated a set of beliefs about the nature of homosexuality. The technique of the case study meant that the perception of cure belonged to the analyst first and foremost, as it was the analyst who had to be convinced by the client that changes had actually occurred. While challenges to these epistemic practices were relatively weak in the early 1950s, stronger challenges to psychoanalysis emerged with the development of the homophile movement, followed by the importation of competing behavior therapies from Britain.

Homophiles Resist the Reorientation Regime

If the Kinsey studies prodded a reaction in the form of the reorientation regime, they also emboldened a movement in support of homosexuals. In 1951 a group of Los Angeles men involved in the Communist Party formed a homosexual emancipation group, the Mattachine Society, built on the secretive and cell-based model of their Marxist organization. While the radical era of this movement would be short lived, during the early years they built a sense of collective identity as an "oppressed minority group." The boundaries of the movement were strongly enforced, and the group developed tactics of direct action to challenge oppressive laws. They also engaged in leafleting and sought to create an "ethical culture" as a group. The early Mattachine Society successfully supported a member through a case of police entrapment, leading to his acquittal.[56] However, such outspoken tactics could not be sustained within the repressive political climate of the McCarthy era.

Allegations in 1953 by a newspaper columnist that the "homophile" movement might be a group of subversives threatened the Mattachines to such an extent that the group transformed its strategies from radical tactics to seeking assimilation and working with sympathetic experts.[57] Although the magazine *ONE* maintained the radical vision, the Mattachines, along with a women's group, Daughters of Bilitis, strove to fit in alongside heterosexuals. Rather than utilizing direct confrontation, they portrayed respectability and worked with researchers, most notably UCLA psychologist Evelyn Hooker, to challenge psychoanalytic orthodoxy through science. The assimilationist strategy of the homophiles made it difficult, however, for the movement to maintain a sense of itself. The result was a contradictory sense of collective identity, a "we" that no longer wished to be separate but that still acknowledged distinction. This made sustaining the homophile movement and knowing its boundaries quite difficult, and made the collaborative work of sympathetic experts even more important. The work between Hooker and the homophile movement fits a model of knowledge production found in hybrid social movements. That is, lay actors and formal experts both brought expertise to the table in the production of knowledge. Homophile group members brought their personal experience and their social networks, while Hooker and her collaborators brought expertise in mental health testing.

One of the difficulties for this movement was that early on homophiles themselves remained divided on whether to challenge the homosexuality diagnosis in the first place. This dilemma surrounded the figure of Donald Webster Cory, whose book *The Homosexual in America* (1951) was a foundational and inspirational text for the movement. Cory, whose real name was Edward Sagarin, had a friendly relationship with psychoanalyst Albert Ellis, who wrote the introduction to his book.[58] Ellis, also a psychologist, departed from many of the views of psychoanalysts opposed to homosexuality. Outspokenly supportive of gay emancipation, Ellis developed the perspective, eventually adopted by Cory, that *exclusive* homosexuality is a form of neurosis. For all human beings to be healthy, Ellis thought they should acknowledge and act on their innate bisexuality.[59] Cory was married with a son when he wrote *The Homosexual in America,* and lived a compartmentalized life, so it was ironic that his work was so important to the homophile movement.

Cory's position notwithstanding, Evelyn Hooker worked with the homophiles and became the first psychologist to publish a study claiming that homosexuality was not necessarily pathological. Her work, and the funding she was able to strategically secure, reveal that the intellectual opportunity structure, while immensely hostile to homosexuality, offered some minimal flexibility within which she could maneuver. Hooker's interest in equality stemmed, in part, from her experiences on a fellowship at the Institute of Psychology in Berlin during the 1930s, when she stayed with a Jewish family, and later traveled through Russia during the Great Purge of 1938 under Stalin. Seeing oppression firsthand in these contexts encouraged her to make social justice a central part of her work.[60] She was persuaded to research the nonpathological aspects of homosexual life by one of her students at UCLA. Working within a scientific world in which homosexuality was considered pathological required that she collaborate with a psychiatric consultant. Her work was eventually funded by a grant from the National Institute of

Mental Health. While UCLA initially required her to do her research on campus, Hooker fought the university to allow her to do the work in her home off campus, since doing this research at the university would not have been possible given confidentiality concerns of participants.[61] Within the context of an intellectual opportunity structure hostile to the idea that homosexuals could be mentally healthy, Hooker strategically followed rules but worked around them when necessary.

Unlike many of her colleagues, Hooker took seriously the homosexual identity asserted by homophile groups, and investigated its positive as well as negative aspects. Hooker echoed the homophile movement's ambivalence about group identity, treating group dynamics that set homosexuals apart from the rest of society as a potential source of pathology, but she also saw that coming out and belonging to a community had important benefits. Rather than a diseased set of attractions and behaviors, homosexuality was something that people could healthfully identify with as needed.

For Hooker, psychoanalytic theories of the individual failed to take into account a number of key social dynamics. In a preliminary analysis of male homosexuals, she claimed that much of the pathology observed in this group, such as depression or neurosis, was likely due to societal oppression:

> It would be strange indeed if all the traits due to victimization in minority groups were, in the homosexual, produced by inner dynamics of the personality, since he is also a member of an out-group which is subject to extreme penalties, involving, according to Kinsey, "cruelties (which) have not often been matched, except in religious and racial persecutions."[62]

Indeed, the question of whether pathologies associated with homosexuality were inherent or were reactions to social stigma would be an important one, as sexual reorientation therapists seized upon higher rates of illnesses among homosexuals as evidence of a need for reorientation treatment.

Hooker found that in her research subjects, "coming out" and adopting a homosexual identity, with connection to a larger community, could be positive for a person's mental health:

> With group support and belongingness some anxieties tend to be diminished. These individuals are, in some aspects at least, mutually supportive. The groups are therapeutic groups in the sense that they give support to the individuals, give a possibility of identification with

a group and thus reduce marginality and isolation, and often afford release of tensions and anxieties.[63]

Through coming out, homosexuals gained access to support and a community social life. However, reflecting the Mattachine Society's push for a collective identity based on assimilation, Hooker noted that living in separate and oppressed communities could create group-induced pathologies. The mutual overexcitation within the segregated group, without sufficient release of tension, led to disturbed behaviors like exhibitionism and promiscuity. Furthermore, marginalization led to rigid rules. What was ultimately needed was full integration into the larger community.

Hooker further expressed the ethos of assimilation in her 1957 psychological research study, "The Adjustment of the Male Overt Homosexual," which directly challenged the diagnosis of homosexuality as a personality disorder. She sought out "well adjusted" homosexual men for her study through her networks in homophile organizations, and matched each one with a heterosexual control on age, education, and IQ. This would be the first study of homosexuals who were not in prisons, clinics, or mental hospitals, and who might show an "average adjustment, provided (for the purpose of the investigation) that homosexuality is not considered to be a symptom of maladjustment."[64] To evaluate personality adjustment, Hooker's study used a set of projective personality tests, including the Rorschach inkblot test and others. A team of internationally renowned experts evaluated the data, and Hooker concluded that homosexuality per se should not be considered a mental disorder. The judges could not do better than chance when trying to discern which Rorschach interpretations came from homosexuals and which were from heterosexuals. In the qualitative portion of the report, Hooker described a homosexual subject who had been misidentified by the judges as a well-adjusted heterosexual:

> This man is in his early 40's and holds two master's degrees in different artistic fields from one of the major educational institutions of this country. He had a long career as a college teacher—long, and apparently successful. He was caught in what was, to the police, suspicious circumstances with another man, and in the space of a few minutes his entire professional career was destroyed. He now is the manager of a magazine. Although in his early life he passed through the "cruising" stage, he now has highly stable personal relationships, including a "homosexual marriage." If one brackets the fact that he is a homosexual, one would think of him as being a highly cultured, intelligent

man who, though unconventional in his manner of living, exhibits no particular signs of pathology. He has never sought psychological or psychiatric help. He has been a homosexual from adolescence, with no heterosexual experience or inclination.[65]

Here was one among many cases of well-adjusted self-identified homosexual men that Hooker presented to the scientific community. Summarizing the data, she concluded that there were many forms of homosexual adjustment, pathological and healthy, and due to this variety, homosexuality in itself could not be considered an illness.

By the mid-1960s, a new spirit in the homophile movement drew ideas and tactics from the civil rights movement. Led by Frank Kameny and Barbara Gittings, and emboldened by Hooker's research, the movement sought to challenge the medical model of homosexuality directly.[66] The new boundaries of the homophile collective identity no longer included people who believed in an illness model of homosexuality. Albert Ellis claimed at a convention that "the exclusive homosexual is a psychopath," to which an audience member retorted, "Any homosexual who would come to you for treatment, Dr. Ellis, would *have* to be a psychopath."[67] Kameny wrote to Cory, who upheld Ellis's view, "You have left the mainstream for the backwaters . . . the senile Grandfather of the Homophile Movement, to be humored and tolerated at best; to be ignored and disregarded usually; and to be ridiculed at worst."[68] By 1966 the newly created North American Conference of Homophile Organizations (NACHO) took on a civil rights posture, and by 1968, the group adopted a resolution and motto modeled after the black pride slogan "Black Is Beautiful," namely, "Gay Is Good." That same year, the first confrontation between activists and psychiatrists took place when a Columbia University student group protested a medical school panel on homosexuality for not including homosexuals.[69]

Undeterred by these developments, psychoanalysts developed strategies to deal with the emergent phenomenon of affirmative homosexual identity. Some psychoanalysts treated homosexual identification as a symptom of deeply entrenched pathology. Lionel Ovesey advised that when selecting male clients, those with homosexual identification should be avoided. While nothing was impossible in therapy, Ovesey argued that those who were so exclusively homosexual that they identified with it were beyond remedy: "Those in the unfavorable group do not often appear in the psychiatrist's office, and when they do, their motivation will usually not stand up to challenge. The problem of selecting homosexuals

Barbara Gittings and Phil Johnson present a booth at the American Psychiatric Association conference in 1972, "Gay, Proud, and Healthy," working toward removal of the stigmatizing "Homosexuality" diagnosis from the *DSM*. Photograph by Kay Lahusen. Courtesy of John J. Wilcox, Jr. LGBT Archives of Philadelphia.

as patients for treatment, therefore, is solved for the most part by the homosexuals themselves."[70]

Charles Socarides, who would become the primary leader in the opposition to removing homosexuality from the *DSM* and later a cofounder of the National Association for Research and Therapy of Homosexuality, took a more direct approach to rising resistance. Socarides's view was that heterosexuality, like homosexuality, was psychogenic. He believed that strong pro-heterosexual social norms with distinct sex divisions had evolved over time in order for children to learn to be properly heterosexual. His opposition to homosexuality thus stemmed from his perception of the need to maintain a set of values necessary for the preservation of society. Consequently, Socarides launched an all-out assault on homosexuality. At a convention of the American Medical Association in June 1968, he described homosexuality as "a dread dysfunction, malignant in character, which has risen to epidemic proportions," and he called on the federal government to create national centers for rehabilitating homosexuals:[71]

> The "solution" of homosexuality is always doomed to failure. . . . Homosexuality is based on fear of the mother, the aggressive attack on the

father, and is filled with aggression, destruction, and self-deceit. It is a masquerade of life in which certain psychic energies are neutralized and held in a somewhat quiescent state. However, the unconscious manifestations of hate, destructiveness, incest and fear are always threatening to break through. Instead of union, cooperation, solace, stimulation, enrichment, healthy challenge and fulfillment, there are only destruction, mutual defeat, exploitation of the partner and the self, oral-sadistic incorporation, aggressive onslaughts, attempts to alleviate anxiety and pseudo-solution to the aggressive and libidinal urges which dominate and torment the individual.[72]

Socarides claimed that half of homosexuals experienced serious mental illnesses and the other half "when neurotic may be of the obsessional or, occasionally, of the phobic type. They may suffer from character disorders, psychopathic personality or some variety of addiction."[73] These strongly articulated views, along with his general theory about sexuality, would propel him to a leadership role in the coming years.

Through the 1960s forces amassed in preparation for a clash over the homosexuality diagnosis. The homophile movement had radicalized, and Hooker and others had provided scientific literature that would be instrumental in that cause. In Great Britain, the Wolfenden Report of 1957 had recommended that homosexuality no longer be considered a disorder. Psychoanalysts developed different postures in response to the growing challenges. One move was quietly made in 1968 prior to the conflict; in the new *DSM-II*, "Homosexuality" was removed from the section on personality disorders and placed in the section on sexual deviations, perhaps in an attempt to make Hooker's personality-based work less relevant. Challenges to the scientific basis of psychoanalysis persisted, however, making room for behavior therapy of homosexuality to be imported from Britain into the United States in the late 1960s. While this was a competing school of mental health, behavior therapists initially joined forces with psychoanalysts in maintaining homosexuality's status as a medical condition.

The Behaviorist and the Physiological Test

While psychoanalysis was the predominant theoretical basis for psychiatry in the United States over the first half of the twentieth century, academic psychology was dominated by behaviorism. The work of this school was primarily confined to academia—mostly research on animals—including teaching rats to run mazes, or teaching animals in a cage known as the "Skinner box" to press buttons for food or to avoid electric shocks. The new innovation of behavior therapy applied these decades of research to the clinical setting with human beings.

Disagreements were plentiful within behaviorism, but there were key shared assumptions. One was bracketing the question of the existence of "mind" or "consciousness" and focusing instead on the body and the brain as the targets of research and therapy. Radical versions of behaviorism assumed there is no such thing as consciousness, casting as epiphenomenal anything experienced as mind. Subsumed within the category of behavior, rational thought was understood to be the product of learning processes and lifelong conditioning.[74] Behaviorists sought to understand causes and effects within the brain, allowing researchers to predict a response, given any stimulus. Likewise, if an organism's response were known, a researcher could predict the stimulus. Behavior therapy conceptualized the brain as malleable and capable of further learning.[75] There was no consensus on the initial causes of homosexuality; behaviorists entertained a range of theories, including treating it as a learned behavior, the result of concentrations of prenatal hormones, and even heredity.[76] Regardless, behaviorists sought to treat, or "extinguish," homosexuality. However, rather than assuming, as psychoanalysts did, that heterosexuality would emerge naturally, behavior therapists believed that it would have to be taught or induced.

Behavior therapy for homosexuality began with male subjects, many of whom were referred for treatment after conviction for sexual offenses. Like psychoanalysts, behaviorists believed that male homosexuality involved a fear of women.[77] This emphasis on fear was one reason why these schools were able to collaborate on treatment. Like the adaptational school, behaviorism assumed that humans are motivated primarily by utilitarian and instrumental concerns: what is good is whatever helps a person attain physical objectives, and what is moral is whatever yields personal gain. A person is a "physical locus of a set of abstract, operationally definable attributes whose sole focus [is] to promote adaptation to immediate social circumstances."[78] Given the many shared assumptions about human nature, including the malleability of homosexuality, the adaptational school of psychoanalysis and the behaviorists seemed to differ mostly on mind/body questions: whether consciousness was real or epiphenomenal, and whether treatment required intervention at the level of the mind or the body. A crucial and consequential difference was in the acquisition of heterosexuality. For psychoanalysts (with the exception of Socarides), heterosexuality emerged naturally once fears were overcome, whereas for behavior therapists the client had to be reconditioned.

The Association for the Advancement for Behavior Therapies (AABT) was founded in the United States in 1966. Many proponents hoped behavior therapy, grounded on scientific method in the laboratory, would replace psychoanalysis. Devoted to evidence-based treatments, the behaviorists invoked the tradition of the experimental method in psychology as the basis for their credibility and professional identity. This approach originated much earlier, however, and its techniques were imported from Europe.

The behaviorist treatment of homosexuality began across the Atlantic in the mid-1950s. The first large study was performed in Czechoslovakia. Kurt Freund, a sexologist at the Clarke Institute of Psychiatry in Prague and connected to the Eysenck group in Britain, conducted the study, with a sample of sixty-seven male subjects. Freund treated the men with a form of "aversion therapy," which would become the most controversial form of treatment. Aversion therapy coupled same-sex imagery with an aversive stimulus as a form of negative conditioning. Freund used an agent to induce vomiting while male subjects viewed still images of nude males. This method was later coupled with positive conditioning, whereby Freund gave men testosterone as they viewed images of nude females. Measuring outcomes in terms of sexual behaviors—whether or not subjects sustained heterosexual relationships—Freund found that at the five-year follow-up, 25 percent of the men were sustaining heterosexual relationships.[79]

In the 1960s British mental health experts interested in maintaining the homosexuality diagnosis had been encouraged by Freund's results. In 1961 Stanley Rachman of the Institute of Psychiatry in London called for the application of behavior therapy treatments for homosexuality among a host of other "sexual disorders," including fetishism, exhibitionism, and impotence.[80] British psychologist Basil James took up Rachman's challenge, treating one male client by duplicating Freund's methods. James reported the outcomes in terms of sexual behavior, but with much more physical detail than the psychoanalysts:

> His relatives describe him as "a new man," and his relations with them as wholly satisfactory and better than at anytime in his life. He himself has felt no attraction at all to the same sex since the treatment, whereas previously this attraction had been present throughout every day. Sexual fantasy is entirely heterosexual and he soon acquired a regular girl friend. Kissing and strong petting occurs regularly, and is

entirely pleasurable, in contrast with the revulsion with which he had previously regarded any heterosexual contact. In these situations he achieves strong erections and has the desire to make further sexual advances. He has ejaculated on several occasions in this situation.[81]

British behavior therapy research advanced in accordance with Rachman's recommendations, moving on to electric shock, or "faradic," aversion therapy. One research team used this technique, applying electrodes built into the floor while one male subject watched nude images, and in this case the researchers narrowed the measure of outcome to masturbatory fantasy content.[82] The subject, who had sought out treatment after seeing news reports on the James study, was deemed a success because he still masturbated to fantasies of sex with women on follow-up. Responding to the charge for evidence-based therapies, behavior therapists would continue to develop increasingly specific measures of sexual attraction. Finally, they applied something called the "phallometric test," then considered to be the best measure of sexual attraction.

Among the first to apply the phallometric test in the treatment of homosexuality was psychiatrist John Bancroft, at St. George's Hospital in London. He derived the concept from earlier work by Kurt Freund. In the 1950s Freund had been commissioned by the Czech government to develop a means to ferret out men who were lying to get out of military service by claiming to be homosexual.[83] He developed the test to monitor genital arousal while subjects viewed still pictures of nude men and women. Freund invented a "penile plethysmograph" device, which encapsulated the penis within a vacuum air chamber while the amount of air displaced by the action of tumescence was recorded on a rotating drum.[84] In his own research, Freund had applied the technique to measure the outcomes of aversion therapy with pedophiles. While adopting Freund's test, Bancroft developed the "mercury-in-rubber strain gauge" to replace the vacuum air chamber, as he thought the chamber produced mechanical stimulation of the penis and was unreliable. Bancroft also claimed his device, which essentially measured changes in the circumference of the penis through the use of an expandable wire loop, was less cumbersome. He initially applied it to test the aversion therapy treatment of a pedophile,[85] but soon after used it in the treatment of homosexuals.[86]

Aversion therapy for homosexuality began in the United States in the late 1960s and early 1970s, at a complicated time for reorientation researchers. On the one hand, psychoanalysts had paved the way for the treatment of homosexuality, and the AABT was a supportive scientific community. However, psychoanalysts still maintained jurisdiction over the field. For behaviorists to gain entry into the market, they would have to rely on the experimental method as the marker of their credibility, and this shaped their research practices. This was also a time when behavior therapies were under attack. Anti-psychiatry writer Thomas Szasz had criticized behavior therapy as denying human freedom,[87] and a cultural backlash appeared in a novel by the British writer Anthony Burgess, *A Clockwork Orange* (1962), which Stanley Kubrick made into a successful film in 1971. Complicating things further for behaviorists, the gay liberation movement launched in 1969 following the Stonewall Rebellion in New York and similar riots across the United States. Forces amassing in the radicalized homophile movement blended with the gay subculture and launched a challenge to psychiatry, calling for deletion of homosexuality in the *DSM* as a means to attain full rights in society. In 1970 Australian psychiatrist Nathaniel McConaghy, a leading practitioner of aversion therapy for homosexuality, was among several psychiatrists publicly admonished at the conference of the American Psychiatric Association in San Francisco, with activists shouting, "Vicious," "Torture," "Where did you take your residency, Auschwitz?," and "We've listened to you, now you listen to us."[88] Thus, behavior therapy of homosexuality came to the United States at a moment of direct confrontation by the people it was supposed to treat, when gays came to understand that aversion therapies were evidence of mental health experts' hostility.[89]

In these circumstances, behaviorists in the United States avoided controversial methods of applying aversive stimuli and attempted to create more humane alternatives. For example, in 1967 Joseph Cautela applied the method of "covert sensitization" to two homosexual subjects. Rather than applying an aversive stimulus, Cautela instructed subjects to imagine they were vomiting as they looked at erotic images. "Systematic desensitization" was another softer technique, in which a subject was gradually exposed to a stimulus that aroused fear. For example, in a "fading" method, a male client became aroused while viewing a male nude, and gradually the image would be faded into a female nude.[90] In one form of systematic desensitization, Gerald Davison developed the technique of "orgasmic reconditioning," also known as "Playboy therapy," initially to treat a client with sadistic fantasies.[91] The therapy directed the male client to masturbate while looking at images of nude women in order to eliminate the unwanted fantasies.

When aversion therapy was eventually applied in behavior therapy research in the United States, it tended to take the form of "avoidance training" with electric shocks. This technique was designed such that the subject had the opportunity to avoid electric shock altogether. Typically a male subject would be shown a slide of a nude male, and if he did not advance the image after a short amount of time, he received an electric shock. The idea was to train the subject to associate the aversive stimulus with spending too much time with the unwanted stimulus. Theoretically, lingering in fantasy about a member of the same sex would become associated with pain.[92]

By the end of the 1960s and into the 1970s, behavior therapists had consolidated their own notion of sexual orientation through their therapeutic and measurement practices, compared to the ideas of psychoanalysts. Through deployment of the phallometric test, male sexual orientation was located in the body, as a learned physiological response to visual stimuli. Importantly, within the rubric of behavior therapy, physiological arousal within a testing scenario was conceptualized as a form of behavior, regardless of one's ability or willingness to control it, given that consciousness was considered epiphenomenal to begin with. While the gay liberation movement shaped therapeutic techniques, leading behaviorists to devise conditioning methods that looked less like forms of aggressive punishment, activists did not shape these measurement practices. The drive toward specificity—measuring arousal directly from the penis rather than any other physiological arousal test—was a product of behaviorists' competition with psychoanalysis, emphasizing the experimental method. Even though a "vaginal photoplethysmograph" device was invented in 1975 to measure women's sexual arousal using an optical device,[93] the vision of behavior therapy for female homosexuality would not come to pass, as these treatments would dwindle with the demedicalization of homosexuality.

Competing Authoritarian Measures of Behavior

Treatable psychogenic homosexuality was, in many ways, a U.S. invention. In the 1950s, within a quite favorable climate that included state and broader cultural support, psychoanalysts in the United States built on the social ameliorationist theory, but distilled it, departing from Freud's theory of drives and asserting that homosexuality had no biological basis. Homosexuality was an acquired disease that could be treated through therapies that cleansed the heterosexual man of pathological homoerotic "contaminants." Case study narratives showcased the therapist's skill and worldview, as clients achieved heterosexual behavior by internalizing a value system. When behavior therapy rose as a competitor to psychoanalysis, it had many similarities with its predecessor: namely, that homosexuality was a complex of fears that could be treated.

However, the subject in behaviorism was an improperly molded body in need of reconditioning. Phallometric testing constituted sexual subjectivity based on visually directed genital arousal response.[94]

With competing measurement techniques, each school located homosexuality in different places within the human subject. Psychoanalysis located it in a system of meaning within the mind, held in place by irrational fears that could be alleviated, but also located it in sexual behaviors expressed by the client. Behaviorism located it in a body that could be reprogrammed, understanding physiological response to erotic imagery as a form of behavior. The psychiatric case study and the behaviorist phallometric test can both be considered authoritarian forms of evidence from the perspective of the client. It was always the therapist, and his technology, who determined the status of the patient, rather than the patient himself. While both settings allowed for negotiations and evasions on the part of the client, it was always on the researcher's terms. In the political climate of the day, the case method addressed pathologies in ways that aligned with hegemonic value systems. By constituting homosexuality as a condition that could be overcome, the treatment of psychogenic homosexuality with ego psychology resonated with the ethos of individualism and self-determination characteristic of dominant American ideologies.

The weakening of psychoanalysis coupled with gradual changes in the political climate made room for behaviorism and the growth of a militant gay liberation movement. As intellectual opportunities in science for pro-gay forces were scant, resistance in this period did little to challenge the epistemic practices of psychoanalysts and behavior therapists, but it did shape theories and therapeutic methods in later years. If anything, the visibility of gay activism initially provided fodder for the view held by therapists that homosexuality was a growing epidemic.

While homophile activists did not shape the dominant measurement practices of reorientation therapists, these practices were influenced by battles over professional jurisdiction. Challenges that psychoanalytic methods were unscientific led the Bieber research team uncharacteristically to adopt controls, statistics, and a large sample to demonstrate experimental rigor. The struggle to challenge psychoanalysis pushed behavior therapists to refine their measurement techniques, using a technology that they argued was the most specific means for capturing sexual arousal. Nonetheless, the ideas and activist networks established in this period would be instrumental in the decade to come, leading to the deletion of "Homosexuality" from the *DSM*.

By 1970 the field of therapeutics was in dramatic flux regarding the issue of homosexuality. Gay activists had come to see the methods of re-orientation therapists as hostile. The more important source of concern, however, was the assumption that homosexuality was something to be treated. Chapter 2 begins with the story of the removal of the "Homo-sexuality" diagnosis from the *DSM*, centering on the career of psychia-trist Robert Spitzer, who became prominent in this process. While this fight was successful and significantly altered the field of therapeutics, the dynamics within this field would take on a new character with the addi-tion of a countermovement of ex-gays. Perhaps one of the most impor-tant legacies of the psychogenic-treatable model of homosexuality would be the emergence of an antithetical and influential model: that of innate and immutable homosexuality.

two

THE EVOLUTION OF DR. ROBERT SPITZER
The Rise of Gay-Affirmative Therapies, 1970–2003

In the history of homosexuality and mental health professions in the United States, psychiatrist Dr. Robert Spitzer has been pivotal. Yet, despite his influence, homosexuality was never the primary topic of his research. Rather, he is most known in the field for his development of psychiatric diagnostic manuals. After leading the revisions of two versions of the *DSM*, Spitzer was active in the development of a third and is known for his leadership role in ushering in psychiatry's contemporary psychopharmacological approach. Earlier in his career, he developed computer tools that facilitate diagnoses in clinical settings.[1] Overall, his thinking has been important for determining what qualifies as a disorder in psychiatry and other mental health fields.

In the early 1970s, when Spitzer was a member of the American Psychiatric Association Nomenclature Committee, he convinced fellow committee members to permit an openly gay psychologist to present scientific research arguing that homosexuality is not a mental disorder. Spitzer's personal decision-making process became influential, and once he came to terms with demedicalization, others on the committee followed suit. Given this central role in the removal of "Homosexuality" from the *DSM*, it might seem surprising that by the late 1990s, Spitzer decided to conduct a study to assess whether gay and lesbian people could be *reoriented* to heterosexuality. Spitzer gathered a sample of two hundred people who claimed to have successfully left homosexuality for at least five years. He performed a telephone survey, asking respondents to retrospectively rate their sexual attractions, behavior, and identity before and after reorientation. Reporting at a conference of the American Psychiatric Association in 2001 and in the journal *Archives of Sexual*

Behavior in 2003, he announced that some highly motivated gays and lesbians could indeed change their sexual orientation through therapy or religious ministry. The media picked up the story and reported it widely. Spitzer's decision to conduct the study left many perplexed, but he emerged as a credible spokesperson for the ex-gay movement, having been central to the demedicalization of homosexuality. Reports about his findings were exaggerated and often transformed by this movement and religious right organizations more broadly, despite Spitzer's attempts to rein in some overstated claims.

Spitzer offered one explanation of his seemingly contradictory actions, namely, supporting gays in the 1970s but promoting ex-gays in the 1990s. During an interview in his living room in Princeton, New Jersey, in 2008, he said:

> I just love controversy. I love people arguing with each other. I've always— when I was fifteen I lived in Manhattan on the Columbus Circle and now it's on Fifty-Ninth Street and Broadway. Now there are cars and there are streets that go through it. But it used to be like Hyde Park in London. People would come there and argue all the political stuff and I used to go there.[2]

In both the 1970s and the 1990s, Spitzer encountered activist groups protesting the American Psychiatric Association, and rather than looking the other way, he listened each time. As a self-proclaimed sympathetic professional for the underdog, he has played a key role in facilitating intellectual opportunities for both gay liberation and ex-gay activists in science, even as each side maintains a certain ambivalence toward him. Spitzer's proclivity for the polemical cannot entirely explain these episodes, however.

In this chapter, Spitzer's two major engagements with the issue of homosexuality, which acted as bookends of his illustrious career, are used as a framework to examine major shifts over three decades in the field of therapeutics with regard to homosexuality. I argue that Spitzer's position, which has been publicly depicted as contradictory and irrational, actually remained quite stable. All along, Spitzer upheld the position that homosexuality is not a mental disorder, but that it is "suboptimal" as an expression of human evolutionary potential. Revealing how dramatically the field of therapeutics changed over these years, Spitzer's position was radically progressive in the early 1970s, but by the 1990s, it was not progressive enough for mainstream science. With the rise of gay-affirmative therapies, the idea that homosexuality constituted

Dr. Robert Spitzer in 2003 in his office at Columbia University, where he conducted his study purportedly demonstrating that some gays and lesbians can change their sexual orientation through reorientation therapies and religious ministries. Photograph by John Chapple. Copyright John Chapple. www.johnchapple.com.

a "normal variant" of human sexuality prevailed in psychiatry by the late 1990s, placing Spitzer's once radical views on the fringe alongside ex-gay therapy practitioners who took an even more pro-reorientation position.

Through the process of moving reorientation from the mainstream to the fringe over these decades, a concept of "core features" of sexual orientation as sexual attractions emerged. In the immediate years after the removal of "Homosexuality" from the *DSM,* mainstream positions against reorientation therapies were primarily couched in ethical terms, denouncing the therapies as detrimental to gays and lesbians. By the late 1990s, Spitzer's study became a high-profile media event and redirected the dispute into a technical matter over how to measure sexual orientation. Spitzer used a composite of identity, behavior, and attractions that he measured with retrospective self-report. However, he used sexual attraction to define the "core features" of sexual orientation and attempted to show that even attractions at the "core" could be changed. As the concept of sexual orientation with "core features" of attractions was consolidated, the question of how to scientifically measure a straight "core" became a deeply contested issue.

The Protracted Process of Demedicalization

"Homosexuality" was officially removed as a diagnosis from the *Diagnostic and Statistical Manual of Mental Disorders* in 1973 in a watershed moment for gay liberation. While this moment might seem definitive, the demedicalization process was gradual. It would not be until the late 1990s that the American Psychoanalytic Association recognized this change. Lingering diagnoses like "sexual orientation disturbance" and "ego-dystonic homosexuality" continued into the 1980s to offer professionals the opportunity to treat clients for homosexuality if it caused them distress, while "sexual disorder not otherwise specified" remained until recently. Moreover, the attitudes of mental health professionals have taken time to change.

While the homophile movement had been interested in demedicalization earlier, direct activism against the American Psychiatric Association ramped up in 1970. No longer content with assimilation politics, gay liberation activists often used "zap" actions of direct public confrontation, disrupting meetings and utilizing theatrical demonstrations. The movement membership was hybrid in terms of professional status, bringing together sympathetic and often closeted gay professionals with lay activists. Openly gay historian Martin Duberman debated psychoanalyst Irving Bieber at Columbia University in 1972:

> Bieber turned out to be a Central Casting version of the portly, pompous psychiatrist, contentedly patronizing everyone else on the panel, imperviously repeating his own circular arguments. When he announced that he had never known a homosexual man who had a "loving, constructive father," one of the gay undergraduates grabbed the microphone to declare that he had had just such a father. Bieber smiled unctuously and told the young man that as an experienced clinician he had long since become familiar with such "distorted self-evaluations." He offered to give the young man a "proper" battery of tests should he be willing to present himself at Bieber's office. At that point, *I* grabbed the mike and in a tone that matched Bieber's in unctuousness, politely offered to test *him* for "advanced symptoms of homophobia" if he would trot round to *my* office. Bieber looked astonished at my insolence and disdainfully moved on to another topic.[3]

Spitzer entered the story in 1972, when he happened to be attending a conference of the Association for the Advancement of Behavior Therapy where activists were protesting. Impressed with the passion and the arguments he encountered, Spitzer agreed to allow a psychologist from the

Gay Activists Alliance to present the case for the deletion of "Homosexuality" to the Nomenclature Committee at the next APA convention in 1973. This psychologist was Charles Silverstein. Silverstein's presentation included the best available scientific evidence that homosexuality does not cause mental distress.[4] He added, however, that the stigma associated with the diagnosis caused significant harm.[5] After considering this presentation, Spitzer was further moved to support demedicalization following a meeting of the clandestine "GayPA," a group of gay professional psychiatrists who remained closeted in order to keep their jobs. Others on the committee followed Spitzer's lead.

Spitzer's sympathy for the gay cause was, in part, rooted in his theory of diagnosis, that a diagnosable condition "either regularly cause subjective distress or regularly be associated with some generalized impairment in social effectiveness or functioning."[6] Under this principle, homosexuality was neither pathological nor normal; rather it was "suboptimal." Spitzer compared homosexuality to other conditions:

> If failure to function optimally in some important area of life, as judged by either society or the profession, is sufficient to indicate the presence of a psychiatric disorder, then we will have to add to our nomenclature the following conditions: celibacy (failure to function optimally sexually), revolutionary behavior (irrational defiance of social norms), religious fanaticism (dogmatic and rigid adherence to religious doctrine), racism (irrational hatred of certain groups), vegetarianism (unnatural avoidance of carnivorous behavior), and male chauvinism (irrational belief in the inferiority of women).
>
> If homosexuality per se does not meet the criteria for a psychiatric disorder, what is it? Descriptively, it is an irregular form of sexual behavior. Our profession need not now agree on its origin, significance, and value for human happiness when we acknowledge that by itself it does not meet the requirements for a psychiatric disorder.[7]

As a basis for demedicalization, this view meant the stigmatizing diagnostic classification could be eliminated, helping gays and lesbians in their struggle for rights. Meanwhile, reorientation therapists could continue their practice for patients who experienced mental distress over their sexual orientation.

In an attempt to appease critics of demedicalization, Spitzer then pushed for a specific diagnosis covering treatment of people with mental distress over homosexuality. The new diagnosis of "Sexual Orientation Disturbance" (SOD) read:

This is for people whose sexual interests are directed primarily toward people of the same sex and who are bothered by, in conflict with, or wish to change their sexual orientation. This diagnostic category is distinguished from homosexuality, which by itself does not necessarily constitute a psychiatric disorder. Homosexuality per se is a form of irregular sexual behavior and, with other forms of irregular sexual behavior that are not by themselves psychiatric disorders, is not listed in this nomenclature.[8]

The inclusion of the phrase "does not necessarily constitute a psychiatric disorder" allowed board members who were reluctant about deletion to feel they were not endorsing the idea that homosexuality was normal.[9] Spitzer stated:

Homosexual activist groups will no doubt claim that psychiatry has at last recognized that homosexuality is as "normal" as heterosexuality. They will be wrong. In removing homosexuality per se from the nomenclature we are only recognizing that by itself homosexuality does not meet the criteria for being considered a psychiatric disorder. We will in no way be aligning ourselves with any particular viewpoint regarding the etiology or desirability of homosexual behavior.[10]

Spitzer expressed a position that did not consider homosexuality to be "as normal as heterosexuality," even as he supported civil rights for gays. The board of trustees, the APA's governing body, passed Spitzer's proposed changes to the *DSM*, and at the same time, it passed a resolution he developed in support of gay rights. It opposed discrimination in areas of "employment, housing, public accommodation, and licensing," called for legislation at all levels of government to ensure equal protection under the laws, and supported the decriminalization of homosexuality.[11] Official demedicalization did not end here, however.

Psychiatrist and reorientation therapist Charles Socarides, author of *The Overt Homosexual* and other reorientation texts, led the opposition to the board's decision. He argued that no one involved in researching the diagnosis for the board was an expert on sexual orientation like himself; thus the board had acted unscientifically. In another unprecedented move, the decision was placed for a vote of APA members. The resulting tally, 58 percent to 37 percent in favor of deletion, upheld the decision, but Socarides argued this slim majority was evidence that gay activist pressure rather than consensus was the reason. Regardless, by 1973, homosexuality as a mental disorder was formally defunct in American psychiatry, and other mental health fields followed.

As a sympathetic professional, Spitzer opened up an unprecedented relationship between the psychiatric profession and a social movement, allowing a member of a diagnosed group to present scientific evidence to the Nomenclature Committee on behalf of demedicalization. Thus, he facilitated a key relationship between science and the public within the intellectual opportunity structure. Making a decision about science on the basis of a vote, a rare occurrence indeed, was a novel institutional form that also presented opportunities for gay liberation activists. The success of gay liberationists at the American Psychiatric Association would prove strategic, as the jurisdictional relationship between this institution and other mental health associations would now play a key role in further demedicalization, as psychiatry and the *DSM* led other fields in determining the definitions of mental illness.

In the ensuing years, a key leader in American psychology was also influenced by gay activist arguments. Psychologist and behavior therapist Gerald Davison was developer of "Playboy therapy," one of the "softer" behavior therapy techniques developed in the United States amid hostility to the aversion therapies discussed in chapter 1. Before leaving a conference of behavior therapists in 1972, Davison attended a panel where Charles Silverstein condemned aversion therapy.[12] He was deeply moved by this encounter, and when he became president of the Association for the Advancement of Behavior Therapy in 1974, he wrote an inaugural speech against reorientation.[13] In this speech, Davison argued that evidence of efficacy or inefficacy was irrelevant—the very existence of treatments for homosexuality was denigrating to gays and lesbians. In a later essay, Davison claimed:

> When trying to garner support for my proposal that we should stop trying to change homosexual orientations, I was interested for some time in documenting the failure of various behavior change regimens in eliminating homosexual inclinations. Of particular interest was the question of whether aversion therapy of various kinds had proven successful (if you will) in stamping out homosexual behavior and inclinations. And indeed, I tend to believe the evidence is still lacking for a suppression of homosexual behavior or ideation via aversive procedures. Nonetheless, even if one were to demonstrate that a particular sexual preference could be wiped out by a negative learning experience, there remains the question as to how relevant this kind of data is to the ethical question of whether one *should* engage in such behavior to change regimens. In discussing this possibility with some students and colleagues, I am convinced that data on efficacy are quite irrelevant.

Even if we *could* effect certain changes, there is still the more important question of whether we *should*. I believe we should not.[14]

This new view was based on two key premises. First, the existence of these therapies necessarily implied that homosexuality is a disease, and second, gays and lesbians did not go voluntarily to treatment; they were often forced into it. Davison's ethical argument became the dominant view regarding the treatment of homosexuality within science for the next two decades. In lieu of raising the issue of evidence with regard to efficacy or harm, pronouncements against reorientation would frequently be made on such ethical grounds.

For those behavior therapists who continued to pursue reorientation in the early 1970s, evidence began to mount that sexual orientation could not be changed with aversive techniques. This is what Davison meant by "evidence is still lacking." Behaviorist studies on men with phallometric testing revealed that through therapy, homosexual arousal could often be extinguished, but heterosexual arousal could not be induced. Utilizing the genital arousal monitor with erotic imagery indicated that men could not be conditioned to be aroused by images of nude women.[15] In a typical aversion therapy study using penile plethysmography, Nathaniel McConaghy and coauthors stated that "from these data, it would seem that there is a decrease in reported homosexual feelings and in associated negative heterosexual feelings following aversion treatment, but there is no actual increase in heterosexual feelings."[16] Because of such treatment failures, a tacit alliance between gay activists and the technology of phallometric testing developed at this time, where phallometry was interpreted to reveal an inner core of fixed attractions rather than a behavior that could be modified. As the impetus for conducting studies of this type dwindled, however, the new Davison view prevailed; evidence was irrelevant because it was unethical to treat homosexuality.

After demedicalization, gay professionals' fears of being discredited diminished immensely, and psychology and psychiatry became increasingly gay affirmative. New professional organizations formed around the affirmation of gay identity, solidifying the demedicalization view in the field of therapeutics within formal institutions. In 1974 Silverstein became the founding editor of the *Journal of Homosexuality*, establishing an interdisciplinary forum that provided a venue for gay-affirming research. The Association for Gay Psychologists, founded in 1973, pushed for further demedicalization. In 1975, the board of directors and Council of Representatives of the American Psychological Association adopted a position statement endorsing the decision of the psychiatrists; their new position statement claimed: "Homosexuality, per se, implies no impairment in judgment, stability, reliability, or general social or vocational capabilities. Further, the American Psychological Association urges all mental health professionals to take the lead in removing the stigma of mental illness that has long been associated with homosexual orientations."[17]

Further entrenching Davison's view, the *Journal of Homosexuality* published papers from a 1977 symposium titled "Homosexuality and the Ethics of Behavioral Intervention." Among these essays, Silverstein's went furthest in condemnation, characterizing reorientation therapy as a form of dangerous sadomasochism. He grouped behavior therapy treatments along with the treatments of neuroscientist Robert Galbraith Heath:

> And "Horrible Heath" (Heath 1972) maintains that we should follow his example and excise bits of brain tissue here and there, connect electrodes to certain internal structures, apply current from time to time, introduce a prostitute into the room, stop shocking, and see what happens. Heath is fascinated with this exercise in professional sadism. I am horrified.[18]

Silverstein was referring to experiments conducted at Tulane University in 1972, in which Heath surgically implanted electrodes into the pleasure centers of subjects' brains and had them self-administer electrical stimuli to make behavioral modifications, including an attempt to change one man's sexual orientation.[19] In his paper, Silverstein also depicted the person who pursues reorientation treatments as a masochist with low self-esteem brought about by rejections in society and the family. He theorized that these primarily male clients are bound by rigid gender roles, and their treatment decision is based on contempt for women and a desire to rid themselves of "feminized" homosexuality.[20] While some reorientation researchers might try to shift the debate from ethics back to evidence,[21] in this climate they could not.

Despite these gains for supporters of gays in mental health institutions, many challenges remained. Laws had been passed protecting gays and lesbians from discrimination in cities across the country, but a conservative backlash ensued. Beauty-queen-turned-activist Anita Bryant's "Save Our Children" campaign was instrumental in rolling back many anti-discrimination laws. She famously argued that because homosexuals cannot reproduce, they must "recruit" young victims.[22] Meanwhile, in mental health fields, some mental health professionals still saw homosexuality as a possible indicator of pathology. A 1977 study of psychiatrists in the United States claimed that 69 percent of psychiatrists believed homosexuality represented some kind of pathology, 60 percent thought homosexual male relationships were less mature and loving than heterosexual relationships, and 70 percent thought the psychiatric problems experienced by homosexuals were due more to conflicts within the individual than to societal stigma.[23] The study was reported in *Time* magazine under the title "Sick Again?"[24] While homosexuality itself was no longer considered a disorder, the subordinated status of homosexuality remained.

Into the late 1970s, Spitzer continued to defend diagnoses in the *DSM* for people experiencing conflicts over their homosexuality, to the chagrin of gay activists and professionals who preferred no mention of homosexuality in the diagnostic manual at all. In his capacity as director of the task force developing *DSM-III*, Spitzer worked to transform all psychiatric diagnoses into "atheoretical" descriptions of symptoms. Revising the *DSM-III* involved the revision of "Sexual Orientation Disturbance." For Spitzer, the category was too general and needed to focus more specifically on homosexuality. He proposed "Homodysphilia" to replace SOD, and the definition he put forward suggested that he maintained at least a partial view of homosexuality as pathological. The new compromise of "Ego-Dystonic Homosexuality" (EDH) eliminated this view and attributed problems to negative societal attitudes. It read:

> A desire to acquire or increase heterosexual arousal so that heterosexual relations can be initiated or maintained and a sustained pattern of overt homosexual arousal that the individual explicitly complains is unwanted as a source of distress. . . . Since homosexuality itself is not considered a mental disorder, the factors that predispose to homosexuality are not included in this section. The factors that predispose to ego-dystonic homosexuality are those negative societal attitudes towards homosexuality which have been internalized. In addition features associated with heterosexuality such as having children and socially sanctioned family life, may be viewed as desirable, and incompatible with a homosexual arousal pattern.[25]

EDH went into the *DSM-III* under the direction of Spitzer, but not without resistance from opponents.

Despite this setback for the pro-gay view, the magnitude of the transformation toward a pro-gay perspective that occurred within mental health professions over the 1970s could be seen in the largely negative reception to a reorientation study published near the end of the decade. *Homosexuality in Perspective* was a highly anticipated work for famed sexologists William Masters and Virginia Johnson. Like their earlier research on heterosexuals, the study involved real-time observations of sexual physiology: subjects in the laboratory engaged in sex acts while connected to electrodes. In addition to providing therapy for various sexual dysfunctions for homosexual participants, the research included a study of reorientation for homosexuals experiencing "dissatisfaction." This clinical work was conducted over the years 1968 to 1977. Consequently, the study had an odd feature: the condition at the center of investigation was a disorder when the study began but not when the study was completed. The results showed a "success" rate higher than any reported before. Masters and Johnson attributed this to the motivation of their clients and the strong screening process, which selected only those interested in complete change.[26]

When released, *Homosexuality in Perspective* was largely panned by the scientific community and the press.[27] Although *Time* ran a story anticipating its release and lauding the authors' reputations, the *Los Angeles Times* gave the book a negative review, stating that it "abounds in fallacies." The reviewer appeared to mock the authors when he stated, "'Conversion' to heterosexuality is possible more than half the time. You could change if you wanted to." Leading psychiatrist John Money noted that members of the sample each paid $2,500, so "you've got a hopelessly biased self-selected sample skewed in favor of success." In addition, psychiatrist Judd Marmor challenged the short treatment time, stating, "I would doubt very much that you could reverse a group of [Kinsey] 6 persons in two weeks." [28] Even Masters and Johnson, who were redefining the field of sex research at the beginning of the decade with their risqué work, were now out of step with current trends in the mental health field on the topic of homosexuality.

The Religious Reformation of Reorientation

Formally locked out of mainstream mental health institutions, many of those interested in sexual reorientation couched their views in the language of conservative Christianity, with its definition of homosexuality as "sin." Because homosexuality could no longer be acceptably viewed in terms of pathology within scientific circles, the intellectual opportunity structure required an alternative knowledge system, and within the United States, evangelical Christianity offered cultural material for a shift of venue. In particular, the ex-gay movement emerged out of the "Jesus movement," which had targeted feminists and other leftists in the late 1960s and early 1970s. Meanwhile, some psychoanalysts continued their secular work on the margins, including Socarides.[29] In the 1980s, the religious ex-gay movement had a favorable political climate in which to grow, as the election of Ronald Reagan marked the beginning of twelve years of social conservatism in the country, including a backlash against the counterculture. The first wave of religious right organizing began with Jerry Falwell's Moral Majority. It combined evangelical television with conservative electoral politics, raising millions of dollars for political campaigns and voter registration drives. The anti-gay rhetoric of these groups became further inflamed during the AIDS crisis.[30]

The growth of the religious ex-gay movement was not only a response to demedicalization. Religion had become an arena of struggle for gay activists with the advent of pro-gay theology. In 1968 Troy Perry founded the Metropolitan Community Church in Los Angeles as a gay-affirming ministry. In 1972 Perry published his autobiography *The Lord Is My Shepherd and He Knows I'm Gay*, beginning with the theological affirmation:

> One thing is sure. We homosexuals must all learn to rid ourselves of the sense of shame that we have been conditioned to accept from the heterosexual world. Such shame is no longer acceptable to any of us. How could we go on being ashamed of something that God had created? Yes, God created homosexuals and homosexuality. It exists throughout history, and all over the world. We homosexuals number in the millions here in the United States alone. We must rid ourselves once and for all of the sense of shame I speak of.[31]

In response to the new pro-gay theology, evangelical Christians reasserted that homosexuality is sinful. One such response was the ex-gay movement.

In 1973 former homosexual Frank Worthen and heterosexual minister Kent Philpott founded Love in Action, the first ministry to "reform" homosexuals. Philpott's *The Third Sex?* was a foundational text used in the development of relatively small ministries across the nation. It provided a template for ex-gay testimony of deliverance from the homosexual lifestyle. Ex-gays Michael Bussee and Gary Cooper worked with Worthen soon after Philpott's ministry was founded, and in 1976 the first ex-gay conference was held at Melodyland Christian Center in Anaheim, California. The outcome of the conference was the founding of Exodus International, which became the largest ex-gay ministry in the United States.[32]

The Third Sex? established the genre of ex-gay testimony. The book includes interviews with three men and three women, and each tells a story of sacrificing the homosexual lifestyle for Christianity. Some still experience homosexual attractions as temptations, while others are asexual, such as "Bob":

> KENT: When you first became awakened by the Holy Spirit, did your living with Ron seem like a problem?
>
> BOB: Yes. That is one of the first things that happened. Initially, when I first had my renewal experience, I hadn't resigned myself to give up sex. That happened a few months later as the Holy Spirit began to convict me. I reached the point where I got so excited about Jesus in my life that I realized I couldn't pursue this life style. Initially I wanted to be able to have my cake and eat it too. But I loved the Lord so much that I was willing to do whatever He wanted me to do, no matter how much it hurt. . . .
>
> KENT: Is the idea of marriage repulsive to you?
>
> BOB: Marriage isn't repulsive. It's just that I can't accept in my own mind, emotionally, the sex act. You see, any kind of sex act is repugnant to me right now.[33]

Here, Bob relinquished sexual pleasure for a relationship with God. Following the interviews were more theoretical and theological chapters. The discussions of the causes of homosexuality tended generally to follow psychoanalytic theories of family socialization experiences, leading to gender nonconformity and subsequent homosexuality. The men had distant fathers and overbearing mothers. The women were socialized in masculine roles and were in masculinizing environments of prisons or the military. In addition to the use of psychology, Philpott viewed homosexuality as a form of demonic possession. It emerged because a person is deceived by Satan: "The origin of homosexuality is found in Paul's classic statement—'they exchanged the truth about God for a lie . . .' (Romans 1:25). Homosexuality was not in the mind of God when He created man. Homosexuality came with the rebellion."[34]

With the growth of the religious ex-gay movement, some researchers began to further bridge the domains of scientific discourse and theology. The term *ex-gay* was first used in scientific literature in 1980, when psychiatrist Mansell Pattison and his wife and research associate, Myrna Loy Pattison, published "'Ex-Gays': Religiously Mediated Change in Homosexuals" in the *American Journal of Psychiatry*. The authors interviewed eleven white men who had participated in a Pentecostal ex-gay ministry. Framing change as "spontaneous," the authors claimed:

> Occasional autobiographical reports have described a spontaneous change in sexual orientation through salutary life experience, which

usually includes religious conversion, and there are individual case reports of spontaneous change without psychotherapy. However, such reports seem to be the exception. . . . The program seemed to offer an "experiment of nature" by which we could investigate this apparently spontaneous change from homosexuality.[35]

In the age of demedicalization, this description avoids terms like *curing* and *pathology*. As a professional, Pattison bridged the worlds of psychiatry and religion, having served as editor of the journal *Pastoral Psychology*, being a licensed evangelical minister, as well as working as a psychiatrist. His experience in these different social worlds allowed him to bring ex-gay ministries into the psychiatric literature.

Although Pattison's research was exploratory, in 1983 Elizabeth Moberly developed a foundational theory that blended theology and psychoanalysis. In her book *Homosexuality: A New Christian Ethic,* Moberly brought together notions of sin with ideas about the etiology of homosexuality. This blend discouraged the outright moral condemnation of homosexual desires and encouraged their "redirection," and because it discouraged condemnation, the book became popular in the ex-gay movement. Moberly argued that same-sex attraction is rooted in something called "defensive detachment," the result of a disrupted relationship with a same-sex parent from an early age. This leads to a strong resentment toward members of the same sex. A natural "reparative drive" compensated for this detachment, however, creating strong emotional feelings toward members of the same sex. These emotional feelings often became eroticized. This pattern was termed "same-sex ambivalence." Superimposing a theological framework, Moberly argued that heterosexuality is also part of God's plan, but she claimed that appropriate parent–child relationships were also part of this design, and when they were thwarted, the "reparative drive" resulted. Healing homosexuality and moving beyond an arrested developmental state involved developing nonerotic same-sex friendships leading to complete heterosexual development and gender identity.[36] Blending these theoretical concepts would enable reorientation therapists to obtain religious clients, while shifting to the safer intellectual venue of theology.

Despite such "blends," many leaders of ex-gay ministries maintained their own theological expertise on conversion. Religious texts tended to see *salvation* as the ultimate goal of reorientation, rather than heterosexuality per se. For example, in *Desires in Conflict,* ex-gay and pastoral counselor Joe Dallas stated:

Let me emphasize from the outset that I know of no universal "cure." Nobody does. Instead I have taken the experiences of men I've worked with and have, hopefully, gleaned some ideas from their journeys that will be helpful to you in your own.

I have tried to position the struggle against homosexual desires as a part of the broader sanctification process all Christians go through. All Christians, of course, don't wrestle with homosexuality, but they wrestle with *something*. That's part of our common human experience.[37]

Dallas's worldview, reflected in the positions of many within ex-gay ministries, placed the sin of homosexuality on a par with other forms of sin. This idea encouraged other Christians to accept former homosexuals into the flock, and it explained how temptation lingers:

But don't ever say that you have arrived. You, like all of us, will continue to struggle against any number of temptations and tendencies as long as you're alive and kicking. Even if you became completely free of any homosexual tendencies, there is a myriad of other issues to deal with. Nothing but your death or the coming of Christ will change that.

Besides, you have no guarantee that you're immune to homosexual struggles. If they are gone, wonderful. But who is to say that they'll never return? Don't get too confident—that's always a sign of danger.[38]

Thus, by circumventing "cure," Dallas and other religious ex-gay leaders competed with secular reorientation therapists by treating salvation as the central goal over and above heterosexuality.

By the end of the 1980s, the religious ex-gay movement was small but growing. It had established testimony as a means of knowing the power of God's work in one's own and others' lives. It had established the alternate goal of salvation rather than full heterosexual desire. From their inception, ex-gay ministries affirmed that people are born heterosexual, but may still experience same-sex attractions as temptation to sin. Developing heterosexual feelings was not guaranteed, but emulating or moving toward heterosexuality was an obligation.

Gay-Affirmative Therapy Ascends

Reflecting on the more gay-affirming 1980s in mental health professions, Charles Silverstein wrote in 1991 that there was a "lessening of the need to speak defensively and to pound one's chest in defiance against the formerly rigid attitudes toward gay people."[39] Support for affirming the mental health of gay and lesbian people was shaped by the AIDS epidemic, which devastated the physical and mental health of many in the gay community. Dealing with the harsh realities of the disease made the pathologization of homosexuality an extremely unpopular idea within mental health communities in the United States. However, the AIDS epidemic was used as justification for moral opprobrium against homosexuality among conservatives. Some within the conservative Moral Majority saw AIDS as "punishment" for "unnatural" behaviors. If the medicalization of homosexuality in mental health terms was untenable, doctors and public health researchers blamed homosexual behaviors for AIDS, implicitly remedicalizing homosexual behaviors within medicine and public health.[40]

In response to general conservatism and mass anti-gay backlash, the decade of the 1980s was a time in which gay rights activists developed national organizations to advance their causes.[41] In line with this trend, new institutions within national mental health institutions provided a setting for the development of theory and therapeutic practices that affirmed gay lives. Emerging out of struggles over demedicalization, in the mid-1970s, the Caucus of Gay, Lesbian, and Bisexual Members of the APA was established within in the American Psychiatric Association and attained representation at its assembly in 1982. This organization became the Association of Gay and Lesbian Psychiatrists (AGLP) in 1985.[42] In psychology, Division 44 of the American Psychological Association was founded in 1985 as the Society for the Psychological Study of Lesbian and Gay Issues, a venue for researching lives of lesbians and gays and gay-affirmative ideas. By the end of the 1980s, the AGLP had founded a new publication, the *Journal of Gay and Lesbian Psychology,* to join the *Journal of Homosexuality* in promoting research on lesbian and gay mental health. The creation of these new institutional forms further solidified the position that homosexuality is not a mental disorder within the intellectual opportunity structure of mainstream science. The very existence of these newly established institutions stood in the way of any efforts to reestablish the diagnosis.

Moreover, the work of these new organizations, particularly the AGLP, contributed to the deletion of "Ego-Dystonic Homosexuality" from *DSM-III.* Writing in the *American Journal of Psychiatry* in 1981, Spitzer defended EDH.[43] Confronted with a challenge to remove the diagnosis, he stated in a letter, "To remove that category would [shatter] that achievement and would be viewed as the acceptance of the view that homosexuality is a normal variant."[44] Prompting from AGLP led to a hearing with Spitzer's workgroup looking at psychosexual disorders for *DSM-III-R,* and as a result, Spitzer recanted. *DSM-III-R* left treatment for those who might be distressed by their sexual orientation as an entry under the heading "Sexual Disorder Not Otherwise Specified," and it contained no reference to homosexuality. According to historian Ronald Bayer, sympathy for the plight of gay and lesbian people during the AIDS epidemic also likely con-tributed to the willingness to remove the last reference to homosexuality from the *DSM*.[45]

Along with these institutional changes, gay-affirmative therapists wrote new therapeutic texts embracing the idea of homosexuality as a "normal variant," and encouraging gay identity formation. Australian psychologist Vivienne Cass wrote the influential essay "Homosexual Iden-tity Formation: A Theoretical Model," published in the *Journal of Homo-sexuality* in 1979. Cass laid out a six-stage model of identity development, created though years of working with gay clients. First, gays discovered their own homosexual desires, and therapy proceeded until there was full integration between identity and these feelings and behaviors.[46] Gay-affirmative psychology texts tended to deal with issues such as devel-oping healthy gay and lesbian relationships, coming out, and attending to relationships between parents and their gay children—all generally assuming that homosexuality is immutable, and thus, the client is best served by learning to develop a gay or lesbian identity. In 1982 psycholo-gist John Gonsiorek assembled the work of several gay-affirming psy-chologists and psychiatrists in the edited volume *Homosexuality and Psychotherapy: A Practitioner's Handbook of Affirmative Models*. In the introduction, Gonsiorek retheorized homosexuality, contrasting it with forms of pathology.[47]

When he was a graduate student in the mid-1970s, Gonsiorek joined forces with three other graduate students to form the Task Force on Sexual Orientation, compiling scientific information about homosexu-ality. The group secured sponsorship from the American Psychological Association, and during the late 1970s and early 1980s, the APA provided programming time at conferences. Evelyn Hooker, John Gagnon, and psychologist and former Gay Activists Alliance member John De Cecco served as mentors. This group presented research, and over the course of the contentiously conservative 1980s, task force members Gonsiorek and James Weinrich noted by 1991 that "most experts in the area have concluded that sexual orientation is set by early childhood." The works they cited to support this claim included a piece by sexologist Richard Green titled "The Immutability of (Homo)sexual Orientation: Behavioral Science Implications for a Constitutional (Legal) Analysis."[48] Discussing the definition and measurement of sexual orientation, Gonsiorek and Weinrich drew on a 1977 literature review by Shively and De Cecco that defined sexual identity in four parts: biological sex as genetic material in chromosomes, gender identity as psychological sense of being male or fe-male, social sex role as adhering to male or female cultural conventions, and sexual orientation as "erotic and/or affectional disposition to the same and/or opposite sex."[49] Here, in contrast to the "inversion" models of early sexologists and reorientation practitioners, Shively and De Cecco conceptualized sexual orientation and gender identity as separate components of one's sexual identity. Gonsiorek and Weinrich also emphasized the importance of the term "sexual orientation" over "sexual preference" because "research findings indicate that homosexual feelings are a basic part of an individual's psyche and are established much earlier than conscious choice would indicate." The term "sexual preference" implies a conscious choice, but sexual orientation, they argue, is established in early childhood.[50] Moreover, while they noted that much research on sexual orientation relies on self-report, they appealed to Kurt Freund's penile plethysmographic method of measurement as "the most rigorous work in this area" to measure sexual orientation, as that device had proved that heterosexual desires could not be induced in reorientation subjects.[51]

In the same volume in 1991, gay-affirmative psychologist Douglas Haldeman sounded the death knell for reorientation programs:

> Psychological ethics mandate that mental health professionals subscribe to methods that support human dignity and are effective in their stated purpose. Conversion therapy qualifies as neither. It reinforces the social stigma associated with homosexuality, and there is no evidence from any of the studies reviewed here to suggest that sexual orientation can be changed. Perhaps conversion therapy seemed viable when homosexuality was still thought to be an illness; at this point, it is an idea whose time has come and gone.[52]

In this essay, Haldeman noted that reorientation studies up to that point "represent inadequate and misleading scientific practice. They are consistently flawed by poor and non-existent follow-up data, improper classification of subjects ('converting' bisexuals who are not primarily homosexual in the first place), and confusion of heterosexual competence with sexual orientation shift."[53] Because insufficient evidence for the efficacy of reorientation existed, it could not be the basis of ethical practice.

In the profession of psychoanalysis, however, the complete demedicalization of homosexuality took longer to accomplish. Bayer attributes this to the fact that psychoanalysis tended to see everyone as afflicted with pathology, given the conflict-ridden nature of normal human development.[54] Charles Socarides remained a prominent advocate of the pathologizing view, publishing books that recycled his theories from the late 1960s on the treatment of homosexuality as a pathology developed in the pre-Oedipal period of early childhood, especially in response to a controlling mother and weak father who do not permit individuation of the young developing child.[55] In 1988 Elaine Siegel published *Female Homosexuality: Choice without Volition,* a study of twelve women, the largest-ever exploration of treating female homosexuality at that time, applying Socarides's pre-Oedipal theories to women. Siegel argued that women experienced less anxiety over homosexuality than did men, and this is why few have sought treatment in the past. Female homosexuality, she argued, was also the result of failure to individuate from the mother.[56] All these works maintained the psychoanalytic case study as the means of evaluating both homosexual behavior and the internalization of therapeutic ideologies. Official demedicalization in psychoanalysis would not be accomplished until 1999, when the American Psychoanalytic Association issued a position statement against reorientation. As an important aspect of this process, resistance within psychoanalysis emerged as new theories explored ways in which homosexuality—especially male—could be understood without its being pathologized.[57]

By the beginning of the 1990s, gay-affirmative ideas in mental health aligned with different strains of gay activism. As gay rights issues increasingly found their way onto the national stage in this decade through the work of organizations such as the Human Rights Campaign, public opinion about the nature of homosexuality became deeply interwoven with views on gay rights. Supporters generally viewed innateness and immutability of homosexuality as a basis for rights, while anti-gay opponents tended to believe that homosexuality was chosen and therefore was not a basis for "special rights."[58] However, promoting fixed sexual orientations was not the only strategy pursued by those who opposed anti-gay bias, as this was also the time when the smaller group Queer Nation was founded, emerging out of AIDS activism. While those who fought for gay rights tended to advocate a notion of fixed sexuality and used assimilationist and professional tactics, queer activists, emerging out of the AIDS Coalition to Unleash Power (now commonly known as ACT-UP), were more theatrical and confrontational, and theorized sexualities as fluid, especially given that fighting AIDS was more a matter of legitimizing marginalized sexual behaviors and rendering them safer, rather than promoting fixed sexual identities. These queer activist perspectives notwithstanding, in the arena of national politics, Tina Fetner characterizes the 1990s as the era of "culture war" over homosexuality.[59] Gays and lesbians, now visible on the national stage, were forced into party politics as a result of the religious right exerting influence on the Republican Party in the 1980s. Homosexuality became a highly charged issue that enabled conservatives to galvanize their base around a threat to "family values." No longer could gay rights be a marginalized "side" issue in politics—they were now on the national stage and everyone had an opinion about them, including national politicians, further legitimating those who took a mainstreaming and assimilationist approach.

Also entering public discourse at this time, widely publicized research studies suggested a biological basis and even biological "cause" of homosexuality. This research, which located homosexuality in the body, contributed to the national conversation about gay rights. Some research was rooted in theories of brain organization, based on levels of androgen exposure during fetal development.[60] The structure of the hypothalamus, comparative finger lengths, ways of hearing, and other bodily effects apparently resulted from this exposure during gestation. Other researchers worked to establish a "gay gene."[61] Even if the researchers did not view their findings as demonstrating that homosexuality was innate and immutable, gay rights supporters often took the work this way. This interpretation only reinforced the gay-affirmative position in mainstream mental health professions that identity needed to be aligned with an innate sexual orientation. It was against this backdrop that a new secular organization was formed to support the research and therapy of homosexuality.

The Founding of NARTH

Perceiving that they were under threat from gay-affirmative views in mental health and innate-immutability ideas in biological science, reorientation therapists founded the National Association for Research and Therapy of Homosexuality (NARTH) in 1992. According to Socarides, an attempt was under way within the American Psychiatric Association to try to declare reparative therapy "unethical," and lawyers had to intervene on behalf of the new organization.[62] In Nicolosi's view, there were going to be attempts to ban reorientation practices across the board. Meanwhile, the American Psychoanalytic Association, moving toward demedicalization, no longer permitted reorientation therapists to have meetings at their conventions.[63] Effectively excluded from mainstream mental health associations as an organization, Nicolosi, Socarides, and psychiatrist Benjamin Kaufman founded NARTH to support therapists who treated clients with unwanted same-sex attractions and to promote diversity of opinion within mental health fields.[64] Those therapists did not lose their accreditation and could still attend conferences as members of professional associations, but NARTH was not welcome as a group. Despite this marginalization within science, the controversy remained in the public, as NARTH provided testimony in legal venues dealing with gay rights, and appeared in various media, declaring themselves experts on the malleability of sexual orientation.

NARTH initially relied on two rhetorical strategies in attempts to establish legitimacy. First, the organization claimed a strict separation between "politics" and "science" and declared that opponents were corrupted by politics. In his book *Healing Homosexuality*, Nicolosi stated:

> It is not our intent to contribute to reactionary hostility. However, there is a distinction between science and politics, and science should not be made to bow to gay political pressure.
>
> The National Association for Research and Therapy of Homosexuality (NARTH) has recently been formed to combat politicization of scientific and treatment issues. NARTH will defend the rights of therapists to treat dissatisfied homosexuals.[65]

Nicolosi also expressed the "right" of therapists to provide reorientation treatment:

> NARTH will defend the right of therapists to study and refine therapeutic techniques for men and women who are struggling with homosexual thoughts, feelings, and behaviors that they do not want to accept as part of their deepest identities.[66]

These positions would be essential for NARTH's critiques of national mental health organizations, charging them with "political correctness" and alleging that they were beholden to gay activism and gay politics. By the late 1990s, this rights discourse extended to the client's right to self-determination in choosing to be reoriented.

In the era of the religious ex-gay movement, Joseph Nicolosi became an important theorist who was able to bridge the secular and the theological. Drawing on Moberly's work, Nicolosi's *Reparative Therapy of Male Homosexuality* (1991) used the concepts of "reparative drive" and "defensive detachment" in the development of individual and group therapy programs. In *Healing Homosexuality*, published two years later, Nicolosi reframed his case studies as "testimonies" to appeal to the religious ethos of the ex-gay movement:

> The Gay Liberation Movement has been very successful through the drama of personal testimony. When all the theoretical arguments were presented to the American Psychiatric Association in 1973, both for and against the idea of homosexuality as pathology, it was the

socio-political perspective that had the most influence. Listening to some gay men's personal stories of frustration in treatment, the psychiatric association omitted homosexuality as a diagnostic category.

Now, exactly twenty years later, we are offering the opposite sort of personal testimony, that of homosexual men who have tried to accept a gay identity but were dissatisfied and then benefited from psychotherapy to help free them of the gender identity conflict that lies behind most homosexuality.[67]

Here Nicolosi has characterized the basis for the decision of the APA Nomenclature Committee as rooted primarily in personal testimony. However, although Spitzer's experiences meeting members of the GayPA group certainly played a role, scientific research studies that included the work of Evelyn Hooker, Marcel Saghir, and Eli Robins were key. In addition to reframing ex-gay case studies as "personal testimonies" to appeal to the religious ex-gay movement, this analysis reduced the decision to remove "Homosexuality" from the DSM to one based on a "socio-political perspective" rather than anything based on science.

During this decade of escalating conflict and transformation, and with the formation of NARTH, U.S. professional associations created position statements challenging reorientation therapies and supporting gay rights. The number of such statements increased in the 1990s, providing one indicator of how the marginalization of reorientation and the promotion of gay-affirmative perspectives escalated from within mainstream mental health and medical professional associations—elements of the intellectual opportunity structure solidifying reorientation's position on the scientific fringe within the field of therapeutics.

If these position statements were not enough of a barrier blocking intellectual entries into mainstream science, NARTH also had to contend with the development of a new genre of testimony challenging the efficacy of reorientation treatments. In his 1991 memoir, Cures, the historian Martin Duberman discussed his reorientation attempt through psychoanalysis in the 1960s, relating how he gradually became aware that his sexual orientation would not change and that homosexuality is not pathological. Duberman described new ideas circulating in gay liberation groups that led him to reject the idea that life as a homosexual meant a life of unhappiness. A few years later, Mel White, former ghostwriter for evangelical ministers Jerry Falwell, Billy Graham, and Pat Robertson, came out as gay and then published Stranger at the Gate: To Be Gay and Christian in America.[68] White recounted decades of attempts at conversion therapy, including aversion treatments and religious counseling,

American Psychiatric Association

1973 homosexuality and civil rights
1984 homosexual issues concerning the military
1988 statement on discrimination based on gender or sexual orientation
1990 homosexuality and the armed services
1992 homosexuality
1998 sexual orientation, psychiatric treatment

2000 "reparative" therapy
2000 same-sex unions
2002 adoption and coparenting of children by same-sex couples
2005 support of legal recognition of same-sex civil marriage

American Psychological Association

1975 discrimination against homosexuals
1976 child custody or placement
1981 employment rights of gay teachers
1987 use of diagnoses "homosexuality" and "ego-dystonic homosexuality"
1988 sodomy laws and APA convention
1991 Department of Defense policy on sexual orientation and advertising in APA publications
1993 lesbian, gay, and bisexual youths in the schools
1993 resolution on state initiatives and referenda
1997 appropriate therapeutic response to sexual orientation

1998 legal benefits for same-sex couples
2004 sexual orientation, parents, and children
2004 sexual orientation and military service
2004 sexual orientation and marriage
2005 hate crimes
2007 opposing discriminatory legislation and initiatives aimed at LGB persons
2008 transgender, gender identity, and gender expression nondiscrimination
2009 resolution on appropriate affirmative responses to sexual orientation distress and change efforts

National Association of Social Workers

1977 policy statement on gay issues (antidiscrimination)
1987 policy statement on lesbian and gay issues (antidiscrimination)

1994 policy statement on lesbian and gay issues (antidiscrimination)
1997 policy statement on lesbian, gay, and bisexual issues (antidiscrimination)

American Counseling Association

1998 appropriate counseling responses to sexual orientation

American Psychoanalytic Association

1992 position statement on homosexuality
1999 position statement on reparative therapy
2008 position statement on gay marriage

2009 position statement on gays, lesbians, and bisexuals in the military

American Medical Association

2000 policy statement on sexual orientation reparative (conversion) therapy

American Academy of Pediatrics

1983 homosexuality and adolescence
1993 homosexuality and adolescence

Pro-gay position statements of U.S. medical and mental health associations, 1973–2009.

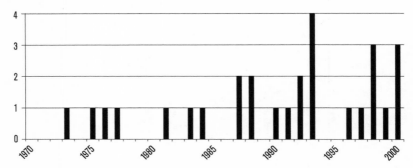

Number of pro-gay position statements approved per year by U.S. professional medical and mental health associations, 1970–2000.

when his sexual orientation would not change and he experienced great despair. White realized that Christian theology does not require the idea that homosexuality is sin, and that this way of life can be seen as a gift from God. Countertestimonials of failed therapeutic change tended to include stories of transforming worldviews, as homosexuality moved from pathology or sin to something healthy and praised.

In this context of increasing hostility to reorientation, NARTH leaders made various media appearances defending their work and promoting the idea that homosexuality is a disorder. NARTH was able to take advantage of the fact that journalists seek opposing views when covering issues, which helps sustain countermovements.[69] For example, in 1994, Charles Socarides appeared on *Larry King Live* (guest-hosted by Nick Charles) opposite Shelly Klinger, director of the American Psychiatric Association Committee on Gay, Lesbian and Bisexual Issues. In the discussion, Socarides promoted the idea that homosexuality is a disorder, while Klinger tried to shift the terms of the debate away from this issue toward questions about the ethics and efficacy of reorientation treatments:

> NICK CHARLES (speaking to Klinger): This debate is all about homosexuality. Is it a treatable disease or not? Briefly outline your argument.
> SHELLY KLINGER: There's no controversy over whether homosexuality is a disease or not. Scientifically it has been proven that homosexuals do not have a mental disorder. The controversy is over whether people should try to treat something that is not a disease with a treatment that doesn't work scientifically and probably causes harm to people.
> NICK CHARLES: Dr. Socarides, agree or disagree with that?

CHARLES SOCARIDES: I heartily disagree with that. Homosexuality is a developmental disorder. There are various forms of homosexuality which have to be separated from each other. There's homosexual behavior, which is not the true condition, and obligatory homosexuality, which we feel is one of the sexual deviations. There's a hard-core group within the American Psychoanalytic Association, mostly psychoanalysts, who believe by suitable analytic treatment, many homosexuals may develop the capacity to love a woman and give up homosexual relations.[70]

In addition to representing all "homosexuals" as men in this comment, it is noteworthy that Socarides characterized homosexuality as a "developmental disorder." Such claims significantly weakened NARTH's credibility in this period, given the prevailing wisdom that homosexuality should not be listed in the *DSM*. However, despite Klinger's assessment of "no controversy," the news coverage created an impression that scientific debate remained open.

Socarides may have attempted to repathologize homosexuality on CNN, but nonetheless, NARTH ran up against the hard barrier that homosexuality was no longer considered a mental disorder in science. One alternative strategy was to point to associations between homosexuality and known pathologies as a means to justify reorientation therapy. In 1997 NARTH leaders used AIDS to promote their work. Citing reports that young men were becoming infected with HIV at an alarming rate, Socarides and coauthors wrote an op-ed in the *Wall Street Journal* titled "Don't Forsake Homosexuals Who Want Help." The authors stated:

Every day young men seek help because they are experiencing an unwanted sexual attraction to other men, and are told that their condition is untreatable. It is not surprising that many of these young men fall into depression or despair when they are informed that a normal life with a wife and children is never to be theirs.

This despair can lead to reckless and life-threatening actions. Many young men with homosexual inclinations, feeling their lives are of little value, are choosing to engage in unprotected sex with strangers. Epidemiologists are well aware that the number of new HIV infections among young men involved in homosexual activity is rising at an alarming rate; within this population, the "safer sex" message is falling on deaf ears. One recent study revealed that 38% of homosexual adolescents had engaged in unprotected sex in the previous six months.

Young men and the parents of at-risk males have a right to know that prevention and effective treatment are available.[71]

In this case, NARTH promoted its treatments in a way that did not pathologize homosexuality per se, but rather, the expression of behavior. Using this strategy, NARTH would cite many other health disparities for gays and lesbians, including suicide, never pointing out that such health disparities might be alleviated by ending anti-gay oppression.

Within the American Psychological Association, psychologists initially responded to NARTH's public statements in 1995 with an attempt to ban reorientation practices. Psychologist Doug Haldeman described this process:

> We tried in 1995 to just prohibit conversion therapy and got shot down, in large part, by the practice community, who said, wait a minute, if we start going down the road of prohibiting certain kinds of therapies without credible evidence that they are harmful, we are heading down a very, very dangerous path here. And we went back then, and thought, OK, what can we say about this prejudice, about these therapists? What kind of warning labels can we put on them?[72]

Through the efforts of Haldeman and others, the American Psychological Association passed the 1997 position statement titled "Appropriate Therapeutic Responses to Sexual Orientation." The statement sought to establish that reorientation therapies have a basis in discrimination, and it made a strong call for informed consent, especially noting that clients should be informed that homosexuality is not a mental disorder. Drawing on Haldeman's research,[73] the statement noted that "societal ignorance and prejudice about same gender sexual orientation put some gay, lesbian, bisexual and questioning individuals at risk for presenting for 'conversion' treatment due to family or social coercion and/or lack of information."[74] Referring directly to NARTH's *Wall Street Journal* op-ed, the position statement added that "some mental health professionals advocate treatments of lesbian, gay, and bisexual people based on the premise that homosexuality is a mental disorder (e.g., Socarides et al, 1997)."

While taking a strong stand against treating homosexuality as pathology, the 1997 American Psychological Association's statement did not yet take a definitive stand on the efficacy of reorientation. Rather, it claimed that "the ethics, efficacy, benefits, and potential for harm of therapies that seek to reduce or eliminate same-gender sexual orientation are under extensive debate in the professional literature and the popular media (Davison, 1991; Haldeman, 1994; Wall Street Journal, 1997)."[75] According to Haldeman, the statement contained careful language about evidence of efficacy because the American Psychological Association strives to make judgments based on the best available science:

That language was criticized by many people who wanted a stronger statement. But at the time we were trying, as I remember it, to be thoughtful about the way we put things and not to say things that we could not defend. Because at that time, we hadn't done this comprehensive review of all the literature. . . . We still refer back to that just to say, here are the ethical implications of what's happening here.[76]

The claim that the status of therapies is "under extensive debate" made this position statement the weakest among all the national professional organizations by the end of the 1990s, leaving an opening in the intellectual opportunity structure whereby reorientation researchers might provide evidence that reorientation is possible.

Spitzer Publishes his Ex-Gay Study

Robert Spitzer's reorientation study entered public discourse at the peak of a major wave of ex-gay activism in the United States. In what Bob Knight of the conservative Family Research Council has called the "Normandy landing in the larger cultural wars," beginning in 1998 religious right groups, including Focus on the Family, funded a massive newspaper and billboard advertising campaign promoting ex-gay ministries. The campaign featured ex-gays with captions professing claims of "change."[77] The initiative grew to the point that *Newsweek* featured ex-gay spokespersons John and Anne Paulk in a cover story that August titled "Gay for Life? Going Straight: The Uproar over 'Sexual Conversion.'" The media campaign also coincided with the founding of Love Won Out, an ex-gay ministry created by Focus on the Family. The organization Parents and Friends of Ex-Gays (PFOX) was also founded as a response to the better-known group Parents and Friends of Lesbians and Gays (PFLAG).[78]

The year 1998 also marked the twenty-fifth anniversary of the removal of "Homosexuality" from the *DSM*, and the American Psychiatric Association acknowledged this event at its annual convention by passing a position statement titled "Psychiatric Treatment, Sexual Orientation." The statement referred to a fact sheet, published in 1997, that claimed there is "no published scientific evidence supporting the efficacy of 'reparative therapy' as a treatment to change one's sexual orientation," and listed several harms associated with such treatments, including depression, anxiety, and self-destructive behavior. Moreover, the position statement opposed any treatment based on the idea that homosexuality is a disorder on its own. The APA convention in Toronto also commemorated the anniversary with a panel titled "Psychiatry: 25 Years Since Depathologizing Homosexuality." Notably absent from the panel, however, was Robert Spitzer, who was not invited. This snub was an indication that, despite his historic work that made the twenty-fifth anniversary possible, his positions on Sexual Orientation Disturbance and Ego-Dystonic Homosexuality and his belief in the suboptimal status of homosexuality had now placed him outside the mainstream.

Meanwhile, NARTH and ex-gay ministries were calling for formal recognition of ex-gay therapies in protests against national mental health associations. While NARTH had previously called for recognition of therapists' rights, these protests now emphasized clients' rights to "self-determination," with ex-gays holding up signs with statements such as "It's my right to change."[79] At the 1999 convention of the American Psychiatric Association, Spitzer encountered a group of protesting ex-gay activists. According to PFOX activist Anthony Falzarano, "[Spitzer] came up and said, 'You guys are out here again'. . . . I asked him if he would consider taking us more seriously and attend our press conference. I told him some prominent ex-gays would give their testimonies. To my surprise, he came."[80] According to Spitzer's accounts, this meeting changed his mind about the possibility of change: "They were claiming that, contrary to the APA position statement, they had changed their sexual orientation from homosexual to heterosexual. I started to wonder: Could it be that some homosexuals could actually change their sexual orientation?"[81] Portraying himself as a skeptic unlikely to believe in reorientation because he had sympathized with pro-gay causes in the past, Spitzer set himself up to be "converted" by a new study into a believer in the possibility of reorientation, which would make him into an immensely credible spokesperson for ex-gays.

Spitzer decided to conduct an ex-gay study to examine change claims further. When he announced this plan, gay activist Wayne Besen of the Human Rights Campaign, sensing the threat, wrote Spitzer a letter to warn him about doing the research. Besen, whose background was in public relations and politics, warned that conducting a research study based on the testimonies of ex-gays would be "scientific suicide" because ex-gays could not be trusted to tell the truth about their sexual orientation. Instead, Besen and the HRC recommended that Spitzer use objective measurements such as the polygraph and the penile plethysmograph. Besen's letter to Spitzer indicates one way in which the Spitzer study helped transform a hotly contested ethical matter into a technical dispute over evidence.[82]

The Spitzer study emerged within an intellectual field that not only included several professional opposition statements to reorientation therapy; new research also threatened preemptively to undermine the credibility of the work. In 2001 psychologists Ariel Shidlo and Michael Schroeder, along with psychiatrist Jack Drescher, coedited *Sexual Conversion Therapy*, a volume addressed to a range of audiences including scientists, therapists, and the general public. They claimed the book was intended to counter with quality science what they called the "infomercial" approach of the ex-gay movement. Shidlo and Schroeder had compiled narratives of harm in a project they called "Homophobic Therapies: Documenting the Damage." Like Spitzer's, their study was developed in partnership with social movement organizations, but with pro-gay groups, not reorientation activists. After their first twenty interviews, they reported that even among people who claimed treatments had failed and were harmful, they found some benefits to reorientation, such as an increased sense of belonging in a community of ex-gays. As a result, the coauthors renamed the study "Changing Sexual Orientation: Does Counseling Work?" and used this more inclusive name in their calls for participants.

The *Sexual Conversion Therapy* volume included Schroeder and Shidlo's summary of alleged ethics violations by reorientation therapists, suggested within the reports of the former patients they interviewed. Subjects said they had been pressured by their therapists to go to the media and tell of their success in changing sexual orientation. In some cases, religious universities threatened to expel ex-gays if they didn't renounce homosexuality.[83] Ex-gays were also deprived of informed consent, as they were misinformed that homosexuality was either a psychological disorder or had not been acknowledged as a healthy condition, drawing on "purportedly scientific, fraudulent information about gay lives and relationships which characterized them as unhappy and dysfunctional."[84] Clients were also not informed about gay-affirmative therapy as an alternative treatment. Schroeder and Shidlo's study suggested that ex-gay claims of change might take a different form if clients had all the available facts. In the field of therapeutics, this kind of work acted as "preventive context" for the Spitzer study, providing intellectual resources for the opponents of reorientation to undermine the self-reported claims of change Spitzer would later use to make his claims for efficacy.

Spitzer began gathering his sample in January 2000. He put out a call for participants with ex-gay ministries and with NARTH, and also appeared on her nationally syndicated radio show with conservative commentator Dr. Laura Schlessinger, who had become known for her opposition to gay rights. According to NARTH, when he appeared on the

Dr. Laura Program in early 2000, Spitzer made the following statements promoting the study and reporting preliminary results:

> I'm convinced from people I have interviewed, that for many of them, they have made substantial changes toward becoming heterosexual. . . . I think that's news.
>
> I came to this study skeptical. I now claim that these changes can be sustained.
>
> I agree that a homosexual who is not able to be aroused heterosexually . . . I think, implicitly, there is something not working.[85]

In addition to filling public airwaves with claims of change, these public statements appealed to the worldview of ex-gays, facilitating the creation of a link of trust between Spitzer and his subjects. This was important because older NARTH members, especially Socarides, were understandably skeptical of Spitzer given his role in demedicalization.[86] As a result, he successfully gathered a sample of 200 people (143 men and 57 women) who met his inclusion criteria, among which was having lived at least five years out of homosexuality.[87]

As Spitzer was conducting this research, the American Psychiatric Association passed a new position statement titled "'Reparative' Therapy." This time, the language was directed more narrowly against the practice of reorientation, and endorsed the view that homosexuality is a "normal variant" of human sexuality:

> To date, there are no scientifically rigorous outcome studies to determine either the actual efficacy or harm of "reparative" treatments. There is sparse scientific data about selection criteria, risks versus benefits of the treatment, and long-term outcomes of "reparative" therapies. The literature consists of anecdotal reports of individuals who have claimed to change, people who claim that attempts to change were harmful to them, and others who claimed to have changed and then later recanted those claims.[88]

The position statement called for ethical practitioners to refrain from practice until real evidence was produced. Spitzer intended to address this new position statement directly and fill this void. At the same conference where the resolution was passed, Spitzer attempted to hold an open debate on reorientation treatments, but the panel was canceled once leaders of the association learned that NARTH was involved in organizing the event. Spitzer decided to hold a press conference to protest the cancellation; several ex-gay leaders joined him, speaking behind a podium with a banner that read "Reparative Therapy is Ethical."[89]

The following year the study created a media firestorm even before Spitzer had the chance to present his unpublished paper. This was because a few days before the conference, the results of the study were somehow leaked to the press. An internationally published Associated Press story overshadowed all other news coming out of the APA convention that year. The story titled "Some Gays Can Go Straight, Study Suggests" began, "An explosive new study says some gay people can turn straight if they really want to. That conclusion clashes with that of major mental health organizations, which say that sexual orientation is fixed and that so-called reparative therapy may actually be harmful."[90] Such coverage of the Spitzer study helped the ex-gay movement more broadly. The public perceived a controversy among scientists, when in fact there was next to none.

On the day of Spitzer's presentation, the *New York Times* likewise carried an account titled "Study Says Gays Can Shift Orientation." This headline, referring to all "gays," gave the impression that Spitzer's conclusions were stronger than he claimed, as he believed that the possibility of change was actually "rare." Journalist Erica Goode wrote:

> A psychiatrist at Columbia University who contends that the mental health profession has "totally bought the idea that once you are gay you cannot be changed" will report today that some "highly motivated" gays can become heterosexual. The researcher, Dr. Robert Spitzer, said his study was based on 45-minute telephone interviews with 143 men and 57 women who had sought help to change their sexual orientation. He and his colleagues found that 66 percent of the men and 44 percent of the women had achieved "good heterosexual functioning," he said.[91]

Although Goode clarified that the study was based on "highly motivated" gays, ambiguous headlines suggested that Spitzer's work referred to all gays. Moreover, percentages of subjects achieving heterosexual functioning might be misread as a success rate, but this study could not produce such a rate. The sample had been carefully selected to meet certain criteria of alleged change.

The Spitzer study is an example of a "partnership model" of research, in which researcher and subject both bring expertise to the table in the production of knowledge.[92] Spitzer's study combined the experience-based knowledge of ex-gays with his own mental health expertise to produce evidence of change. However, while Spitzer was conducting a secular study, sexual orientation measures often took on different significance for subjects reporting on the power of faith. Exodus International executive vice president Randy Thomas downplayed the Spitzer study as "secular," but he argued that the testimony he provided would still be credible:

> Exodus Executive Director Alan Chambers and I were two of the people (Exodus and non-Exodus) interviewed for Dr. Spitzer's study.
>
> When I learned that the very doctor who had removed homosexuality from the DSM (Diagnostic and Statistical Manual) list of disorders wanted to research those of us living beyond homosexuality it was one of those uh-oh moments. I thought *Is this a set up? Or is this a fair interview?* As with all interviews, those of us that participated in the Spitzer study sought to honor the Lord by being completely honest. He only calls us to give an account; we are not responsible for what is done with our testimony by other people. . . . So what is a nice faith based ministry like us doing hanging out with secular therapists? We were giving testimony to the righteousness of Christ of course.[93]

In such cases, the survey response acts as a "boundary object." These are "objects which are both plastic enough to adapt to local needs and the constraints of the several parties employing them, yet robust enough to maintain a common identity across sites."[94] As a boundary object, the sexual orientation rating could span Spitzer's secular scientific worldview and the religious worldview of his subjects, who attach a spiritual and supernatural significance to their experiences. Although an awkward partnership, the blend of expertise produced powerful rhetoric.

Media exaggerations of Spitzer's claims prompted a response from mainstream psychiatry. According to psychiatrist Jack Drescher, some media figures were even stating that Spitzer had broadly "changed his mind," potentially misleading the public into believing that Spitzer actually favored putting the diagnosis of "Homosexuality" back into the *DSM*.[95] To quell this perceived problem, Drescher and others encouraged the American Psychiatric Association medical director to issue a statement on behalf of the association. The statement reiterated the 1998 and 2000 position statements, again claiming, "There is no scientific evidence supporting the efficacy of reparative therapy as a treatment to change one's sexual orientation."[96]

Such developments led Spitzer to feel compelled to regain control over the public interpretation of his study. After all, he was trying to demonstrate that there was merely *some* evidence of change, challenging the claims of "no evidence" in position statements, not to buttress the religious right political agenda with claims that homosexuality was always a choice. In an op-ed in the *Wall Street Journal* two weeks after the presentation of his paper, Spitzer clarified his views:

What I found was that, in the unique sample I studied, many made substantial changes in sexual arousal and fantasy—and not merely behavior. Even subjects who made a less substantial change believed it to be extremely beneficial. Complete change was uncommon.

My study concluded with an important caveat: that it should not be used to justify a denial of civil rights to homosexuals, or as support for coercive treatment. I did not conclude that all gays should try to change, or even that they would be better off if they did. However, to my horror, some of the media reported the study as an attempt to show that homosexuality is a choice, and that substantial change is possible for any homosexual who decides to make the effort.

In reality, change should be seen as complex and on a continuum. Some homosexuals appear able to change self-identity and behavior, but not arousal and fantasies; others can change only self-identity; and only a very few, I suspect, can substantially change all four. Change in all four is probably less frequent than claimed by therapists who do this kind of work; in fact, I suspect the vast majority of gay people would be unable to alter by much a firmly established homosexual orientation.

I certainly believe that parents with homosexually oriented sons and daughters should love their children—no matter how their children decide to live their lives—and should not use my study to coerce them into unwanted therapy.[97]

Following these concerns about people exaggerating his findings, Spitzer went on in the op-ed to defend the practice of reorientation, claiming that the decision to enter into treatment could be a "rational, self-directed goal" rather than a result of societal pressure. Drawing on NARTH's framing of client rights, Spitzer stated that "such a choice should be considered fundamental to client autonomy and self-determination." This op-ed also signaled that Spitzer defined attraction patterns as the "core features" of sexual orientation, beyond identity and behavior, and claimed that these features could be accessed through self-report data.

A year after Spitzer's presentation, Ariel Shidlo and Michael Schroeder published their full outcome study, "Changing Sexual Orientation: A Consumers' Report," which presented another side of the story. This study also attracted media coverage, albeit to a much lesser extent than Spitzer's. Of the 202 participants in Shidlo and Schroeder's study, 26 reported that they were a "success." However, all these success cases continued to use what the authors called "homosexual behavior management" techniques: cognitive and behavioral tools learned in reorientation therapy to minimize homosexual desire and maximize heterosexual desire, such as reading the Bible or imagining getting AIDS from same-sex encounters. Shidlo and Schroeder's findings raised further suspicions about the veracity of self-report claims by ex-gays. Their subjects still experienced same-sex attractions, and they often had incentives to misrepresent their heterosexual attractions. To assess harms for those in the "failure" category, the authors used an open-ended qualitative interview format rather than a quantitative instrument. As a result, they assessed *meanings* of harm attributed by clients to their own experiences and did not claim to have definitive scientific evidence of harm.[98]

Also in 2002, while preparing his paper for publication, Spitzer met with another researcher who published competing work on experiences of ex-gays and ex-ex-gays in the *Sexual Conversion Therapy* volume. A. Lee Beckstead, a psychologist from Salt Lake City, had been through a failed reorientation attempt in a Mormon ministry. His chapter in *Sexual Conversion Therapy* was drawn from his doctoral dissertation, in which he examined the motivations and experiences of reorientation clients. Beckstead had also trained at the Kurt Freund Phallometric Laboratory at the University of Toronto, and those experiences shaped his understanding of male sexuality rooted in physiology. The interviews Beckstead conducted challenged the depth of heterosexual feeling in reorientation therapy "successes." For example, "Clint" was an allegedly "successful" ex-gay respondent who was married and experienced a form of emotional other-sex attraction, only with his spouse. In his dissertation Beckstead wrote:

> Overall, participants noted that a generalized heterosexual arousal was not as important to them as closeness to their partner or spouse. Clint discussed a common theme reflected by others who experienced their intimacy with their partner as "warm and comfortable":
>
>> I use the comparison of a campfire versus a forest fire. That maybe my emotional response to men would be like a forest fire and that it's very . . . it's been very intense and dangerous and out of control and perhaps damaging or hurtful. But my relationship with my wife is more like the campfire. It's warm and comfortable and happy and reassuring and protective and although it probably doesn't have the same emotional intensity that the physical relationship with a man might bring, you know, I think maybe it's good.[99]

To Beckstead, Clint's characterization of his heterosexual attractions meant that he really did not achieve a heterosexual result, but an asexual result at most; Spitzer, however, would consider this a success. His meeting with Beckstead enabled Spitzer to anticipate critical arguments in his publication, and he dedicated a long section of the conclusion of his article to challenging Beckstead's views.

Spitzer's study was finally published in 2003 in the *Archives of Sexual Behavior* along with twenty-six peer commentaries. Editor Kenneth Zucker decided to publish the paper with these commentaries rather than putting the paper through an ordinary peer review process that likely would have failed. Zucker, whose own work involved "curing" children of gender identity disorder, aligned with the theories of reorientation therapists and was another sympathetic professional providing an intellectual venue for the ex-gay movement in his capacity as editor of the journal. Spitzer displayed his results in the paper using bar graphs showing dramatic shifts in identity, behavior, and attraction before and after treatment. To more clearly define therapeutic efficacy, he created a variable that he called "Good Heterosexual Functioning," and he declared that 66 percent of the men and 44 percent of the women in his sample met this standard. According to Spitzer, this was an improvement over previous research, which failed to adequately define a full success. Good Heterosexual Functioning included the following criteria:

> (1) During the past year, the participant was in a heterosexual relationship and regarded it as "loving"; (2) overall satisfaction in the emotional relationship with their partner (at least 7 on a 1–10 scale where 10 is *as good as it can be* and 1 is *as bad as it can be*); (3) heterosexual sex with partner at least a few times a month; (4) physical satisfaction from heterosexual sex at least 7 (the same 1–10 scale); (5) during no more than 15% of heterosexual sex occasions thinks of homosexual sex.[100]

Spitzer constructed this variable based on criteria he believed would provide face validity. It did not include generalized arousal to the other sex, and consequently, a respondent such as "Clint" in Beckstead's study might have qualified as a success by this definition.[101] Spitzer's construct reveals norms about ideal heterosexual relationships, including emotional content, fantasy life, and minimum ideal sexual requirements such as monogamy. It stands in contrast to what he claims is Beckstead's poorly delineated and arbitrary definition of heterosexuality, thereby attacking interview methods that lack standardized measures. Here was a distinct difference between researchers on where to draw "the straight line."

As a whole, the peer responses published in the issue along with Spitzer's paper were overwhelmingly negative, both in terms of the ethics of the study and its methodology, and generally deemed it nonscientific. The ethical concerns primarily centered on how Spitzer neglected to assess harm in his research, especially in the wake of findings by harm researchers Shidlo and Schroeder. One commentary even claimed that the study violated the Nuremberg Code principles of human experimentation established in the wake of Nazi atrocities.[102] Psychiatrist John Bancroft, who had once used aversion therapies to treat homosexuality, joined several others in condemning the study for reinforcing the idea that homosexuality is a mental illness.[103] And several commentaries explained that the research would be used to further oppress gays in society by making it look as though homosexuality is a "choice" and therefore not a basis for rights.[104]

But much of the criticism of the Spitzer study was pitched in terms of methodology. Spitzer's method, gathering a sample of ex-gays and asking them to retrospectively report on their attractions, behavior, and identity before and after therapy, was suspect not only because a retrospective study cannot demonstrate causality but also because ex-gays were not deemed capable of reporting these aspects of themselves. Criticizing "subject selection bias," Kenneth Cohen and Ritch Savin-Williams pointed out that Spitzer had chosen a sample of people he knew would be likely to agree with his hypothesis, and excluded people who would disagree.[105] Other commentators hypothesized that subjects in a religious sample would be pressured into exaggerating claims of change. This was often couched in terms of "cognitive dissonance" theory, whereby respondents resolved psychological distress brought about by the conflict between religious values and same-sex attractions by denying those attractions.[106] At times, the tendency to misrepresent sexual orientation change was understood as due to "internalized homophobia,"[107] but more often it was due to religious pressures to demonstrate change, witness to others, and affirm faith.[108] Psychologist Gregory Herek questioned the ethics of the study on these grounds, claiming that Spitzer had not used safeguards to eliminate key sources of bias in his research subjects and, as such, he had unethically promoted faulty research.[109]

Taking a different approach to the veracity of self-reports, six critics called for "objective" physiological measures of sexual attraction to accompany untrustworthy self-reports.[111] Criticizing self-report measures in a hypothetical case of a male subject, Bruce Rind stated:

> In short, these measures, it seems, assess surface rather than core change. The man's beliefs are tied to the surface, to the role he feels compelled to play, and to the extent that the core differs, his self-reports are self-deception. What is needed are measures of involuntary response to various actual stimuli, rather than just self-reports that reflect essentially volitional behavior. Put the man back into tempting

DISAGREE			AGREE, but with a weaker position	AGREE	
Methods	Methods and Ethics	Ethics		Methods	Methods and Ethics
Carlson	Bancroft	Dresher	Krueger	Hershberger	Byrd
Cohen and	Beckstead	Tye	Klein		Nicolosi
Savin-Williams	Gagnon		Wakefield		
Diamond	Hartmann		Yarhouse		
Friedman	Herek				
Hill and DiClementi	Rind				
McConaghy	Wainberg et al.				
Rodriguez Rust	Worthington				
Strassburg					
Vasey and Rendall					

Twenty-six commentaries in *Archives of Sexual Behavior,* published with the Spitzer study in 2003, offered disagreement or agreement with Spitzer's conclusions (there is now evidence for the efficacy of reorientation therapies; they should be pursued if desired by the client) on the bases of methodology and ethics.[110]

situations of the kind that formerly aroused him or expose him to gay pornography of the type that used to excite him. Measure his arousal with plethysmography. Expose him to heterosexual situations that he claims attract him or expose him to heterosexual pornography and then measure the arousal in the same way.[112]

While this was an important concern for many, some thought physiological testing was not the way to get better objectivity. For example, Gregory Herek stated in an interview, "I do recall that a number of people did raise [phallometric testing] as a possibility. It's not where my head goes." Herek leaned toward better self-report techniques:

There's some research that suggests that by using different kinds of questioning techniques we can get more honest self-reports of sexual attraction and sexual behavior. For example, when people are interacting with a computer, they are more likely to disclose their own stigmatized sexual behaviors as well as other kinds of stigmatized behaviors than when they are interacting with a person. So there are techniques like that that we can use.

Herek voiced skepticism of reorientation efficacy research in general: "I am not sure that I see great value in devoting a lot of research resources to the issue in the first place. So, in a way, coming up with the gold standard is several steps removed from that."[113] While mainstream critics did call for phallometric testing on this issue, Herek's response is an ethical rejection of the research program altogether. His chief complaint about the methodology of the study was that it could not show causality; he was joined by others in this concern.[114]

Other critiques were more theoretical. Lisa Diamond criticized the sexual orientation "taxonomy" built into Spitzer's research question that asked if homosexuals can be turned into heterosexuals. This, Diamond claims, divides the world into "sheep" and "goats" in a way that Kinsey had warned against, as sexualities are much more complex.[115] Paula Rodriguez Rust further questioned the content of sexual orientation as a construct:

> The real challenge Spitzer poses, therefore, is not the assertion that changes in sexual identity, feelings, and behavior occur, but the assertion of a core sexual orientation that is, although core, amenable to change. If a core orientation can change, what defining characteristic renders it "core"? The proposition that a malleable core sexual orientation exists is untestable. Its function is not scientific, but psychological; it allows individuals undergoing reparative therapy to hope that they will, ultimately, be able to live without fear that their same sex desires will resurface.[116]

Some commentators agreed with Spitzer, however, at least in part, and a few celebrated the study wholeheartedly. Most enthusiastic were NARTH's Dean Byrd and Joseph Nicolosi, who defended the research both in terms of methods and ethics. Ethically, the research supported the principle of the client's right to choose reorientation therapy. Methodologically, Nicolosi defended Spitzer's measure of sexual attractions in light of Beckstead's challenge. From Nicolosi's perspective, a "campfire" may be more desirable than a "forest fire":

> Almost all the clients I have known who transition away from homosexuality describe a more subtle heterosexual response, one which has, as my former client says, less "zing." But even though they are of less intensity, these experiences are richer, fuller, and more emotionally satisfying. These men describe a feeling of "rightness" and a natural compatibility. As one ex-gay and now-married client said, "When I compare my intimate experiences with my wife to my homosexual experiences, it seems like we were little boys playing in the sandbox." Rather than feeling depleted, he is renewed, feels good about himself, and experiences himself as an integral part of the heterosexual world.[117]

Such claims defended Spitzer's use of self-report. Indeed, Nicolosi, Byrd, and Potts had published a study a few years earlier in the journal *Psychological Reports* with a similar self-report method.[118]

After these critiques, Spitzer backpedaled. In the same issue in which the study appeared, he published a separate response to the commentaries, saying that he had asked the wrong research question in his research study:

> Instead of the research question "Can some gays change their sexual orientation?" the primary question should have been "Contrary to conventional wisdom, do some ex-gays describe changes in attraction, fantasy, and desire that are consistent with true changes in sexual orientation?" The credibility of the subjects' self-report, as it is in all treatment efficacy studies that use self-report becomes an additional issue to be considered.[119]

Spitzer then refined his conclusion:

> In the paper, I wrote, "The study provides evidence that change in sexual orientation following some form of reparative therapy does occur in some gay men and lesbians." With the benefit of time and the many thoughtful commentaries on my study, a more accurate assessment is the following: The conventional wisdom in the mental health profession is that reorientation therapy can get some gays to identify themselves as "heterosexual" and therefore "ex-gay," but few, if any, will report changes in sexual attraction, fantasy, and desire consistent with true changes in sexual orientation. The study findings call this view into question. In a sample of 200 ex-gays, the majority reported changes in sexual attraction, fantasy, and desire that are consistent with what would be expected if true changes from predominantly homosexual to predominantly heterosexual orientation had occurred. Although some response bias could have occurred, it is unlikely that it can explain all of the reported changes in sexual orientation.
>
> The study provides the level of evidence appropriate to the initial stages of therapeutic evaluation with regard to an important and controversial issue. What is needed is a prospective outcome study in which a consecutive series of volunteer subjects are evaluated before starting reorientation therapy and after several years.[120]

Thus, according to Spitzer's own conclusion in this response to the commentaries, the position statements of professional mental health organizations remained intact. No definitive evidence existed for the efficacy of reorientation therapy, even by his own admission. However, ex-gay and other conservative groups had a resource available to them that could be compelling for public audiences: a research study in a scientific journal that claimed to have demonstrated that reorientation works in certain cases.

At the same time that Spitzer's study was published, activist Wayne Besen published a book that targeted it directly. *Anything but Straight: Unmasking the Scandals and Lies Behind the Ex-Gay Myth* was a tour de force in debunking reorientation, ending with a hard-hitting critique of the Spitzer study. On the cover of the book was a photograph of ex-gay activist John Paulk, who had appeared on the cover of *Newsweek* a few years before. Besen got word late one night that Paulk was at a gay bar in D.C. and hurried to the bar. Paulk found out he had been spotted, but Besen managed to photograph him as he fled the scene. Besen used the image of the "fallen" ex-gay Paulk represented as further evidence that reorientation programs were fraudulent. Besen's criticism of the Spitzer study described the letter he sent him while at the Human Rights Campaign, calling for physiological testing including penile plethysmography. He challenged the political and monetary motivations of Spitzer's research participants, saying many were likely bisexual. Spitzer himself was duped by the religious right, Besen claimed, and he was just seeking some media attention at the end of his career. Besen stated:

> In the end the real loser is Dr. Spitzer. Whether he was an over-the-hill stage horse galloping toward the limelight or a court jester hoodwinked by a scheming religious right is unimportant. What matters is that Spitzer's embarrassing travesty of scholarship will surely go down as his defining work, a professional pockmark that will indelibly taint his once splendid career.[121]

Here Besen tried to contain further damage to gay rights that the Spitzer study might cause, but religious right groups would inevitably use it to their own ends.

Proponents Take the Study and Run

In various public policy venues, opponents of gay rights immediately used the Spitzer study to characterize homosexuality as an immoral "choice" that should not be a basis for rights. In 2003 Dr. Jeffrey Satinover, member of the NARTH scientific advisory committee, testified before the Massachusetts Senate Judicial Committee studying gay marriage and cited the newly published study.[122] Even back in 2001, when the study was first announced, members of the Finnish Parliament suggested that

Spitzer had "changed his mind" about whether homosexuality should be a mental illness diagnosis in the *DSM*.[123] In an attempt to rein in this misuse, Spitzer wrote an open letter to Finnish MP Kari Kärkkäinen just days before the parliamentary vote on a bill allowing same-sex partnerships, which was predicted to lose:

> I am disturbed to hear (although not surprised) that the results of my study are being misused by those who are against anti-discrimination laws and civil union laws for gays and lesbians.
>
> My study, based on a very unique sample, indicated that—contrary to the current view of most mental health professionals—some homosexuals can change their sexual orientation to a significant degree. However, I also indicated in the discussion section of my presentation, that such results are probably quite rare, even for highly motivated homosexuals. I also said that it would be a serious mistake to conclude from my study that any highly motivated homosexual can change his or her sexual orientation, or that my study shows that homosexuality is a "choice."
>
> Whether or not some homosexuals can change their sexual orientation is a scientific issue that to me, is totally irrelevant to the ethical issue of whether homosexuals are entitled to anti-discrimination laws and civil union laws. As a citizen (not as a scientist), I personally favor anti-discrimination laws and civil union laws for homosexuals.[124]

Following Spitzer's clarification, the Finnish Parliament narrowly passed the same-sex partnership bill.

NARTH president Joseph Nicolosi also used the study in an attempt to get the American Medical Association to change its position on reorientation. During this exchange, Nicolosi used statistics drawn from the Spitzer study to try to establish that reorientation is effective in many cases:

> Dr. Spitzer found that, contrary to most psychiatric opinion, individuals who have undergone reorientation therapy can experience positive changes from homosexual to heterosexual orientation. Of those he studied, most indicated that they still struggled with homosexual attractions to some degree, but 11% of the males and 37% of the females indicated a complete change from homosexual to heterosexual orientation.[125]

Nicolosi used Spitzer's data as though the study were a representative sample of people going through treatment. Furthermore, the outcome data ("11% of the males and 37% of the females indicated a complete change from homosexual to heterosexual orientation") are only mean-ingful as success rates in a longitudinal random sample of people at-tempting therapy, not in a retrospective study of a convenience sample of people who claim their therapy worked. Likewise, religious right groups utilized the study to promote reorientation and anti-gay public policy. Alluding to the study even before it was published, Dr. James Dobson of Focus on the Family stated, "We applaud Dr. Spitzer for having the cour-age to examine and then expose the myth of inevitability."[126] Regardless of the backpedaling in Spitzer's response to the many commentaries, the study was published and available for advancing anti-gay causes.

Spitzer: Standing Still While the World Changes

The period of the 1970s through the early 2000s spans immense changes in the field of therapeutics regarding reorientation. A reorientation ther-apist at the beginning of this period would be considered at the leading edge of the field, but by the end, would be on the scientific fringe, per-haps looking to religious groups for allies and clients. Robert Spitzer stands as a pivotal figure, not only because of his role as a sympathetic professional for movements seeking to influence science, but also be-cause he helped set in motion many of the changes in the intellectual opportunity structure more broadly, even those that led to his margin-alization. His "in between" position on the "suboptimal" status of ho-mosexuality enabled him to take on these roles. While it is unclear how Spitzer's views may or may not have changed regarding the efficacy of therapy, his own "conversion" on the issue of whether change was pos-sible was intended to boost the credibility of his work on ex-gays. Yet his position on the status of homosexuality as a nondiagnosable condition has remained steadfast across these decades. This view has left many on both sides of the debate feeling rather ambivalent toward him.

Over these years the intellectual opportunity structure changed dra-matically, gradually strengthening barriers to any movements seeking to redefine homosexuality as an illness in the United States. Once ho-mosexuality had been demedicalized, new institutions, including gay-affirmative subsections of professional organizations as well as journals, were established that would have to be disbanded were the old view to take hold again. New position statements and ethics codes solidified re-orientation's place on the fringe. And new credibility hierarchies of evi-dence began to take shape, as penile plethysmography reentered the re-orientation debate with criticisms of the Spitzer study. Spitzer may have been a sympathetic professional for ex-gays and a boon for them within the public, but the credibility of his study was shattered within science, even leading him to retreat from his own conclusions.

Despite Spitzer's efforts to contain the interpretation and impact of his study within public circles, he had published his study in a scientific journal. This resource was available for ex-gay ministries, religious right organizations, and gay rights opponents to use in various political venues. The ways in which the Spitzer study came to be used in the public domain illustrate a principle of science and technology studies, as Bruno Latour claims: "The fate of facts . . . is in later users' hands; their qualities are thus a consequence, not a cause of collective action."[127] In other words, the transformation of Spitzer's study into a demonstration of the general "effectiveness" of reorientation therapy remained a possibility if those who deployed it could create that reality. Given ambiguities in the 1997 American Psychological Association position statement, it would take even more effort among mainstream professionals to draw the line of the boundaries of science on this issue—a process that would take shape beginning in 2007. After that time, Spitzer would once again become a major public figure regarding his ex-gay study, eventually issuing a public apology.

The late 1990s and early 2000s were an important time for honing a conceptual understanding of sexual orientation as involving "core features" of sexual attraction. Yet a number of problems remained in the broader field of therapeutics, including where to draw "the straight line." Was a person who described his attraction to his female sex partner as an emotional "campfire" really straight, or was less "zing" to be expected? Would physiological testing be required to demonstrate that "core features" had changed, or would self-report of masturbatory fantasy or attraction suffice? Within science, retrospective self-report of sexual attraction change did not meet the burden of proof, and because of various concerns raised about the veracity of ex-gay testimony, such claims could not be trusted. The tacit alliance between pro-gay professionals, gay activists, and phallometric testing, which began with the failed behavior therapy studies of the 1970s, found stronger expression with explicit calls for physiological testing of ex-gays intended to reveal an inner core of fixed same-sex sexual orientation. While phallometry began to increase in importance, by no means was there any consensus that this was the most important measure of sexual orientation to be utilized in the field. At the same time, claims of harm reported by ex-ex-gays, especially recounted in the work of Shidlo and Schroeder, began their rise to prominence in the debate, but did not yet gain the status of scientific proof of harm.

When I interviewed Spitzer for the first time in 2008, he cited the influence of evolutionary psychology in forming his views on homosexuality in recent years, particularly the theories of Steven Pinker. He also appealed to the ideas of Jerome Wakefield on the meaning of disorder:

> [Jerry Wakefield] argues that there are two components to a disorder. One is that there's some naturally evolved function that is not working, and the second is because of that, there is some harm to the individual. So if you applied that standard criterion to homosexuality it seems to me it's hard to avoid the notion that something is not working which is the evolution of heterosexual capacity for arousal. So in a way I do believe it's a disorder, even though I'm known as the person who got the homosexuality out as a disorder, which is, I don't like to publicly say what I just said, but I admit to it, that's the way I see it.[128]

Today, gay rights are entrenched with notions of "pride" and of homosexuality as a "natural variant." Spitzer's view demonstrates that support for gay rights need not include a wholesale acceptance of these gay-positive views.

Over these decades, the ex-gay movement grew with a generally peaceful division of labor between secular reorientation therapists and religious ministries. For the most part, these groups could hold together if the goal, ambiguously stated, was "change" from homosexuality. Psychoanalytic concepts could be mapped onto religious interpretations of family dynamics, and homosexuality could pass back and forth between "sin" and "illness." As the debate turned more acutely to evidence and the meaning of change, this alliance would be harder to sustain. Ultimately the frame dispute over the true goals of reorientation would lead to fragmentation.[129] During these early years, when Joe Dallas and other ministers challenged the idea that a full change in sexual attractions was needed and Socarides claimed full change was possible, this difference in definitions of reality could unite a broader constituency, as a benefit of a frame dispute.

If Spitzer's study did not change the scientific record on the efficacy of reorientation, it raised the stakes of the debate. No longer simply an ethical matter, reorientation research now played a more prominent role, as discussions turned more acutely to evidence or the lack thereof. Rather than simply saying that reorientation should not be performed, mainstream scientists needed other means to discredit self-reports of ex-gays besides relying on undermining their character. As attention to scientific evidence grew, the solutions proposed by mainstream scientists would

strain the already uneasy alliance between secular reorientation therapists, who sought complete sexual orientation change, and religious ex-
gay ministry leaders, who placed emphasis on salvation as the primary
goal of ex-gay ministries. In addition to a renewed focus on how to scientifically define and measure sexual orientation, another form of evidence
would help facilitate this cleavage: collective testimonies from an organized movement of ex-ex-gays.

three

EX-EX-GAYS MATCH TESTIMONY WITH TESTIMONY, 2004–2007

Evangelical Christian psychologist Warren Throckmorton produced the documentary *I Do Exist* in 2004 as a means to help American audiences connect with the conversion testimonials of ex-gays. Although Throckmorton intended the film as an informational documentary, various churches used it as a ministry tool, and ex-gay activists used it for outreach, even getting it broadcast on television stations. Throckmorton intended to give a voice to ex-gays as a group of people who were not being heard. *I Do Exist* featured five ex-gays telling their stories of transformation from gay to straight. It also included an interview with Dr. Robert Spitzer, telling of his own transformation from skeptic to believer in the possibility of reorientation through his own research process. Noe Guttierez Jr., whose narrative was most prominent in the film, described being able to have heterosexual feelings as a result of reorientation and the power of faith.

But by 2007, Throckmorton had undergone a transformation of his own and retired his influential film. In part, this was because Guttierez had decided to leave the ex-gay movement. While remaining private about his sexual orientation, Guttierez was reported by Ex-Gay Watch as saying:

> I do not regret my words on-screen. I am a person who believes in change, especially that espoused by an active Christian faith. However, I do regret the divisive message of the ex-gay movement and that my story became a vehicle for that message. I personally have had a change of heart in the matter of a person's sexual orientation. It has been my experience in the years since joining (and later leaving) the ex-gay movement that a person's sexual orientation may or may not be an

area impacted by the change that comes by way of a diligent Christian faith.[1]

Gutierrez, like John Paulk and others, became fodder for anti-reorientation activist blogs, fitting the trope of the "fallen ex-gay" as evidence that ex-gay programs were a sham. Before retiring the film, Throckmorton wrote in a Frequently Asked Questions page on his website:

All documentaries become dated the day after they are released. People pass through seasons of change and perspectives shift. I think all who purchase the video should recognize that a documentary is a snapshot in time. I cannot say what each person profiled would say about their situation now. Nor should I.

Throckmorton added his newly formed position on reorientation:

I now believe durable change in basic attractions is very infrequent. I also believe that some people, women most often, experience change in their attractions quite spontaneously without therapy. I believe therapy to change sexual orientation is not likely to be successful if the objective is complete change of attractions. Clients who desire assistance and support to live in accord with their religious views may find help with a willing therapist but change of orientation seems unlikely.[2]

This was a remarkable shift for the creator of this film, given that Throckmorton's video promoting reorientation had become so influential in churches. It appears that seeing his video participants leave the ex-gay lifestyle led Throckmorton to reconsider. It is also noteworthy that Throckmorton drew on ideas about women's sexual fluidity to develop his new view of the nature of sexual orientation.

Throckmorton's change of heart can be seen as part of a convergence that took shape during the middle years of the 2000s. On all sides of the debate, moderate groups began moving toward positions acknowledging that same-sex attractions cannot be therapeutically eliminated, but nonetheless, people might choose to live with a heterosexual identity and still be mentally healthy. Religious members of the ex-gay movement began asserting that same-sex attractions are unlikely to change through reorientation. Throckmorton, a professor at the evangelical Grove City College in Grove City, Pennsylvania, took a position similar to that of other religious scholars who maintained connections to the ex-gay movement but were not formally affiliated with NARTH. Further public admissions of lingering same-sex attractions by ex-gays included the Reverend Ted Haggard and were echoed by leaders of Exodus International. And the convergence toward this view did not happen among ex-gay leaders alone. "Ex-ex-gays," who had gone through reorientation but claimed that it failed, began telling their stories on the anti-reorientation side of the debate, yet called for more compassionate understanding of ex-gay experiences. Meanwhile, mainstream professionals, who worked with clients struggling with conflicts between their same-sex attractions and religious faith, began drawing on more complex notions of human sexuality. These professionals began to acknowledge that a mismatch between an adopted heterosexual identity and fixed same-sex sexual attractions might be mentally healthy in some circumstances where religious values are central.

The dynamic of convergence analyzed in this chapter, in which actors from different social worlds began forging a middle path between polarized views, should be understood as the beginning stages of the development of a new definition of "sexual orientation" within science regarding the reorientation issue.[3] A necessary step toward convergence was the development and in some cases exacerbation of frame disputes on both sides of the debate, enabling more moderate groups to break ranks with more hard-line activists.[4] These negotiations unfolded during these years following the Spitzer study, but prior to the American Psychological Association task force. Moving toward a new definition of sexual orientation as a fixed set of attractions, independent of identity, not only required moderate activists to come together but also required communication between scientific researchers and more moderate social movement communities.

Rather than happening solely in a top–down fashion, this convergence took place with the partial buy-in of multiple parties from mainstream psychology, religious ex-gay groups, and some gay rights advocates.[5] Within the ex-gay movement, the alliance across secular and religious groups began to unravel as increasing focus on the meaning of "change" in the debate exposed different understandings of successful reorientation outcomes across these intellectual venues. The increasing visibility of ex-ex-gays had a major impact on religious ministries, which were concerned about losing followers if they became disappointed in the level of their sexual orientation change. With increasing scientific scrutiny on the meaning of *change,* religious ministries leaders faced stronger incentives to come forward with the reality of lingering same-sex attractions. As the ex-gay movement began to fragment over whether changing physical attractions or achieving salvation was the ultimate goal, those religious groups and researchers that valued salvation over sexual orientation change became part of the moderate convergence and experienced more intellectual opportunities to wield influence within mainstream psychology. The increasing visibility of ex-ex-gays came about with the founding of an ex-gay survivor movement—part of a broader mobilization of anti-reorientation activism in the wake of the Spitzer study.

Anti-Reorientation Activists Mobilize

During the mid-2000s, gay rights activists began a more focused opposition to reorientation, responding not only to the mass deployment of the Spitzer study but also to other successes of the ex-gay movement that occurred in its wake. Such successes can be described as "critical events," occurrences that escalate the mobilization of opposing movements.[6] Anti-reorientation activists who took a more hard-line approach attempted to prove to the public that all forms of reorientation were fraudulent, especially expressed in the work of activist Wayne Besen and his new organization, Truth Wins Out. On the other hand, new ex-ex-gay organizers used a softer testimonial approach, explaining that reorientation did not work for them personally and had harmed them. Many ex-ex-gays maintained ties to the ex-gay movement, and they could not always dismiss ex-gay therapies as simply scams. They saw them instead as risky endeavors with high stakes.

The approaches of Truth Wins Out and ex-ex-gays certainly overlap. In 2000, Besen had put together the first large compilation of ex-ex-gay narratives, *Finally Free,* while he was working at the Human Rights Campaign. This document included the testimonies of ten men and four women, discussing how their therapy did not work and how it harmed them. Jeffry Ford, former director of the ex-gay ministry OutPost, explained how electric shocks during his therapy would catapult his arm into the air. Catherine Wulfensmith, a former client of the Love in Action reorientation ministry, described becoming immensely depressed, leading to her being kicked out of the organization, becoming suicidal, and ultimately homeless.[7]

Once ex-ex-gays began organizing themselves, however, differences in style took shape between those activists who had previously had religious ex-gay experiences and those who had not. Here a frame dispute between the ways of characterizing the ex-gay movement existed, but it was easily managed. Those taking a more hard-line approach maintained strict opposition to reorientation therapies and worked to discredit ex-gay practitioners as fraudulent. Meanwhile, ex-gay survivors tended to promote respect for the decisions of adults to enter treatment. Ex-ex-gays even met with ex-gay leaders to tell their own stories, and they maintained personal ties with friends in these ministries with whom they shared a common faith and many similar experiences. In the end, both approaches would make contributions to the new middle path perspective, as Truth Wins Out's advocacy included pressure for the physiological testing of ex-gays, and ex-ex-gays' advocacy included recognizing the validity of pursuing a heterosexual identity.

One critical event that focused mobilization of gay activists on the reorientation issue in this period was the "Zachary Stark affair." Ex-gay ministries had successfully extended their outreach to minors and their parents. The Refuge program, part of Love in Action, was a live-in ministry to which parents could bring their teenage sons or daughters to have them renounce their homosexuality. At the age of sixteen, Zachary Stark was taken there by his Christian parents after he told them he was gay. While at the camp, Stark wrote in a MySpace blog entry:

> Somewhat recently, as many of you know, I told my parents I was gay. . . . Well today, my mother, father, and I had a very long "talk" in my room where they let me know I am to apply for a fundamentalist christian program for gays. They tell me that there is something psychologically wrong with me, and they "raised me wrong." I'm a big screw up to them, who isn't on the path God wants me to be on. So I'm sitting here in tears, joining the rest of those kids who complain about their parents on blogs—and I can't help it.[8]

Along with this story, Stark posted the rules of the camp. Doors had to be left open at night, possessions were searched for gender inappropriate or gay lifestyle items, and participants were constantly monitored for same-sex sexual contact. News of Stark's situation traveled virally, and filmmaker Morgan Jon Fox, who knew Stark, organized a protest outside the camp. The protest group called itself the Queer Action Coalition and wrote press releases and alerted state authorities. In 2011 Fox published a documentary chronicling these events, *This Is What Love in Action Looks Like.*

The protests attracted media attention and legal action by the state of Tennessee. Protesters sought to affirm gay identity with slogans like "It's OK to be Gay." One protester held a handmade sign with a quote represented as an American Psychological Association Position Statement: "Research findings suggest that efforts to repair homosexuals are nothing more than social prejudices garbed in psychological accoutrements." Others read, "Jesus Is No Excuse for Hate" and "This Is Child Abuse." Protesters compared the Refuge program and its rules to the

1999 satirical film *But I'm a Cheerleader,* which lightheartedly depicted a reorientation camp coercing young people out of homosexuality through imposed gender norms and discipline.[9] While adults might choose ex-gay ministries, protesters were particularly incensed by the practice of forcing young people to change. Moreover, they expressed outrage over the way in which Love in Action lumped homosexuality with other problems, including sex addiction and drug abuse, as if homosexuality were a pathological addiction.[10]

The *New York Times* featured the story "Gay Teenager Stirs a Storm" on July 17, 2005. *Good Morning America* and CNN also ran stories on the ethics of forced reorientation for minors. In the midst of the controversy, John Evans, cofounder of Love in Action, who had become ex-ex-gay himself, wrote to the leader of the program, John Smid, dramatically explaining that he had changed his position: "In the past 30 years since leaving the 'ex-gay' ministry I have seen nothing but shattered lives, depression and even suicide among those connected with the 'ex-gay' movement."[11] In the midst of the media exposure, Tennessee officials ultimately investigated Refuge to determine whether it was administering therapy without a license.[12]

Responding to these events in mid-2006, the National Gay and Lesbian Task Force (NGLTF) published Jason Cianciotto and Sean Cahill's *Youth in the Crosshairs: The Third Wave of Ex-gay Activism,* a hard-hitting attempt to discredit ex-gay programs. The seventy-eight-page paper alerted readers to the coerced reorientation of youth, explaining that as part of a larger campaign against gay marriage, they were being used to demonstrate that homosexuality could be unchosen. The NGLTF report begins with the Stark story, followed by the case of another teen, D. J. Butler, who reportedly was driven to Love in Action facilities in handcuffs. In response to the Stark affair, Cahill attended a Focus on the Family "Love Won Out" conference in October 2005 and reported on the meetings. Cianciotto and Cahill emphasized how ex-gay experts targeted male youth through the concept of the "prehomosexual" boy, who is not adequately masculine.[13] In addition to alerting readers to the issue of the coercion of youth, *Youth in the Crosshairs* also argued that ex-gay leaders target parents with misinformation about the gay lifestyle leading to alcoholism, unhappiness, and domestic violence. The report also informed parents about harms experienced by ex-ex-gays.[14]

While the Stark incident had proved galvanizing, especially concerning the coercion of youth, a second critical event spurring gay activists into action centered on federal marriage policy. Exodus president Alan Chambers had been working with an organization called the Marriage

Amendment Project, a coalition seeking to "preserve marriage as it is intended." The Federal Marriage Amendment (also known as the "Marriage
Protection Amendment") was introduced in 2005, and the following
year, when a vote was near, the Bush White House invited Exodus leaders Chambers and Randy Thomas to a press conference to discuss the
proposed amendment.[15] Chambers was also invited to provide testimony in the Senate. In his testimony he reasoned that if gay marriage
had existed when he was homosexual, he never would have had the incentive to live his current heterosexual life.[16]

In response to the White House invitation and these public displays of
ex-gay testimony, Wayne Besen founded Truth Wins Out (TWO) in 2006
to home in on discrediting reorientation. Unlike the efforts of NGLTF,
which were part of a set of broader pro-LGBT strategies, Besen developed
this organization with a more focused target. The organization name reconfigures the name of Focus on the Family's ex-gay ministry Love Won
Out. Besen explained:

> I started [Truth Wins Out] after Alan Chambers was invited to the
> White House from Exodus stumping for the Marriage Amendment.
> But it was actually a very natural process to make because I was still
> working every single day on this issue whether I cared to or not. People
> were coming to me, whether it was reporters, or shrinks, or victims of
> this stuff, for advice, and it was just a natural extension of it. I thought
> I might as well make an organization out of it.[17]

Given Besen's prior work on this issue with the Human Rights Campaign
and his success with his analysis of the ex-gay movement in his 2003
book *Anything but Straight: Unmasking the Scandals and Lies of the
Ex-gay Myth*, Truth Wins Out was indeed a natural extension. Besen
sought to paint the ex-gay movement as fraudulent, exploiting unwit-
ting gays, and promoting lies in the policy arena. In 2013, TWO's website described itself as a group that "monitors anti-LGBT organizations,
documents their lies and exposes their leaders as charlatans," and it invites visitors to "help TWO uncover the next 'ex-gay' swindle."[18]

Truth Wins Out subsequently became an organizing hub for a network of anti-reorientation organizations, including *Box Turtle Bulletin*,
founded in 2004, as well as older groups Ex-Gay Watch and Soulforce.
TWO organized protests outside NARTH conventions and ex-gay ministry meetings.[19] At one colorful protest of a NARTH convention in
Orlando, Florida, activists adopted Disney themes, wearing duck cos-
tumes and using duck call whistles to paint reorientation therapists as
"quacks." Protesters also held signs declaring "NARTH is Goofy," and

one protester dressed as the Disney character. TWO demonstrated its political strength by facilitating a scandal in 2006 that cast NARTH as a hate group. The episode involved remarks made by experts on the NARTH website. Canadian psychiatrist Joseph Berger had "called for allowing schoolchildren to shame and ridicule classmates who don't act according to stereotypical gender roles." At the same time, New York psychologist Gerald Schoenewolf "asserted that slaves may have been better off in chains than in 'savage' Africa."[20] Besen described how the new TWO network was useful in facilitating the scandal:

> It's a very small community of people who talk about [challenging ex-gay programs], and I think we generally complement each other's work because we can't just all do it ourselves. There's not that many hours in a day. I think it's good that we quote each other's work. If one person comes up with something we all do our thing. A perfect example is the NARTH slavery issue. That first appeared in Ex-Gay Watch, but then I used my PR background to do a PR campaign. I took it to National Black Justice Coalition, got a letter from them, which I could then send to the Southern Poverty Law Center. I got a story placement, and so I have enough to take to the *LA Times.* There you go, NARTH's screwed, just like that.[21]

The scandal reinforced a public image of NARTH as bigoted. Following this publicity, NARTH president Joseph Nicolosi apologized for the postings, removed them from the website, and publicly stated that the organization did not support bullying or slavery.

Besen's group also took an active role in opposing misrepresentations of the scientific record. Starting in 2007, TWO asked scientists, "If your research has been deliberately misused to harm the gay, lesbian, bisexual and transgender community, please report these infractions to us. Only by shining a bright light on these lies, can we hold violators accountable and protect legitimate science from being deliberately skewed."[22] Among the researchers providing testimonies on TWO's new "Respect My Research" website were Judith Stacey and Carol Gilligan, who explained how their work had been misappropriated by right-wing organizations. Spitzer used the site as an opportunity to speak out against how Focus on the Family and other anti-gay groups had misused his research:

> It's understandable that Focus on the Family would be delighted with the results of my study because the study did indicate that there was evidence that some gays can change not only their sexual identity but [also] their sexual orientation. . . . What they failed to mention, and it's

Members of Truth Wins Out (TWO) protest a NARTH conference in Orlando, Florida, in 2006, using a Disney theme to portray reorientation therapists as "quacks." Besen on left. Courtesy of Wayne Besen, Truth Wins Out.

not, I guess, a big surprise, is that in the discussion, I noted that it was so hard for me to find two hundred subjects to participate in the study, that I have to conclude that although change is possible and does occur, it's probably quite rare, and of course they don't want to mention that.[23]

Spitzer went on to warn potential clients of reorientation treatments that their possibility of change in arousal and fantasy was quite small:

As far as the gay person who is thinking about change, the gay person wants to know not only can some people change, but how likely is it if I go into some kind of therapy or program. So my study, I think, does indicate that some gays can change, but it also suggests that it's probably pretty rare. So the gay who is thinking about entering some kind of a program to change should know that the likelihood of success is probably quite small. And of course, Focus on the Family doesn't want to say that.[24]

After so much work done by reorientation opponents to discredit Spitzer's study, it was ironic that Truth Wins Out was now presenting Spitzer promoting the idea that some gays can change their orientation. However, because the misinterpretations of his work had extended so far, just getting Spitzer to express his opinion on his own research was needed to correct these misuses.

Besen maintained a position that physiological testing was essential as part of any ex-gay research study. He had made this point in *Anything but Straight,* and in a personal interview, he reiterated:

> And I will say right now that any future study that does not include physical measures such as the penile plethysmograph . . . no-lie MRI, and you can throw in a third, whatever you want, polygraph, . . . or maybe microexpressions to see if they're lying. To not use physical measures in a test particularly when you have people who have a . . . conflict of interests, is to pull the wool over people's eyes. I mean it's not credible. You must, when talking about changing sexual orientation, you must, must, must have physical measures to back it up. If you don't have physical measures the paper you're writing is not worth the paper it's on unless you recycle it.[25]

Here, Besen echoed calls for the phallometric test like those of several psychologists in the wake of the Spitzer study, including Lee Beckstead. This idea of fixed sexual orientation, primarily rooted in concepts of male sexuality, was thus shared between hard line anti-reorientation activists and some gay affirmative psychologists.

In contrast to the aggressive fact-finding and fraud-exposing approach of Truth Wins Out, the "ex-gay survivor" movement formed in 2007 and consolidated a softer testimonial approach. The self-help and advocacy group "Beyond Ex-Gay" claims on its website:

> We believe that ex-gay experiences cause more harm than good. Certain people who currently identify as ex-gay say they are content as such. We don't seek to invalidate their experience. For us such a lifestyle was not possible or healthy.[26]

Key here is the assertion that these ex-ex-gays do not seek to invalidate the experiences of ex-gays. Rather, they strive to warn potential clients, families, and religious leaders about the dangers of reorientation by sharing their own personal testimonies. According to this argument, it does not matter if reorientation works for anyone because the dangers are so great that no one should even attempt to change his or her sexual orientation.

Christine Bakke and Peterson Toscano, cofounders of Beyond Ex-Gay, trace the origins of the organization to a one-actor play, *Doin' Time in the Homo No Mo' Halfway House: How I Survived the Ex-gay Movement.*

Promotional poster and DVD cover for Peterson Toscano's play *Doin' Time in the Homo No Mo' Halfway House* (2008). Performances of this play helped develop an ex-gay survivor network, leading to the cofounding of Beyond Ex-Gay by Toscano and Christine Bakke. Artwork by Tina Encarnacion.

Toscano launched this play in 2003 as a means to work through the anguish of his experiences. He had participated in the same Love in Action ministry in which Zachary Stark had been held against his will, but had gone there as a willing adult. The title of the play is the source of the term "ex-gay survivor," as Toscano wanted to indicate that he had been through a traumatic experience and had endured. His narrative highlighted his seventeen years and more than thirty thousand dollars spent on three different continents, unsuccessfully trying to eradicate his homosexuality. His efforts included participating in exorcisms, attempting to conform to traditional gender roles, and marrying a woman. Having left evangelical Christianity, he became a Quaker and worked through the relationship between his homosexuality and his faith.[27] In his play, Toscano took on various personas of people living in an ex-gay ministry, the "Homo No Mo' Halfway House," a phrase used by many clients of Love in Action. Although often serious and somber about the struggles of gay people in the time of AIDS, the play is a humorous tour through the absurd practices of ex-gay ministries: forbidding bananas in the men's dorm kitchen, limiting time spent in the restrooms to prevent masturbation, conducting exorcisms, and fostering gender conformity to eliminate same-sex desires.[28]

Others who had had similar encounters with ex-gay ministries approached Toscano after performances of the play and asked if there were any kind of group they could join. Nothing existed, so Toscano began developing a network of ex-ex-gays interested in sharing experiences.[29] In a 2007 interview in *Glamour* magazine, Christine Bakke credited the play with raising her awareness about her own failed ex-gay attempt, giving her the courage to come out as lesbian and eventually cofound Beyond Ex-Gay with Toscano.[30] Tosacano was invited to participate in the protests of Love in Action during the Zachary Stark incident, and appeared in and helped to produce Morgan Jon Fox's film *This Is What Love in Action Looks Like.*

According to Bakke, the *Glamour* magazine article launched their organization onto the national stage.[31] After the article was published, Bakke was invited as a guest on *Good Morning America,* and Toscano appeared on the *Montel Williams Show* and the *Tyra Banks Show.* Beyond Ex-Gay hosted the first ever national ex-gay survivor conference on the campus of the University of California at Irvine in the summer of 2007, working in conjunction with the UC Irvine LGBT Resource Center and Soulforce, the gay activist group led by former Jerry Falwell ghostwriter Mel White.

The Beyond Ex-Gay conference included self-help sessions for ex-gay survivors, a session for writing personal narratives to place in the media, and a session devoted to allies of ex-ex-gays. In one event called a "chalk talk," ex-gay survivors wrote about their experiences on a large piece of butcher paper. Some reminisced about harmful therapy experiences, while others wrote about the benefits.[32] Following the conference, survivors took framed collages they had created to the offices of the Thomas Aquinas Psychological Clinic in Encino, California. The collages incorporated poems, prayers, personal photos, and statements of harm and struggle in overcoming the effects of ex-gay programs. For example, Toscano's collage included the statement, "I ended up depressed, discouraged, and depleted. It left me contemplating suicide and distressed that I might lose the faith I fought for and cherished."[33] While this event achieved press coverage, Toscano hoped that giving NARTH members gifts that were difficult to destroy would be a more effective way of raising reorientation therapists' awareness about the harms of their work.[34] The event also coincided with an Exodus International conference that was being held at nearby Concordia University. Ex-ex-gays met with ex-gay leaders at their conference to share stories and build community. By targeting the opposing movement directly yet compassionately, ex-ex-gays attempted to use their own experiences to change hearts, rather than seeking to expose their opponents publicly as frauds.

The tactics of Beyond Ex-Gay primarily involve the use of personal testimony, much like the tactics of ex-gay ministries. Tanya Erzen has called such practices "testimonial politics," and describes them as "narratives of sin, redemption, and personal transformation."[35] Testimonial narratives of ex-gays and ex-ex-gays are also, however, about psychological harm and healing, and in many ways they are "illness narratives," modern-day stories told by people who suffer illness and pain and then experience healing. These accounts have pedagogical functions, evoking emotional responses and moral obligations toward those who suffer.[36] Ex-gay testimonies will often include stories of pain that is due to dissatisfaction inherent in the "homosexual lifestyle," the struggle for autonomy in a world that does not recognize that homosexuals can change, and ultimate healing through deliverance from homosexuality. Ex-ex-gay narratives match these structural elements but have different content: they tell of pain that is due to ineffective and barbaric therapies, the struggle for autonomy against an oppressive anti-gay culture, and healing that accompanies deliverance from a reorientation program.

Because this kind of narrative is so common in the ex-gay movement, the continued use of the testimonial genre by former ex-gays can be seen as a kind of "social movement spillover," a means by which groups that address different issues may end up sharing tactics, personal networks, and activism styles.[37] The associations of ex-gay survivors with people still in reorientation ministries effects the tactics they deploy. Unlike hard-line anti-reorientation activists, ex-gay survivors maintain meaningful ties with people whom they met in these ministries, and do not wish to undermine the legitimacy of ex-gay experiences or treat them as fraudulent. Ex-ex-gays have many shared experiences with ex-gays, having been through similar conflicts between religion and sexual orientation. And while ex-gays experience marginalization in the evangelical Christian community, ex-ex-gays also experience some difficulty integrating into the gay community.[38] In addition to taking testimonial tactics from the ex-gay movement, the close ties maintained by ex-ex-gays have enabled them to hold meetings with ex-gay leaders that hard-line anti-reorientation activists could not arrange. It should be noted that Beyond Ex-Gay is not representative of the tactics of all ex-ex-gays, but to date it has been the only national organization representing this group in the United States.[39]

As ex-ex-gay activism coalesced, their work increased the public visibility of harm narratives even as it promoted empathic understanding of ex-gays' decisions to enter reorientation therapy and religious ministries. As promoters of this kind of empathy, ex-ex-gays were part of a convergence toward a middle path approach. Anti-reorientation activists with stronger debunking strategies also contributed to the middle path insofar as they were advocates of the idea that sexual orientation cannot be changed. But for hard-line anti-reorientation activists, the idea that living with incongruity between a heterosexual identity and homosexual attractions would be further evidence for fraud, especially given the stakes in the policy arena where the existence of reorientation threatened the granting of gay rights.

Divisions Surface within the Ex-Gay Movement

When ex-gay leaders appeared on the national stage in the late 1990s, the meaning of "change" in reorientation advertisements was ambiguous. Yet, with increasing publicity of ex-ex-gay stories and skepticism about change, ex-gay ministries needed to keep people from leaving. Evangelical psychologist Mark Yarhouse developed a perspective to help this problem by acknowledging lingering same-sex attractions within a Christian framework. In the book *Sexual Identity: A Guide to Living in the Time between the Times,* Yarhouse and his coauthor, Lori Burkett, claimed that despite poor methodology in efficacy studies, reorientation research showed a 30 percent success rate at best, leaving most people with lingering same-sex attractions. Conservative Christians needed a way to manage their lives despite these attractions, and this book was offered as the solution. Yarhouse and Burkett argued that shifting the goal to sexual identity change rather than orientation change would ensure fewer disappointments. For Yarhouse and Burkett, sexual identity consisted of "(1) sense of gender as male or female, (2) sexual preference, for example, toward the same- or opposite-sex, and (3) behaviors or intentions in light of their sexual attraction."[40] They defined sexual orientation as "the *directionality* of a person's attractions toward the opposite sex, the same sex, or both" and claimed that "by writing a book to help people who struggle with their sexual identity, we are not primarily focusing on helping people change their sexual orientation, though sexual orientation or sexual preference is one of the three main things that make up sexual identity. So we do not ignore sexual orientation, but we are not focused exclusively on changing it either."[41]

In 2004 Yarhouse founded the Institute for the Study of Sexual Identity at the evangelical college Regent University, and developed what he called "Sexual Identity Therapy"—a technique for managing sexual identity in an evangelical Christian framework when same-sex attractions persist. This approach does not preclude the possibility of attraction change, but rather shifts the overall emphasis to identity. In 2006 Warren Throckmorton and Yarhouse further formalized this approach within a new set of evangelical therapeutic guidelines that included reorientation therapy as an option. Regarding the evidence for the efficacy of reorientation treatments, the authors based their position on the ambiguity surrounding the best way to measure sexual orientation. Throckmorton and Yarhouse stated:

> Prior to outlining the recommendations, let us define what they are not. They are not sexual reorientation therapy protocols in disguise. Although some investigators (e.g., Spitzer, 2003) have attempted to examine sexual orientation change, numerous criticisms have been leveled at client self-report as a means of assessing such change. Currently, no other means of sexual orientation assessment has found wide acceptance. A consensus about accurate assessment and measurement of sexual orientation would be required in order to empirically test therapies purporting to produce sexual orientation change. At present, such consensus does not exist.[42]

Furthermore, the authors called for client satisfaction and general mental health as the best outcome measures:

To varying degrees, some clients may come to believe change has occurred in their sexuality while some will believe little or no change
has occurred. These perceived changes can be examined but we do not
view such change as a determinant for the success or failure of sexual
identity therapy. Instead, client satisfaction and overall mental health
improvement are more efficiently assessed.[43]

Throckmorton and Yarhouse's guidelines proposed that a person may
live an identity that is incongruent with the person's sexual attractions as long as he or she is satisfied, especially if he or she belongs to
a religious community. However, the guidelines no longer asserted that
sexual attraction change is the definitive outcome of reorientation, as
Throckmorton had suggested two years earlier in his film.

By this time, Exodus International leaders were also adjusting their
views about lingering same-sex attractions, developing ideas about
change that were more identity centered. In 2006 Exodus provided an
elaborate statement of the meaning of "change" in the book *God's Grace
and the Homosexual Next Door*.[44] Addressed to the wider Christian
community, this book was largely intended to convince other Christians
that homosexuality is a "sin" like all other sins. Furthermore, it argued
that homosexuals are capable of redemption and are worthy of outreach,
but the book took the sympathetic view that same-sex attractions are not
chosen. As Tanya Erzen argues, ex-gays have been marginalized within
the larger Christian community, which often views them as incapable
of true change and often sees homosexuality as more severe than other
sins.[45] If homosexuality were a typical "sin," then admitting to lingering
same-sex attractions could be understood as another aspect of living in
a world fraught with all kinds of enticements, with homosexuality being
just one of them.

God's Grace and the Homosexual Next Door contained an essay titled
"Is Change Possible?" by Mike Goeke, Exodus vice president of operations. Goeke provided an identity-centered explanation, challenging the
view that successful change should be based on shifts in sexual attractions, but he stopped short of admitting lingering same-sex attractions
in this essay. First, Goeke encouraged trust in God rather than in human
ideas, since "God can work change *in whatever way He desires*" and "un-
realistic expectations easily breed and grow doubt." Acknowledging that
establishing strong heterosexual feelings is rare, he claimed that "true
change isn't so much behavior focused, attractions focused, or demon
focused, . . . true change is *heart* focused. It's a change of *identity* from
the inside out."[46] The change should be toward a Christian identity rather

than a heterosexual identity. Goeke took the position that "ex-gay" is a "false identity," because "identity change should not be based on former sin" but "on the fully righteous, fully holy identity bestowed on [one] via the Cross of Jesus Christ."[47] Once one has developed a Christ-centered heart and changed identity and behavior in line with God's will, shifts in attraction will usually emerge. However, the new desire is frequently for "connection and intimacy" and "longing for a healthy, intimate relationship with the opposite sex in marriage."[48]

While this definition of change left the issue of attractions rather vague, Exodus president Alan Chambers publicly admitted to the widespread existence of lingering same-sex attractions among reorientation ministry participants during a scandal involving the Reverend Ted Haggard. In November 2006, Haggard, president of the National Association of Evangelicals and director of the fourteen-thousand-member New Life Church in Colorado Springs, stepped down from his leadership after being accused of paying a male escort for sex over a three-year period and using crystal methamphetamine.[49] After a confessional letter acknowledging sexual immorality followed by a three-month silence, Haggard claimed that "Jesus [was] starting to put him back together" after three weeks of reorientation treatment. Tim Ralph from Haggard's church claimed that Haggard was now "completely heterosexual."[50] This claim was met with predictable skepticism, and even Chambers expressed doubt, stating, "The truth is it's not my story, and it's not the story of anyone I've ever met. . . . It doesn't sound like something that is really the case."[51] Chambers's comment was followed the next year with Haggard's acknowledgment of his continued struggles with homosexual desires. His willingness to be forthcoming about lingering same-sex attractions, acknowledging them as a potentially lifelong struggle, and Chambers's skepticism about complete change are exemplary of the convergence toward the middle path view. Disavowing the term *ex-gay*, Chambers stated in the *Los Angeles Times* the following year, "By no means would we ever say change can be sudden or complete."[52]

The Haggard scandal happened during a particularly difficult year for the ex-gay movement regarding its public image. Richard Cohen, president of PFOX, founder of the International Healing Foundation and author of *Coming Out Straight: Understanding and Healing Homosexuality*, appeared on CNN earlier that year demonstrating his therapeutic techniques. One of these included "touch therapy," in which Cohen held and cuddled his same-sex client to re-create a nonsexual father–son bond. Cohen also demonstrated "bioenergetics" on the program, repeatedly hitting a pillow with a tennis racket while shouting, "Mom, why did you do that to me?!" to release deeply felt memories.[53] Cohen had been permanently expelled from the American Counseling Association in 2002 for violations of the ethics code, including actions that "seek to meet [counselors'] personal needs at the expense of clients," violate "the trust and dependency of clients," and promote therapy in a deceptive way.[54] CNN's coverage was a blow to the movement's credibility, as NARTH and Exodus leaders had to distance themselves from these approaches, which became fodder for media satirists.

Identity as the primary marker of change was again emphasized at the Exodus International West Coast Regional Conference I attended in Fresno, California, in 2008. The event, held in a large church, was a three-day worship service that included gender-segregated breakout sessions. With around two hundred attendees, the conference was a jubilant celebration complete with a Christian rock band set up on the church stage with song lyrics projected onto a back wall. Attendees raised their hands in a Pentecostal style of charismatic worship, feeling the force of divine power and breaking into tears. Chambers emphasized identity change in his sermons, and some women, but mostly men, shared their testimonies of leaving the homosexual lifestyle. Books were sold in the lobby, including some secular reorientation books but mostly ones describing religious approaches. In addition to acknowledging lingering same-sex attractions, Exodus leaders Chambers and Thomas both drew attention to what they perceived was effeminacy in their own mannerisms and speech. Reiterating the reorientation concept that male homosexuality involves a fear of taking on a masculine role, Thomas explained that these feminine expressions were an "accent" left over from when he was gay.[55]

Perhaps the most consequential statement of lingering same-sex attractions within the ex-gay movement has been in a research study published by evangelical researchers Stanton Jones, of Wheaton College, and Mark Yarhouse in 2007. This is often considered the best study by members of the ex-gay movement, although the book was not peer-reviewed. Touted as making up for widely perceived shortcomings of the Spitzer study, this Exodus-funded study measured sexual orientation over a two-year period, with a sample of seventy-three religious respondents. The data, based on self-reports of identity, behavior, and attraction, showed significant changes in behavior and identity change, but shifts in attraction were relatively small. The authors used the Kinsey scale as a measure of attraction and reported an overall mean shift from a Kinsey 4 to a Kinsey 3 over the period.[56] They also claimed that no one reported harm, but several people left the study and no follow-up was done with those who left.[57] The authors claimed that one-third of their sample achieved reorientation "success," but over half of these were living in celibacy and continued to experience same-sex attractions.[58] Jones and Yarhouse argued against physiological testing on the basis of its methodological shortcomings, and added that evangelical Christian subjects and researchers should not be exposed to erotic imagery that violates their values.[59]

These shifts in interpretation of change within the religious wing of the movement can be attributed, in part, to the emergence of public ex-ex-gay narratives. As Yarhouse and Burkett argued, lowering expectations of physiological change might keep disappointed people from leaving ex-gay ministries. But calls for physiological testing may have also contributed to shifts in this rhetoric in the religious wing of the movement. While no physiological tests of reorientation therapy outcomes had been conducted since the 1970s, the reassertion of the need for such tests may have had a performative effect on self-reports of physiological attractions. In an analogous case of a technology that purportedly measures "truth" from the body, Ken Alder argues that the polygraph has been less of a lie detector and more an extractor of confessions—as long as people believe that a device can extract truth from the human body independent of the will to hide it, the polygraph works.[60] In the case of ex-gays, the phallometric test may have altered the claims of change within ex-gay activism and reorientation research to include acknowledgment of lingering same-sex attractions.

In a personal interview in 2008, when Exodus was still in full operation, Chambers offered a response to the idea of using physiological data to test outcomes:

> Are there ways to determine whether someone's attractions are in one place or another? Sure. Some people who have cancer undergo chemotherapy, and it cures them of cancer; whether it comes back or not, people can be cured of cancer. Psychology and therapy cannot cure people of sin. It's just not possible. Therefore, if someone hooks me up to some type of an electrode or does a scan of my brain while I am looking at homosexual pornography, they would likely see that it stimulated senses. From the age of eleven I spent so much time giving in to homosexual thoughts and urges that my brain, no doubt, would recognize that stimulus. I would imagine there are numerous stimuli that would do the same thing. In fact, heterosexual pornography would likely produce a reaction. I'm married and I am physically and sexually attracted to my wife. Heterosexuality is something that

has been strongly developed in my life. And while I have a wonder-fully satisfying outlet for that attraction to my wife, I have to be careful there too now that there has been a reorientation of sorts. . . . While I think such a study is an interesting way to determine attraction level, I am unsure [of] the purpose of it. I don't think there's any beneficial purpose in it. For me, it absolutely would not redefine who I am or have any bearing on me or the life that I have both chosen to lead and love leading. I don't need a test to tell me what I already know about the strength of my memory and the addictive patterns that I once was beholden to. Nothing invalidates the life that I lead today. Nothing can invalidate the identity change, the radical unbelievable identity change that's happened in me and so many others. It cannot invalidate the change in orientation that's happened in me. It just would simply point to the fact that for a significant period of time I had an unquestionable attraction to the same sex. It's not so earth-shatteringly surprising that I might still find the same sexual stimuli appealing today. I will never be as though I never was. Regardless of the stimuli, I believe that is true of all humans and the significant behavioral patterns they have left behind.[61]

It is noteworthy here that Chambers professed to some heterosexual attraction changes at this time yet admitted to lingering same-sex attractions. Nonetheless, the logic behind Christian conversion and the equation of homosexual desire with ubiquitous temptation to sin placed physiological tests of the body at the bottom of a hierarchy of evidence for sexual orientation in Chambers's worldview. In a world where God created human beings to be tempted by sin, physiological testing would just reveal the pervasiveness of temptation rather than a basis for identity.

While religious groups were exploring the emphasis on identity change, NARTH members continued to assert the possibility of full reorientation. At the NARTH conference I attended in Dallas in 2007, Joseph Nicolosi presented his theory of the "double-bind/double-loop" approach that he and his colleagues used with male reparative therapy clients.[62] While NARTH members employed a variety of theories and techniques, Nicolosi's has been particularly influential. As I noted in the introduction, this theory equated male homosexual desire with failed and inferior masculinity. Because Nicolosi believed same-sex attractions derived from feelings of gender inadequacy, any gender-shaming experience could lead a man to feel such attractions and potentially engage in "homosexual enactment." When a man experienced shame, his mind became divided against itself, and he became divided from others; this is the "double bind." In this state, a man experienced a lack of masculinity, and sought to draw masculinity from other men, eroticizing that which seems exotic to him. He was at the mercy of the "reparative drive." To get out of the "shame" state, a client had to process the source of the shame by grieving. His mind would then experience a "double loop," returning to an "assertion state" with no same-sex attractions, feeling connected to himself and to others.[63] Nicolosi argued that through addressing gender shame, the sexualization of unmet needs from same-sex peers would dissipate and natural heterosexual attractions would emerge.

At the Dallas conference, NARTH made the ethical case for inclusion within science and for the recruitment of reorientation clients by emphasizing values supported by mainstream professionals. These included client "autonomy" and "self-determination," both terms in the American Psychological Association Code of Ethics. Denying access to reorientation therapy was, NARTH argued, a violation of these principles. At a protest at the American Psychological Association in 2006, ex-gay clients held signs invoking these values, including, "You don't have to be gay," "Self-determination," and "Change is possible!"[64] At this time, NARTH members presented a petition and letter to APA president Gerald Koocher. The letter (written by Joseph Nicolosi) began:

> Today, I bring to the American Psychological Association a petition with 75 names on it—including my own. We all are APA member-psychologists who are professionally committed to the right to assist men and women who are transitioning out of their unwanted same-sex attractions. Most importantly, we are committed to protecting client autonomy and self-determination.
>
> As psychologists, all of us need to listen, and listen respectfully, to men and women who turn to us for understanding, support, and professional assistance in their effort to diminish their unwanted attractions and to develop their heterosexual potential.[65]

Nicolosi also implored Koocher to meet with the protesters, all of whom had rejected a gay identity:

> To simply tell them[,] "Abandon your hope for change; your biology is your destiny!" or "Keep working or getting rid of your internalized homophobia!" is not only uncompassionate, but scientifically unsupportable. We can no longer reduce the important issues of worldview differences and client self-determination to that glib phrase "homophobia."
>
> We need to be frank with ourselves as scientists: a gay lifestyle is not for everyone with same-sex attraction. "One size does not fit all."[66]

In a protest at the American Psychological Association convention in 2006, ex-gay activists call for the APA to recognize sexual reorientation therapies and the right to pursue sexual orientation change as self-determination. Photograph from Exodus International.

Professional mental health associations continued to reject NARTH as incapable of respecting the dignity of gays and lesbians. Yet, what "autonomy" and "self-determination" truly entailed for clients interested in reorientation remained contested, and these would be issues that a new American Psychological Association would have to take up in the years to come.

Contrary to the position statements of all professional mental health associations in the United States, NARTH claimed that it had evidence for reorientation change, but it was ignored because of political bias. In February 2007, the governing board of NARTH adopted the "Leona Tyler Principle," named after a former APA president who advocated a commitment to scientific data in psychological practice. Linda Nicolosi wrote this description for the NARTH website:

> In essence, the principle states that when psychologists are speaking as members of their profession, any advocacy in which they engage should be based on scientific data and demonstrable professional experience. Perhaps Dr. Tyler, then APA's president, was able to foresee the day

when organized psychology would be influenced by activism, and she wanted to ensure that psychology as a profession would not be eroded.

"Ironically," noted NARTH Scientific Advisory Chairman A. Dean Byrd, Ph.D., "since the enunciation of this principle, the national mental health associations seem to have been taken over by ideologues whose activist agendas show little concern for science or professional experience. In fact, this principle seems to have been repeatedly violated by APA itself."[67]

Thus, NARTH portrayed itself as committed to science in its advocacy, unlike the APA. In representing itself as scientifically objective, however, NARTH shifted attention away from the fact that its treatment of homosexuality as an unwanted condition was a value orientation.

In an interview, NARTH therapist David Pickup argued that mainstream psychology was problematically interwoven with-gay affirmative values. Value orientations, he stated, corrupt all psychological research:

Every good psychologist knows [psychology] is not a hard science, it's a soft science. In my opinion we need to talk about these kinds of issues both as scientifically as we can and anecdotally. We can't, until we can put a human being literally in the test tube and [have] hard science, figure things out in the classic scientific sense. Everyone knows that. Everyone—gay therapists, nongay therapists, whatever. But we must be as scientific as possible so that we can be as credible as possible. So that's one reason why there's so much debate on this scientific study or that scientific study. So naturally a gay-affirmative therapist is going to interpret scientific findings [and] scientific studies that we do as skewed or different, and we, of course, with our professional bias, may, like they (unless we're really careful), look at their evidence and see that their evidence is not credible. It is incumbent upon each individual to look at the evidence knowing this is a soft science.[68]

The logical conclusion would be that all value orientations should be included in science until the fateful day when the hard truth of human beings is finally revealed. In an effort to demonstrate his own scientific objectivity, Pickup added that NARTH was willing to consider any kind of evidence to show that complete change is possible. When asked about phallometric testing and brain scanning, he answered:

No one here is afraid of that. We would love it. In fact, moving towards that is exactly what NARTH is doing. I'm not saying that tomorrow we're going to institute exactly those programs, but we certainly would be open to it.

It was a key NARTH tactic to assert the contradictory position that value-neutral scientific objectivity required the inclusion of research practices that devalue homosexuality. This position stood in contrast to one articulated by evangelical researcher Stanton Jones, who argued that because science and values are inevitably interwoven, science can be rooted in evangelical Christian values that include the assertion that homosexuality is a "sin."[69]

Illustrating tensions between professional therapists and religious ministries, NARTH members also challenged the overall effectiveness of religion-based approaches, claiming that approaches such as prayer cannot solve core issues underlying same-sex attraction. Pickup argued:

> So in general, the Exodus community is dealing more with the spiritual aspects of the soul and so they're going more through techniques of behavioral things. Obviously they're going to be talking the majority of the time about homosexuality as sin, and against God's will and that kind of thing, and so they will seek healing from homosexuality through prayer. . . . Obviously in reparative therapy we don't do that. We believe we go to the underlying causes, and the other organizations don't really do that. What we deal with is the underlying nature of the thing, and then Christianity deals with the spiritual, in terms of the relationships with God and the removal of sin. . . . I do think, without realizing it, some very good-hearted Christians call transformation out of homosexuality just stopping of behavior.

Pickup made an additional claim about the origins of ex-ex-gays:

> I believe that spirituality really only addresses right and wrong and how one can be in a pure relationship with God, and that's wonderful as it is, if people want to do that, but neither can I call that a fundamental shift in personality, or fundamental shift in one's feelings, in my opinion. That's why a lot of guys are out there who call themselves ex-ex-gays because unfortunately they haven't had that deeply transformative experience that deals with the causes of homosexuality, so they still dealt with temptations, and wondered why God didn't heal them, and there was suffering, because they felt these feelings for other guys and they made a choice to be true to their emotional makeup and live a gay lifestyle.

Such claims illustrate the frame dispute between secular reorientation, rooted in the goal of full attraction change, and religious ministries, seeking salvation and Christian identity above all else.

At the 2007 NARTH conference, participants acted out many of the formal rituals of scientific meetings. The fifty or so attendees favored professional attire. In the program, presenters listed accreditation suffixes, such as "LCSW, BCD, ICADC, Psy.D.," in a display of scientific authority. But realizing they may be vulnerable to infiltration, during the first session, all attendees in the main hall were asked to stand and explain who they were and why they were there.[70] As at the Exodus conference, a book sale table contained movement literature, but with titles emphasizing secular approaches. Author Dawn Stefanowicz was also present to promote her story and her book *Out from Under,* in which she claimed harm from being raised by a gay father. Life coaching was emphasized at the conference as a newly burgeoning supplement to reorientation therapy. One life coach described himself as "more than a therapist and less than a friend," being on call for discussions whenever a client was experiencing significant danger of homosexual enactment.[71]

During one session titled "Homosexuality 101," NARTH president-elect Julie Harren-Hamilton described a new way of thinking about the "gay gene," shifting causal understandings of homosexuality away from bad parenting. While many theories of reorientation focus on overbearing mothers and distant fathers, the new focus of the ex-gay movement on recruiting minors meant that parents were primary consumers for their sons and daughters, and theories that blamed parents might be a difficult sell. Harren-Hamilton argued that the so-called gay gene does not cause homosexuality, but rather it really causes an oversensitive temperament. While parents might be perfectly fine in the ways they interact with their children, those children who inherit a gene for hypersensitive temperament may misinterpret good parenting in harmful ways, leading to homosexuality rooted in gender identity fears. However, Harren-Hamilton did not rule out environmental causes altogether, including parents, peers, and traumatic experiences, as each person's experiences are different. Such theorizing simultaneously rationalized away biological explanations for homosexuality while perhaps making reorientation more palatable to parents who might consider reorientation treatment for their son or daughter.

The keynote speaker at the conference, Stanton Jones, presented results of his longitudinal ex-gay study with Mark Yarhouse to great applause, and he was presented the Charles Socarides Award.[72] The lauding of Jones and Yarhouse's work at this conference, which provided immense evidence for lingering same-sex attractions among participants in Exodus International, suggested that NARTH shared some appreciation for the middle path approach. Signs of serious fragmentation between Exodus and NARTH were beginning to show, however. Alan Chambers, who was slated to speak at the event, opted not to attend, as did Throckmorton. While Nicolosi attended the Exodus International Regional Conference in Fresno, his stay was very short and he left immediately following his presentation.

"Discovering" Women's Sexual Fluidity

Although women have sought out sexual reorientation therapy since its inception, and have also been reorientation therapists, they have been largely invisible in the literature on reorientation, and on mainstream studies of the nature of sexual orientation. Writing in the *Counseling Psychologist* in 2004, psychologists studying the ex-gay movement noticed this:

> Generally speaking, women have been ignored in the literature on conversion therapies. The reasons for this are unclear, but this may have to do with a greater tolerance of same-sex attraction and behavior on the part of women among the religious and psychoanalytically oriented practitioners who have been the primary advocates of conversion treatments. Male privilege in patriarchal religions may actually be a double-edged sword in that because of that privilege, men (particularly White, economically privileged men) hold a central role in the church structure and may draw more attention when they do not conform; because of women's auxiliary status, their sexuality may be less visible and their deviation less salient.[73]

These authors pointed not only to the invisibility of women but also to the lack of research on racial minority groups. Whether the literature reflected the actual demographics of reorientation therapy clients was unknown, but organization meetings tended to be populated primarily with white men. These demographics were reflected in the ex-ex-gay movement as well.[74] But as new research on women's sexuality emerged, it introduced ideas about mismatches between attraction and identity that could be useful for developing more moderate approaches. Moreover, this research examined the role of emotion in sexuality in ways not previously emphasized. Research on women would provide additional resources for thinking beyond the polarized divide.

Within the ex-gay movement, Janelle Hallman has practiced therapy in Westminster, Colorado, specializing in sexual reorientation therapy for women. She published a series of articles on this topic in the *NARTH Bulletin*. Hallman summarized her approaches in *The Heart of Female Same-Sex Attraction* (2008):

Therapy is rarely, if ever, focused on the *direct* eradication of a woman's same-sex feelings or orientation. A woman's SSA [same-sex attraction] is not a neatly compartmentalized aspect within her life that can be easily isolated and simply extricated; it is rarely a behaviorally based phenomenon that can be objectively observed, quantified or controlled, although it certainly has behavioral components. Female SSA is an extremely complex multidimensional biological, cognitive, emotional, behavioral and relational *dynamic* that may or may not reach into a woman's core identity.[75]

Change process occurred differently for women because of the alleged innate difference between men's and women's sexuality:

Because female sexuality is more emotionally than physically based, sexual arousal and attraction patterns can and do change as a woman's emotional connections change. Core beliefs that often drive a woman's same-sex intimacies—such as the belief that only women are able to emotionally connect—can be challenged and often change. The content and frequency of a woman's sexual fantasies can change. Behavioral aspects of a woman's sexuality, especially if there is a compulsive component, commonly change.[76]

For men, unmet emotional needs from other men became sexualized due to a feeling of inferiority. But for women, excessive emotional connection between same-sex peers led to homosexuality. The idea that women's sexuality is more "emotionally based" than men's is widely shared among the ex-gay movement. The complex mismatches between feeling and identity that Hallman described included lingering same-sex attractions and conceptualized them as part of a multidimensional "dynamic" that may not be connected to identity. Thus, theories of sexual reorientation of women introduced ideas that could be useful for conceptualizing a middle path between the extremes of full sexual orientation change and gay-affirmative therapy.

Ex-ex-gay Christine Bakke, cofounder of Beyond Ex-Gay, described what gender differences in understandings of sexual orientation meant for women in her organization:

[Ex-gay programs] feel like women's relationships are emotionally dependent, unhealthy enmeshed relationships, and so basically we're counseled to not be close to other women, to rely on God as our source of everything, to not even have a close mentoring relationship with another woman in many ways. It is not hard and fast throughout the ex-gay movement, but for people who do work with women, you'll hear them talk a lot about emotional dependency issues and enmeshment.[77]

As a result, women who were ex-gay survivors had to contend with a specific kind of harm, namely, learning to view other women again as trustworthy friends:

So what happens . . . because of that is . . . a lot of people feel that they've blocked the ability to maintain good friendships. So for me it took a long time, years, to start to repair that and I'm just feeling that in the last couple of years I'm back to where I probably was before the ex-gay movement, where I'm able to be close to somebody and depend on somebody else. I've had to learn a lot about interdependence.[78]

In the ex-gay movement, the idea that women's sexuality was more emotionally based was accompanied by the idea that women's sexuality is more "fluid" than men's.

This idea of gender differences in sexual fluidity has been shared across many social worlds, including within mainstream pro-gay psychology. Lisa Diamond, a psychologist at the University of Utah, has written extensively on women's sexuality. Her book *Sexual Fluidity,* also published in 2008, is a thirteen-year longitudinal study of a sample of eighty-nine women with same-sex attractions. Diamond defines fluidity as follows:

Sexual fluidity, quite simply, means situation-dependent flexibility in women's sexual responsiveness. This flexibility makes it possible for some women to experience desires for either men or women under certain circumstances, regardless of their overall sexual orientation. In other words, though women—like men—appear to be born with distinct sexual orientations, these orientations do not provide the last word on their sexual attractions and experiences. Instead, women of all orientations may experience variation in their erotic and affectional feelings as they encounter different situations, relationships, and life stages.[79]

Sexual fluidity may involve a sexual response to a particular person in whom a woman has become emotionally invested, or it may involve an exploratory phase. Diamond distinguished between the "spontaneous" fluidity experienced by her clients and the "effortful" fluidity that one might try to experience when going through reorientation therapy. Like Hallman, Diamond's ideas proved useful for thinking about mismatches between identity and attraction, making her work a key intellectual resource for theorizing the middle path. It is noteworthy that Diamond's model, like the dominant understanding of male sexuality in psychology, still involved fixed sexual orientations from birth for women, but a layer of fluidity existed atop this orientation.

Because it acknowledged fluidity, Diamond's work was predictably taken up to support the possibility of change in reorientation programs. Some reorientation proponents at the NARTH conference pointed to the fact that her work demonstrated the possibility of sexual fluidity, without attending to the distinction between spontaneous and effortful fluidity. In her book, Hallman stated:

> Many contemporary studies support the notion that female sexuality in general is fluid or flexible rather than rigid or fixed and that it is structured differently from male sexuality. While the concept of sexual *fluidity*—the *spontaneous* evolution or transformation of one's sexual attractions, behaviors or identity—is not identical to the concept of *changeability*, which involves *intentional* effort directed toward altering or changing one's sexual attractions or behaviors, it does support the notion that *sexual feelings and behaviors are not absolutely immutable or unchangeable.* It does *not* however directly translate into proof that *any* woman with SSA can easily change or alter her same-sex attractions or orientation.[80]

Hallman was more careful than many within NARTH when citing Diamond's work. Yet these appropriations led Diamond to speak out against the misuse of her research on the Truth Wins Out "Respect my Research" website. Although Diamond acknowledged in her video that research on sexual fluidity is "open to distortion," she addressed NARTH's claims that her research supported reparative therapy: "This is a willful misuse and distortion of my research. Not an academic disagreement, not a slight shading of the truth. It is a willful distortion, and it's illegitimate, and it's irresponsible, and you know that, and you should stop."[81]

The emphasis on women's sexuality during this period helped consolidate a set of gendered understandings of sexuality across social worlds, namely, that women's sexuality is more fluid and emotional, whereas men's is physical. The religious ex-gay movement tended to blur this distinction, since even men's conversion might lead to nothing more than a set of emotional attractions, from which physiology may follow. In my interview with Diamond, she reiterated that after presenting her work, male ex-gays have come up to her and said that they personally resonate with her model of sexual fluidity and wonder if it could be applied to men, especially the idea that fluidity might be person centered through emotional connection.[82] Nonetheless, Diamond's work provided alternative understandings beyond the polarized positions, contributing conceptual material to a convergence of ideas at an intermediary position.

Gay-Affirmative Professionals Clear a Middle Path

In the face of widespread publicity of ex-gay research and testimony, some mainstream professionals working with clients experiencing acute conflicts between religious values and same-sex attractions began exploring ways to partially accommodate ex-gay perspectives. In a 2004 special issue of the prominent journal *Counseling Psychologist,* psychologists explored alternative therapeutic approaches for this population. John Gonsiorek, who had done so much to help establish gay-affirmative therapy in psychology, was one of the commentators and perhaps the most cautious voice in the issue. He summarized the development of a middle path:

> These integrative solutions offer no decisive resolution but rather a process of persevering in the attempt to craft a solution by valuing both sexuality and spirituality, addressing psychological conflict and distortion when they appear to be interfering, and trying to find a middle path where no component of the individual is violated or disparaged.[83]

The issue included three empirical studies and four commentaries, followed by a collective response by researchers. As the issue departed from strict gay-affirmative therapy ideals, the researchers indicated that the peer-review process was difficult, and reviewers had expressed concerns about pro-reorientation bias.[84] These authors explained, however, that they were devoted to opposing conversion therapies and were dedicated to pushing the American Psychological Association to follow the lead of other professional associations and declare full opposition to reorientation.[85] This determination notwithstanding, they earnestly intended to begin clearing a middle path, given the struggles of clients caught between religious values and sexual feelings.

Central to the special issue was the empirical research of A. Lee Beckstead and his dissertation adviser Susan Morrow. Rather than trying to eliminate their own perspective from the work, they disclosed their assumptions as a commitment to a "horizons of understanding" model of research. Beckstead disclosed his history as a participant in the Mormon reorientation ministry Evergreen International, spending six years attempting to become heterosexual, coming out as gay, and working with clients experiencing conflict over their sexual orientation. Beckstead's ex-ex-gay status provided him with an "insider affiliation," which "gave him access to investigate areas that others might have over-looked." Morrow also declared her perspective as a lesbian feminist.[86] In a later interview, Beckstead discussed his work with an organization in Salt Lake City called Healing the Great Divide, in which Mormon and non-Mormon therapists met to try to work through polarization on con-troversial issues; this involvement, he felt, demonstrated his capacity for compromise. He added that his view that reorientation therapy might have a range of negative and positive effects allowed him to communi-cate across different perspectives.[87]

Beckstead and Morrow's paper on the experiences of Mormons who had sought reorientation change contributed to the scant research in-vestigating the features of those seeking reorientation therapies. This study included interviews, focus groups, and personal journals from four women and thirty-eight men of Mormon faith, including people who sup-ported or opposed the ex-gay movement. The paper broadly described a developmental process common to all members of their sample, whether the therapy worked or failed. Highlights from their model included first experiencing an environment with various anti-gay factors, including shaming by family and peers, stereotypes of the "gay lifestyle," and anti-gay religious ideologies, which led to a feeling of being different. These feelings typically led to maladaptive coping mechanisms until people in conflict hit rock bottom and found their way into reorientation therapy. Beckstead and Morrow identified aspects of reorientation programs that were positive for respondents, even for those who became opposed to the movement. These included connecting with others and coming out of the shroud of secrecy, having a feeling of relief and hope when heterosexual-ity was a perceived outcome, and general increases in self-esteem and social functioning. However, opponents of therapy in the sample also reported harms that included suicidal thoughts and attempts, as well as confusion when family patterns were blamed for homosexual feelings.

As Beckstead had done in the chapter he published in the *Sexual Conversion Therapy* volume edited by Shidlo, Schroeder, and Drescher, Beckstead and Morrow claimed that no one from the entire sample ex-perienced significant heterosexual arousal, although many experienced emotional feelings for their spouses. John, a proponent of reorientation, stated:

> My feelings for her are not sexual, they are emotional and every once in a while there is a twinge that I can see that I am allowing that part of the sexual relationship to develop. But I'm not stressing about it. . . . I mean you can train anybody to do anything. You can train for instance

any animal to be sexual or not sexual. . . . I don't feel unsexually attracted to her. In other words, there are times when she has done to
me what a man has done. She's gotten close, kissed my neck, kissed my
ears, and I've felt that arousal.[88]

As discussed in chapter 2, such findings led the researchers to claim
that they found no evidence for the efficacy of reorientation treatments.
Because Beckstead upheld a notion of sexual orientation that incorporated male physiology, descriptions of emotional attraction like the pre-
ceding would not be significant evidence in his worldview for therapeutic
efficacy. After putting forth a model of identity development through and
following therapy, the authors acknowledge the limitations of their own
self-report data, but defended themselves as being primarily interested
in research subjects' understandings of their own experiences. Beckstead
and Morrow argued that although heterosexual arousal was not achieved
by proponents, "we must accept that participants' self-identifications and
constructed perspectives are valid for them because they fit for them."[89]

Doug Haldeman also contributed a piece to the middle path special
issue with three case studies from his practice that did not fit easily into
gay-affirmative "out gay" or reorientation "ex-gay" models. Haldeman, an
openly gay psychologist, frequently worked in his private practice with
clients recovering from reorientation. His first case, Phil, was an African
American man with same-sex attractions who believed that he did not fit
into the gay world because of his race, and who felt a strong need to live
a celibate life to remain connected to his extended family and religious
community. The second, Michael, was a Caucasian man from a rural fundamentalist background who gave up reorientation after several years
in ex-gay ministries and needed to resolve several problems. Religious
integration, for example, was crucial for Michael's identity development,
and he needed to correct misconceptions about gay relationships to determine how he would proceed. Finally, John was a married Caucasian
man experiencing homosexual attractions, but he did not wish to leave
his heterosexual family. His role as a parent was important to him, and
although his marital sex life was functional, his wife expressed anxiety
over his homoerotic attractions. In these cases, Haldeman described
treatment as "client centered," encouraging therapists not to demean
prior choices or experiences. In the third case, Haldeman even cited the
"sexual identity therapy" work of Mark Yarhouse, as John needed to acknowledge the reality of his same-sex attractions before he could manage his behaviors and identity. The approach also included working with

the client to decide what identity to pursue, while acknowledging that same-sex erotic feelings are not likely to change.[90]

Among the commentaries in the special issue, psychologist Roger Worthington, who would also later serve on the APA Task Force on Appropriate Therapeutic Responses to Sexual Orientation, articulated what would become an influential statement for reconceptualizing sexual orientation. Citing earlier research studies on ex-gays, Worthington noted that proponents of reorientation are often ambiguous about the meaning of change and that researchers fail to define their terms consistently:

> The term *sexual orientation* should refer to a person's sexuality-related predispositions (especially attraction and arousal) toward and away from persons with specific gender characteristics (whether those predispositions are genetically, biologically, environmentally, socially determined or constructed). In contrast, Worthington, Savoy, Dillon, and Vernaglia (2002) defined *sexual orientation identity* as a more precise term regarding one's acceptance and recognition of sexual orientation.[91]

Using the mismatches in Beckstead and Morrow's study as support for this distinction, Worthington described "sexual identity development" as a negotiated process of self-definition that includes the acceptance of sexual orientation identity. Given this fractured ontology, Worthington then claims:

> It is difficult, if not impossible, to disentangle sexual orientations from sexual orientation identities when the method of assessment is self-reported data (Diamond, 2003; Worthington & Navarro, 2003).[92]

Because of this entanglement, self-reports of sexual orientation can only be understood as expressions of sexual orientation identity rather than as transparent windows into true attractions. Worthington then noted, "Even some proponents of sexual reorientation treatments have recently acknowledged that their target of change is sexual identity and sexual orientations are relatively immutable (M. Yarhouse, personal communication, December 2, 2002)."[93] This quotation, with its citation of Yarhouse, reveals one way in which communication across the divide of gay-affirmative and conservative evangelical professionals contributed to this convergence of ideas.

Even with the assertion of fixed sexual orientations, taking a middle path was met with reservations from some in the mainstream mental health community. John Gonsiorek, who was known for his work developing gay-affirmative therapies (as discussed in chapter 2), supported the middle path but argued strongly that this move should not be an invitation to support sexual reorientation therapies, which he viewed as an attempt by conservative Christians to control science through "theocracy in scientistic drag."[94] As evidence that internalized homonegativity was the primary motivator, Gonsiorek pointed to Tozer and Hayes's report in the special issue on a quantitative survey of clients' motivations to enter reorientation treatment.[95]

The *Counseling Psychologist* special issue marked an important moment in consolidating new understandings about therapy and those caught between sexual feelings and religious ideals, but it did not yet have the kind of force in setting the boundaries of science of the position statements from professional associations. While these articles pushed beyond the statements of other associations such as the American Psychiatric Association and National Association of Social Workers by incorporating ideas from the ex-gay movement, more work would be required to modify scientific orthodoxy, in terms of both officially articulating this compromise and solidifying the American Psychological Association's stance on reorientation treatments. The pledge by researchers in the issue to oppose sexual reorientation reflected arguments to set limits to the "big tent" philosophy of the American Psychological Association, calling for firmer boundaries to be drawn in the intellectual opportunity structure that would exclude NARTH if this compromise was going to work.

As these psychologists were forging the middle path, it is noteworthy that gay-affirmative psychiatrists, by contrast, were at work painting reorientation therapy organizations as hate groups, using tactics more aligned with Truth Wins Out. The documentary film *Abomination: Homosexuality and the Ex-Gay Movement,* created for the general public by the Association of Gay and Lesbian Psychiatrists, used ex-ex-gay testimonies to reinforce the links among ex-gay ministries, reorientation therapists, and hate groups. In the opening montage, a preacher can be heard admonishing, "Be not deceived, neither fornicators nor adulterers nor idolaters nor effeminate . . ." while angry protesters march against gay rights. Someone yells "Go to Hell, fag!" while protesters from the Westboro Baptist Church of Topeka, Kansas, hold signs showing "Matt in Hell" (a reference to hate crime murder victim Matthew Shepard). The documentary uses other emotion-evoking devices such as sinister music as background to ex-ex-gays' descriptions of their therapies, and sad music to accompany harm narratives.[96] *Abomination* also illustrates how reorientation opponents within psychiatry tended to take a stronger debunking position, unlike their counterparts in psychology. While psychiatry has played an important role in developing the science of sexual orientation, it has largely ceded jurisdiction over talk therapy to the discipline of psychology as a result of the psychopharmacological revolution. It is within the American Psychological Association that this contest over reorientation treatments would unfold more formally in the years to come.

Convergence but Not Consensus

This chapter has explained how convergence toward new definitions of "sexual orientation" and "sexual orientation identity" began with the partial buy-in from parties across multiple social worlds. These events formed the intellectual backdrop for the American Psychological Association task force that would convene in 2007. Between the extreme poles of promoting gay-affirmative therapy and complete sexual reorientation, gay-affirmative professionals, ex-gay ministry leaders, and ex-ex-gays converged toward more "integrative solutions." While moderates cleared a middle path in the field of therapeutics, it should be noted that this was a process of convergence rather than the development of a clear consensus. Thus, there were many middle paths being proposed between the "out gay" and "ex-gay" extremes.

The negotiation of a middle path was made possible not only by social movement fragmentation, but also through the opening of opportunities in the intellectual opportunity structure for some ex-gays. Gonsiorek attributes the interest in integrative solutions to the increasing appreciation for multiculturalism in psychology, yet the experiences of clinicians paying close attention to the needs of their clients also played a role. It should be noted, however, that while intellectual opportunities were opening for religious ex-gays that admitted to lingering same-sex attractions, in many ways, this strategy of the mainstream psychologists helped to fragment the ex-gay movement further by drawing closer attention to the meaning of "change." However, these new ideas were not yet part of official APA policy. The APA position statement of 1997 left open the question of evidence for the efficacy of reorientation treatments. Further negotiations of the boundaries of science would first require the formation of a task force, which would be highly contested by NARTH members; this is the story told in chapter 4.

four

REORIENTATION'S LAST STAND
Showdown at the American Psychological Association

Just six years after leaders of Exodus International participated in the promotion of George W. Bush's Marriage Protection Amendment at the White House, a series of high-profile events marked a dramatic decline in the ex-gay movement's public power in the United States. First, in May 2012, Robert Spitzer issued a public apology to the gay community for having conducted his reorientation study. The apology, reported on the cover of the *New York Times* and published in the *Archives of Sexual Behavior,* undermined much of the public credibility of the study. One month later, Alan Chambers, president of Exodus International, also announced in the *New York Times* that he no longer believed in the merits of reorientation therapies, and even said that practicing gays could achieve Christian salvation. The following year, Chambers announced that Exodus International was closing its doors. In a dramatic and tearful meeting with ex-gay survivors, Chambers read an apology for the harms caused by Exodus International and expressed hope for reconciliation. Since then, bans on conversion therapy for minors have become law in two states.

To understand this decline, it is important to consider the role of a key report issued in 2009 by the American Psychological Association. With immense press coverage, the APA was unequivocal in its opposition to reorientation programs, stating in a new position statement that "there is insufficient evidence to support the use of psychological interventions to change sexual orientation," and "although sound data on the safety of SOCE [sexual orientation change efforts] are extremely limited, some individuals reported being harmed by SOCE. Distress and depression were exacerbated. Belief in the hope of sexual orientation change followed by the failure of the treatment was identified as a significant cause of distress and negative self-image."[1] Utilizing much of the logic established in the 2004 special issue of *Counseling Psychologist,* the APA report was written by the six-member Task Force on Appropriate Therapeutic Responses to Sexual Orientation, some of whom contributed to that issue discussed in chapter 3. The new report was a devastating blow to the scientific credibility of self-reported evidence of reorientation change, while at the same time it boosted the credibility of ex-ex-gay reports of harm. Yet, building on the middle path compromises that had been established in the years before, the APA offered an official compromise: as long as clients were aware that their sexual orientation would not change, and as long as they and their therapists did not hold anti-gay stereotypes, clients might choose whatever sexual identity was most suitable. The new model, intended to affirm both sexual orientation and religious diversity, was called "sexual orientation identity exploration."

The Spitzer apology and the Exodus International closure must be understood, then, as aftermath of this major change in the credibility hierarchy of evidence. The Spitzer study, the Jones and Yarhouse study, and Exodus International's positions were all based on self-reported testimony. With these self-reports undermined, the credibility of these positions could not stand. However, undermining self-reports as evidence of efficacy of change alone could not catalyze these shifts. Harm testimony of ex-ex-gays was also important, and an additional product of the APA task force report was to elevate these self-reports of harm to the status of scientific evidence.

As discussed in the introduction, a key element of the intellectual opportunity structure that can block social movements from influencing science is the boundaries of credibility set for persons and for kinds of evidence. Such boundaries do not occur spontaneously, but must be established and enforced through what Thomas Gieryn calls "boundary work." When describing this process, Gieryn draws on a set of metaphors for mapmaking. He claims that in publicly debated science, various actors will "map" the cultural landscape to distinguish science from other ways of knowing. Such cultural representations include "compelling arguments for why science is uniquely best as a provider of trustworthy knowledge, and compelling narrations for why my science (but not theirs) is bona fide."[2] In addition to establishing the boundaries of science, this work provides maps for the public to differentiate the "genuine scientists" from the "false prophets." Who draws the prevailing maps of science? Gieryn uses the term "second-order" boundary work to describe the struggles to designate which "cartographers" are deemed credible.[3]

The story of the 2009 APA task force report includes boundary work at multiple levels. In struggles over determining who would map the boundaries of science, the National Association for Research and Therapy of Homosexuality clashed with the APA when none of its nominees were selected as task force members. In response, NARTH produced a "countermap" of science supporting its view that reorientation was efficacious and safe. Within the scientific community this was a weak challenge from the margins, but in the world outside, NARTH's expertise has had a significant impact. To maintain the credibility of the APA report as scientific and not merely the product of "gay activism," the task force would have to establish that its work was grounded in valid scientific principles.

In this chapter, I argue that the task force report, which both deflects and partially incorporates the ex-gay movement's ideas, came into being largely because of that movement's successes. The popularization of dissent and the ensuing concerns raised by gay rights activists required a response from mainstream psychology.[4] Subsequently, the boundary work of the APA and the task force set the cultural boundaries of science through a series of strategic intellectual moves that, in effect, elevated the physiological testing method of phallometry above self-report in the credibility hierarchy of evidence, and also raised reports of harm to a scientific status never seen before. By redefining sexual orientation primarily in terms of male physiology, and determining "the straight line" on a basis of physiological evidence, the APA effectively reinforced a world of fixed sexual orientations ready made for use in mainstream gay rights arguments in the United States. These events represent reorientation's last stand in trying to garner scientific credibility the U.S. field of therapeutics, as the boundary work of the APA was catastrophic for the movement.

The Decision to Form a Task Force

Unlike other professional associations, the American Psychological Association remained equivocal in 2007 about whether there was evidence for the efficacy and safety of reorientation treatments. While the 1997 APA position statement raised ethical concerns about conversion therapies, it claimed the ethics, efficacy, and potential harm of these therapies were "under extensive debate" in science and the media.[5] This left the organization without clear positions on efficacy or harm, and it remained open to claims on either side. Clinton Anderson, director of the Office of Lesbian, Gay, Bisexual and Transgender Concerns, recalled:

> It was an issue that needed to be [addressed], because our [1997] reso-
> lution does not deal with the issue of efficacy or harm from an empiri-
> cal perspective at all. It's purely grounded in ethics.[6]

This meant an intellectual opportunity was open for reorientation groups
to make claims publicly while the APA had no clear position.

The Office of LGBT Concerns that Anderson runs is part of the APA's
Public Interest Directorate in Washington, D.C. The directorate consists
of a set of offices whose stated mission is to apply "the science and practice of psychology to the fundamental problems of human welfare and
social justice [and] through education, training and public policy . . . promote equitable and just treatment of all segments of society."[7] Other offices of the Public Interest Directorate address areas such as aging, ethnic
minority affairs, and violence prevention. The Office of LGBT Concerns
works "to advance the creation, communication and application of psychological knowledge on gender identity and sexual orientation to benefit society and improve lesbian, gay, bisexual and transgender people's
lives."[8] It is built into the very purpose of this office to oppose practices
that deem homosexuality to be a disorder, and is another institutional
barrier to the medicalization of homosexuality.

In Alan Irwin's terms, the APA's Public Interest Directorate and Office
of LGBT Concerns foster "citizen science," a vision in which scientists and
citizen groups engage in open dialogue.[9] In terms of intellectual opportunity, this institutional arrangement provides gay activists with an avenue
to influence business at the APA. With a commitment to honoring gender
and sexual diversity and combating discrimination and stigma, the Office
of LGBT Concerns facilitates dialogue among groups concerned about
these matters and the field of psychology. In addition, the office provides
an institutionalized location from which the APA can take public policy
positions on various issues affecting LGBT people. Citizen science in this
case, however, is geared toward attending to concerns on the pro-LGBT
side. The Public Interest Directorate does not have an office designed to
facilitate dialogue with people expressing religious or ex-gay concerns,
but Division 36 of the APA, whose members are interested in the psychology of religion, does provide a forum for scholars interested in the
intersection of theology and psychology. Division 36 does not have the
kind of institutional structure for facilitating relationships between science and the public that the Public Interest Directorate does. As such,
the structure of the APA directorate facilitates intellectual opportunities for direct public engagement with pro-gay groups, but direct public
engagement with ex-gay groups is less formally institutionalized.

According to Clinton Anderson, three major factors contributed to the decision to request a task force to reconsider the 1997 statement:

> The first was that there had been some empirical publications on the issue since we did our report, and some of them got a good bit of media attention. Secondly, [while] we were probably the first professional association to adopt a position, . . . NASW and the American Psychiatric Association and others have as well, and [we wondered] where are we in relation to them? And the third [factor] was that community organizations, particularly PFLAG [Parents and Friends of Lesbians and Gays] and the NGLTF [National Gay and Lesbian Task Force], continued to articulate a high level of concern about the issue, about particularly . . . their belief that the reparative therapy rhetoric was having an impact on young people and on the social climate and context for young people.[10]

As an exemplary case of citizen science, the office facilitated dialogue between activists and psychology over the rising influence of reorientation. One of the activists who approached Anderson about APA revisiting the issue was Ron Schlittler, then president of PFLAG. Schlittler described his motives:

> I was becoming more and more concerned that these folks [reorientation proponents] were becoming more sophisticated and more forceful in how they were presenting this whole reparative therapy thing, and I just expressed my concern. I said, "Clinton, this is really alarming what they're doing, and it is time for the APA to take a look at what you've put out so far, and is there any updating or refreshing that's called for based on the way that the discussion is unfolding? Are there things being claimed that there's no science to back up, or vice versa? What's real and what's not?" Because as advocates and activists, what we need is accurate quality information so that we can make our case in the court of public opinion as well as school districts, or wherever it may be.[11]

Schlittler viewed psychological science as an important resource to be used in public places where claims by the association have influence. When talking with Anderson, Schlittler and Jason Cianciotto of the National Lesbian and Gay Task Force expressed alarm over the advancing ex-gay movement and claimed that LGBT members of the public, especially youth, needed the APA's support in the form of a statement.[12] In this case of opposing social movement dynamics, the success of the ex-gay movement required gay rights groups to consort with the APA, but in this case, the opportunity for gay rights groups to influence action was quite open.

From the point of view of Anderson's committee in the Office of LGBT Concerns, the publicity for reorientation therapies and reorientation studies was not emanating from the ex-gay movement alone:

> The NARTH publicity machine is very much connected, [but] NARTH alone would not have . . . the capacity to generate [the publicity necessary to inspire a Task Force]. . . . It's their linkage to Focus on the Family and other organizations that do have a lot of ability to communicate to their audiences. So there continued to be this idea in certain media that research had proven that conversion therapies worked, and we weren't sure how good the research was.[13]

Because the APA Public Interest Directorate's mission included educating the public about the status of science in psychology, the widespread circulation of efficacy claims, combined with requests from gay activists, was a challenge significant enough to require APA to solidify its position on the matter. Here, the public promotion of fringe science "fed back" into the work of mainstream scientists, requiring them to clarify the content of scientific facts.

In the same interview, after describing the empirical work that was out there, including the Shidlo and Schroeder study, Beckstead's dissertation, and the Jones and Yarhouse study, Anderson said, "We're not talking about a vast body of research." It is noteworthy that Anderson did not mention the Spitzer study, despite its massive publicity, when asked about this research. Minimizing the body of relevant literature is a boundary work strategy for those who claim there is no evidence for the efficacy of reorientation.[14] Likewise, when I explained my research for this book to psychiatrist and APA task force member Jack Drescher, he expressed the view that my study could fit on one page, given the dearth of scientific literature on the topic.[15]

NARTH Advances Nominees

When the APA sent out a call for psychologists to apply for a position on the task force, NARTH offered four candidates: two from the reorientation world, and two evangelical psychologists. The NARTH website presented the qualifications for each of the four, emphasizing professional credentials and areas of expertise. "Stanton Louis Jones, PhD is Provost and Dean of the Graduate School and Professor of Psychology at Wheaton

College, Wheaton, Illinois. He is co-author of *Homosexuality: The Use of Scientific Research in the Church's Moral Debate.*" "Mark A. Yarhouse, PhD is Professor of Psychology, Doctoral Program in Clinical Psychology at Regent University in Virginia Beach, Virginia. Dr. Yarhouse is co-author of *Homosexuality: The Use of Scientific Research in the Church's Moral Debate* and has published many peer-reviewed articles on homosexuality and treatment for SSA [same-sex attraction]." "A. Dean Byrd, Ph.D., MBA, MPH heads the Thrasher Research Fund and is affiliated with the University of Utah School of Medicine, Department of Family and Preventive Medicine, Department of Psychiatry. Dr. Byrd is considered one of the foremost experts on same-sex attraction and reparative/reorientation therapy. Dr. Byrd has published numerous articles on SSA and change, as well as gender and parenting issues." Finally, "Joseph Nicolosi, PhD has been involved in researching sexual orientation and treating individuals with unwanted SSA for more than 25 years. He is a California-licensed psychologist, founder of NARTH and author of *Reparative Therapy of Male Homosexuality, Healing Homosexuality: Case Stories of Reparative Therapy* and *A Parent's Guide to Preventing Homosexuality.* Dr. Nicolosi is a pioneer of reparative therapy and is one of the world's foremost experts on the successful treatment of same-sex attractions."[16]

Despite these listed credentials, the group's nominations were unlikely to be considered from the onset. Although Nicolosi and Byrd were both APA members, being leaders of a group founded on the idea that homosexuality is a disorder undermined their credibility. Anderson stated:

> NARTH, since its beginning, has been an organization that we (the American Psychological Association as a whole, not just my office) have deliberately worked to avoid any association with. When they had their inaugural meeting, we participated in a press conference in opposition to them. . . . They've approached us, there's a status within our convention called non-affiliated groups, so groups can ask to meet in conjunction with us, even though they're not affiliated with APA. We have refused them that status. They have asked to advertise their meetings and their conferences in . . . the APA *Monitor,* and we've chosen to not allow them to do that.[17]

Even though NARTH may have avoided explicitly stating that homosexuality is a disorder in recent years, Anderson claimed that

> their founding principle on homosexuality was that it was a developmental disorder, and we have decided that we cannot allow ourselves

to be perceived in any way in association with an organization that takes that position. And so that's what we have [done], and we've been very clear in our letters to them. . . . What they say is that now their membership includes people who no longer believe that homosexuality is a developmental disorder. . . . Their rhetoric now is that they're not about trying to stigmatize gay people. If people want to be gay, that's fine. They are now about providing services to an underserved population, which is that population of people who have same-sex attraction but do not want to be gay, and so it doesn't take very long interacting with those people before their pejorative attitudes and sentiments and actions are quickly revealed.[18]

Because of perceived anti-gay views, those forming the task force believed that NARTH members would not be able to comply with the APA Code of Ethics, which requires honoring various forms of diversity, including sexual orientation. Task force chair Judith Glassgold stated:

One thing that is foundational is that APA's policies are affirmative of sexual orientation diversity. Anybody who sat on that committee had to be [affirmative], that's its policy, that's where we are coming from. This was not a committee to debate different things. This was a committee that was charged with coming up with affirmative perspectives, and affirmative solutions, and affirmative recommendations on therapy. That helped define who the members were. That was part of the charge.

[How does APA define affirmative, what does it mean to be affirmative?]

That homosexuality is not a mental illness, or a disability, and is equivalent to heterosexuality, in all those ways.[19]

Thus, linking the NARTH organization and its associates with the pathologization of homosexuality was an important strategic component of exclusion.

Stanton Jones and Mark Yarhouse were not members of NARTH, however. The fact that NARTH nominated them likely did not help their chances, though. Rather than being anti-gay, task force members believed their nomination was based on "faulty" scholarship. Member Lee Beckstead explained:

Our advocacy was grounded in scholarship. And that's, I think, the criticism: that anybody else who wanted to be part of the club, that their scholarship wasn't [adequate], or their advocacy wasn't based on scholarship. Like the Jones and Yarhouse [study], there are problems with it. We had actually quite a lengthy critique of the study.[20]

Similarly, Glassgold explained that Jones and Yarhouse's research was considered "gray literature," having never been published in a scientific journal, and that the members of the task force felt it was methodologically flawed:

> [Jones's] book with Yarhouse is pretty poor. . . . The research is awful. . . . I think it's . . . their methodology—they don't know how to do statistics, they don't know how to do sampling. . . . So if . . . you don't use appropriate statistical analysis to analyze your data, you kind of ruin your credibility. And when you make some errors in how you define sexual orientation. . . . So I'd say that there were some serious flaws in their work that we ended up not going into . . . You do have to meet some basic standards.[21]

In addition to problems in the quality of research, Glassgold considered Jones to have an "ideological bent" and accused him of having an "anti-scientific streak in some of his earlier work."[22] Moreover, she said:

> I think the danger of Yarhouse and Throckmorton is that they're leaning towards relativism. [They believe] that all ideas are equivalent and equal and that's not true. . . . Larry Summers, the former president of Harvard who now is involved in the Obama administration, says that in a free society all ideas should be heard, but not all ideas should be adopted because they are not all equal. . . . And that's what I think they refuse to see. I think that's what Stanton Jones . . . and NARTH refuse to see is that though they have ideas, [it] doesn't mean their ideas are equivalent. They have to really validate their ideas and so far they haven't.[23]

Thus, as a rationale for exclusionary boundary work in the selection process, the NARTH candidates were rejected on the basis of values out of step with the task force charge, in addition to concerns about the quality of their research.

At the end of the vetting process, APA president Sharon Stephens Brehm appointed six people, selected on the basis of their qualifications, expertise, and ability to work according to the APA Code of Ethics and other policies. The result was a task force with four "clinicians" and two "methodologists." The clinicians were Judith Glassgold (chair), Lee Beckstead, Beverly Greene, and psychiatrist Jack Drescher, and the methodologists were Roger Worthington and Robin Lin Miller. Only Robin Lin Miller had not been involved with the reorientation issue before; as editor of the *American Journal of Evaluation,* she was brought in as the neutral research specialist to review the science.

Those who were selected for the task force brought some form of scientific expertise that aligned with the concerns and tasks raised in the charge, including expertise in diversity, as well as familiarity with the issue of sexual reorientation. They also demonstrated an ability to be affirmative in the ways required by the charge. And they all had different roles. For example, Lee Beckstead noted:

> I think my role was constantly making sure what they were saying was accounting for the people that I knew either personally or professionally or I knew from this other perspective, so I wanted to make sure that they weren't just going to reinforce this gay affirmative stance, but we needed to find some framework that allowed conservative religious individuals to be part of the tent, to be part of the treatment plan. So I would constantly make sure [to say:] we can't just discard this, we can't just discard this. We have to keep including these viewpoints. I think that was what my role was.[24]

To a large degree, Beckstead, as an ex-ex-gay himself, was a partially sympathetic professional for the ex-gay movement, insofar as he did not outright condemn reorientation programs as fraudulent. Coming from Salt Lake City himself, he knew the power of the Mormon faith up close, and knew how much it could mean to a person's self-identity.

Psychiatrist Jack Drescher brought another set of concerns to the task force, especially regarding the implications of the issue for the larger political context. Drescher, a psychoanalytically trained psychiatrist working in New York City at the William Alanson White Psychoanalytic Institute, was author of *Psychoanalytic Therapy and the Gay Man.* That book, published in 1998 when the American Psychoanalytic Association was rethinking its position on reorientation treatments, not only reconceptualized psychoanalytic theory and practice in ways that could be beneficial for gay men but also addressed the historic conflict between gay and lesbian rights and psychoanalysis more broadly. He has also written numerous essays and articles critical of reorientation.[25] Some APA members wondered why a psychiatrist would be participating in this committee, but Drescher's work as an advocate for psychotherapy within psychiatry, and his publications, were used to defend his appointment. Drescher described his expertise regarding the larger political context:

> I probably was the most senior member of the task force. I had been actively involved in the culture war aspect of this issue as a public spokesperson. So my role as it evolved was sort of to bring a kind of awareness of what we were doing within a larger social context. They

already understood it was important to do this, but . . . I brought a kind of historical perspective to . . . understand this is a clinical issue that has been subsumed for political purposes. And you can't just talk about the clinical issues without having some understanding that there are political agendas being pursued.[26]

Drescher understood that the concerns the task force was dealing with did not end at the clinical setting but were part of larger political battles. He described the terms of the war as follows:

We're all in the middle of a culture war. I'm just a spokesperson for a certain viewpoint. Homosexuality is not an illness. Homosexuality can be normal. Gay people should have the same rights and privileges as other people, and shouldn't be discriminated against. Those are controversial issues.[27]

Thus, the positions of Beckstead and Drescher represented an important tension from which the report emerged: Beckstead was focused on reconciliation while Drescher was a voice of caution considering the political ramifications of compromising too far.

Judith Glassgold, the chair of the committee, had developed affirmative therapeutic approaches for lesbian clients. As chair of Division 44, which focuses on LGBT issues, she worked to reconcile differences between that division and the Division of Psychoanalysis, as the latter had not completely eradicated psychoanalytic approaches that pathologized homosexuality. Glassgold's experience in leadership and in developing compromises enabled her to play an intermediary role:

Jack Drescher works more with gay men who are struggling, [but] their struggles with their sexual orientation may be more with personality issues and internalized homophobia. Lee works in Utah and with exclusively religious clients, so that was his point of view. . . . Just a few years before I was appointed to the task force, I worked with Orthodox Jews who were struggling with these issues. I had an article in press at that time on that issue. So I was kind of the middle person, I think, between Lee and Jack. And I had credibility as a gay activist, where Lee may be viewed with suspicion by gay activists. . . . Jack's a brilliant guy when it comes to understanding dynamics and process, and Lee has the experience of watching people struggle. . . . I think it was a great synergy.[28]

In this intermediary role, Glassgold was able to work with Beckstead on exploring literatures that dealt with the psychology of religion while still keeping a focus on the larger political ramifications of the report.

According to Glassgold, Beverly Greene, a clinician in private practice and member of faculty in the Department of Psychology at St. John's University in Queens, New York, seemed to fit into the task force "more on the side of Jack [Drescher]." Greene's areas of specialization center on understanding ways people contend with intersecting identities and using this knowledge in the context of the therapeutic encounter. As part of her research, Greene has examined psychodynamic theories for racist and homophobic content. In addition, she has written about diversity within gay and lesbian communities, as well as therapy with sexual minority clients of color.[29] Clearly Greene's role on the committee involved challenging oppressive ideas within reorientation therapies. She also brought a perspective on other forms of marginalization.

One of the two people Glassgold described as "methodologists" on the panel was Roger Worthington, at the time a member of the Department of Educational, School, and Counseling Psychology at the University of Missouri, where he was also the chief diversity officer. Worthington has written on the sexual orientation therapy debate and has developed theories of sexual identity development. His research has emphasized diversity across "race, class, gender, sexuality, and religion," and investigates "multicultural counseling competencies."[30] In addition, Worthington has written on the topic of sexual identity within psychological research.[31] Along with advising on methodology, he made a contribution to theorizing "sexual orientation identity" as an entity distinct from "sexual orientation," as described in chapter 3.

When asked about the evaluation of the literature in the APA task force report, Drescher, Beckstead, and Glassgold all referred to Robin Lin Miller as the one who did the primary work of evaluating the sexual reorientation therapy studies. Miller is a faculty member in the Ecological-Community Psychology program at Michigan State University. Her work has involved HIV/AIDS prevention and evaluating community service organizations, including the Gay Men's Health Crisis in New York.[32] She was editor of the *American Journal of Evaluation* from 2005 to 2009, and she has served on the editorial board of several other journals.

When these six task force members were selected, NARTH strongly dissented, claiming that reorientation proponents who applied for the position had been willfully excluded and only "gay activists" were chosen. Nicolosi stated: "The gay-affirmative make up of this task force offers a compelling reason for ex-gay organizations across the U.S. to protest at the annual APA Convention this August in San Francisco."[33] On the NARTH website, each task force member was described with a short counterbiography. Drescher is a "well known gay-activist psychiatrist, serves on the *Journal of Gay and Lesbian Psychotherapy* and is one of the foremost opponents of reorientation therapy"; Beckstead counsels LGBT people from traditional religious backgrounds and "although he believes reorientation can sometimes be helpful, he has expressed strong skepticism"; Greene was "founding co-editor of the APA Division 44 series, *Psychological Perspectives on Lesbian, Gay, and Bisexual Issues*"; Miller "worked with Gay Men's Health Crisis in New York City and has written for gay publications"; finally, Worthington won the "'2001 Catalyst Award' from the LGBT Resource Center, University of Missouri, Columbia, for 'Speaking up and often regarding LGBT issues' and co-authored a piece titled 'Becoming an LGBT-Affirmative Career Advisor.'"[34]

Speaking to the media, Nicolosi framed the candidates as activists uncommitted to "intellectual diversity." In a press release titled "American Psychological Association Appoints Political Activists to New Committee," Nicolosi blasted the selections:

> This new APA task force was created to monitor "reorientation therapies"—therapy for people who want to decrease their homosexual attractions and develop their heterosexual potential. *But the APA has sent the foxes to guard the henhouse.* Reorientation therapy is for people who don't want to be gay—and it is now being monitored by gay activists who believe there is no such thing as a formerly gay person![35]

Nicolosi also complained about a lack of "diversity" on the committee:

> My impression, looking over this list, is amusement—and then anger. First, the amusement: the APA never stops talking about its passion for "diversity." Where is the worldview diversity on this list?
>
> Next, the anger. We offered a strong list of candidates. All were rejected.
>
> Judging from these members' backgrounds, I do not believe this task force will be fair in its analysis of appropriate therapies. By rejecting any real reorientation therapist for the task force and stacking it with so many gay-affirmative opponents of sexual reorientation, the committee has already pre-determined what it will find.
>
> I predict that this task force will recommend ruling that reparative therapy is unethical and harmful to individuals and should be banned by the APA.
>
> Such a conclusion will inevitably violate patient autonomy and self-determination, and will silence intellectual diversity.
>
> We will fight this effort with all of our resources.[36]

NARTH had aligned itself with Nicholas Cummings, former president of the APA and a strong critic of the organization. In his writing and advocacy, Cummings has criticized the structure of the APA, which allegedly promotes "political correctness" run amok. Contributors to the book *Destructive Trends in Mental Health: The Well-Intentioned Path to Harm* (2005), coedited by Rogers Wright and Cummings, expressed various concerns about how the APA had been hijacked by leftist political ideologies. In an essay titled "Psychology's Surrender to Political Correctness," Cummings and William O'Donohue voiced dissent:

> The field of psychology is severely fractionated into almost sixty formal divisions and fifty state associations, which compete for seats on the organization's governing body, the Council of Representatives. These divisions range from the subfields within psychology, such as experimental psychology, clinical psychology, counseling psychology, military psychology, and psychopharmacology, to the more ideological groups, such as the Society for Consumer Psychology, humanistic psychology, Society for the Psychology of Women, Society for the Psychological Study of Lesbian, Gay and Bisexual Issues, ethnic minority issues, peace psychology, and international psychology. Originally intended as units organized around special interests and concerns within psychology, they have become power bases and self-interest groups that fiercely vie against one another for the limited number of seats on the Council of Representatives in order to influence the course and commitments of the APA.[37]

Because one must be a member of a division or a state psychological association to vote for the Council of Representatives, Cummings and O'Donohue, as did NARTH leaders, argued that this structure has contributed to the development of "politically correct" positions that are not based on science. From the point of view of NARTH, it is no surprise the APA would choose task force members who reflect a pro-gay ideology because the Council of Representatives is so biased. Alternately, we might analyze the institutional arrangement of the APA as part of an intellectual opportunity structure fostering commitment to particular values, including being affirmative of sexual orientation diversity.

At the APA Convention in Boston, in 2008, NARTH leaders seized an opportunity to influence leaders of the association at the APA President's Town Hall Meeting. Several NARTH members attended the meeting, including Nicolosi, and expressed their frustration at feeling excluded from the organization as a whole. One by one, advocates made statements to the president and ended with the query, "Is there a place for me in the APA?" David Pickup, a formerly gay man training under Nicolosi at the Thomas Aquinas Psychological Clinic, also voiced his concern. At the meeting, he stood and said, "I am an ex-homosexually oriented man who provides reorientation change therapy for men who want this. I my-self have greatly benefited from this type of therapy, so I guess I would ask the same question that the other gentlemen asked, that is, is there a place for me in the APA?"[38]

The meeting became tense, and at the peak of this tension, Arthur Goldberg, director of JONAH (Jews Offering New Alternatives to Homo-sexuality) and member of NARTH, asked APA president Alan Kazdin why qualified reorientation proponents, including Nicolosi, were rejected from the task force. Kazdin deferred to Clinton Anderson, standing in the back of the room with a microphone. Anderson answered, "No one was rejected. Rather people were selected, and I think the board of direc-tors would agree that the set of people who were selected were highly qualified people."[39] At this, Nicolosi cut him off and shouted, "That's the kind of double-talk that turns people off from the APA right there!"[40] In contrast to the kind of citizen science relationship experienced by gay activists, these professional ex-gay activists were generally told that their proposed candidates for the task force were underqualified.

Once the board of directors approved the formation of a task force, the charge given by the APA leadership included three primary tasks. While the first was to review and update the 1997 resolution, the second was to generate a new report discussing "appropriate application of af-firmative therapeutic interventions" for people who desire sexual reorien-tation. A third task was to discuss "the presence of adolescent inpatient facilities that offer coercive treatment designed to change sexual orienta-tion or the behavioral expression of sexual orientation." The charge also called for discussion of "stereotyped gender normative behavior to miti-gate behaviors that are perceived to be indicators that a child will de-velop a homosexual orientation in adolescence and adulthood."[41] After completing its discussion of appropriate therapies, the task force was di-rected to inform the APA how it should respond to groups that promote reorientation and how it should support "affirmative" therapeutic inter-ventions. The charge did not call for any review of the scientific literature on efficacy or harm, however.

NARTH Creates a Version of the Literature

In another dramatic moment at that 2008 President's Town Hall Meet-ing, Nicolosi challenged President Kazdin to take NARTH's work more seriously. He held up a thick, bound manuscript, stood, and stated, "I'm asking you if you would consider reading this document. As a representative of many dissatisfied APA members, would you look at this document, read this document, and respond to us?" Kazdin agreed, "I will read the document."[42] Then, in a seeming breach of informal rules about space during professional conference meetings, Nicolosi boldly walked up to the panel and laid the bound volume on the table before the president. The document painted a landscape of the boundaries of science from NARTH's point of view, presenting research studies over a span of 125 years. It was a "countermap" of the boundaries of science, anticipating anti-reorientation conclusions of the forthcoming APA task force report. By citing hundreds of efficacy studies, NARTH attempted to set up an army of cited authors to be challenged in order for NARTH's position to be undermined. Bruno Latour has described this tactic as "enrolling allies" in order to fortify one's position.[43]

Not long after the town hall meeting at the APA in 2008, NARTH published its literature review. The review used a language of scientific neutrality and was published as volume 1 of the organization's newly created publication, the *Journal of Human Sexuality*. The cover of the bound journal bore the title "What Research Shows: NARTH's Response to the APA Claims on Homosexuality." The report is divided into three sections, and because it enrolls hundreds of studies, it is difficult to review each here. The following summary analyzes many of the report's primary claims.

Section I of "What Research Shows" began with a discussion of how "change" in sexual orientation had been measured in the literature:

> Clinicians and researchers typically defined "successful" treatment as an intentional shift in sexual desire from homosexuality to heterosexuality, either through self-reporting or through measurements such as penile plethysmography or the 7-point Kinsey scale (Kinsey, Pomeroy, & Martin, 1948), the multi-item Klein Sexual Orientation Grid (KSOG) (Klein, 1978), or other measures (Sell, 1997). Since there is no consensus of what constitutes a successful outcome, various authors maintain their own autonomy in how to define an outcome as successful.[44]

Deferring to researchers' varying definitions of successful outcomes allowed NARTH to include studies with myriad outcome measures. These included therapist assessment (typical in psychoanalysis) and client self-report (as in the Spitzer study). The many studies presented predominantly relied on these two forms of reporting.

Survey	Number (and percentage) reporting exclusive opposite-sex attraction shift fully successful
Nicolosi, Byrd, and Potts (NARTH consumer satisfaction study, 2000), 318 participants	114 (36%)
Shidlo and Schroeder (initially titled "Documenting the Damage," 2002), 202 participants	8 (4%)
Spitzer (2003), 183 participants	96 (52%)
Total of 703 participants	28 (31%)

Data from NARTH's "Compilation and Overall Average Outcome of Recent Surveys of Reorientation Therapy Consumers," from "What Research Shows," published as James Phelan et al., "What Research Shows," *Journal of Human Sexuality* 1, no. 1 (2009): 15.

The historical review of efficacy research was presented in the format of an inventory. Each short paragraph began with a name followed by a publication year and a description of the research. For example, the entry for work by Edmund Bergler read:

> Bergler (1956) reported that in his 30 years of practice, he had successfully used psychoanalysis to help approximately 100 homosexuals change their orientation, and that a real shift toward *genuine heterosexuality* had occurred. Using psychoanalysis, Bergler and his associates reported a 33 percent cure rate—that is, following treatment these patients were able to function as heterosexuals, where before treatment they were exclusively homosexual. Eidelberg (1956) reported that two out of five cases were still successfully functioning as heterosexuals three years after treatment.[45]

At the 2007 NARTH convention in Dallas, James Phelan, lead author of "What Research Shows," read through the entire list from this report in a roll call fashion. As he read, conference attendees nodded their heads in affirmation (and at times shouted "Yeah!") with the announcement of each new citation.[46] Phelan and coauthors folded together the rates of "fully successful" change from three "recent consumer surveys"—the NARTH study (by Nicolosi, Byrd, and Potts, 2000), the "Documenting the Damage" study (by Shidlo and Schroeder, 2002), and the Spitzer study (2003)—to compile an overall "success rate" for these studies.[47] By folding results from the Shidlo and Schroeder study into these other studies, Phelan and coauthors transformed it from a study that has generally been used to challenge reorientation therapies into one that helps to demonstrate a near one-third "success rate."

NARTH's version of the landscape of scientific studies demonstrating efficacy was vast, covering a broad array of therapeutic interventions and outcome measurements. The document stated: "Section I of this treatise is a brief overview of 125 years of clinical and scientific reports documenting that volitional change from homosexuality toward heterosexuality is possible." The studies reviewed varied considerably in their methodological rigor. Demonstrating perhaps the loosest case, Nicholas Cummings made a ballpark estimate of reorientation among thousands of clients in his practice, many of whom he did not treat himself. Of sixteen thousand clients, "approximately 2,400 clients successfully reoriented their sexuality to heterosexuality." While these data might be substandard, the inclusion of Cummings on the list allowed the entry of a former APA president as a credibility marker.[48] On the other hand, Jones and Yarhouse's research was treated as the most methodologically rigorous by contemporary standards. The review points out that their self-report study utilized standard outcome measures and was particularly credible because of the "self-criticisms, alternative explanations, and painstaking efforts to neither exaggerate nor minimize the meaning of their findings."[49]

For all of the allies enrolled in section I, this part of the report conspicuously downplayed the contributions of aversion therapists to the literature. This is ironic given that behavior therapists once were major contenders in sexual reorientation research and practice. A few major aversion therapy studies were listed, but they were separated from the rest of the literature review, where the authors stated, "Although aversion therapists were successful in treating a variety of unwanted homosexual thoughts, feelings, and behaviors, . . . aversion therapies are no longer used for sexual reorientation because of ethical considerations."[50] Instead, the review lists studies using other therapeutic techniques, including pre-Freudian hypnosis (studies spanning 1882–98), psychoanalysis (1920–94), behavior and cognitive therapy (1935–86), group therapies (1954–80), sex therapy (1972–84), pharmacological interventions (1940–2009), religiously mediated reorientation (1992–2007), and spontaneous reorientation (1948–2007).

Section II of the document responded to the charge that reorientation therapies are harmful. In contrast to its vast landscape of studies on how reorientation is effective, NARTH claimed that the number of studies that claimed to show harm was small. They again upheld Jones and Yarhouse's study as the "most methodologically rigorous study to date" and stated that "no evidence was found to support the claim that attempts to change sexual orientation caused harm to participants." (The document did not mention that some people dropped out of the study and that the authors had not followed up.) The landscape included only one claim of harm from one study, the paper by Shidlo and Schroeder. Although these researchers reported that clients who felt their reorientation therapy failed experienced high rates of suicide attempts and ideation, the NARTH document countered this by citing another paper, presented by Whitehead at a NARTH convention, claiming that the suicide rates were "likely lower" after reorientation therapy, because homosexuality itself causes suicide. Next the coauthors countered the claim that reorientation therapies contribute to homophobia in society. They presented evidence that despite the existence of ex-gay therapies, there had been growing belief in the idea that homosexuals are "born that way," along with evidence of improved attitudes toward gays and lesbians in society.[51] The authors rounded out the discussion of harm by claiming that even greater harms may befall clients if they are not offered reorientation therapies.

Finally, NARTH challenged a claim attributed to the American Psychological Association that "there is no greater pathology in the homosexual population than in the general population." This claim is an altered version of a statement in an APA brochure: "Research has found no inherent association between any of these [lesbian, gay, or bisexual] sexual orientations and psychopathology." The term *inherent* was operative in the APA statement but missing from the NARTH claim. This transformation of the relationship between homosexuality and pathology allowed the coauthors to use any correlations in research on health disparities for sexual minorities (usually attributed to oppression) as evidence to refute their version of the "APA claim." Instead they suggested (without explicitly claiming) that homosexuality is innately pathological, and that consequently, reorientation treatments are a needed remedy. The health disparity literature reviewed included mental health disparities (youth suicide, depression, substance abuse, eating disorders, relationship difficulties) and medical health disparities (HIV/AIDS, sexually transmitted diseases). Homosexuals were especially prone to other forms of deviance in their review, including promiscuity, sexual addiction, rape, child molestation, and violence.[52] Finally, the authors pointed out that some homosexuals participate in risky and unconventional sex practices, including those involving scat, "water sports" (sexual activity involving urine), fisting, and bestiality. Anilingus among homosexual men is a risk factor for hepatitis A, the authors claimed, and "the act of analingus [*sic*] is not found among heterosexuals (McWhirter & Mattison, 1984)."[53]

Once this report was delivered to Kazdin, it was passed along to the still-deliberating task force. Beckstead explained how and why the group generally rejected NARTH's analysis:

> They didn't even mention my study. . . . That is, like, well, wait a minute, how can this be based on science if they don't include science? And they included Karten's dissertation; it's an interesting dissertation, but it's not that many people, and it's not a rigorous qualitative study. Again they're using data without questioning the data to support their agenda. . . . I love what Robin [Lin Miller] did. . . . Robin is the editor of the top statistical journal. She looked at those studies and saw how flawed they were. You can't do meta-analysis of flawed data. It's like looking at a broken thermometer and asking what's the temperature outside?[54]

Beckstead likened NARTH's refusal to acknowledge the claims of harm made by clients to the dynamics of sexual abuse perpetrators and victims. In these dynamics, the abuser may say to a victim, "Now you're getting angry with me, there's no need to get angry, what's the anger all about?" In Beckstead's characterization, such an approach effectively dismisses any harm and "[puts] it back on the person with the less power" to deal with. In a sexual abuse scenario, Beckstead claimed that this rationalization enables a perpetrator to continue his or her actions while it disempowers a victim. Regarding NARTH, he stated, "If they were truly trying to understand it, they would do studies or investigations of the harm of their approach."[55]

The APA Draws the New Boundaries of Science

Although the initial charge for the task force did not require a review of the scientific literature to determine whether or not reorientation was effective or safe, the group decided it was imperative to provide one: "The debate over SOCE [sexual orientation change efforts] has centered on the issues of efficacy, benefit, and harm. Thus, we believe it was incumbent on us to address those issues in our report."[56] Contrary to NARTH's claims about "what research shows," the task force created APA's map of science. In two chapters, one providing an overview of SOCE research and "methodological limitations," and another on "outcomes," the report addressed whether change efforts have been efficacious and whether they are harmful. These chapters were largely the work of meth-odologists Robin Lin Miller and Roger Worthington.

The literature review held a high scientific standard. As a first prin-ciple, research included in the review had to have been peer-reviewed, which excluded the Jones and Yarhouse study, even though it has been touted by NARTH as the "most methodologically rigorous." The group divided studies into "experimental," "quasi-experimental," and "non-experimental" categories, depending on their design. Only the ex-perimental and quasi-experimental studies were considered capable of demonstrating causality. For studies to be considered sufficiently ex-perimental, "participants are randomly assigned to treatment groups such that individual differences are more equally distributed and are not confounded with any change resulting from the treatment. Experiments are also rigorous because they include a way for the researcher to deter-mine what would have happened in the absence of any treatment (e.g., a counterfactual), usually through the use of a no-treatment control group." By contrast, quasi-experimental studies "do not have random as-signment but do incorporate a comparison of some kind. Although they are less rigorous than experiments, quasi-experiments, if appropriately designed and conducted, can still provide for reasonable causal conclu-sions to be made."[57] Of the eighty-three studies collected, only six were deemed "experimental" and three were "quasi-experimental." All nine studies were conducted in the late 1960s and early 1970s.

These nine studies were all tests of aversion therapy, and they all showed general therapeutic failure. They demonstrated that it was possi-ble to reduce homosexual arousal but not to induce heterosexual arousal. It is tremendously ironic that the work of researchers who conducted aversion therapy studies, historically seen by gay liberation activists as unethical forms of "torture," was, years later, now enrolled in a docu-ment that challenged all reorientation practices. Based on these "early period" studies, the task force claimed that reorientation is likely to fail in all cases:

> We concluded that the early high-quality evidence is the best basis for predicting what would be the outcome of valid interventions. These studies show that enduring change to an individual's sexual orienta-tion is uncommon. The participants in this body of research continued to experience same-sex attractions following SOCE and did not report significant change to other sex attractions that could be empirically validated, though some showed lessened physiological arousal to all sexual stimuli.

The majority of these studies used phallometric testing as their outcome measure. Elevating the credibility of phallometry, the report states, "In men especially, physiological measures are considered more dependable for detecting sexual arousal in men and women than self-report of sexual arousal or attraction."[58] Thus the tacit alliance between reorientation opponents and phallometric testing, which had developed at the time of the demedicalization of homosexuality, became formal when evidence for the inefficacy of reorientation was needed.

The APA review also solidified a crucial distinction that had been proposed in earlier writing by gay affirmative psychologists to discredit self-report. The task force claimed that self-report studies do not adequately distinguish between the construct of "sexual orientation" and "sexual orientation identity." The task force officially defined sexual orientation as "an individual's patterns of sexual, romantic, and affectional arousal and desire for other persons based on those persons' gender and sex characteristics."[59] By contrast, "sexual orientation identity" is defined as "acknowledgment and internalization of sexual orientation and reflects self-exploration, self-awareness, self-recognition, group membership and affiliation, culture, and self-stigma."[60] Rather than undermining the claims of ex-gays as self-deceptive or intended to deceive, the task force invalidated self-report on the basis of poor "construct validity," effectively invalidating recent research that relied on this method. By this logic, a person's report of his or her sexual attractions can only be understood as an expression of identity. The report stated:

> Considered in the context of the conceptual complexities of and debates over the assessment of sexual orientation, much of the SOCE research does not adequately define the construct of sexual orientation, does not differentiate it from sexual orientation identity, or has misleading definitions that do not accurately assess or acknowledge bisexual individuals. Early research that focuses on sexual arousal may be more precise than that which relies on self-report of behavior. Overall, recent research may actually measure sexual orientation identity (i.e., beliefs about sexual orientation, self-report of identity or group affiliation, self-report of behavior, and self-labeling) rather than sexual orientation.[61]

According to the task force, recent research, based on self-report measures, could not provide scientific proof of efficacy, and could only be used for other scientific purposes, such as understanding people's motivations for pursuing SOCE or providing evidence of harm.

Indeed, all the task force members interviewed for this book expressed an affinity for phallometry in studying the outcomes of reorientation therapies. Glassgold stated, "I think if you wanted to have a real empirical study, you hook people up with a plethysmograph."[62] Beckstead, who previously worked in a phallometric laboratory with Ray Blanchard and coauthored a phallometric study of pedophiles, had been a proponent of this technique throughout the debate, even if he also acknowledged some of the limitations of phallometry:

> I also think there has to be an objective [assessment], . . . like a phallometric assessment, something that would measure physiologically their arousal pattern. That itself is controversial because some people say that sexual orientation is not just arousal. In fact, . . . arousal patterns for women don't necessarily match their sexual identities or sexual behaviors or sexual relationships. But for men, they tend to.[63]

Drescher offered an analogy:

> The other cavalier thing that [Spitzer] did was, he said something like, we didn't have any money to do phallometric testing. So I said, OK, so let's say there's a Dr. "Spritzer" who's a world famous cardiopulmonary internist who years ago did some of the seminal research on deleterious effects of secondhand smoke, and he was the one who discovered that secondhand smoke could have a harmful effect, but Dr. Spritzer is also a libertarian so when New York City passes its anti-smoking laws prohibiting people from smoking in bars, he's against it for political ideological purposes, so he decides to do a study to see whether or not everybody is harmed by secondhand smoke, and so he stations himself outside a cigar bar, and he asks patrons on their way out the door if they would like to participate in a study, and he asks them have you ever been harmed by cigarette smoke. But he doesn't have any money to do any chest X-rays. That's the Spitzer study.[64]

Such calls for tests of the body are aligned with the task force's use of aversion therapy studies from the 1970s that failed to demonstrate conversion, as phallometric testing had been used in most of them. The position statement concluding the task force report invoked these studies when it stated:

> There are no studies of adequate scientific rigor to conclude whether or not recent SOCE do or do not work to change a person's sexual orientation. Scientifically rigorous older work in this area (e.g., Birk, Huddleston, Miller, & Cohler, 1971; James, 1978; McConaghy, 1969, 1976; McConaghy, Proctor, & Barr, 1972; Tanner, 1974, 1975) found that

sexual orientation (i.e., erotic attractions and sexual arousal oriented to one sex or the other, or both) was unlikely to change due to efforts designed for this purpose. Some individuals appeared to learn how to ignore or limit their attractions. However, this was much less likely to be true for people whose sexual attractions were initially limited to people of the same sex.[65]

This rhetorical work has "materialized" the male body in the course of the discussion. Whereas physiological response to erotic imagery might be ignored or downplayed by reorientation proponents, emphasizing this kind of evidence has the effect of bringing the body back into being as a meaningful entity to be perceived and acknowledged.[66] This emphasis also has the effect of erasing the sexual subjectivities of women, if male sexuality is used as the source of the universal definition of "sexual orientation" to suit a set of policy concerns.

In contrast to the rigor in measuring efficacy, measures of harm, previously considered "anecdotal," were given a credibility boost by the task force report, which homed in on suggestions of harm, finding it in studies that did not even pose it as a research question. To achieve this, the task force looked for people dropping out of studies, for iatrogenic effects, for client reports of harm, and for evidence of indirect harms. For example, one early aversion therapy study was characterized as containing examples of harm:

> In McConaghy and Barr's (1973) experiment, 1 respondent of 46 subjects is reported to have lost all sexual feeling and to have dropped out of the treatment as a result. Two participants reported experiencing severe depression, and 4 others experienced milder depression during treatment. No other experimental studies reported on iatrogenic effects.[67]

The nonexperimental studies, considered useless for providing evidence of efficacy, were fair game for evidence of harm. For example:

> A majority of the reports on iatrogenic effects are provided in the non-experimental studies. In the study conducted by Bancroft (1969), the negative outcomes reported include treatment-related anxiety (20% of 16 participants), suicidal ideation (10% of 16 participants), depression (40% of 16 participants), impotence (10% of 16 participants), and relationship dysfunction (10% of 16 participants). Overall, Bancroft reported the intervention had harmful effects on 50% of the 16 research subjects who were exposed to it. Quinn, Harrison, and McAllister (1970) and Thorpe et al. (1964) also reported cases of debilitating depression,

gastric distress, nightmares, and anxiety. Herman and Prewett (1974) reported that following treatment, their research participant began to engage in abusive use of alcohol that required his rehospitalization. It is unclear to what extent and how his treatment failure may have contributed to his abusive drinking. B. James (1962) reported symptoms of severe dehydration (acetonuria), which forced treatment to be suspended. Overall, although most early research provides little information on how research participants fared over the longer term and whether interventions were associated with longterm negative effects, negative effects of treatment are reported to have occurred for some people during and immediately following treatment.

High dropout rates characterize early treatment studies and may be an indicator that research participants experience these treatments as harmful. Lilienfeld's (2007) review of harm in psychotherapy identifies dropout as not only an indicator of direct harm but also of treatment ineffectiveness.[68]

It is also noteworthy that the task force used the phrase "10% of 16 participants," which would be 1.6 people, suggesting that the use of percentages was an effort to appear more scientific. Adding these findings to the more recent studies that explicitly addressed harm (Shidlo and Schroeder 2002; Beckstead and Morrow 2004), the report concluded, "Studies from both periods indicate that attempts to change sexual orientation may cause or exacerbate distress and poor mental health in some individuals, including depression and suicidal thoughts."[69] With client self-reports of harm elevated to a scientific status, this work lent more credibility to harm narratives of ex-ex-gay activists within the field of therapeutics more broadly.

New Therapeutic Guidelines for Identity Exploration

The task force set out to provide a set of scientific guidelines for therapists working with clients struggling with their sexual orientation. To do so, it had to reconcile a number of factors. On the one hand, its charge and the need to adhere to the APA Ethics Code more broadly required the task force to develop therapeutic guidelines that were "affirmative" of LGBT people and diversity. On the other hand, the American Psychological Association had taken some recent turns toward formal acknowledgment of religious diversity, including respect for the religious values of clients and research subjects. The task force also had to respond to NARTH's claims that clients had a right to "self-determination" and "autonomy" in the therapeutic encounter, so denying clients the "right" to have their homosexuality reoriented by a therapist had to be justified.

The task force worked within the framework of the APA's "evidence-based practices in psychotherapy" (EBPP), defined as "the integration of the best available research with clinical expertise in the context of patient characteristics, culture, and preferences."[70] The use of this framework further illuminates why the task force felt compelled to review the literature: based on this review, the proposals for therapy could incorporate established facts that sexual orientation is unlikely to change in therapy and change attempts can be harmful. Yet, it is noteworthy that there was no evaluation in its report of scientific evidence for the efficacy of gay-affirmative therapies, and it is unclear when an evidence-based standard is necessary for making therapeutic recommendations; nonetheless these standards were applied to reorientation.

The task force members also looked to new work in the field of the psychology of religion for guidance. The elements of the report dealing with these matters were heavily influenced by the work of Lee Beckstead, who stated:

> Judith [Glassgold] and I started exploring more about the psychology of religion, again trying to figure out, incorporate this piece, learning more about the other side so to speak. . . . We really were able to integrate a scientific viewpoint of religion.[71]

The report acknowledged that psychology had historically held negative views of religion but that new research had demonstrated ways in which religion can be a positive coping resource. Two 2007 APA resolutions regarding religion were particularly pivotal. The first was the "Resolution Rejecting Intelligent Design as Scientific and Reaffirming Support for Evolutionary Theory." Crucial in this position statement was a boundary marker:

> While we are respectful of religion and individuals' right to their own religious beliefs, we also recognize that science and religion are separate and distinct. For a theory to be taught as science it must be testable, supported by empirical evidence and subject to disconfirmation.[72]

Because religious belief cannot be falsified, it therefore cannot be scientific according to this resolution, and this principle of falsifiability justified the APA's scientific authority on the matter. The other key document was the "Resolution on Religious, Religion-Based, and/or Religion-Derived Prejudice." It provided a general affirmation of religious diversity, but also demarcated psychology and religion as separate epistemological domains:

It is important for psychology as a behavioral science, and various faith traditions as theological systems, to acknowledge and respect their profoundly different methodological, epistemological, historical, theoretical, and philosophical bases. Psychology has no legitimate function in arbitrating matters of faith and theology, and faith traditions have no legitimate place arbitrating behavioral or other sciences.[73]

By stating that psychology could not arbitrate matters of faith, this statement was intended to prevent psychology from explaining away religious experiences as merely secular psychological epiphenomena.[74] In terms of the intellectual opportunity structure, these position statements affirming religious diversity were crucial for shaping the task force's approach to people whose religious commitments might be more important to them than their sexual feelings, ultimately helping usher in the compromise of "sexual orientation identity exploration."

Given these resolutions, a general commitment to opposing discrimination on the basis of religion was important for the task force's work. There are, however, different ways religion can be the basis for discrimination. People may discriminate against members of a religion; alternately, religion itself can be a source of prejudicial views. Although the resolution condemns both of these forms of prejudice, the line between "religion-derived prejudice" and religious beliefs worthy of respect can be difficult to draw. Glassgold described a way in which Clinton Anderson proposed that the task force proceed on this distinction:

Clinton has struggled with that and came up with this separate idea of the social impact of religion versus judging the validity of the beliefs. And in different individuals the beliefs have different impact, and some individuals or beliefs don't have necessarily a negative impact on their sense of themselves, and for other people it does.[75]

Thus, the task force could criticize particular prejudicial religious beliefs if they had a negative social impact.

Given these new resolutions, the principle of being "affirmative" of diversity, derived from the APA Ethics Code and part of the task force charge, was tricky. Two competing priorities have been relevant for people experiencing conflicts over their sexual orientations. Religion-affirming models emphasize "telic congruence," living in accordance with religious values, while gay-affirming models have emphasized "organismic congruence," living in alignment with the experienced self. The report suggested that understanding these philosophical differences may lead to deeper understanding across worldviews:

> It is important to note that the organismic worldview can be congruent with and respectful of religion . . . and the telic worldview can be aware of sexual stigma and respectful of sexual orientation. . . . Understanding this philosophical difference may improve the dialogue between these two perspectives represented in the literature, as it refocuses the debate not on one group's perceived rejection of homosexuals or the other group's perceived minimization of religious viewpoints but on philosophical differences that extend beyond this particular subject matter.[76]

While it is perhaps difficult to bridge the gap described here, passages such as this express a tone of rapprochement that the report attempted to foster.

The therapeutic recommendations went on to provide an "affirmative" approach intended to respect both religious and sexual orientation diversity. Within the new model of "sexual orientation identity exploration," a client should be free to pursue either "telic" or "organismic" congruence in therapy. But, the report specifies, "Many religious individuals desired to live their lives in a manner consistent with their values (telic congruence); however, telic congruence based on stigma and shame is unlikely to result in psychological well-being."[77] Contrary to NARTH's "What Research Shows," which used evidence of heightened pathology within gay communities as evidence of the damaging effects of homosexuality, the task force claimed that therapists utilizing an affirmative approach must acknowledge empirical research that demonstrates the impact of stigma and minority stress on sexual minorities, creating distress and health disparities. Pointing to the distinction between a fixed "sexual orientation" and a malleable "sexual orientation identity," they extended the concept of "affirmative" to include a range of therapeutic outcomes through identity exploration, including heterosexual identity if the client so chose. This was a significant change from "gay-affirmative" models of the past, which encouraged clients with same-sex attractions to accept and embrace a gay identity. As a compromise, the guidelines stated that sexual orientation does not change and that pursuing a life in congruence with religious values can be mentally healthy in some cases. Some treatments marketed as "sexual identity therapies" thus now carry a stamp of approval from the American Psychological Association—as long as they do not include efforts to change orientation.[78]

Finally, the concept of providing "affirmative" approaches to therapy became a key resource for the task force when responding to claims about ex-gays' right to therapy based on "self-determination" and "autonomy." The concept of "affirmative" incorporates aspects of the "self-determination" claims of reorientation proponents, but it includes a crucial caveat: for a client to experience true self-determination and autonomy, he or she must be provided full informed consent. This means that clients must be informed of the facts that sexual orientation is highly unlikely to change and that the attempt may be harmful. Furthermore, true self-determination and autonomy require a community environment and a clinical setting free of anti-gay bias and coercion. Therapists and clients should be disabused of any anti-gay stereotypes for there to be true autonomy in sexual orientation identity exploration.[79]

Spitzer's Apology and the Remnants of the Ex-Gay Movement

By August 2009, the American Psychological Association task force had set new terms for the boundaries of scientific knowledge and practice in the field of therapeutics. Self-report evidence for reorientation had been discredited, while testimonies of harm had been granted a bolstered status. Sexual orientation was understood in terms of physiological response that could not be therapeutically altered. Fixed sexual orientations existed in humans, although the ability or willingness to acknowledge them might vary, and therapists were now encouraged to defer to clients' self-definition of their identity in therapeutic processes. The APA stopped short of calling for disbanding ex-gay organizations, but it had driven a wedge between components of the movement that differed over the importance of attraction change, exacerbating the frame dispute over goals. The stage was set for the beginning of the decline of the ex-gay movement in the United States.

Just a few months before the APA report was issued, ex-gay organizations in the United States had become associated with anti-homosexuality activists in Uganda seeking a death penalty for homosexuality, resulting in negative press in the United States. Widespread condemnation of involvement of the U.S. ex-gay movement in these developments led leaders such as Alan Chambers and evangelical minister Rick Warren to distance themselves from these developments. Being held responsible for a harsh anti-gay initiative like this was a severe liability in the United States. The movement was also rocked by scandal again in 2010, when George Alan Rekers, a member of the NARTH scientific advisory board, was caught with a male escort whom he had found on the website rentboy.com. Rekers resigned from the NARTH board, and the movement was forced to do damage control as the story was passed around late-night talk shows.[80]

In the midst of the declining credibility of the movement and rising visibility of ex-gay survivors, Robert Spitzer issued a public apology for his ex-gay study. He decided to do this in 2012, after he was interviewed at his home by Gabriel Arana, a reporter for *American Prospect* who had been through a failed reorientation therapy attempt with Nicolosi. In his article "My So-Called Ex-Gay Life," Arana described how the therapy led him into such a suicidal state that he committed himself to a mental hospital, resulting in the delay of his self-acceptance as gay. During his time in the ex-gay world, he had been encouraged to participate in Spitzer's study.[81] As reported in the *New York Times,* Spitzer decided at four in the morning to write his letter of apology. In the interview for the story, he stated, "You know, it's the only regret I have; the only professional one."[82] In *Archives of Sexual Behavior,* Spitzer wrote:

> I believe I owe the gay community an apology for my study making unproven claims of the efficacy of reparative therapy. I also apologize to any gay person who wasted time and energy undergoing some form of reparative therapy because they believed that I had proven that reparative therapy works with some "highly motivated" individuals.[83]

Spitzer further claimed that "there was no way to determine if the participants' accounts of change were valid."

Interpretations of Spitzer's apology varied, especially regarding what it meant for the scientific record. In the public, whether or not the study was "retracted" became a crucially important factor regarding its use as a resource in debates. Gabriel Arana reported that Spitzer wanted to retract the study but that Kenneth Zucker, editor of *Archives of Sexual Behavior,* had declined his request. Arana wrote:

> Spitzer was growing tired and asked how many more questions I had. Nothing, I responded, unless you have something to add.
>
> He did. Would I print a retraction of his 2001 study, "so I don't have to worry about it anymore"?[84]

In turn, various media outlets and gay activists have reported that Spitzer "retracted" the study. Since the apology, Spitzer appeared in a new video produced by Truth Wins Out. In the video, he never used the term *retracted,* yet the website framed the exchange as an "interview with Dr. Robert Spitzer[,] who discusses retracting his infamous 'ex-gay' study." In this interview, Spitzer asked various reorientation and religious right organizations to stop using videos of him saying he believed in the study's results. In Spitzer's living room, a placard was placed behind his couch that read in large letters "Unmasking the 'Ex-Gay' Myth" as he explained that now that his study has been taken away from these conservative groups, "I would think that's a pretty rough place to be in."[85]

NARTH president Christopher Rosik claimed, however, that Spitzer's apology did not amount to a "retraction." Instead, Spitzer had "reassessed his interpretation" of his findings.[86] Rosik pointed to statements by editor Kenneth Zucker, who claimed there was never a request for a retraction; rather, a discussion took place concerning how best to proceed now that Spitzer had a different interpretation of his findings. Zucker countered by saying:

> You can retract data incorrectly analyzed; to do that, you publish an erratum. You can retract an article if the data were falsified—or the journal retracts it if the editor knows of it. As I understand it, he's just saying ten years later that he wants to retract his interpretation of the data. Well, we'd probably have to retract hundreds of scientific papers with regard to re-interpretation, and we don't do that.[87]

According to these views, Spitzer's study was not retracted but rather reinterpreted. Rosik claimed that the language of retraction was politically motivated, and even appealed to the merits of Spitzer's study: "The case for the credibility of participants' account of change still remains."[88]

Spitzer responded to this controversy over whether or not he had retracted his study in a second interview with me at his home in 2013, at which time he explained his position. He first indicated that the word *apology* was itself carefully chosen:

> In terms of making my views known, the use of the term *apology* was terrific, just terrific, because it gives an emotional thing to it. It's not just saying that he's changing his views on something but I know I've hurt people and I want to apologize. I feel very good about that.[89]

Contrary to the Arana story, Spitzer said that he did not request a "retraction" from Zucker but rather talked with him about options for moving forward now that he had reinterpreted his results. Regarding whether or not the study was retracted, he attempted to clarify:

> You don't hear about scientists retracting a study very often. Practically never. This is kind of interesting. I went out of my way to make my misgivings public. Usually when you think of retracting a study, you think of how the author realizes he made a mistake or something. Was this a retraction? It wasn't a retraction of the data or anything. It was a retraction of my views in the conclusion of the study—the significance.[90]

This response raises the question: is a study technically "retracted" when the author no longer accepts his or her own interpretation? Clearly Zucker does not think so. Spitzer does believe the data were accurate and should be part of the scientific record, but he says we should not believe his earlier interpretation. In the end, there has been no formal retraction: the publication, which was not peer-reviewed, remains in the scientific record along with several predominantly negative commentaries and a response paper by the author that backpedals from his initial conclusions, followed by an author's apology for the study written ten years later.

Soon after Spitzer's apology became public, Exodus director Alan Chambers announced that Exodus International was now denying the effectiveness of reorientation therapies. In an article in the *New York Times* titled "Rift Forms in Movement as Belief in Gay 'Cure' Is Renounced," Chambers explained that the new position reflected the views of both himself and the board of directors. Chambers claimed that like all "ex-gays" he still harbored some form of same-sex attraction and that ex-gays should not be afraid to admit they would have a struggle for life. The *Times* reported, "Only a few years ago, Mr. Chambers was featured in advertisements along with his wife, Leslie, saying, 'Change is possible.' But now, he said in the interview, 'Exodus needs to move beyond that slogan.'" Exodus was singling out homosexuality and treating it differently from other forms of sin, as the church does not require people to change from the sins of pornography or lust in quite the same way. Illustrating the movement's "rift," the *New York Times* reported that critics of Chambers still thought change was completely possible. Therapist David Pickup claimed that restricting the therapy could be harmful to patients "'by making them feel that no change is possible at all.'" Parents and Friends of Ex-Gays and Gays leader Gregg Quinlan claimed that Chambers was just tired of his struggle and was "'making excuses.'" Yet, the article also tied the change in Exodus's policy to opposition to anti-gay laws abroad. One Exodus board member, Dennis Jernigan, was forced to resign because of his support for Jamaica's anti-sodomy laws, and the board vowed its opposition to laws criminalizing sexual acts between consensual adults, including the proposed law in Uganda.[91]

In a more recent trend toward making reorientation therapists into national pariahs, the state of California passed a ban on conversion therapy for minors. Other states around the country have proposed similar bans, and one passed in New Jersey. The ban in California, upheld by the Ninth Circuit Federal Court of Appeals, made the practice of reorientation therapy with clients under the age of eighteen punishable by delicensing. California Senate Bill 1172 cited the APA task force report and the APA resolution accompanying that report among statements from several professional associations in the United States, and a position statement by the Pan American Health Organization as a regional affiliate of the World Health Organization. It pointed to the APA report as the leading basis for the claim that sexual reorientation therapies pose "critical health risks" for LGBT persons, and the bill concluded that there is a compelling state interest to protect "the physical and psychological well-being of minors, including lesbian, gay, bisexual, and transgender youth" from the harms of conversion attempts.[92] This state regulation of therapeutic practice, now also present in New Jersey and proposed in other states, is a new element of the intellectual opportunity structure that prohibits reorientation researchers from producing knowledge about reorientation of minors in these states, and it further undermines for the public the credibility of reorientation as a dangerous practice.

Almost a year later, in June 2013, the Oprah Winfrey Network aired an episode of *Our America with Lisa Ling* featuring Alan Chambers apologizing for the harm caused by Exodus International's false promises of change. The episode was filmed in the basement of the First Presbyterian Church of Hollywood and included several ex-gay survivors in a group setting with Chambers and his wife, Leslie. Chambers read an apology, which also circulated in the press and on his blog. The apology acknowledged the harms caused by Exodus but characterized them as unintended and inadvertent. After having read many stories of ex-gay survivors since renouncing reorientation, Chambers said that he was sorry his organization had caused those harms and had not spoken out more within the church:

> More than anything, I am sorry that so many have interpreted this religious rejection by Christians as God's rejection. I am profoundly sorry that many have walked away from their faith and that some have chosen to end their lives. For the rest of my life I will proclaim nothing but the whole truth of the Gospel, one of grace, mercy and open invitation to all to enter into an inseverable relationship with almighty God.[93]

Chambers stopped short of apologizing for his own views that homosexuality is not within God's plan. Ex-gay survivors in the room had strong reactions and said the apology was not enough. Chambers would have much farther to go, and Exodus International needed to cease operations. And this is exactly what happened next. At its thirty-eighth annual conference, Exodus International announced that it would be closing its doors on June 20, 2013. In an interview about the apology with the *Huffington Post*, Chambers claimed that Exodus International was never about "curing" homosexuality, but he admitted that within the theological framing of the organization, the suggestion of "change" implied cure, and this was harmful.[94]

In the wake of Exodus International's folding, the remnants of the ex-gay movement are in many ways much weaker. Love Won Out and Love in Action have closed, and Evergreen International has been absorbed into the Mormon group North Star. Ex-gay ministries have reorganized under the name the Restored Hope Network, directed by Anne Paulk. NARTH and Focus on the Family are both affiliated with this group. The organization continues to offer reorientation therapy blended with theology, but with more moderate religious groups now absent, the division of labor between secular and religious sides has been rejoined. Meanwhile, these developments have given rise to another offshoot movement called "Side B Christianity," a loose term for gay celibacy.[95] Given the widespread acceptance in the United States of the idea that homosexuality cannot be reoriented, some ministries are promoting gay celibacy as a means to live within God's plan. Emerging out of a community called the Gay Christian Network, "Side A" allows for practicing gay people to be Christian, and "Side B" views gay sex as sinful but gay sexual orientation as acceptable. The terminology "Side B" has been applied to Courage, a Catholic organization that implements the Vatican's policy on gay celibacy as well: it is OK to be gay but not to act on it. While it appears that the ex-gay movement is fragmented and significantly weakened in the United States, pastor Mel White has warned that it may become stronger and go underground in light of recent negative publicity.[96]

At the time of this writing, NARTH continues its operations and has brushed off the decline of Exodus International as insignificant. NARTH reduced the organization to a "public relations voice and referral clearing house," and explained that the affiliated ministries were already reorganizing under the Restored Hope Network anyway.[97] The organization's website narth.com has also been rebranded as the "NARTH Institute," with older materials archived at narth.org. While part of the Restored Hope Network in the United States, NARTH has now been subsumed within the neutrally named "Alliance for Therapeutic Choice and Scientific Integrity."[98] When I interviewed Pickup in 2009, he was eager for NARTH to continue pursuing research to demonstrate the efficacy of reorientation. Since this time, psychologist Michael Bailey at Northwestern University has offered his lab to the ex-gay movement as a venue for proving reorientation can work—if this is what such therapists wish to do. This lab has both phallometric and brain scan equipment available to test sexual orientation. To this date, such evidence has not materialized.

But what if physiological testing of ex-gays' sexual orientation were to materialize, and it were to show that change is possible? In my interview with Lee Beckstead, I posed such a scenario. If NARTH researchers were to conduct a test and present results of efficacy with phallometric data, for instance, would there then be some evidence for the efficacy of reorientation therapy? To this Beckstead replied:

> Keep going further, though, because sex offenders can fake it. I would want to make sure that in the phallometric assessment the participants aren't pumping, or they're not doing mathematics in their heads to not get aroused. I would want to consider the type of phallometric assessment. There's just more to it than that. The data's going to be important, the arousal data, but if they're showing something, I would want to keep making sure that the design took into account all that we're talking about. Not just one view of it. So it is evidence, but there are so many pieces of this puzzle that to really claim something you have to account for all of it.[99]

"Pumping" is a form of "faking" the phallometric test in which the subject produces an erection through voluntary muscular contractions.[100] Regarding where to set the criteria for the "straight line," it seems we could go on forever. How can we ever really know what is going on in each subject's mind—could he be fantasizing about things other than the erotic imagery he is viewing? This factor would be relevant for brain scanning as well. Somehow the credibility of evidence inevitably involves issues of trust between people who produce evidence (including research subjects) and the people who evaluate that evidence.

A Newly Formalized Sexual Dichotomy

Materializing bodies as physical indicators of sexual arousal, the APA task force report definitively shifted the kinds of objects that could be perceived within science in this field. Once the new dichotomy of sexual orientation/sexual orientation identity was formalized, subjects' self-reports could no longer speak for sexual orientation, but rather for sexual orientation identity, and bodies became necessary to truly evaluate orientation. The report also introduced the innovation of drawing evidence of harm from studies not intended to investigate this issue. In effect, the report reflected convergence of moderate worldviews found in ex-ex-gay organizations and gay-affirmative therapy and activism. The former upheld claims of harm as the highest form of evidence, making efficacy claims irrelevant. The latter tended to uphold physiological testing above self-report. The APA report melded these views, providing a document that reorientation opponents could unite behind. And although the championed Jones and Yarhouse study was rejected as unscientific "gray literature," the APA task force report offered several olive branches to members of the social world of religious ex-gay ministries, most notably "sexual orientation identity exploration."

By the close of the first decade of the twenty-first century, mainstream science in the field of therapeutics had completely excluded the efficacy claims of sexual orientation change efforts as unscientific, and raised many questions about the ethics of these practices. While the APA may be the "prevailing cartographer" of the scientific landscape, legal issues prevent banning reorientation altogether, so clients may still pursue SOCE if they desire. The task force report provides particular "recommendations" to psychologists, but these recommendations do not necessarily restrict professional behavior. With the exception of the treatment of minors in a couple of states, there is nothing legally or professionally stopping an expert from promising complete attraction change, so it is unclear whether clients will be able to give informed consent. However, at the time of this writing, a consumer fraud lawsuit is pending in New Jersey, brought by the Southern Poverty Law Center on behalf of a former client of Jews Offering New Alternatives to Homosexuality; this lawsuit could change the landscape for reorientation even further.[101] It remains unclear whether clients will be provided the opportunity to experience what the APA considers to be true self-determination, based on access to scientific information and being free to make choices in a context free of anti-gay bias. Insofar as anti-gay sentiments reign supreme in areas of the United States, reorientation therapies will continue despite the APA's claims, and reorientation proponents will continue to say the APA is beholden to gay activism. It remains to be seen what effect the APA report will have in policy arenas or in "the court of public opinion," but given the cultural authority of science in the United States, the effect is likely to be positive for opponents of reorientation, even if reorientation continues. Yet, despite these losses for the ex-gay movement within the United States, an anti-gay transnational advocacy network has had numerous gains abroad. Chapter 5 turns to the global stage to investigate the impact of this shift in focus, with particular attention to developments in Uganda.

five

A NATIONAL MOVEMENT AGAINST "HOMOS"
How Reorientation Concepts Traveled to Uganda, 2009–2014

At the Kololo stadium in the capital city of Kampala, approximately thirty thousand people from the East African nation of Uganda poured into a political rally and celebration for the passage of the Anti-Homosexuality Act. In its final form, this law made homosexuality punishable by life imprisonment and also outlawed any pro-gay advocacy. Historian Rebecca Hodes, who attended the event, described a day complete with festivities, including acrobats and school choirs. This stadium has been a symbol of national pride since the British flag was lowered there in 1962. A nationalist connection was made in speeches—the passage of the bill was given the status of defining Uganda—with calls for Western leaders to respect national sovereignty. Speaking to the crowd, President Yoweri Museveni drew support from a report written by scientific experts from the Ugandan Ministry of Health, and he described homosexuality:

> It is not genetic. It is not congenital. It is behavior. It is not nature, it is nurture. It is not because somebody is born like that, it is because of the way somebody is brought up. That's why I said I am going to sign the bill because I am convinced with the available information that these people are not born like that, they just learn and they can unlearn what they have learned.[1]

This was a case where understandings of the science of sexual orientation and the making of public policy could not be more explicitly interwoven. Despite its passage in February 2014, the Anti-Homosexuality Act has since been ruled unconstitutional by a Constitutional Court under the charge that there was not a quorum present in Parliament when it passed, but at the time of this writing that judgment is on appeal to the

Ugandan Supreme Court, with much national support behind the measure. Members of the Ugandan Parliament are also vowing to revive a new version of the bill.[2]

Attention to anti-gay transnational connections across the United States and Uganda in relation to this bill erupted in the U.S. media in 2009. In the series of stories titled "Uganda Be Kidding Me," MSNBC host Rachel Maddow reported on a conference on the "homosexual agenda" hosted in Kampala by the local organization Family Life Network, including ex-gay and anti-homosexual leaders from the United States. One of these activists was Scott Lively of Abiding Truth Ministries. Lively's ministry has been discredited as a "hate group" by the Southern Poverty Law Center in the United States, but he could still find a powerful and receptive audience in Uganda, where he has had ties for years. He is coauthor of *The Pink Swastika,* which alleges that fascism is caused by male homosexuality because it ultimately leads to the fetishization of a cold and cruel masculinity.[3] At the conference in Kampala, Lively claimed that homosexuality was behind the Nazi Holocaust and likely other acts of genocide in Africa. He also claimed that homosexuals indoctrinate children to accept homosexual feelings and identify as gay, despite the fact that these feelings will go away in adulthood. Moreover, at the conference, Lively promoted NARTH as the preeminent authority on scientific research on homosexuality and the effectiveness of reorientation therapies. Ex-gay leaders from the United States were also present, including Don Schmierer of Exodus International and Caleb Lee Brundidge of the International Healing Foundation. Various documentaries and news reports in the United States point to these activists and other U.S. evangelical Christians as responsible for inspiring and even writing the Anti-Homosexuality Bill. Such accusations miss acknowledging the motivations of people in Uganda who draw on ideas from abroad to develop their own positions that are strategic both locally and on the global stage; after all, these U.S. activists were invited by the Family Life Network to attend their conference.

The passage and presidential signing of the new Ugandan law directly thwarted the positions of various Western leaders, Westernized international governmental organizations, and global mental health associations supporting gay rights around the globe. Such leaders included United Nations Secretary-General Ban Ki-moon and then-Secretary of State Hillary Clinton,[4] who have made speeches on gay rights as human rights. President Barack Obama called the Ugandan bill "odious," while British Prime Minister David Cameron threatened to pull aid from any country that denied gay rights.[5] And in 2011, the UN Human Rights

Council narrowly passed a Gay Rights Protection Resolution.[6] Within mental health fields, the American Psychiatric Association and International Federation of Social Work passed resolutions condemning the bill, and the World Psychiatric Association's president Dinesh Bhugra, who had recently come out as gay himself, said the profession of psychiatry should apologize to gay people.[7] Within Uganda's postcolonial context, such statements have often been interpreted as evidence of Western influence and condescension, as the anti-homosexuality movement has successfully framed homosexuality as a culturally imported practice and has conflated it with rape, child molestation, and particular sex acts. While the Psychological Society of South Africa also provided a statement in opposition to the bill,[8] in Uganda, psychology is still establishing itself as a profession, and South Africa's statement may be seen as excessively influenced by Westernized gay activists.[9] Popular Kenyan literary figure Binyavanga Wainaina, on the other hand, defiantly declared "I am homosexual" and has stated, as a Pan-Africanist, that he would travel the continent despite laws criminalizing homosexuality. Claiming that leaders use homosexuality to deflect attention from other issues, Wainaina offered LGBT rights proponents across the continent additional support that could not be dismissed as Western influence.[10]

Uganda is one of several countries where there has been a backlash against gay rights in recent years. When delegates from France and the Netherlands introduced a European Union–backed gay rights declaration to the UN General Assembly in 2008, delegates were dramatically split, with several Arab and African countries among sixty member states opposing.[11] At the end of 2013, the Supreme Court of India reinstated laws established in 1861 criminalizing homosexuality,[12] and Russia has been embroiled in controversy over laws against homosexual "propaganda."[13] Similar developments have been reported in many countries in Africa. In Nigeria, a new law criminalized same-sex marriage, as well as prohibited both pro-gay gatherings and displays of same-sex affection.[14] A man in Cameroon who was convicted for sending a text message to another man stating "I am very much in love with you" died in prison. Lawmakers in Zambia have been seeking a constitutional ban on homosexuality.[15] Zimbabwe president Robert Mugabe claimed in an alarming speech that he would never accept gays, who are "worse than pigs, goats, and birds"; he declared, "If you take men and lock them in a house for five years and tell them to come up with two children and they fail to do that, then we will chop off their heads."[16] Approximately eighty countries around the world have laws criminalizing homosexuality, with at least seven imposing a death penalty in some cases.[17] To understand these developments, it is important to note the specific local justifications for anti-gay views, since each nation has a different historical, cultural, and political context, while anti-gay ideas and resources traverse complex webs of transnational alliances.

In this chapter, I continue to examine shifting meanings of "sexual orientation" and the ways in which scientists draw the line between gay and straight, but in a very different national context. To explain how the Uganda Ministry of Health could come to the conclusion that homosexuality is a behavior in need of regulation, I will explain three primary factors underlying the flows and transformations of science in this context.[18] First, the National Association of Social Workers of Uganda (NASWU), with its close connections to both the anti-homosexuality movement and Parliament, has acted as a direct pathway for definitions of homosexuality and concepts drawn from NARTH research to have strong legislative influence, backed up by local expert authority. Second, numerous aspects of the intellectual opportunity structure in Uganda have thwarted any pro-gay science-based strategy, as position statements from Westernized scientific institutions can be dismissed as "foreign influence." Finally, Ugandan psychiatrists and psychologists, some of whom participated on the Ministry of Health panel, have had to walk a tightrope between the demands of their global professions, on the one hand, and local needs, on the other. These local concerns include threats to their personal liberty, as the Anti-Homosexuality Act contained provisions against pro-gay advocacy. Crucial in these struggles has been the success of the anti-homosexuality movement in culturally defining "homosexuality" to encompass child molestation, rape, and other brutal sex acts. To understand the shapes science has taken in Uganda, I first examine the dueling dynamics of the ex-gay and gay rights movements as transnational advocacy networks, since they have facilitated global flows of knowledge about homosexuality and sexual orientation more broadly.

Opposing Transnational Advocacy Networks

Some have characterized moral conflicts over homosexuality around the world as "exports" from the West, often with one side or the other of the U.S. "culture wars" to blame. A so-called Gay International, exemplified by global gay rights groups such as the International Gay and Lesbian Human Rights Commission based in the United States, draws on essentialist ideas about gay identity to call for the rescue of naturally occurring gay and lesbian populations abroad through human rights advocacy. This has led to the attempted exportation of a homo-/heterosexual binary from the West to other contexts around the world where such distinct binaries did not exist. Cultures in the "non-West," which have frequently included some forms of fluid same-sex homoerotic behavior without identification, are forced to impose a gay/straight binary through neo-colonialist human rights law. Thus, one could argue that global gay rights advocacy is to blame for anti-gay nationalist reactions and the harsh imposition of a strict heterosexuality in many countries around the world. "In undertaking this universalizing project," Joseph Massad has stated, "the Gay International ultimately makes itself feel better about a world it forces to share its identifications. Its missionary achievement, however, will be the creation not of a *queer* planet but rather a *straight* one."[19] From Massad's perspective, anti-gay backlash around the world is less about a morality-based condemnation of same-sex sexual behavior and more about opposing the imposition of an imperialist model of modern sexual identity categories tied to an apparatus of rights. While there is some truth to this perspective, it ignores the harsh historical context in which gay rights discourses have emerged, as a reaction to medicalization and forced treatment—a relationship I have explored in this book.

Another version of "culture war" export portrays the religious right in the United States as predominantly responsible for orchestrating homophobia abroad. In addition to media coverage of the links between U.S. ex-gay leaders and the Anti-Homosexuality Bill, journalist Jeff Sharlet has written about the ties between Ugandan member of Parliament David Bahati, the sponsor of the bill, and the "The Family," a secretive evangelical Christian organization composed of policy makers in Washington, D.C., who share a fundamentalist Christian ideology and pull strings around the world.[20] Documentaries such as *Missionaries of Hate* and *God Loves Uganda* further this narrative, portraying Uganda as extremely homophobic and corrupted by Western missionaries, in contrast to an allegedly tolerant and enlightened West.[21] From this perspective, Ugandans are primarily puppets of Western right-wing financing and influence. And there may be some truth to this assessment as well. Scott Lively has even taken credit for inspiring the sentiment behind the recent Russian anti-gay laws, as he claims he encouraged the pursuit of such legislation during his speaking tour of fifty cities in the former Soviet Union.[22] Such views, however, certainly disregard the levels of anti-LGBT sentiment within Western countries and understate the capacity to resist that local sexual minority activists have developed.

Moreover, all these claims of "culture war exporting" demonstrate a misunderstanding of the capacity of people in Uganda to formulate their own perspectives, to draw on available cultural ideas floating around the world, and to accept, develop, and/or resist them. Pastor Martin Ssempa, religious leader of the anti-homosexuality movement in Uganda, has alleged that portrayals of Ugandans as puppets of the West are racist.[23] In an interview, Bahati responded to the idea that Westerners inspired the Anti-Homosexuality Bill:

> It's not only not true, but it's also very insulting. . . . If one suggested for Ugandans to do something good for their country they have got to get it from somewhere, we live in a global world. We share knowledge and share experiences, but I think we know what's good for the children of Africa and what's good for Uganda, so therefore it's not true. While it's true that we have friends in the U.S., I don't think that we do what they do. We relate around the blood of Jesus.[24]

Law professor Sylvia Tamale, who has been a leading supporter of LGBT rights in the country, agreed: "This is one rare occasion when I agree with Ssempa. It is true that evangelical groups from abroad have an influence, and that they are financially supporting the homophobia movement. It is no coincidence that they had that conference in March and the bill was tabled in October. But they found fertile ground in Africa."[25] Nonetheless, both the anti-homosexuality and pro-LGBT movements within Uganda have sought to undermine their opposition by declaring the other to be corrupted by Western influence.

Rather than looking at flows of ideas as one-directional exports, I study both the LGBT and anti-homosexuality movements as "transnational advocacy networks." Such networks involve complex linkages of actors with imperfectly aligning interests. Transnational advocacy networks are organizational forms centered on principled ideas and values that blur boundaries between "a state's relations with its own nationals and the recourse both citizens and states have to the international system."[26] These networks share knowledge and resources, and to promote a principled cause, they must be flexible in their tactics. Typically, there will be bidirectional flows of funds, services, and training between charitable foundations and nongovernmental organizations. The range of actors in the network may include NGOs, local social movements, foundations, media, churches, and governmental sectors.[27] In the case of the anti-gay transnational network, the anti-homosexuality movement in Uganda has drawn on financial and intellectual resources from evangelical Christians in the United States. The pro-gay transnational advocacy network encompasses local LGBT activist groups, including Sexual Minorities Uganda (SMUG) and the lesbian organization Freedom and

Roam, also with links to international human rights organizations and global LGBT activist groups, some of which provide funding.

Global transnational activism involves the development of collective action frames that are resonant with constituencies across national borders and cultures. This process of "global framing" takes what are traditionally seen as local issues and connects them to a broader concern on an international scale. Activists may broaden their network through "frame bridging," that is, connecting issues so that they are seen as part of a common cause.[28] Gay rights activists have deployed global framing by asserting that a population of LGBT persons live in all nations and share an interest in survival; activists have utilized frame bridging by connecting these concerns to a broader human rights framework. Anti-homosexuality activists, rooted in the ideology of evangelical Christianity, have also employed global framing by connecting their concerns to a broader struggle for human salvation that transcends national borders. By connecting homosexuality to Western imperialism, African anti-homosexuality groups bridge their fight with larger concerns about Pan-African ethnicity and local nationalisms. Although solidarities may exist between the local anti-homosexuality movement and evangelical groups abroad, the intricacies of local needs require the development of particular ideas and tactics.[29] In this sense, sexual cultures and political activism in local context may blend ideas from abroad with local tradition and ideas, in the process producing forms of sexual and political "hybridity." In Uganda I am interested not only in the transnational links made by ex-gay and gay activists, but also in the specificities of the local meanings of homosexuality, reorientation, and political activism.

Fertile Ground for Anti-Homosexuality Views

Many critics of Ugandan president Yoweri Museveni allege that his opposition to homosexuality is a form of scapegoating, intended to deflect attention away from problems of poverty and his semiauthoritarian leadership. President Museveni rose to power in 1986 as leader of the National Resistance Army after a chaotic time, toppling the socialist regime of Milton Obote. His government instituted a one-party system, but was perceived as a beacon of hope moving toward democracy. He brought numerous factions together, and under his leadership there have been decreases in poverty and improved status of women, including increased numbers of women in the legislature. By 2005 maintaining democratic legitimacy required instituting multiple parties, and Museveni's administration became a patronage system. In part, Museveni's legitimacy as ruler has derived from his fights against a number of insurgencies, most notably the Lord's Resistance Army led by Joseph Kony, accused of many atrocities against children and others.[30] Museveni has also vowed to stop al-Shabaab, an Islamic extremist group based in Somalia responsible for attacks against civilians in 2010 in Kampala. But given that Museveni seized power in a civil war, leaving office could mean exile or other threats for him. Unlike democratic governments, under which leaders exit office with generally peaceful ceremony, it is not as easy in a semiauthoritarian regime. Museveni, who has been in power for over two decades, has been accused of rigging elections. The need to quell opposition, especially to prevent Arab Spring–style uprisings, means human rights are precarious and can be revoked quite arbitrarily. When I was in Uganda during 2011, opposition leader Kizza Besigye had been placed under house arrest. Crackdowns on protest movements have been harsh. In these circumstances, homosexuals may indeed make convenient scapegoats.

Many Ugandans describe the national culture as maintaining strong taboos against the open expression of all forms of sexuality in general. Alluding to the sexual openness of the West more generally, President Museveni has claimed that he would lose his position in office if he were to kiss his wife openly in public. The Ministry of Health report described a threatening fad of "sexual exhibitionism" that is "alien and repugnant to most African cultures." Along with strong taboos, sexuality carries with it an aura of scandal. On street corners throughout the capital city of Kampala, tabloid newspapers such as *Red Pepper* routinely report sexual escapades of many kinds. Along with the Anti-Homosexuality Act, leaders have also passed legislation banning women from wearing miniskirts and showing cleavage, and have outlawed pornography. A headline in the *Guardian* during the period when Museveni was considering his signature on the Anti-Homosexuality Bill read "Given Uganda's Homophobia, Why Does It Lead the Way in Googling Gay Porn?" The British paper reported that according to Google's search statistics, Uganda is one of the top countries where gay pornography is sought online.[31] These kinds of contradictions between repression and fascination characterize how Uganda's attitudes toward homosexuality have taken shape.

Culturally, the influence of evangelical Christianity, and of Pentecostal charismatic churches in particular, has grown steadily in recent years, also contributing to an overall anti-gay and generally sex-negative climate. Christian missionary work in the country had been primarily conducted by more moderate denominations, yet much of the nation has been undergoing an evangelical revival. Smaller churches known as *biwempe* were the first wave of this movement among the poor, and new megachurches have been built with an influx of funds beginning in 2005. These churches emphasize youth as a sign of hope and renewal for the country, especially given the HIV/AIDS epidemic, which is blamed on older generations. This religious revival is unusual in Uganda because it has attracted members of the middle class and major politicians.[32] The new Ugandan Pentecostalism has also emphasized nationalism.[33]

Explaining links between the United States and this religious revival, a report by Kapya Kaoma, an Anglican priest from Zambia working with the Boston-based think tank Political Research Associates, illuminates connections among revival churches in the United States and church leaders in Uganda.[34] Several churches, including the worldwide Anglican Communion, have undergone schisms over the ordination of gay priests. In these conflicts, African religious leaders have overwhelmingly united with conservative bishops from the United States in opposition to homosexuality, and attendees at an international Anglican conference in 1998 voted that homosexuality is not compatible with scripture. Seemingly in exchange for this political support, conservative churches in the United States have sent large sums of money to African counterparts, convincing many that mainline churches are on the wrong religious path. According to Rev. Aaron Mesigye, the provincial secretary in the Ugandan Archbishop's office, U.S. conservative churches had been "contributing towards the remuneration of salaries of the provincial staff since 1998. . . . American conservatives provide money to Africans not as donors but as development partners in mission."[35] In addition to independent donors, the U.S. federal government also funds conservative African churches through the President's Emergency Plan for AIDS Relief (PEPFAR), which provides money for abstinence programs.

Following the devastation wrought by HIV/AIDS beginning in the 1980s, many social conservatives around the world looked to Uganda as a model nation for prevention. Behavior modification programs discouraged multiple sex partners through a "zero grazing" policy.[36] When the U.S. PEPFAR program was implemented in 2004 under George W. Bush, Uganda was a major aid recipient, including funding for antiretroviral treatments. Funds were funneled into churches and faith-based organizations to implement HIV prevention strategies defined by abstinence outside marriage and being faithful within. According to reports in 2006, new infections had shifted toward older demographic groups, prompting the belief that older people are morally lost. It was thought, therefore, that a revolution among young people would build the future. While initial HIV prevention efforts were implemented under the ABC (abstinence, be faithful, use condoms) model, condoms were eventually dropped because Museveni and his Pentecostal wife, Janet, opposed condom promotion. As founder of the Ugandan Youth Forum, Janet Museveni has been particularly prominent in advocating abstinence among youth in the country.[37] PEPFAR policies implemented under the Bush administration encouraged this shift, and condom advertising disappeared. New campaigns emphasized abstinence and behavioral change. Advertisements throughout the capital, present when I visited in 2011, encouraged people to "get off the sexual network." However, by 2012 HIV rates were on the rise, especially among married older couples, threatening Uganda's success story.[38] Uganda became the only country receiving PEPFAR funds where HIV rates were increasing. Heightened concerns about HIV made this a particularly salient part of the debate over homosexuality, with proponents of the bill pointing to HIV risks associated with same-sex sexual behaviors and opponents claiming the bill would make HIV prevention more difficult.

Under circumstances where homosexuality is considered an abhorrent sin, it has been almost impossible for people in Uganda to publicly identify as gay. Although there are LGBT support groups in urban areas and this network is growing, local gay activist Frank Mugisha described how there are people in villages who maintain a veneer of ambiguity about their personal lives:

> You go to a place here in Uganda, and they will tell you that a man never gets married. He doesn't have kids. He could be a homosexual, or he could be impotent. It could be his lifestyle. People ignore the person. . . . So if someone built their own house by the family house and he is having affairs with guys, people would ignore him. They wouldn't do anything like that. But if you come from a lower family, you are thrown out of the village.[39]

Similarly, one Ugandan psychiatrist I spoke with also described some people in villages living asexual lives that may involve the suppression of same-sex behavior and desire:

> I was of the strong view that homosexuality does not exist in Africa, until somebody asked me a question and said, are you sure everybody is married in Africa? I said no. He said, have you ever thought about those people who have no reason for not being married but they are not married, and I am sure there are people like that in every African village. It was certainly true in my village. So the question is what about those people? And I want to leave it to you that maybe some of them might be homosexual but not expressing it. So not with the opposite

sex at all. But they're not enemies of anybody, and they're not actually caught going with people of the same sex. You want to call them asexual? I don't know.[40]

These descriptions seem to support Joseph Massad's assertion that the growth of the Gay International and the imposition of a sexual identity system abroad has led in developing countries to a tiered system of sexual expressions for people with attractions to members of the same sex; those with ties to the West, who are often from the middle class, have the ability to resist anti-gay nationalism and to enact a gay identity, whereas people in lower classes and nonurban areas are most likely to experience persecution and unfulfilled desires.[41] Female homosexuality is not accepted in Uganda, but it is seen as less threatening than male homosexuality, which is the primary target of moral opprobrium. South African scholar Kopano Ratele attributes this disparity to a widespread hegemonic masculinity ideal involving the demonstration of sexual prowess through large numbers of female sexual partners and their level of physical attractiveness, common across many African countries.[42] Despite this need to demonstrate prowess, Uganda's culture makes it difficult to talk about sexuality openly, except in the form of scandal. Together, these political and cultural forces have provided fertile ground for the successes of the anti-homosexuality movement in Uganda, enabling it to define homosexuality as an unwanted behavior in the popular imagination.

The Ugandan Movement against Homosexuality

In February 2010, thousands of people poured into the streets in the small town of Jinja, just outside the capital city of Kampala, to engage in the "Million Man March against Homosexuality." Holding signs with slogans such as "Sodomy Is Evil," "Homosexual Repent," and "Parliament Unite against Sodomy," protesters called for an end to homosexuality in the country and chastised U.S. president Barack Obama as the face of Western influence promoting gay rights. Pastor Martin Ssempa, who organized the march, spoke during the rally, conflating homosexuality with child molestation:

> People keep saying yes homosexuals can change, yes we can make a law that protects our children and we have also asked a simple question: if you do not want the death penalty for pedophiles, what punishment do you want? Otherwise are you a defender of pedophiles? Or are you a protector of children?[43]

One protester said in a media interview, "I have a verse in the Bible in Leviticus 20 verse 13, it says that homosexuals should be put to death . . . yes." In response to threats of withholding foreign aid, one placard read, "Obama to hell with your aid!" Pastor Ssempa, who had been on television claiming that Uganda's reserves of oil and uranium can be its vehicle to financial power and independence, claimed at the rally, "Obama, even if you do not give us money for medicine for our people, to hell with that money, we would rather die but die in dignity." Voicing a nationalist theme, he added, "This is Uganda and we also have our rights just like the Americans have theirs. We decide for ourselves what is good for us. So these leaders should leave us alone to make our own legislations that are good for us."

According to Sylvia Tamale, dean of the Makerere University School of Law, this wave of strong anti-homosexuality sentiment was not the first, as there had been a few over the past decade. Museveni had ordered the arrest and prosecution of all homosexuals in 1999 when it was reported that a gay wedding had been performed. In February 2003, a new outpouring erupted after Tamale publicly recommended the Equal Opportunities Commission recognize gay rights, and she sustained many personal attacks in the media. The most recent wave occurred prior to the filing of the bill, and much of this has been a response to the 2008 attempt by delegates from France and the Netherlands to advance gay rights with the UN General Assembly. After the Family Life Network conference in March 2009, the local press reported that UNICEF was distributing sex education books called *The Teenagers Toolkit* in schools without the approval of the Ugandan Ministry of Education. Opponents of the books claimed they promoted homosexuality as "normal," effectively recruiting youth into the lifestyle.[44]

Once the Anti-Homosexuality Bill was filed, anti-gay intimidation and violence escalated. The nascent tabloid newspaper *Rolling Stone,* along with others such as *Red Pepper,* published names, photographs, and contact information for gays and lesbians with titles such as "100 Pictures of Uganda's Top Homos Leak." *Rolling Stone* included the words "Hang Them" on the cover of one issue. Editor Giles Muhame claimed that he included these words not to incite violence but rather to reflect the widespread belief that gays should be put to death through the legal process.[45] The images on the "Hang Them" cover were of gay activist David Kato, then director of Sexual Minorities Uganda, and Bishop Christopher Ssenyonjo, a pro-LGBT Anglican pastor who is heterosexual but has been vilified as homosexual. Kato and other activists filed a grievance against *Rolling Stone* for violating human rights and won a judgment from the

One of several tabloid newspapers that targeted gays with names and addresses. Giles Muhame, editor of *Rolling Stone* (no connection to the U.S.-based music magazine), claimed that the words "Hang Them" on the cover were not a threat but rather echoed a widely held sentiment. On the cover of this issue, published October 9, 2010, are activist David Kato and Bishop Christopher Ssenyonjo. Benedict Desrus/Sipa Press/uganda_rolling_stone. 024/1011292230 (Sipa via AP Images).

Ugandan Judiciary ordering the tabloid to stop publishing names, effectively leading to the demise of the newspaper. Although this ruling seemed like a victory for the gay rights movement, Kato was murdered by an intruder in his home in January 2011.

A major leader of the anti-homosexuality cause, Pastor Ssempa is founder of Makerere Community Church, and he conducts Sunday services in a classroom at Makerere University in Kampala.[46] For many years, he has held Saturday night poolside abstinence rallies on campus. In his speeches and press conferences, he has equated homosexuality with child rape, and has often reduced homosexuality to men's acts of anal sex that have pernicious physical consequences. *Homosexuality* has become a code term for men forcibly penetrating rectums, especially those of the innocent, behavior allegedly leading to incontinence and other disorders in addition to HIV infection. In a press conference featured in the British documentary *Vanguard: Missionaries of Hate,* Ssempa, flanked by Christian and Muslim leaders, stated:

I've taken time to do a little research on what it is homosexuals do in the privacy of their own bedroom. One of the things they do is anal licking, where man's anus is licked like this [licking fist] by the other person, like ice cream, and then what happens, even poopoo comes out, the other one poopoos out, and then they eat the poopoo. The other one they do is they have a sex practice called fisting, where they insert their hand into the other man's [anus] . . . all the way and it is so painful they have to take drugs, but they enjoy it.[47]

Ssempa then proceeded to show pornographic images allegedly depicting these practices. He also demonstrated fisting, a fetish practice by no means limited to or practiced by a majority of gay men. Pornography depicting white men engaged in this practice illustrates the racial meaning of homosexuality for Ssempa, as a white Western import inflicted on black Africans. He stated, "We do not want this sickness. It is sick and therefore deviant, and we don't want it." The documentary also included a sequence with Ssempa showing gay porn images in a slide show during a church service, claiming that homosexuality involves partners smearing feces on each other's face, as well as eating feces. He then stated, "As Africans, we want to ask Barack Obama to explain to us, is this what he wants to bring to Africa as a human right, to eat the poopoo of our children?"; the congregation roared out in response, "No!" Such tactics dehumanize gays to nothing more than these actions. Ssempa has maintained that homosexual practices are culturally un-African, comparable to "bringing a pig in a mosque in Saudi Arabia."[48] During my trip to Uganda, I tried to interview Pastor Ssempa, attending his church service and going down to his church office, but he declined because he felt the British documentary cast him in a "negative light," despite his willingness to be open. Nonetheless, the anti-homosexuality movement in Uganda, largely led by the Family Life Network, Pastor Ssempa, and David Bahati, has contributed to a national culture in which homosexuality is understood to incorporate child rape, result in anal incontinence, and may even be a form of genocide against Africans through the Western promotion of nonreproductive sexuality, including the recruitment of children.

These waves of anti-homosexuality activism, which predate the filing of the bill, challenge the idea that U.S. activists merely came in to the country in 2009 and inspired it. The ties between the Family Life Network and Pastor Scott Lively also extend back much earlier than the 2009 conference, to March 2002, when Stephen Langa, director of FLN, organized a conference against pornography and obscenity. According

At a press conference on January 15, 2010, flanked by Christian and Muslim leaders, Pastor Martin Ssempa shows gay pornography and demonstrates fisting, one of the sexual activities he claimed Barack Obama was forcing on the childen of Uganda. Notable here is the whiteness of the porn actors: homosexuality is framed as an import from the West and un-African. Benedict Desrus/ Sipa Press/ uganda_bill.082/1105311844 (Sipa via AP Images).

to one FLN member, at that time "pornography was being used to induce homosexual experience; a very large outpouring of pornography in our schools. It was being used as a recruitment tool in our schools to sexual deviance."[49] As a moral entrepreneurship organization, FLN includes the Uganda National Parents Network and works in coordination with other family values groups such as the Uganda Coalition for Moral Values. The organization claims to be a secular lobbying group, although it works in conjunction with religious organizations. It is not distinctly Christian because FLN members must also reach out to the local Muslim minority. Lively spoke at their 2002 conference, later describing Langa as "the country's leading champion of the family and Uganda's equivalent of Dr. James Dobson." Together Lively and Langa then made several media appearances that year on state-run television and radio and conducted an abstinence seminar with students. Lively also appeared on a talk show, speaking about the dangers of homosexuality and plugging his book *The Pink Swastika.* In a report chronicling the trip, Lively described the most pertinent dangers facing Ugandan society, including a Western leftist agenda to make the nation accept "perversion and promiscuity" by making aid dependent on the promotion of "safe sex" and condom use. The dangers also included HIV/AIDS, which would spread if Ugandans were to accept "safe sex."[50]

Rather than being cut of whole cloth in 2009, the Anti-Homosexuality Bill was actually intended to extend earlier legislation. In 2007 Parliament passed a bill calling for the death penalty for the crime of "aggravated defilement," defined as having sex with a person under the age of fourteen when HIV positive. According to Ssempa, the death penalty provision of the 2009 bill was intended, in part, to extend the "aggravated defilement" law to homosexual acts. "We have a problem," he said, "of men who have HIV/AIDS and women who have HIV/AIDS who are told by sorcerers that if they want to get to get healed from HIV/AIDS then they must rape a virgin. This demonic, deviant, and evil disgusting activity is practiced in Uganda, Tanzania, Zambia, even South Africa."[51] Supporting this claim, Topher Mugumya of the African Network for the Prevention and Protection against Child Abuse and Neglect argued in a UN news story, "'About 10,000 cases of defilement are reported to the police every year; this [proposed law] is a welcome development."[52] However, it is unclear why a new bill was necessary given that "aggravated defilement" law covered sexual relations by any adult with anyone under the age of fourteen. Nonetheless, linking the Anti-Homosexuality Bill to this earlier legislation further characterized homosexuality as encompassing child rape.

Although anti-homosexuality proponents have frequently stated that homosexuality is a "learned behavior that can be unlearned," the term *ex-gay* is relatively new in Uganda, according to the gay activists with whom I spoke. While the conference in Kampala was an important moment for importing ideas, the global ex-gay movement has been minimally involved in the country. "Exodus Global Alliance," an organization spun off but separate from U.S.-based Exodus International, has no office there, and NARTH's global initiative, the International Federation for Therapeutic Choice, remains small. Thus, there is in Uganda no ex-gay movement with group ministry and personal testimony like in the United States. According to members of the FLN, it would be too shameful for "ex-gays" to come together in the country to share such transformative experiences. Instead, individual ex-gays are often placed before television cameras or before crowds to talk about how they were recruited into the practice of homosexuality. One pastoral counselor I met at FLN headquarters claimed that homosexuality could be managed in one-on-one therapy, but never in a group setting. In a press conference, Ssempa introduced "Sandra," who as a young schoolgirl was allegedly recruited into homosexuality at the age of sixteen, after living with three lesbians. Sandra reported that members of a gay activist group gave her money and gifts (a laptop and an iPod) to explore lesbianism.[53]

The most influential case of individual ex-gay testimony in Uganda has been that of then-twenty-six-year-old George Oundo, a sex worker who previously went by the name Georgina, and testified on national television station NTV in 2009 about his "homosexual recruitment" practices with youth:

> I was a very strong LGBT activist. The name Georgina is known worldwide. . . . I was initiated into homosexuality when I was twelve years of age through friends. . . . We used books, but also we used different practical things. Especially when lesbians are teaching about sex, you can use water-based lubricant, then you get a dental dam. . . . So when we get one person in a school or two and we initiate them into homosexuality, that is finished. I recruited many, many boys in Jinja because my formal school was in Jinja. The whole school will understand what is homosexuality. We teach these boys and we give them these lubricants, and they go with these lubricants in schools. . . . These lubricants are brought into Uganda by an international organization.[54]

Oundo then described how he would infiltrate schools and approach young boys to recruit them by getting close to and touching them. He has since returned to a gay lifestyle and has been up front about the money he received from Ssempa for making these statements. Yet Pastor Ssempa still maintains this testimony on his personal blog.[55] One gay activist claimed in 2011 that at that time Oundo was no longer welcome in the LGBT community because of the damage he had caused.[56] Thus there is no concept of "ex-ex-gays" in this context. The story of George/ Georgina Oundo also reveals how the label "homosexuality" can encompass more gender nonconformity in Uganda.

As members of the anti-homosexuality movement have successfully linked homosexuality to a dangerous set of vices in the popular imagination, advocates prescribe behavioral management for homosexuals. A representative of the Family Life Network elaborated further:

> Our position on that is people choose their sexual behavior and that is very important. Whatever orientation it is, they choose it, and that is important for them to understand. Point number one: people choose their behavior. They can choose to change, but they can choose not to change. They are people, not animals. . . . [When saying their desires cannot change], you are devaluing them. It is like an addiction

to marijuana. That is so demeaning when you think about it from any angle. So we believe in the value of the human mind.[57]

Calling the brain "the biggest sex organ," this representative of FLN responded to the question of how we know whether a person has been cured of homosexuality:

When you throw your pesticide onto the weeds how do you know the weeds are gone? You look. When you look on the surface they are gone. Now the biggest part is underneath that you live with for the rest of your life. They pop up when you least expect them.[58]

He then compared the bill's pressure to overcome homosexuality with giving a jump start to a car in winter, and compared the process of leaving the vice behind to a musician's overcoming a case of stage fright. In this regard, homosexual desire is an unimportant phenomenon to be devalued and ignored, even if it never changes; what is most important is to suppress homosexual behavior.

The malleability of sexual behavior has been frequently invoked by the movement, but not always within a scientific frame. When asked in a personal interview in 2011 about the scientific evidence used to support the bill, Bahati answered:

I think that homosexuality is wrong both in science, in law, and in divinity, because it is very clear from the Bible, from the Koran, that it is evil. It has also been proved that it is not inborn, it is learned, and can be unlearned and it is a behavior like drug addiction that can be learned and it can be unlearned. So that's it. And also there is some conclusive research, scientific research, that points to the fact that if you are homosexual you are prone to getting HIV/AIDS three times more than an ordinary person because of the friction in the anal organs and stuff like that. If actually it was inborn probably it would have spread evenly across the world.[59]

When asked which of the scientific claims was most important, Bahati pointed to the "health aspects" of HIV because there "was no controversy on that." In a society where HIV rates were on the rise, and where attempts to "cleanse" HIV through sex with virgins allegedly occurred, science on HIV could be mobilized to promote the legislation in 2011. In the public, the science of sexual orientation change took a backseat to the morality of theology, since deliverance from evil did not require scientific proof that it was possible.

A primary accomplishment of the anti-homosexuality movement in

Uganda has been the cultural definition of homosexuality as pernicious sex acts inflicted on children and other vulnerable populations. This has created immense interest in reorientation ideas, especially in terms of considering homosexuality as a behavior to be controlled. It has also contributed to an immensely harsh climate for anyone supporting the idea that homosexuality is a normal variant not in need of modification. Such ideas have been met with cultural ostracism within the media and within the public more generally, often with the threat of violence. At the same time, NARTH's reorientation concepts that were raised in the FLN conference were taken up by the National Association of Social Workers of Uganda (NASWU).

Social Work Brings NARTH to Parliament

Also in attendance at the 2009 FLN conference was NASWU president Charles Tuhaise, whose job also entails conducting research for the Ugandan Parliament (in whose building he has a private office). Tuhaise has been the leader of a thriving profession in Uganda with a long history of working with the state. In an interview in his office, he described a bit of the profession's history:

> Social work training began around 1954 in Uganda. It started at the level of diploma and certificate training, basically to provide the workers in government offices that deal with social welfare. So degree-level training started in the 1960s, around maybe 1963; that's when Makerere University started offering degrees in social work. So since then every year they have people graduating in social work. The numbers are now much bigger because there are now more than thirty universities, so the numbers of social workers have gone up. All these universities teach social work.[60]

Of the major mental health fields, social work has the highest numbers of practitioners and is the most integrated into the machinery of state policy, especially on the issue of homosexuality. As a service field, social work has generally had a complex relationship with science, and for outlining any course of action has often relied on pragmatic rules of thumb derived from experience rather than established scientific fact. The International Federation of Social Workers emphasizes human rights, and the use of "theories of human behavior and social systems" as a basis for its policies.[61] In contrast, NASWU claims that social work "is a profession that deals with the study of human life and human relationships and effective prevention, solutions and management of social problems to promote optimum well-being and social harmony."[62] NASWU's vague declaration of a broad knowledge basis, "the study of human life," is flexible enough to encompass multiple knowledge systems beyond science, including theology.

At the 2009 Family Life Network conference, Tuhaise provided participants with an overview of the legal status of homosexuality in Uganda. Laws against homosexuality were established during the period of British colonial rule. Nonetheless, Tuhaise claimed, the law did not fully deal with the magnitude of the threats posed by the "homosexual agenda," because the penal code vaguely called for the punishment of "carnal knowledge against the order of nature." This language was outdated and could be challenged in court, so a new law was needed.[63] In our interview, Tuhaise expressed the view that homosexuality poses three primary problems for society. First, because it is justified on the basis of accommodating sexual urges, it might open the door to permitting other deviant sexual expressions like pedophilia and bestiality. Second, because society is interconnected, "like an organism," young people may be influenced to engage in homosexuality just by observing that homosexuals are accepted. Third, allowing male homosexuality poses an extreme HIV risk. On this point, he claimed:

> In our opinion, HIV/AIDS should not be used as an excuse to affirm homosexuality as a lifestyle, as a normal lifestyle in the community. We have a huge challenge of HIV/AIDS, but we know that if homosexual behavior is normalized, we shall have a bigger problem, from what we have experienced over the last twenty years. If this behavior is normalized and practice increases, we shall have a worsening problem of HIV/AIDS, even if we had the best interventions.[64]

Tuhaise blended two strains of ideas in these analyses. He sees society as a coherent organism that social workers must help to function more harmoniously. He also sees behavior therapy as a basis for individual behavior modification to pursue these ends. Homosexuality is a learned behavior that must be unlearned for the harmonious functioning of society, he asserted.

In line with NARTH reasoning, NASWU represents itself as a purveyor of objective information that it provides as a public service to society, because professional perspectives supporting gays are corrupted by political influences. The document NASWU produced for Parliament in support of the Anti-Homosexuality Bill is labeled a "statement" rather than a "position statement," unlike the approach of professional associations in the United States and abroad, in order merely to "provide much needed information on this subject."[65] Tuhaise articulated a commitment to impartiality:

> Our position is to put out information as people who have studied and understand the social vector. We put out information for people to study and decide. We are always worried [about] taking positions, taking sides, although when something comes out really clearly that we need to inform the public about, we will not be reluctant. We will do that if we think the public needs to know something. As you can see in the statement, we put out information, but we come out with the advice on what we think should be done.[66]

Tuhaise claimed that the commitment to neutrality was so strong, the NASWU transcended the kinds of politics that bedeviled the United States:

> I've been looking at information from the United States and I think that the problem there, the reason why we have all these young people committing suicide and so on, is because there are two sides of the issue. There are those who say you can overcome homosexuality and live a normal sexual life, and then there is this camp that says no, you don't need to do that, you can live a gay life and lead a normal gay life. So many people are caught in between. Many young people look at these two warring camps, and the psychological problems involved really have to do with the conflict when there are these two warring camps. . . . So that is why there is so much tension. In our opinion, that's why we need to have accurate information. We need to have proper information on what is proper, what is possible and so on. And we really avoid this. It shouldn't be a political issue where you have two warring camps.[67]

While Tuhaise expressed sympathy for people caught in the middle, his organization's position against homosexuality seemed clearly to place it within one of the "camps."

The statement was composed by an executive committee that Tuhaise explained was elected by NASWU members. The organization responded to numerous phone calls from within Uganda and around the world asking for information, he said, and the group also consulted with the Uganda National Parents Network and Uganda Coalition for Moral Values, both part of FLN. Describing the process, he claimed:

> We looked at many professional organizations including medical-based organizations, and many of them have taken positions which we think

overlook basic facts which we think the public should know, and we don't think that it is professional for certain organizations to be influenced by some of the activists. . . . We believe there has been some level of influence by the political side of some of the issues, to see that even professional organizations come out in support of certain positions and so on, but we think as professional organizations we have a responsibility to the public to ensure that they have accurate information.[68]

The NASWU statement claimed that science from the United States supporting homosexuality cannot be trusted, because it has been corrupted by gay activists beginning with the work of Alfred Kinsey. Citing the work of Judith Reisman, an author from the United States who has written extensively against Kinsey, the statement alleged that Kinsey exaggerated the amount of homosexuality in U.S. society, invented the term *sexual orientation* to describe homosexuality and bisexuality, and made them equivalent to heterosexuality in order to "create political clout for the homosexual movement."

Blending concepts from NARTH and evangelical Christianity, the statement then argued that the social work profession must intervene in cases of homosexuality. Citing NARTH to the effect that "hundreds of people have overcome homosexuality and achieved appropriate social functioning," NASWU called on social workers to help clients with same-sex attractions to gradually achieve heterosexuality. Primarily couching sexual development in behaviorist terms, the statement claimed that human behavior is conditioned by "reinforcers" such as orgasm and is socially learned from others, so people must abstain from homosexual behavior. However, sexual behavior also has a spiritual dimension that social workers should attend to. Demonic forces can drive a person's behavior beyond his or her control, or be linked to behavior despite the seeming existence of control. Jesus cast out demons in a person whom psychologists today would diagnose with "schizophrenia." Furthermore, Mary Magdalene's prostitution was demonic until she encountered Jesus. Thus, "Social Work training should include the study of the spiritual dimension of life and how it may be applied to promote well-being and social functioning."[69] The statement claimed that human behavior exists at the level of the soul, consisting of the mind, will, and emotions. The mind must be used to understand behavior so that the will can be cultivated to rein in emotions. In sum, rather than homosexuality being a human right, NASWU claimed that clients have a right to information on homosexuality, cast as a form of demonic possession that can be healed through behavior therapies.

Confident that homosexuality could be treated in all cases once proper motivation has been achieved, Tuhaise argued:

> Even if a person has been a practicing homosexual, they can actually eventually change and behave differently, it's a process. Human behavior does not change overnight. It really involves commitment and motivation from the person involved. That's why in counseling we have what is called client therapy determination. The person who seeks behavioral change must be committed. Otherwise it is unlikely that they will achieve that outcome. So there has to be an understanding about how human behavior works. Human behavior certainly does change. As to whether it should be, say a person who has feelings for the same sex can change to have feelings for the opposite sex, there is information that it has happened in some situations. But as I said, for that to happen there has to be all these dynamics. Personal motivation—the client who is involved they must really want to do this. That means they have not been pushed by their parents—that you must change or we will throw you out of our house—if it is a teenager or what. But once there is personal motivation, people almost [always] change, like a person who has been an alcoholic, and they say they do not want to be an alcoholic.[70]

Thus, the proper motivation included the internalization of the idea that homosexuality must be eliminated. The NASWU statement called for reporting exemptions for social workers, and Tuhaise also described how the association had hopes for expanding the counseling professions in Uganda:

> We still have to organize the behavioral professions like counseling, social work, psychiatry, psychology. Right now many universities are training in those areas, but we have to organize the practice. The practice area is not yet very well organized. We need laws that can properly provide on how people can provide professional services in this area. Matter of fact, for social work we are now working on a draft bill which we hope will be able to establish how social workers can offer their services. How they can be regulated, to establish a council on social welfare, which will ensure that practitioners . . . have an institution to see how they can do this work.[71]

Moreover, he claimed that therapeutic success should be measured in terms of gradual improvement in sexual behavior: no longer seeking out same-sex sexual encounters.

Extending the cultural definition of homosexuality to include pathology and child rape, the NASWU statement calls for supporting the Anti-Homosexuality Bill because of public health risks and child protection. It notes that the U.S. Food and Drug Administration prohibits blood donation by men participating in same-sex sexual behavior because of public health risks of HIV and hepatitis transmission. Additional risks cited include fecal incontinence, rectal and oral gonorrhea, and (again based on NARTH) general risks to physical and psychological health; health risks are not attributed to living in an anti-gay society but rather to the condition itself. The document calls for the passage of the Anti-Homosexuality Bill because of rampant child abuse, George Oundo's admissions of recruitment, and reports of UNICEF distributing a pro-gay sex education booklet. Given the growing strength of the global gay rights movement, NASWU argues that licensed professional counselors should be exempt from mandatory reporting requirements so that people will seek help.[72]

Importantly, a key element of the international intellectual opportunity structure that has made the NASWU statement possible has been the open policy of the International Federation of Social Workers, of which NASWU is a member. Tuhaise stated:

We are members of the International Federation of Social Workers, and being members, we came out with a position which was contrary to theirs. So when they asked us for our statement, which we provided them, and they did certainly say that they had a contrary view, and that they were going to put out their own position, which they did, they published their own statement. The good thing is that they respected our opinion. In their statement they did respect that countries are free. National associations are free to take their own position on those issues. So that was good.[73]

That IFSW policy statement, issued by then-president David N. Jones, claimed that the IFSW recognizes the "territorial integrity" of national social work associations. It went on to state that the IFSW ordinarily does not engage with such local matters, but the organization had to oppose the Anti-Homosexuality Bill on the basis of human rights and various treaties. The statement also asserted that child abuse is a serious issue, and IFSW would work with the NASWU and the Ugandan Parliament on that matter.[74] A second letter with similar language followed from IFSW president Gary Bailey following the passage of the bill on December 20, 2013.[75] Nonetheless, the IFSW's commitment to national integrity meant that NASWU maintained its status in the association as a member in good standing despite these differences.

The NASWU statement was presented to the Ugandan Parliament and became part of the official parliamentary record on the bill. In effect, the NASWU, with its close links to the anti-homosexuality movement, has been a key conduit for bringing NARTH research and concepts directly to Parliament, backed up by the professional expertise of social work in that country as a whole. The intellectual opportunity structure that facilitated this includes a close relationship between NASWU and the movement, the permissiveness of the IFSW, and a broader culture that makes the concepts of homosexuality used within the report acceptable to NASWU leaders. I now turn to the pro-LGBT movement and its connections to the global gay rights movement to explain how flows of science, accepted in the West, are rejected within this policy context.

Sexual Minorities Uganda

In the town of Entebbe, where the Uganda international airport is located near the shores of Lake Victoria, activists organized the first Gay Pride march and gathering in Ugandan history in the summer of 2012. Activist Frank Mugisha, director of Sexual Minorities Uganda (SMUG), called himself "Captain Pride" and wore a sailor suit with a sash. Some carried signs with slogans such as "African and Gay. Not a Choice," and some chanted "We are here" to counter the idea, often touted by the anti-homosexuality movement, that there are no gays in Africa. Hundreds turned out for the event, which was relatively peaceful until the police raided the gathering after the parade, suspecting a gay wedding was being performed.[76] Unlike Western media portraying Uganda as a place of suffering for gays, Ugandan LGBTI activists have taken pride in their creation of effective resistance and community support. Activist Val Kalende argued that the idea of desperation is often used by well-meaning Westerners but pits Ugandans against one another.[77] In alignment with the International Lesbian and Gay Association, the acronym used by sexual minority rights activists in Uganda includes an "I" for intersex: LGBTI. Uganda Beach Pride was held again in August 2013, while the Anti-Homosexuality Bill was pending, and again in 2014 after it passed and was later overruled by a Ugandan court.

Prior to the filing of the bill in 2009, sexual minority activism in Uganda existed primarily as a support network with connections to gay rights and human rights groups abroad. In 2003 Sylvia Tamale described a set of organizations, including Gay and Lesbian Alliance, Gay Uganda, Spectrum, Right Companion, Lesgabix, and Integrity, primarily acting

The third annual LGBTI Beach Pride was celebrated in August 2014 on the shores of Lake Victoria in Entebbe, Uganda. These celebrations occurred after the Anti-Homosexuality Act was overturned by a Ugandan court; appeals are still pending. AP Photo/Rebecca Vassie.

as support groups, with a handful of activists working to improve the status of the community. Integrity was started by activist David Kato but ceased operation following his death. In the early 2000s, homosexuality was already illegal, and the Internet provided a key means for people to form networks while maintaining public heterosexual personas.[78] The primary activist organization in recent years has been Sexual Minorities Uganda. In addition to public advocacy, SMUG coordinates a network of smaller chapters and additional groups across the country, including Freedom and Roam, a lesbian group, and Icebreakers Uganda, providing social support and resources for displaced persons. Because of the oppressive circumstances, members of these groups not only police a gay/straight binary but also tend to promote gender conformity in public places, although blurring gender boundaries may occur behind closed doors. Moreover, bisexual persons may be frowned upon. One activist cast doubts on whether a male sex worker who had sex with men would be part of the community, as not being authentically gay.

Given widespread narratives about the pernicious nature of homosexuals, a primary strategy of SMUG and other LGBTI activists has involved making personal connections and appearances to counteract the negative portrayals. Frank Mugisha explained:

In Uganda you can give someone a brochure, but you have to talk to them; otherwise they are going to use these brochures and materials for other things. . . . Our project here is talking to people. Speaking. Here in Uganda the issue has to be in people's face. If it's not in their face, they don't talk about it, they don't think about it. Otherwise it is an issue that, when it comes up, it is difficult to speak about it. If we talk about it everyday it becomes a little bit easier.[79]

When using this strategy, Mugisha says that he faces the challenge of convincing people that gay is not simply "white," and that black people can be gay and black simultaneously. Sylvia Tamale described this personal connection strategy as appealing to *ubuntu*, a term denoting "humaneness"—a concept that was important during the struggle against apartheid in South Africa. This form of activism involves demonstrating to others that LGBTI people are fellow human beings with experiences that are worthy of dignity and respect, rather than being dehumanized child molesters and vectors of disease. Ugandan AIDS activist Leonard Okello, who has consulted SMUG on this matter, given his work on confronting the stigmas against HIV-positive persons, told me:

I have told members of SMUG [to] keep hope alive. First you have got to build yourself into people of integrity. Anything that is attempted to be [said] about you, to undermine, or demean you, you should stand up against it. The way you interact, the way you behave. Any time you are involved in any public misconduct whatsoever, because you are gay, the case against you will be seen as bad. You need to be seen as people who are normal. When you do a job, do it well. Do your job well. So you provide a positive public face of who you are. So when you get to the next stage . . . nobody then uses your sexual orientation, tries to link it to something else. . . . It will take time, I know.[80]

Mugisha believed that through this bottom–up strategy of building trust, gay rights would eventually have to pass as a result of popular support. Although this was the prevailing domestic strategy when I visited, it had to be conducted carefully to protect activists. The office manager for Icebreakers Uganda described threatening phone calls he received at their unmarked facility whose whereabouts could only be known through word of mouth. The group has conducted seminars on how to tone down gender nonconformity. They use coded language like *church* to refer to a gay bar or the remote term *kuchu* to refer to LGBTI persons. Both SMUG and Icebreakers Uganda have had to move their headquarters periodically because of police raids.

Given its cultural prominence, religion has been a key venue in which activists have had to struggle to define the meaning of homosexuality for popular audiences. Bishop Christopher Ssenyonjo, who retired in 1998 and was excommunicated in 2001 for his LGBTI advocacy, has been a major leader on this front. He also has worked as a religious counselor, as an important referral for persons seeking some kind of support. His counseling and advocacy have been articulated primarily in theological and human rights registers. He and his son have both been accused of homosexuality although they do not identify as gay. In an interview segment with the *Huffington Post*, Ssenyonjo made clear that he opposed the preaching of U.S. missionaries and Ugandan anti-gay pastors, drawing on a different set of religious concepts:

> "Gospel" means "good news" but when you tell people that if you don't change being what you are, you are going to destroy maybe the country like Sodom and Gomorrah was destroyed, you cause a lot of hatred. . . . God called me to go and make clear to my people, even my church, that these people shouldn't just be persecuted. Trying to see that gay people, who are able to listen, can understand that God did not only create heterosexuals but also LGBTQ people. And they are real people. I have met them by counseling and I have not just read about them. And I know who they are. And I know young people would have committed suicide but by trying to help them understand themselves, know they are human beings like me, like any other person. Those churches should speak out and say being gay is not, per se, a sin. Because many people think that being LGBTQ in itself is a sin, whereas you can't say being heterosexual is a sin. The way you try to live your life is not in itself a sin if God has created you like that; you have to use what God has given you in the way you think will give glory to you and to your God. . . . The churches should be clear about sexuality. Human sexuality in itself is not a sin.[81]

With these ideas, Ssenyonjo aligned with mainline Christian churches in the United States and has completed a tour of U.S. universities and churches, speaking about the status of LGBTI persons in Uganda and his advocacy. It is noteworthy that his position includes a theological version of essentialism, attributing sexual orientation to how God creates people.

In Ugandan LGBTI activism, advancing the science of homosexuality as a "normal variant" that cannot be changed has taken a backseat to other forms of advocacy. According to Mugisha, working at the grassroots

level has been most important because "the population on the ground
does not care about science. The only thing they care about is religion, of
course." Brian Nkoyooyo, director of Icebreakers Uganda, made a similar
observation:

> You've watched *Kuchus of Uganda.* In the film, medical students, in-
> stead of taking science facts to defend their position, they are bring-
> ing the Bible. There is a big, big contrast between the science and the
> religious views, and most of the people here are very clouded by the
> religion. We have tried to push the science of how homosexuality is not
> a disease and not a mental illness, but they always go back to the Bible.
> That's why we look at science as not being effective.[82]

Nkoyooyo was referring to an event in this documentary in which SMUG
members participated in a panel at a medical school, and medical students brought out Bibles and admonished members of the panel for their
sinful ways.[83] According to Mugisha, however, David Bahati had consulted prominent Ugandan psychiatrist Seggane Musisi about homosexuality; Musisi said that science did not support the bill. SMUG did
not publicize this because it did not seem as though it would be particularly effective in public advocacy.

In addition to this bottom–up strategy, Ugandan LGBTI activists
have worked in connection with a transnational advocacy network of gay
rights and human rights activists. In part, this has involved importing
Western activist strategies. Nkoyooyo of Icebreakers Uganda described
how the organization started when gay activism was building in the
country around the year 2004:

> I met Frank [Mugisha] around 2000. . . . He had the idea of starting
> up something. We had both gone through a lot. We met this organi-
> zation Icebreakers Manchester and we really liked the activities they
> were doing—support group, sharing around the circle, and drop-in
> center. And so we got interested. What if we had something like that in
> Kampala? What if many youth who have been going through what we
> have been going through came to share what they are going through?
> And it would give them encouragement. Frank started researching
> how we develop a support group and that is how we came up with
> Icebreakers Uganda. We got in touch with David Armstrong, and we
> used [the name] "Icebreakers Uganda" because everything we were
> doing was "Icebreakers Manchester" in the UK. We have never met in
> person, so it was all by email. He has never visited. We started meeting
> in bars and then people [shared] their situations and we would learn

from how they dealt with their situations, and we shared our situations and people would learn and many people came on board.[84]

Nkoyooyo also described how his organization receives operations funding from global human rights organizations. Moreover, as global gay rights organizations such as the International Lesbian, Gay, Bisexual, Trans, and Intersexual Association (ILGA) and the International Gay and Lesbian Human Rights Commission (IGLHRC) have worked to make gay rights part of a broader human rights agenda, their efforts have enabled SMUG to be connected to a broader transnational network. Mugisha was awarded the 2011 Human Rights Award from the Robert F. Kennedy Center for Justice and Human Rights,[85] and the U.S-based Center for Constitutional Rights filed a lawsuit on behalf of SMUG against Scott Lively for "crimes against humanity."[86] Clearly both sides of the struggle over the Anti-Homosexuality Bill have ties to "the West."[87]

However, one liability that has come along with working with the transnational network is that the ILGA has struggled with a past association with pedophilia organizations. ILGA lost its UN consultancy status in 1994 when Senator Jesse Helms (R-N.C.) pointed out that the organization included pedophile advocacy groups, including the North American Man/Boy Love Association (NAMBLA). Since that time, ILGA has worked hard to distance itself from pedophile organizations, purging NAMBLA and two other groups from the organization that year. In 1995 the group altered its charter to include a commitment to the UN Covenant on the Rights of the Child and developed a screening process in 1996 to prevent groups that did not align with their goals from joining.[88] When ILGA reapplied for NGO status with the UN again in 2006, the application was denied because the group was still associated with pedophilia. ILGA then published a statement[89] addressing its commitment to the protection of children and has since participated in a protest of the Vatican in 2010 after a Roman Catholic cardinal declared a link between homosexuality and pedophilia.[90] Through this anti-pedophilia work, ILGA-Europe regained its Economic and Social Council consultancy status with the UN in 2006, and ILGA as a whole regained this status in 2011, yet this history has made severing links between homosexuality and pedophilia in some places in the world more difficult to achieve.

With some exceptions, Ugandan LGBTI activists did not utilize legal human rights strategies in Uganda in the years prior to the passage of the bill, and left these tactics for heterosexual allies within the country. According to Sylvia Tamale, the Civil Society Coalition on Human

Rights and Constitutional Law changed over time to incorporate gay rights largely under the influence of foreign donors:

> Well, our coalition today has over forty member organizations. There are many mainstream human rights groups. Before the bill you wouldn't imagine these groups talking about the rights of homosexuals. We talk about women's rights and the rights of sexual minorities; slowly human rights organizations requested to join not because they are less homophobic but because their donors are asking if they are part of the coalition. There is a silver lining to this, as once they have joined many of them began to change. But only because their donors are asking if they are part of the coalition.[91]

Under the Museveni regime, however, this sector has been subject to state power through registration requirements to assure that these groups are not engaged in political work. Scholars of human rights argue that a culture of fear within the general population undermines the fight for human rights and prevents keeping the administration accountable for previous rights transgressions.[92]

Since the passage of the bill, SMUG has compiled information on violations of human rights through hate crimes. According to this group, hate crimes against gays increased tenfold in the first four months after the bill became law.[93] These acts have included attempted lynchings, burning of homes, beatings, and rapes. One seventeen-year old boy committed suicide over the law because he felt his life had no value. Meanwhile, cuts to aid from Western countries, including the United States, the Netherlands, Norway, and Denmark, have taken their toll. As a first adverse consequence, eighty-seven health-care workers lost their jobs in the Ministry of Health as a result of cuts from the U.S. government over the anti-gay law.[94]

The struggle for gay rights in Uganda has not been without strain within the transnational advocacy network. Tamale noted:

> The international response to the bill is disturbing. For years, Africans have been shouting ourselves hoarse about so many issues, the lack of free elections, free expression, freedom of assembly, and the international community looks the other way. But with this Anti-Homosexuality Bill, my goodness, we wish you responded this way all the time! It leads me to think that just as religious leaders and politicians have been using homosexuality as a political tool, even international politicians are doing the same. It's annoying! Even the threatening of economic sanctions is so problematic because it reinforces

a geopolitical hierarchy. It reinforces the myth that homosexuality is [part of] a Western agenda, importing a decadent agenda. And it reinforces an image that the rights of homosexuals are more important than other rights. There is a petition that we have been signing, sexual rights activists around the continent, condemning this selective activism.[95]

In addition to the problem of needing to consider a broader range of rights in this region, local LGBTI activists explained that when people come from outside the country to help, they often ignore the concerns of SMUG and other organization leaders. These outsiders, while well intentioned, often believe that local activists should be lobbying and fighting for state rights, and often conduct research without consulting local LGBTI leaders regarding its design.[96]

In working with activists abroad, a rights strategy has been particularly useful, especially in the United States. In March 2012, as mentioned earlier, the U.S.-based Center for Constitutional Rights filed a lawsuit against Scott Lively on behalf of SMUG, alleging that Lively has conspired with Ugandan officials to deprive Ugandan LGBTI persons of fundamental rights.[97] Allied activists in Springfield, Massachusetts, with the Stop the Hate and Homophobia Coalition, constructed a mock coffin with an image of David Kato and carried it in front of the café that Lively owns there, Holy Grounds Coffee House.[98] In December 2014, a federal appeals court ruled against Lively's petition to dismiss the lawsuit, and the charge of crimes against humanity remains pending at the time of this writing.[99]

Further extending this network, one psychologist I talked with from outside Uganda works with an NGO and, like Ssenyonjo, serves LGBTI clients. Because of the dire situation, group therapy meetings have been held under the cover of financial seminars or other types of meetings to keep outsiders from knowing what was going on. This therapist, who wished to remain anonymous, was part of a small underground network of pro-LGBTI counseling psychologists. This psychologist stated, "I do a great deal of therapy with LGBTI clients, but when I do, I never write in their files that they are LGBTI because I do not want this in their records. It's just too dangerous." The therapist added that there was a problem in that some people would come to the organization claiming to be LGBTI and demanding services with a sense of entitlement to relocation, requiring the group to have to differentiate between genuine and disingenuous cases. Even when things had been sorted out, this therapist felt LGBTI clients could express an excessive sense of entitlement:

In March 2012, in Springfield, Massachusetts, members of the Stop the Hate and Homophobia Coalition march with a mock coffin dedicated to the memory of activist David Kato, murdered in Uganda in 2011. In support of SMUG's lawsuit against Scott Lively, their march took them past his place of business, Holy Grounds Coffee House, where he holds religious gatherings. AP Photo/ *Springfield Republican,* Don Treeger.

> Well, an interesting question is about this feeling of rights, where does it come from? I have seen it in group sessions. People can party without consequences; because you are gay you can do anything, and because you are part of a minority it is good that people do things for you. It takes away people's responsibility, and they become a threat to themselves. They become more vulnerable and more dependent.[100]

Like Okello's counseling of SMUG to act respectable, and Icebreakers Uganda's seminars in gender conformity, this therapist encouraged clients to cope with danger by toning down any behavior that might suggest transgression.

In a key contest over cultural meanings of homosexuality in this activism, the history of homosexual practices in Uganda also continues to be contested, given the refrains that homosexuality is a "Western import" and "un-African." Sylvia Tamale has compiled a number of academic sources that chronicle homosexual practices in African history:

> When we turn to the past, we find that, contrary to popular belief, homosexuality in Uganda predates colonialism and other forms of subjugation (Murray and Roscoe, 1998). Historically, as was the case elsewhere in the world, homosexual practices were neither fully condoned nor totally suppressed (Feminist Review, 1987). Among the Langi of northern Uganda, the mudoko dako "males" were treated as women and could marry men (Driberg, 1923). Homosexuality was also acknowledged among the Iteso (Laurance, 1957), the Bahima (Mushanga, 1973), the Banyoro (Needham, 1973) and the Baganda (Southwold, 1973). Indeed, there is a long history of homosexuality in the Buganda monarchy; it was an open secret, for example, that Kabaka (king) Mwanga was gay (Faupel, 1962). Trends both in the present and the past reveal that it is time for Africans to bury the tired myth that homosexuality is "unAfrican."[101]

Given the need to illustrate to a broader audience that "homosexuality has existed in Africa," Tamale applied contemporary notions of "gay" and "homosexual" to some of these relationships that are "gender based," as in the case of the *mudoko dako,* illustrating a broader inclusion of gender nonconformity within the category "homosexual" for those on the pro-LGBTI side.[102] In the case of King Mwanga, who had sixteen wives and ten children, the term *gay,* as an identity, cannot capture the complexities of the king's sexual behavior with male subjects. In a Western context such a constellation of behavior might be considered "bisexual" or unidentified "MSM" (men who have sex with men). Nonetheless, Tamale's evidence shows that historically in Uganda, people born into a particular sex have had sexual relationships with people of that same sex, even if it was not exclusive and not labeled with an identity.

Using King Mwanga as evidence for homosexuality in the history of Uganda is also complicated by the legendary story of the Christian martyrs. Monuments are erected in two Ugandan cities for these martyrs, young men in Mwanga's court whom missionaries had converted to Christianity and whom the king burned alive because, in part, they refused to have sexual relations with him.[103] The mythology surrounding these events works for both sides of the debate over homosexuality in the country. Pro-LGBTI activists use the story to prove the existence of homosexuality in the country prior to colonial rule, and anti-homosexuality activists point to it as evidence of the barbarity and depravity of homosexuals, emphasizing the martyr role of Christians.

One area in which science had gained some persuasive power in advocacy against the Anti-Homosexuality Bill, at least while the bill was delayed, was in HIV/AIDS prevention. The fact that HIV prevention had been a matter of national pride, and now rates were increasing, made this a crucial arena of struggle. Moreover, the Ministry of Health, which had been the only office of state government acknowledging the existence of same-sex sexual relationships, provided a local form of expertise that could not be dismissed as "foreign influence." Sylvia Tamale was consulted when those changes were made in the Ministry of Health in the early 2000s:

> There was a very big grant from UNAIDS to the Ministry of Health to work on HIV prevention and advocacy, millions of dollars, and when the proposal ran out, the new proposal was rejected because it did not address the needs of the LGBT population. The ministry came running to me: "Sylvia! You understand this community. Can you write a paragraph for our proposal?" And I said that you have the LGBT community knocking at your door. They have documents. I asked SMUG to give me their document on HIV/AIDS and I asked sex workers who are very organized for their document and I sent it to them. They incorporated this into their document because they were desperate for the funds.[104]

Although members of the Ministry of Health might be homophobic, these funding streams required them to incorporate MSMs into their HIV prevention strategies. With these prevention policies set in place, opponents of the Anti-Homosexuality Bill could use them as a resource, pointing out that the bill would make HIV prevention more difficult. While Bahati pointed to the risks of anal sex as a reason to criminalize homosexuality, Action AIDS activist Leonard Okello argued that the bill would make HIV prevention more difficult by adding risks for women in marriages whose husbands secretly had sex with other men. Clauses in the bill that made homosexual activity a higher crime if the person was HIV positive, he said, stigmatized all HIV-positive persons in the country.[105] In the end, however, these arguments did not prevent the Anti-Homosexuality Bill from passing.

Unlike gay rights activists in the United States, LGBTI activists in Uganda did not see placing pressure on Ugandan mental health professionals as a viable strategy prior to passage of the Anti-Homosexuality Act, given the lack of relevance of these sciences for the masses that they were trying to persuade. As a result, psychologists and psychiatrists participating on Museveni's panel had little exposure to the issue. While fighting along the lines of community engagement and theology, cultural opportunities to shape popular understandings of homosexuality have been scant. I now turn to the views of other mental health experts, including Ugandan psychologists and psychiatrists who were among those who wrote a report for Museveni.

Psychiatry and Psychology Walking a Tightrope

Psychiatrists in Uganda quote a staggering statistic of shortage: there is one psychiatrist per million people. Psychology, which does not have PhD-granting institutions in the country, largely serves as an aid to psychiatry. Seggane Musisi, chair of the Department of Psychiatry at Mulago Hospital, explained that the reason for the menial investment in mental health professions dates back to the colonial period. Faith healers once treated the whole person, but during colonization, Western medicine introduced a mind/body dichotomy. The colonists funded treatment of the body but neglected the mind, setting up the current circumstances as a legacy. With the shortages of practitioners, psychiatrists were designing a triage system where people with dire cases of mental illness would be sent to the city hospitals, and nurses could be trained to work in rural clinics on less severe problems. Psychiatrists also faced competition from village faith healers.

When I visited Uganda in 2011, I had the opportunity to interview some members of the faculty at Makerere University and Mulago Hospital. It was at this school that members of SMUG were admonished by medical students holding Bibles during a discussion panel. I passed the lecture hall where this occurred on my way to the psychiatry department, where I met with Musisi, who would later be asked to serve on the President's Ministry of Health panel on homosexuality in 2014. In our interview, Musisi explained that homosexuality was not a very common topic in his work, and he noted that his training in Australia before working in Uganda fostered his expertise in cross-cultural psychiatry. In Uganda, mental health treatment cannot be targeted at the individual, as Ugandan culture involves more family and community integration. Musisi and much of the staff at Makerere specialized in the treatment of mental health problems associated with HIV/AIDS, and Musisi noted that problems like war and poverty were major contributors to mental health issues.[106]

While there was diversity of opinion, many psychiatrists and psychologists saw homosexuality to be a nonissue given all the other things they were dealing with. The psychiatric dimensions of HIV/AIDS, malaria, and tuberculosis, the widespread traumas of war, and dealing with depression were issues on the forefront. Moreover, homosexuality was rarely discussed because people hardly ever came out as gay or sought treatment from Ugandan professionals for something so widely stigmatized. For these professional respondents, homosexuality seemed a rather odd thing to be talking about. As part of the intellectual opportunity structure here, there was almost no contact between these mental health professionals and gay activists or LGBTI clients, a barrier of unfamiliarity between science and the public. Because of the widespread stigma against homosexuality, all practitioners I talked with endorsed some form of treatment of homosexuality, albeit hypothetical, especially in circumstances in which a person would face immense persecution, and especially if the client were younger and sexually inexperienced. They were well aware of the positions of groups like the American Psychiatric Association and the World Psychiatric Association on homosexuality, but argued that Ugandan culture required different approaches. Psychiatry and psychology were not poised to take positions against the bill, given the wide range of opinions among professionals, and also because speaking out against the bill could yield prison sentences. Musisi noted:

> People have written to me saying I should lead the psychiatric fight against this bill, and I've said no. We have other pressing mental health issues. Human rights activists can take it up. I'm a human rights person hopefully, so I can make my views known from that perspective, but I won't lead this.[107]

Musisi was of course familiar with the fact that the *DSM* and the World Health Organization's *International Statistical Classification of Diseases and Related Health Problems (ICD-10)* did not classify homosexuality as an illness. While he did not think that homosexuality is a disease he told me, "We have no official view. Many doctors tend to follow three things: the world medical view, their religious teachings, their cultural teachings." Given the lack of an official position of Ugandan psychiatry, the diversity of positions among mental health professionals in the country, and the precarious position of the resources for his profession, he had to tread carefully in forming his position.

Psychiatrists at two hospitals revealed that some professionals maintain strong anti-gay views, especially given that homosexuality has been widely defined in terms of predatory recruitment. One psychiatrist specializing in child development particularly worried about the coercion and recruitment of children:

Being a homosexual here raises a lot of anxiety. They recruit a lot of people to make their society bigger. . . . So if you go to schools recruiting and training students to be homosexual to me that is not acceptable.

[Have you seen evidence of that happening?]

I have had to go to a number of schools where there were packages of literature from the outside world and of course children will experiment, and there is pornography on the Internet they wish to know, and if you say it is not a problem to students they will perceive that it is not a problem. . . . I have had to deal with students who have been sexually abused, sodomized. They said they got this literature in the school, and they pass it on, and then they have an economic aspect to it. If you are recruited you are paid. That is not acceptable. That is concerning to the school authorities and to human rights activists and the government.[108]

This psychiatrist compared the cultural insensitivity of UNICEF sex education literature to the idea of making Muslim women be like the Western popular music star Madonna.

The psychologists I spoke with seemed more moderate. Paul Bangirana, who also later served on Museveni's panel, disagreed with the idea that homosexuality is a behavior that is learned through recruitment. He thought sexuality developed in different directions for a variety of reasons, depending on the circumstances. This ranged from some people having a biological basis for homosexuality, to others having a psychological or environmental basis. He was critical of Pastor Ssempa's church for putting the issue in "black and white" terms. Social psychologist Paul Nyende took a similar stance. While psychology training was developing in the country, he hoped for including psychology education in secondary schools to give people skills to evaluate issues through this lens. He noted through surveys in his classes that students come into psychology classes often with very anti-gay views, but by their third year, students often had different perspectives.

Given these circumstances, neither the Ugandan Psychiatric Association, the Uganda Counselling Association, nor the Uganda National Psychological Association took a position on the Anti-Homosexuality Bill. Regarding the last organization, Nyende stated:

You need a critical mass and very powerful advocate to push that agenda to influence legislators . . . but we haven't had very many post graduate students, we need to have more people at that level. Classes at the graduate level are a little bit small, 10 maybe 15, so not that many are out there to have this powerful influence but as we continue graduating these it will sway because the issue of numbers if very important.[109]

Yet he believed that any position against the Anti-Homosexuality Bill would be out of the question for the association:

> I think they considered taking up that issue [, but] nothing was said. It is a bit sensitive because coming out and putting up a statement to push is [difficult]; the actions were very strong in the papers and people were really very angry. We know it is very harsh so we are also saying that the organizations that are supporting will also be punished. That was the bill. That was the advocates as well, so people were kind of turned back by those kinds of statements. . . . Also I think Christian values are very strong in Uganda and definitely when people fall back on those values they opt out. If they come out and maybe put a strong position to support human rights and homosexuality they will be heavily criticized by even their own family members, and as a Christian how do you say that somebody has a right to be gay? So that would deter them from coming out strongly. . . . We actually have a few publications sometimes that can be very ruthless. Certain newspapers have attacked certain people, and they may not argue things rationally. So they could actually turn everything that your members of your association are gay and that is why they do support the rights of the gay. . . . So people have to be very careful to come forward because it is a very sensitive issue to take a stand on.[110]

Given the lack of consensus in the profession, there was little chance that local mental health professional associations could lead a charge against the bill. Even if psychologists or psychiatrists were united in support of gays, they would have faced the dangers of being identified as homosexuality advocates by the state or even accused of being gay by the tabloid media. As a form of regulation of science by the state, this aspect of the intellectual opportunity structure shaped what was possible for scientists in Uganda to say, further undermining any support that may exist for the pro-LGBTI movement, and further undermining a science-based strategy for LGBTI activists.

In a country where anti-gay ideas were dominant, even those psychiatrists and psychologists who might otherwise be sympathetic to gay rights took pragmatic positions on the diagnosis and treatment of homosexuality. Considering that people might face extremely dire circumstances, including the need to leave homosexuality for survival in the community, Musisi upheld a diagnosis no longer acceptable to the West for some cases:

> The old notion . . . I think it was *DSM-II* or *DSM-III* that talked about ego-dystonic homosexuality. That was acceptable. In other words, one

is homosexual but is uncomfortable with their homosexuality and may want some help.[111]

Cognitive behavioral therapy, especially the work of Aaron T. Beck, was the most-cited approach. While the idea of treating homosexuality in some circumstances seemed ethical to these professionals, given the harsh circumstances and difficulties in coming out as gay, this type of therapy was not something they practiced because people rarely came to them admitting these feelings.

Musisi said he would treat a person who had ego-dystonic homosexuality:

> If they say they are gay and society is mistreating me, I can help that person. I deal with psychological pain from whatever source. If someone is happy and gay, I want them to be aware of social and cultural reactions to that type of orientation and what he or she should expect, just like if someone comes with ego-dystonic homosexuality, I could tell them what they could do to become heterosexual, or behave in a heterosexual way.
>
> [Do you think they could change their attractions?]
>
> I'll give you the example of stealing, if somebody likes to steal, or if somebody likes to drink alcohol, and they desire to drink, they could be told to avoid drinking. But wanting to drink can't be removed. If somebody likes women, if a man likes women. Sexual addiction therapies, they should give them to Tiger Woods. But that doesn't remove their desire. They could tell them not to act on it. Same as eating. You teach people to avoid obesity. It doesn't mean they stop loving to eat those things. Just tell them moderation.
>
> [To become heterosexual one would need to reduce homosexual feelings; they would need to get heterosexual feelings. How would someone become heterosexual?]
>
> If you believe in all or none, then you have the view that they cannot change, but if you believe in a gradation like I told you about, then there is a training, the cultural system you are brought up in. Just like someone can be trained to run. Anybody can fight. Some are not very good fighters. That is my behaviorist view. I have not talked about drugs to change the biochemical nature, I don't think those things are correct.[112]

Even Nyende, who seemed among the least anti-gay, thought change might sometimes be necessary and possible:

I think when people are young and they are still in their formative stage and their identity is still in a formative stage we could make a change in them. That is what I am saying with the relative approach of timely adequate sex education and guidance. I think somehow we need to lead them into what we think might be best for them given our culture in Uganda. If your child took a homosexual orientation they are going to live like thieves—they are going to hide. And once they were discovered, there will be hostility. You will be a target of hostility.[113]

In such harsh conditions, these professionals felt that a person's behaviors could be modified through the power of reinforcement in cognitive behavioral therapy for the purposes of survival.

Psychiatrists and psychologists at Makerere were interested in neuropsychiatry and biological models of the brain. When asked how an outcome study of treatment for homosexuality would best be evaluated, Bangirana alluded to brain scanning as a means to measure behavior:

For a client who changes, it definitely has to be behavior. People measure different things. They can measure behavior based on client report, based on observation, and they can also measure the behavior based in terms of the origin of the behavior, or based upon the brain. Let's look at the brain. Let's see what kinds of arousals are taking place in the brain. What kinds of arousal to heterosexual and homosexual imagery are taking place in the brain? And it would be best to have controls. They have done the same tests for controls to know what is the standard reaction for the person who is straight to heterosexual and homosexual imagery, so they can say OK this is the activation. There is still probably some arousal to homosexual imagery. If someone is aroused by homosexual imagery are they homosexual? I think you would have to look at that and the behavior.[114]

Here Bangirana emphasizes physiological responses of the brain as the basis of behavior, the most important variable defining homosexuality, as something to be managed through reinforcement. Considering the issue hypothetically, Bangirana said treatment for homosexuality, if performed, would first involve "psychoeducation," explaining to the client the basis for the unwanted thoughts, and then it would involve exposure therapy:

The goal would be, if they are saying, "I'm having same sex thoughts and I want to change this," then we would do what the client wants. Most interventions are behavioral and cognitive methods. We would probably use some kind of exposures, exposure to the same sex and then some exposure to the other sex. It would be quite a challenge. I have never done this kind of work and am not an expert in changing sexual orientation. However, evidence that sexual orientation can be changed through therapy is not conclusive.[115]

Although Bangirana had never conducted reorientation therapy, these hypothetical ideas convey the predilection for cognitive behavioral therapy and neuropsychiatry, seeing malleable brain responses as expressions of behavior. This perspective on physiology is much different from that of pro-gay advocates in the United States, who appeal to physiological data as a measure of fixed selfhood. Here, Bangirana, like the behavior therapists of the 1960s in the United States and Europe, look to the body's physiological responses as an indicator of behavior that can be modified.

Musisi and Bangirana became part of the eleven-member Ministry of Health scientific panel consisting of psychiatrists, psychologists, medical doctors, and geneticists.[116] Museveni called for this group in late 2013, once the bill had passed Parliament, to advise him on whether or not homosexuality was genetic in origin. Given Musisi's and Bangirana's backgrounds and the tendency for LGBT persons to avoid Ugandan health professionals, it is likely that those on the Ministry of Health panel in 2014 were similarly distant from LGBT-identified people. Despite this distance, the authors of the panel's report that was formally presented to President Museveni cited primary documents from the reorientation debate from Western publications, including the Spitzer study, responses to the Spitzer study, Spitzer's apology, other essays from the *Journal of Gay and Lesbian Psychotherapy,* and even the *Report of the American Psychological Association Task Force on Therapeutic Responses to Sexual Orientation.* This literature was used to claim that while homosexuality may have different causes from person to person, *"It is not a disease that has a treatment."*[117] The report presented to Museveni did consider hypothetical reasons why homosexuality might be genetically determined, but claimed there was no clear evidence for this cause. Homosexuality in animals was declared "uncommon," and research studies on brain structure differences were inconclusive. In contradiction to the claims of the anti-homosexuality movement that homosexuality has not existed in Africa, the report acknowledged the existence of homosexual practices in all societies, including precolonial Africa, but viewed homosexuality as a learned behavior.

The report shifted from the American Psychological Association's position by redefining homosexuality as a behavior "based on" a set of attractions. Speaking to the popular understanding of homosexuality circulating in Ugandan culture, the authors of the report did not distinguish between homosexuality as a basis for consensual adult relationships and various forms of sex crimes involving force and coercion. "Homosexuality" encompasses a set of behaviors, including coercion, and it should be regulated for the betterment of society. In the last section, "The Need to Regulate Sexualities," the authors concluded that "human sexuality needs to be regulated especially as it is the core of the family and hence the nation." Given that "daily scandals and rapes of this world including sexual and gender based violence or human trafficking for sex" exist, all forms of sexuality need regulation. This section then summed up: "African cultures had contained sexual vices. Maybe we need to revisit them to contain the present explosion of overt and coercive homosexual activity with the exploitation of our young children."[118] The Ministry of Health report did not consider the mental health consequences of an Anti-Homosexuality Act for LGBTI-identified persons, but was instead preoccupied with protecting populations it viewed as vulnerable to homosexual teaching or coercion, including children. According to a press release from the National Resistance Movement Caucus, Museveni, following the presentation of the report by the panel, "declared that he would sign the Bill since the question of whether one can be born a homosexual or not had been answered." He then "emphasized that Promoters, exhibitionists, and those who practice homosexuality for Mercenary reasons will not be tolerated and will therefore be dealt with harshly."[119]

Unlike the National Association of Social Workers of Uganda (NASWU), which took a radical stance out of step with its global representative body, the International Federation of Social Workers (IFSW), here were professionals walking a tightrope between the local needs of the Ugandan population with a particular cultural understanding of homosexuality, and the demands of a Westernized global profession that saw it as a "normal variant" in support of gay rights. The sentiment underlying entertaining the idea of hypothetical treatment for homosexuality for people in dire circumstances was not unlike the views of therapists in the United States during earlier decades, and the solutions they recommended at times seemed like the compromise of "sexual orientation identity exploration" of the American Psychological Association. However, belief in the power of behavior modification, and the definition of homosexuality as a set of behaviors that included coercion, are elements of the belief system that enabled some of these professionals to support the bill.

Defining *Homosexuality* in Uganda

What does *homosexuality* mean according to dominant scientific, legal, and moral discourses in Uganda? Defined in terms of behavior, and encompassing rape, child molestation, deliberate HIV infection, and other forms of coercion, it is often understood as a form of evil. While scientific research on homosexuality in Uganda is scant, and reorientation research is nonexistent, one can presume that homosexuals have become "reoriented" in Uganda once they have corrected their "faulty" behavior. Indeed, the intellectual opportunity structure characterized by such a strong law against homosexuality will present immense challenges for anyone seeking to do scientific research supportive of LGBT people in the country.

Defining homosexuality in terms of behavior has enabled links to other social problems in Uganda. Anxieties about HIV/AIDS, child sexual exploitation, the integrity of the nation in the face of Western development pressures and crushing poverty can all find an outlet in denigrating gays in this context, as symbols of the individualism of the decadent West. These trends reinforce development discourses that tend to emphasize heterosexual reproduction as normative in various settings in the Global South.[120] They also help promote nationalism in a postcolonial setting.

In addition to broadly held religious sentiments, the NASWU's ability to bring NARTH research to Parliament and the ability of Ministry of Health experts to reinterpret science from Western institutions played key roles in the passage and signing of this bill. The anti-homosexuality movement helped make this possible by successfully shaping the meaning of homosexuality in the country, and by taking advantage of an intellectual opportunity structure in which the NASWU could take a position independent of the IFSW and still remain a member in good standing within the global body. The interpenetration of the movement, social work, and the state, seen especially in the figure of NASWU president Charles Tuhaise, was also key. Looming penalties for homosexuality advocacy and the threat of shaming by the tabloid media shaped the approaches of local mental health and medical experts, both in their avoidance of the issue and in their 2014 report to Museveni. Moreover, dominant understandings of human behavior in the school of behaviorism and widespread cultural understandings of homosexuality also shaped these views, as Ugandan mental health professionals walked a tightrope between their global profession and their need to maintain legitimacy in a local setting.

New laws against homosexuality in Uganda, Russia, and Nigeria, which are now among more than seventy other nations with such laws, demonstrate that the strategy of claiming that gays are "born that way" is precarious for securing and ensuring rights in the world. The imposition of a system of sexual types has not been well received in places where individualistic identity categories run up against more fluid and unlabeled sexual practices, or where conservative religions have taken hold. This case crucially illustrates how definitions of homosexuality are central factors in rights struggles. While physiological evidence may be useful in the United States to validate a set of attractions that define selfhood, this case also shows how that same kind of evidence could be read as a propensity toward bad behavior, especially if homosexuality is conflated with other social ills. After all, physiological testing was invented by behaviorists who considered arousal to be malleable behavior and not indicative of innate selfhood. Furthermore, if gay rights are to ever advance in Uganda, there is a strong need to disaggregate discussions of adult consensual homosexuality, on the one hand, and rape, pedophilia, child molestation, and exploitation, on the other. Given these acute limitations, looking forward may require considering other platforms for sexual rights besides essentialism.

conclusion
SEXUALITY IS A MATTER OF PERSPECTIVE

In the United States, people often argue that objective science can represent their version of the truth in public moral disputes, even if most scientists have formed a consensus that differs from that point of view. While it is not a given that we will look to scientific evidence to resolve a moral issue, heated ethical concerns such as reorientation often become redirected into technical disputes. Evidence is invoked to literally make a claim "evident," rather than being seen as an opinion or perspective allegedly tainted by politics. Bringing together pieces of evidence to bear on truth is never, however, a simple matter of "letting the facts speak for themselves." A relationship must always be established between the body of evidence and the claim it purports to support. This "metonymic" relationship is never straightforward.[1] In science a tremendous amount of work goes into scientific training, construction of laboratories, and development of scientific facts in order to convince readers of science that claims and the evidence used to support those claims have credibility. Even when scientists have established a consensus, scientists are forever burdened by establishing relationships of trust, not only in themselves as experts but also in the quality of the methods and the relevance of their experimental results. There is always a human element.

When psychologist A. Lee Beckstead described the sexual reorientation therapy debate, he alluded to how limitations of immediate human perception drive disagreement. A well-worn metaphor he used to think about these conflicts was that of trying to perceive a giant elephant:

> Some people hold the tail, some people have the tusks, some people have the skin, and we're all blind men so to speak. And I think all of us have to be talking to one another to see what the elephant really looks like. Most people have been holding on to one part, such as the leg,

saying this is what the elephant is. The more we can hear, understand, but not really take things at face value, and the more we can understand where people are coming from, then we can see the full picture.[2]

Although this metaphor is strong, there is something about it that is perplexing. It suggests that there may be a common object everyone is trying to see, yet we may consider whether, given the differing cosmologies of people engaged with this issue, a common object could ever come into view.

At the risk of mixing my elephant metaphors, it is worth considering what might be the "elephant in the room" for different actors across the terrain this book has covered, insofar as it illuminates how each carries different metaphysical worldviews. First, according to NARTH's responses to the American Psychological Association, sexual orientation should now be understood as being on a continuum, and sexual orientation change experienced by individuals at the level of attractions should not be invalidated. Reorientation challenges the "born this way" essentialism of gay rights advocates and reorientation opponents. Even so, NARTH adherents have their own essentialism, viewing innate heterosexuality as unencumbered once the corruption of gender anxieties has been overcome.

For most religious ex-gays, the ultimate goal of ministry is achieving salvation in an afterlife through obedience to Jesus Christ as Lord. Living outside either heterosexual marriage or celibacy results in living outside God's kingdom for eternity. In this metaphysics, science that does not align with these principles is human folly, and evidence that reorientation does not work is just the worldly persistence of temptation to sin. Such temptations must be resisted in line with theological principle and reading of scripture. Within the remnants of the ex-gay movement in the Restored Hope Network today, it is unclear whether cooperation can be sustained across its long-lived frame dispute, as secular reorientation therapists maintain the belief in sexual attraction change, whereas religious ministries remain more preoccupied with salvation.

On the other side of the debate, anti-reorientation activists have taken the APA task force report as proof that reorientation does not work and is often harmful. Sexual orientations are innate and immutable, based on physiological attractions, and they cannot be therapeutically altered. New activist initiatives have emerged in the wake of this change in the field of therapeutics. Truth Wins Out has developed the website LGBTscience.org, which compiles evidence for the biological basis of sexual orientation differences, including interviews with biologists and geneticists. From this group's perspective, gay and lesbian people deserve rights because homosexuality cannot be changed. Truth Wins Out has also helped develop "The NALT Christians Project," where NALT stands for "not all like that," to advance the idea that Christians can support full LGBT equality on theological grounds. This network includes supportive church groups and ministries. According to NALT, homosexuality and salvation are compatible.

Looking across these worldviews, we can see that the metaphor of the singular elephant does not work. These competing worldviews suggest that objects like "homosexuality" and "reorientation therapy" act more as boundary objects across disparate social worlds, where each term has different meanings and fits differently into a unique cosmology.[3] As sexual orientation research continues, evidence and precisely where to draw the "straight line" will continue to be contested across camps when these do not fit into a system of thought. For people to recognize scientific evidence as meaningful, there must be established relationships of trust. Steven Epstein notes:

> One of the important findings of the sociology of science is that experiments do not, in the simple sense usually understood, "settle" scientific controversies. Nothing inherent in an experiment definitively establishes it as the "crucial" test of a hypothesis. Rather, scientists negotiate precisely what counts as evidence, which experiments represent a hypothesis adequately, and whether an instance of replication is a faithful recreation of a prior study.[4]

Indeed, in a contentious climate, an allegedly "decisive" experiment can drive controversy rather than settle it.[5] We cannot escape a politics of trust and distrust layered upon the production of scientific discourses. Establishing credibility may involve showing credentials, or it may involve community building, but it always involves convincing people that you and your evidence are trustworthy.

Time and time again, interlocutors in the reorientation debate have resorted to claims that "we" have objective science, but "they" are corrupted by politics. The National Association for Research and Therapy of Homosexuality and the National Association of Social Workers of Uganda have claimed that the American Psychological Association's positions are merely beholden to gay activism. Meanwhile, members of the APA task force claim that NARTH is homophobic and its members' research is not methodologically rigorous. Contrary to the idea that there can be a "pure" science, credibility demands mean that some kind of politics always plays a role in scientific work. While the popular story about science is that it should not be "corrupted" by undue influences, science always involves tacit assumptions that are built into research:

> The . . . expert must be seen as a necessarily "partisan participant" in a political debate, not as an apolitical arbiter of . . . truth, and this implies a radical review of the expert's role in therapeutic evaluation. It also opens the way to an active and acknowledged evaluative role for non-experts, for patients and the public at large, in the processes of assessment and decision making.[6]

With this perspective in mind, claims that someone's science has been simply "corrupted" by politics make no sense. Establishing credibility often requires demonstrating that one's research might have provided findings contrary to one's hypothesis or expectations. It also requires adhering to shared values, such as being "affirmative" of diversity. This analysis may seem unsettling, if it evokes images of scientists falsifying or skewing their data to achieve a partisan political agenda, but of course good science still requires the use of practices that maintain accountability to evidence even contrary to one's expectations, and also convincing others that such measures have been followed. Science is *not* just politics by other means, but science and politics are forever interwoven because science involves human beings in the processes of knowledge construction, negotiations of conceptual tools, and the establishment of credibility.[7] For instance, removing homosexuality from the *DSM* was not merely a political decision but rather a scientific decision, interwoven with changing political values that included the choice to see certain forms of research, including the work of Evelyn Hooker, Marcel Saghir, and Eli Robins, as valid scientific evidence.

Tracing the shifting straight line, I have followed processes of bringing evidence to bear on "sexual orientation" over several decades in the United States and abroad. The credibility of evidence has been shaped by the dynamics of opposing social movements, professionals jockeying for jurisdiction over sexuality, and historical context. With some exceptions, this evidence has centered primarily on male-identified bodies and psyches. Male sexuality has been used to represent "sexual orientation," often without anyone qualifying or explaining why it is the key category. The cultural preoccupation with a heterosexual/homosexual binary, primarily male, was identified by Eve Kosofsky Sedgwick as part of Western cultures more broadly, so it is perhaps no surprise to see it manifest within science.[8] Mainstream scientists in the United States and in Westernized global institutions have reinscribed male sexualities as mechanical in nature and fixed. Female sexualities appear to be fluid, emotion based, and

diffuse, and are often ignored because they do not fit the same assumptions. Penile plethysmography as a measurement technique is perhaps
most emblematic of this idea of sexual nature and gender difference. Even
as the APA created the compromise of "sexual orientation identity exploration," which allows for more fluidity of identity, it is based on a male-
oriented model of fixed sexual orientations rooted in innate physiology.

The study of dominant measurement techniques over the years in
these debates reveals how the consolidation of sexual subjectivities has
involved particular power relations embedded in measurement practices.
During the era when homosexuality was considered pathological in the
United States, the psychoanalyst ruled. The dynamic between the expert
and the subject reinforced the primary subjectivity of the analyst, who
decided when the client had become heterosexual. Moreover, psychoanalytic theory depicted the client as helplessly blind to his unconscious
motivations. One became straight only when the analyst's theory was internalized, heterosexuality seen as natural, and homosexuality viewed as
pathology. In addition, the indicators of heterosexuality were linked to behavior. If a client needed to convince a therapist that he or she was heterosexual, the evidence could be feigned through personal narrative. Yet the
general homophobic circumstances led many people to internalize the
view that homosexuality was pathological and to desperately seek cures.

Starting in the 1960s, behaviorists questioned whether the psychoanalytic interpretation was truly scientific and offered physiological data
as a replacement. Experimental studies using aversion therapy and later
covert sensitization therapy meant that an authoritative instrument
would speak for whether or not a client was "cured." Phallometric testing
with penile plethysmography tied erotic imagery and erection to sexual
orientation. To be a straight man meant having a physiological response
to pornography intended to represent heterosexual desire. It also meant
to have no physiological response to homoerotic imagery. Here technology mediated the relationship between experimenter and subject. If a
subject wanted to convince the researcher he was straight, talking was
not enough. He would have to fake desire and produce an erection by
thinking about something else, or by engaging in "pumping" muscles to
produce tumescence. He might also distract himself while viewing homoerotic imagery. Phallometric testing practitioners have ways of preventing these problems, but they cannot be eradicated.

Once homosexuality was demedicalized, the ex-gay movement took
several years to consolidate new evidence in the form of self-report studies. In this kind of research, both professional experts on reorientation research and subjects as lay experts on their own change played significant

roles in the construction of knowledge—the professional brought methodology while the subject brought personal experience. Advocates saw this kind of research as the most democratic. Critics viewed it as coercive, alleging that those who participated in these studies were motivated by fear and a need for inclusion within homophobic institutions. As a result, it was argued, subjects exaggerated their heterosexual desires. Without physiological tests, ex-gays were considered incapable of testifying to their own change.

Eve Kosofsky Sedgwick has provided a crucial insight for considering such power relations. She claimed, "To alienate conclusively, *definitionally,* from anyone on any theoretical ground the authority to describe and name their own sexual desire is a terribly consequential seizure. In this century, in which sexuality has been made expressive of the essence of both identity and knowledge, it may represent the most intimate violence possible."[9] Sedgwick made this claim in 1990, at a time when gay and lesbian lives were heavily marginalized in the United States. Back then, it was inconceivable that state legislatures might be passing bans on reorientation therapies. In the contemporary period of marginalizing reorientation and developing gay affirmative policies, Sedgwick's statement takes on a different and interesting new valence. Is it indeed a form of "intimate violence" to tell ex-gays that they cannot name their own sexual desire? Perhaps, but so is telling same-sex attracted persons that their sexual desire is invalid and pathological. As scientific psychology has been important for defining the individual in the modern state in the United States, it is no wonder that moral disagreements over homosexuality would come to such an impasse. Perhaps it is time to move away from coercive tactics that place people within extreme binds of either/or choices. Before considering such alternatives, I now turn to further analysis of opposing social movements in struggles over scientific knowledge.

When Opposing Social Movements Target Science

The case of reorientation has revealed a number of tactics characteristic of social movements that involve hybrid levels of expertise and that target science. It is quite commonplace to see claims made by such movements that "our" science is objective while "their" science is corrupt without accounting for the fact that all science is situated, contingent, and rooted in a range of ethics and values.[10] Another common tactic used to establish a position as objective is to enroll as many allies as possible, regardless of their strength or acceptability within the scientific community. For example, NARTH's document "What Research Shows," brought together

hundreds of studies discredited in mainstream science, but required readers to challenge every single one.[11] A corollary tactic is to minimize the
number of allies of an opponent. NARTH attempted to minimize the
number of reputable allies on the issue of harm, by pointing to very few
studies, while the APA task force did the same by reducing the number
of reorientation studies worthy of review. Actors in controversies over
sexual reorientation have also been actively engaged in reinterpreting
and redeploying scientific findings. The best example was when NARTH
and religious right organizations utilized the Spitzer study as evidence
of the effectiveness of reorientation therapies for all gays and lesbians,
although Spitzer intended only to demonstrate a possibility for a few
highly motivated individuals. In social movements operating on the
fringe, language and other symbols of science have been utilized in the
performance of scientism. NARTH uses the neutrally titled *Journal of
Human Sexuality*, complete with issues and volumes and its own editorial board, and NARTH conferences are replete with formalities and the
flashing of credentials. As the name NARTH has become publicly linked
to anti-gay bias, it has created a new parent organization with the neutral name "Alliance for Therapeutic Choice and Scientific Integrity." It is
not that mainstream scientists do not deploy these same tactics, for they
do, but the difference is that they have emerged victorious in credibility
struggles.

In addition to these tactics, claimants on both sides of reorientation
therapy debates have routinely used metaphors to make their claims
more vivid and to link their position with more well-established issues in
their discussions of homosexuality, reorientation, and research. Homosexuality is like alcoholism, stealing, or smoking if you believe it is a pathology to be treated, or it is like eye color, handedness, or height if you
believe it is an innate characteristic deserving of rights. Sexual reorientation therapy is like treatment for alcoholism, rehabilitation, or surgery if
you are a proponent, or it is like torture or something out of *Clockwork
Orange* if you are not. Such deployment of metaphors is not surprising.
Yet these metaphors cannot settle the controversy, and alternatives are
needed if we are to move beyond the impasse.

With all these tactics at play, the fate of claims in these disputes has
been shaped by the intellectual opportunity structure within the field of
therapeutics. In the United States, the institutional apparatus upholding
the idea that homosexuality is a normal variant of human sexuality stands
firmly against the therapeutic treatment of homosexuality as pathology. It
includes the removal of "Homosexuality" and all references to same-sex
desire from the *DSM*, and the establishment of position statements, ethics

codes, journals, and professional LGBT therapeutic groups. Notions of "autonomy" and client "self-determination" do not apply when reorientation clients lack informed consent about the possibilities for gay affirmation. While testimonial evidence of change was first undermined by discrediting ex-gay claims as generally untrustworthy, this credibility hierarchy of evidence was later established on the basis of scientific construct validity and the new sexual orientation/sexual orientation identity dichotomy. Ex-gays simply could not access the truth of sexual orientation through testimony, but could only express an ex-gay identity. This move effectively exacerbated the frame dispute between factions of the ex-gay movement. Clarifying the meaning of *change* meant that the frame dispute could no longer be sustained through ambiguous uses of that term. Suddenly, religious ex-gay ministry leaders, with the goal of identity change, might be more affirmed by science if they only abandoned the goals of secular reorientation therapists, and a wedge was driven between these factions.

By contrast, in Uganda, the intellectual opportunity structure has facilitated the uptake of some reorientation concepts in science, also fueled by the influence of the wider cultural understanding of homosexuality established by the anti-homosexuality movement. That movement has, to a large extent, conflated homosexuality with child rape and other social ills, which must be disaggregated if gay rights are to proceed in the country. The prevalence of evangelical Christianity has also facilitated this uptake. In the postcolonial context, secular Western science can be assigned the status of "foreign influence," negating the statements of professional associations even from Westernized international government organizations. The permissiveness of the International Federation of Social Workers and the close relationship between the National Association of Social Workers of Uganda and the Ugandan Parliament have been key institutional relationships enabling the uptake of NARTH concepts, imported during the 2009 Family Life Network conference in Kampala. While transnational networks have been important, the specific version of anti-homosexuality ideology in Uganda blends nationalist concerns with ideas about protecting a young population in the context of growing HIV rates. While much of this is specific to Uganda in the early twenty-first century, it should be noted that there are many similarities between these developments and the historical climate within the United States, where sodomy laws were only overturned by the Supreme Court in 2003. While homosexuality and child "recruitment" are closely conflated in Uganda, this discourse, which was prominent in the United States in the 1970s, still resurfaces from time to time.[12] Finally,

Ugandan mental health professionals in psychology and psychiatry, regardless of their viewpoints, faced pressure from the state to lend some kind of support to the regulation of homosexuality, especially given that the Anti-Homosexuality Act contained provisions against homosexuality advocacy.

The final component of an intellectual opportunity structure, as I have defined it, is the existence of an opposing social movement. In many ways, the dynamics of opposing social movements targeting science are analogous to the dynamics of opposing movements targeting the state that sociologists have observed. For example, in the United States, venue shifting has been an important dynamic, as the victory of gay liberation in demedicalization led ex-gays to shift from the intellectual domain of science to that of theology. By emphasizing a definition of homosexuality as "sin" rather than "pathology," those seeking to change their sexual desires toward heterosexuality could maintain some legitimacy under the banner of religious freedom. The anti-reorientation movement has responded to the shift of venues by highlighting theological perspectives in which homosexuality is theologically supported. As in other opposing social movement struggles, the media have played an important role in exacerbating conflict. While scientists have formed a general consensus that there is no evidence for the efficacy of reorientation therapies, and that they are potentially harmful, media outlets have continued to pit experts against one another as though there remains a burning scientific controversy. For example, in 2011, NPR ran a story titled "Can Therapy Help Change Sexual Orientation?" that presented the testimony of ex-gay Rich Wyler against ex-gay survivor Peterson Toscano, and claimed that the debate still rages despite the APA decision.[13]

Through back-and-forth processes of dialogical framing, a middle path was created in the United States between the extremes of "out gay" and "ex-gay" for clients struggling with conflict. The concept of "sexual identity therapy," initially put forth by Mark Yarhouse and Lori Burkett, has in part become mainstream, although the capacity to therapeutically alter sexual orientation has not been supported. Through this process, the idea of an underlying "sexual orientation," rooted in bodily experienced physiology and emotion, was gradually consolidated. Indeed, the intellectual opportunity structure provided key openings that allowed this convergence to take place. Among them were the 2007 position statement within the APA that recognized respect for religious diversity, and the inclusion of A. Lee Beckstead, an ex-ex-gay with extensive experience in religious communities and with psychology of religion, on the APA task force on appropriate therapeutic responses to sexual orientation.

One thing that is particularly noteworthy in this conflict, which may not always be present when social movements target science, is the complex relationship between human kinds produced in science and the collective identities of these social movements. At the heart of the contest over the efficacy of reorientation therapy is a contest over the validation of notions of selfhood. Inevitably, whenever a social movement unsuccessfully targets science, members of the movement risk being seen as out of touch with the reality that science validates. In this case, the intellectual opportunity structure blocked not only the construction of facts but also the validation of selves integral to the collective identity of social movements. Whether or not an "ex-gay" is delusional and whether or not "gay" people are suitable for full inclusion into society have been stakes in these struggles with mental health institutions. The compromise promoted by the APA of "sexual orientation identity exploration" offered a way to validate aspects of ex-gay lives: one can have a straight lifestyle and identity in line with one's religious beliefs while realizing that at the level of attractions, one will always feel gay. While this position begins to offer a way out of the "culture war," it still precludes a fuller range of understandings of sexual and gendered selves. To better illuminate how this preclusion works, I first will look at how essentialism and the evidence used to bolster it make sexualities appear to exist independent of culture. I will then further explore what it means to understand sexualities as culturally learned and how that idea might still be used to advance gay rights.

"Nature" Manufactured for Assimilationist Politics

In the United States, the relegation of reorientation to the scientific fringe has emerged along with a cultural surge in essentialism around sexual orientation. Whether it is Lady Gaga proclaiming, "I was born this way" or Mary Lambert singing, "I can't change, even if I tried, even if I wanted to" in the Macklemore song "Same Love," essentialist ideas about the innate and immutable nature of sexual orientation are fashionable. Amin Ghaziani has described U.S. culture as moving toward a "post-gay" era, in which sexual orientation becomes so inconsequential that gays and lesbians are integrated into straight spaces.[14] In the era of gay marriage, gays in the military, and hate crime protections, gay and lesbian identities are becoming increasingly accepted as forms of sexual citizenship. While the politics of assimilation involve playing down cultural differences, they are based on essentialist differences. It is not only the belief that gays and lesbians can't change that makes assimilation more tenable; the idea that straights are "uncontaminated" by gay biology also facilitates the comfort levels needed for assimilation. As Suzanna Walters has argued, essentialist politics can only get gay rights so far, since it produces "tolerance" rather than full acceptance. We learn to tolerate many annoying things, such as the side effects of medication, and saying same-sex desire is something that just "can't be helped" is another way of devaluing homosexuality. Alternatively, we might imagine reasons to culturally value same-sex attractions and behavior as part of the human condition for many people.[15] As essentialism reinforces this idea of "tolerance," it is worth further examining how this discourse extracts biology from culture, seen in the new campaign LGBTscience.org put together by Truth Wins Out.

This organization has recently posted numerous interviews with scientists to document evidence for the origins of sexual orientation. The website seeks to explore the biological basis for sexual orientation, what scientists say about changing sexual orientation, and the ethics of research. The most highly publicized research in this area took place in the early 1990s, when studies by Simon LeVay, Dean Hamer, and Michael Bailey made headlines. Many believed these studies suggested that a "gay gene" on the X chromosome, in a region labeled Xq28, was responsible for causing homosexuality. Back then, some gay activists wore charm bracelets with the Xq28 moniker, and T-shirts were made saying "Thanks Mom for the gay gene." Truth Wins Out has interviewed these three scientists and several more, some of whom have been engaged in more recent research.

Research on the biology of sexual orientation centers on two paradigms. One, "brain organization theory," asserts that sexual orientation is the product of sex hormones acting on the fetal brain during gestation. These hormones are responsible for forming internal and external genitals out of the same preliminary structures, and are thought to also shape the brain such that being male means being attracted to females, and vice versa for being female. Sexual orientation is but one of many attributes thought to be the product of these sex hormones; a range of gendered behavior and identity is also being attributed to this cause, such as women's mediocre spatial reasoning skills, which are supposed to account for their underrepresentation in science fields.[16]

Exploring the brain organization thesis, Simon LeVay examined the hypothalamus in brains of deceased homosexual and heterosexual men, as well as women. It had long been thought that this region of the brain affected sexuality in animals, so extending this work to humans was plausible. LeVay found a statistically significant difference in the sizes of the INAH3 region of the hypothalamus for homosexual and heterosexual men. While the trend for having smaller structures was statistically significant, it was not absolute—some gay men had INAH3 clusters on the high end of the scale, while some heterosexual men had clusters on the low end. The study was criticized because most of the gay men had died of AIDS, whereas the majority of the heterosexual men had died of other causes. There is no plausible reason, however, why HIV/AIDS would shrink this region of the brain. LeVay even controlled for this factor in heterosexual men and found no effect.

The second paradigm, which is often linked to brain organization theory, is the idea of a "gay gene," inherited from the mother, which causes homosexuality. Through a genetic study in 1993, Dean Hamer and his team of geneticists at the National Cancer Institute claimed to have found a gene within the Xq28 region of the X chromosome, though no specific gene has been identified. While Hamer and his colleagues had a nuanced explanation of the relationship between the suspected gene and behavior, the media reported a simplistic causal story. Meanwhile, Michael Bailey and Richard Pillard conducted a twin study of homosexuality, in which pairs of monozygotic (identical) and dizygotic (fraternal) twins were studied for homosexual identity. The researchers found that if a person with an identical twin was gay, the twin was also gay, at a rate of 52 percent. Meanwhile, if a person with a fraternal twin was gay, the fraternal twin was gay at a rate of 22 percent. These two paradigms of the "gay gene" and the "gay brain" can be linked if the gay gene somehow regulates the hormones that circulate in the fetus during brain development, perhaps through effects on the gonads.

In the interviews on LGBTscience.org, scientists present their views on the evidence pertaining to the biological causes of homosexuality for a public audience. Typically, these interviews include *narratives* that do the work of relegating sexualities to the domain of nature, outside the realm of culture, rather than treating these domains as interwoven. For example, LeVay states, "The science really backs up the notion that being gay or being lesbian or being straight for that matter is really a kind of central part of your nature."[17] Psychiatrist Milton Diamond explains the meaning of his phrase "nature loves variety":

> Nature when it makes its products, whichever they are, either human beings or animals or plants or whatever, makes them in many different

forms. In fact, we wouldn't have evolution if that didn't happen. So, nature loves variety. The problem is, it's unfortunate that many societies don't like variety, they want everybody to be the same. They want everybody to think the same and have the same religion, have the same thoughts. Well, I think that wouldn't be reality. It's reality for the society that they want things the same. It's not the same for nature. Nature wants variety. And that's the way it progresses.[18]

Like the sexological tradition going back to Kinsey, these narratives pit a natural sexuality against an oppressive cultural morality. It is rather commonplace to place nature and culture in opposition like this; such discourses are ready made to fit into modern state politics, which are often premised on the idea that politics and culture are antithetical to nature. Bringing "what nature wants" into the political realm of acceptance seems to suggest that nature can be seen in an unmediated fashion through the transparent window of scientific research. Yet, a major argument of this book is that notions of sexual orientation, including how they are measured, labeled, and classified, emerge historically. I explore the ramifications of this idea in the next section.

Meanwhile, these research programs have been the target of numerous criticisms, and the original studies have not been replicated. There is no way to explain how genes would produce same-sex sexual desire, and the gay gene theory also lacks a more nuanced incorporation of the reality that genes and environment interact. Nonetheless, this theory has taken on a life of its own, even finding its way into scientific databases as an organizing framework.[19] The popularity of this idea outside science says more about its political utility than about its status as scientific fact. At the same time, gay genes are a precarious strategy for sexual equality, as they could potentially lead to genetic screening. Brain organization research, as in the LeVay study, is not clearly linked to the gay gene except through rhetoric. If there is indeed a measurable difference in brain structures, these differences do not point to a genetic cause, but may be evidence of the brain's plasticity. Any biological differences should not be understood independent of culture, but rather, the scientific vocabularies and methodologies, including grouping people into "heterosexuals" and "homosexuals," are deeply culturally bound. To move beyond the impasse of nature versus nurture, it is imperative to realize that science is not outside the world in which we live. To do so is not to question the value of gay rights, but rather to open up consideration of a broader range of sexual and gender expressions.

Therapy for Binaries

In the Spitzer study, sexual orientation was measured as a composite of behavior, attraction, and identity measures, with attraction being considered the "core feature." The creation of a sexual orientation/sexual orientation identity binary, confining sexual orientation to attraction and the realm of nature, has been a strategic move that works well for policy concerns. Sexual orientation/sexual orientation identity has been brought into being to join the various binaries populating the modern world, including male/female, masculine/feminine, nature/culture, mind/body, technology/society, and many others. This strategic move bears many similarities to the severing of "gender" and "sex," which was important for second-wave feminists but later subject to critique. But as a form of essentialism, fixing sexual orientation within the body, separate from identity, precludes some ways of being human.

Second-wave feminists relied on the sex/gender dichotomy to argue that the malleability of the cultural construct of gender could challenge inequality between the sexes. They argued that gender ideologies of active "masculinity" and passive "femininity" were not a product of "nature" like male and female sex but that gender was socially constructed.[20] Judith Butler has argued that cultural gender does not merely map onto a fixed and natural sex binary but that cultural notions of gender are necessary for the social construction of sex. That is, a cultural binary of gender is mapped onto a continuum of bodies that range from male to female, confining sex to a binary, resulting in the exclusion of intersex categories. This is best illustrated by surgeries on infants with ambiguous genitalia, which historically have been assigned sex and surgically altered on the arbitrary basis of capacity for heterosexual intercourse.[21] For Butler, gender is performative, meaning that people enact gender in ways that make their biological sex seem like an essence. Furthermore, she argues, any gender performance is really a "copy of a copy" with no original, and she considers drag performance to be support for this notion. For Butler, the performativity of gender is built within a "heterosexual matrix" that is normative in society; people are encouraged and even *coerced* to enact gender in ways that make the gender and sex binaries supporting reproductive heterosexuality seem inevitable and natural. In her critique of the heterosexual matrix, sexual orientation categories, which rely on notions of biological sexes to delineate "object choices," are subject to the same criticism. A category like "gay man" relies on an essentialist notion of who belongs in a "male" sex, furthering the exclusion of intersex categories and taking the natural binary of sex for granted.

The logic of Butler's critique of the gender/sex dichotomy can be further applied to the sexual orientation identity/sexual orientation di-chotomy newly formalized by the American Psychological Association. In other words, sexual orientation identities can be viewed as performa-tive enactments of essentialized sexual orientations. Identities of "gay," "lesbian," "bisexual," and "heterosexual" reinforce the idea of an under-lying biological essence. For heterosexual men, this means eschewing anything that might look like homosexual desire, and for gay men, this might mean donning an Xq28 bracelet or eschewing anything like het-erosexual desire. Like gender, cultural expectations of sexual orientation expression can also be coercive. However, if sexual orientation identities are similarly performative, then the rehearsal of desire expressed within them is always a "copy of a copy" with no original. For many men in the era of phallometry, this may mean understanding the physiology of erec-tion as automatic in the presence of key object choices, and perhaps ex-periencing anxiety when it is not. Even learning to say that one was "born that way" becomes part of the performance. Yet, as in the case of the erasure of intersexuality through binary sex, a category system limited to "gay" and "straight" erases other experiences and possibilities such as bisexuality, attraction to a person who does not easily fit into "male" or "female," or attraction to a person simply because of who the person is (or some other reason) rather than the person's sex category. Sexual ori-entation essentialism, rooted in notions of binary sex, also creates chal-lenges for the inclusion of transgender persons within the sexual orienta-tion identity categories of gay, lesbian, straight, or bisexual.

By invoking behaviorist studies using phallometric testing as the best evidence that reorientation does not work, scientists have effectively used a notion of male sexuality as a stand-in for all human sexuality, characterized by fixed sexual orientation. Because female sexuality is often theorized as being primarily emotion based, with emotional con-nection leading to sexual desire, women's sexuality is often understood to be more fluid. In her longitudinal study of women and changes in their sexual identity, expression, and desire, psychologist Lisa Diamond has developed a pragmatic model of women's sexuality in which women are understood to have an underlying fixed sexual orientation, but a layer of fluidity rides on top of this fixed foundation. While this model is useful to make sense of Diamond's data while supporting contemporary gay rights discourses, it still excludes sexual subjectivities characterized by spontaneous fluidity without any fixed sexual orientation foundation. A narrative in which a person is 100 percent heterosexual at one time and 100 percent homosexual at another time is not possible within the cur-rent regime of fixed sexual orientation, even with Diamond's "layer of fluidity." Thus, while notions of fixed sexual orientation undermine the therapeutic reorientation of people into heterosexuality, they come with a cost of undermining some possibilities of conceptualizing spontaneous fluidity of sexual orientations that may occur.[22]

At the same time, Diamond has also encouraged thinking about sexual desire in much more complicated ways. Whereas genital arousal testing reinforces a very mechanical notion of desire, Diamond has encouraged thinking about the ambiguity of the term *sexual desire*. Referring to research on what this term means to young women in qualitative interviews, Diamond provides a number of examples:

> "Liking to look at a woman's face or body"; "the urge to have sex"; "a fluttery feeling in my belly"; "wanting to be physically near someone"; "not needing to care about her personality"; "feeling really really happy around someone"; "electric energy"; "wanting to talk all night long."[23]

Diamond offered this list to criticize Spitzer's use of self-report, given that his attraction scale did not really define the meaning of desire, and it seems to scratch the surface of possibilities of what "desire" might mean to different people. We might also consider how it can complicate notions of male sexual desire limited to visually stimulated erection. What does it mean for a man to feel "really really happy around someone," "electric energy," or "wanting to talk all night long" even if an erection is not present? Such forms of male sexual desire are precluded if the truth of desire is reduced to erections produced by pornography. We might also consider other means by which men become sexually aroused beyond visual stimulation, including touch and emotional connection.

Not all sexual classification systems are based on fixed "sexual orientations," however. The contemporary system in the United States is quite rare historically and cross-culturally, although it has been expanding in influence. To move past the impasse of essentialist views of gay rights politics versus heteronormative conservatism we should reconsider what it may mean for sexualities to be learned.

How Sexualities Still Involve Learning

A key talking point for proponents of the Anti-Homosexuality Act in Uganda was that homosexuality is learned behavior that can be unlearned. This perspective has prompted opponents to look to essentialism for a response. The scientific panel that advised President Museveni noted that no definitive evidence exists for the claim that homosexuality is genetic. When it has been used to justify a bill containing the death penalty for homosexuality, it is understandable that the idea that sexual orientations are "learned" seems extremely dangerous. Indeed, at the time of this writing, controversy rages over a new billboard erected in Richmond, Virginia, by the group PFOX depicting a set of twins and the caption, "Identical twins: One gay. One not. We believe twins research studies show nobody is <u>born</u> gay."[24] At the same time, the idea that there is an element of learning in sexual orientations is a key component of the argument of this book, as it is based on social constructionist theory. However, it does not follow that adopting a position that sexualities are learned means that one supports anti-gay measures, nor does it mean that sexual feelings can just be changed at will.

In the introduction, I explained two constructionist perspectives on how sexualities are learned that I have brought together for this analysis. John Gagnon and William Simon point to particular "sexual scripts" circulating throughout society, which teach us the how, what, when, and where of sexual enactment and desire. We are not born knowing what "sexual" means or how a sexual encounter is to unfold appropriately, and the many things that are considered sexually attractive change over time and from culture to culture. Sexual arousal and orgasm are only possible if a situation is understood to be sexual by participants.[25] Gagnon and Simon likened the adoption of a sexual identity to adopting a career, within which people learn to succeed. Thinking in these terms leads to the question "what is sexual?" There is much ambiguity regarding this category, and its boundaries shift from time to time.[26] For Foucault, sexualities were consolidated as human types through scientific discourses beginning around the end of the nineteenth century. Foucault described the shift from a juridical mode of power to a medico-scientific regime. With this shift, we learned that people who engaged in same-sex sexual behaviors become "homosexual" while those who did not were "heterosexual." This category system, rooted in Western sexology, delineates human kinds, and creates a set of discourses available for our own self-fashioning. In late modernity, people increasingly look to science to understand the many components of their sexuality and self-identity; thus these essentialist ideas have become ever more firmly entrenched.[27] Through a Foucauldian lens, sexual identity is learned because we enter into a world with limited options for sexual expression and identification.[28] Moreover, Gagnon and Simon speculated that people likely adhere to universalized essentialist notions of gender and sexuality because they cannot cope with the existential reality that what it means to be human, including patterns of emotion, thought, and desire, have continually changed throughout human history.[29]

Conceptualizing sexualities as learned and historically contingent, however, does not necessarily mean that all people simply have a "choice" to determine their sexual desires. If we abandon for a moment the idea that sexual orientations are biologically determined, the social shaping of this thing we call "sexual orientation" could be just as strong. Internalizing a cultural idea of fixed sexual orientation can have immense implications for one's life choices. At the cultural level, scripts are created for sexual orientation categories that are difficult to resist. The repeated rehearsal of sexual orientation as essence is likely to accompany bodily effects like any other deeply ingrained practice. At the same time, as long as both a strong gender binary and gay/straight binary exist, reinscribed by a scientific "straight line," it is likely people experiencing fixed sexual orientations will continue doing so.[30] Imagine an openly gay activist who subsequently wants to explore a relationship with a woman; if she finds out about his past, would she trust that he could actually have a sexual relationship with her, given his innate and immutable "nature"? Would anyone believe in the authenticity of their relationship? What might happen to his feelings of attraction for her when subjected to such societal doubt? Yet, with increasing transgender inclusion in society, and with an understanding of the performativity of sexual orientation identities, perhaps a destabilization is possible to allow a broader range of sexual expression beyond the gay/straight dichotomy, especially for men. The scripted ideals, including relationship styles and notions of success, associated with static sexual orientation identities could give way to new possibilities.

To say that sexuality is learned also does not undermine the idea that it has a biological component. Sexual orientation identities might better be thought of as nature–culture composites rather than cultural signifiers for natural sexual orientations. Encouraging us to consider that the body has some meaningful role in sexualities, Elizabeth Wilson has analyzed Simon LeVay's data and acknowledges the statistically significant difference between heterosexual and homosexual hypothalamic structures. Taking an intermediary position, she argues that it is important to take seriously both the differences along with the continuities across the structures LeVay observed, as a starting point for thinking about the complexities of how sexual desires are neurologically embodied.[31] As philosopher Ian Hacking has argued, human categories constituted through science have "looping effects." Reinforcing human kinds can have effects on the people who adopt these identities, resulting in changes in behavior that can, in turn, affect scientific research on those identified groups.[32] If persons are diagnosed with a mental illness, for instance, that illness diagnosis may change behavior in ways that affect research on people with the diagnosis. Applying this concept to sexual orientations, the scientific view that men's sexual orientations are binary, fixed, and based on erectile response may limit other forms of sexual expression. If men adopt this characterization of their sexuality as objective unmediated scientific fact, it will then be reinscribed in scientific research when they participate in studies. Scientific research alleging that women have greater potential for sexual fluidity may actually create more openings for women's sexual exploration. If the brain differences LeVay identified are real, they may be the results of these looping effects more than any "innate" difference in human types—that is, they may be an effect, not a cause.

The learning of sexualities is further illustrated by the fact that the Western system of classifying sexual orientations, based on object choice, is not the only way of classifying sexualities. Some other sexual systems in the world seem to permit (or even require) sexual fluidity among men. In Indonesia, the words *gay* and *lesbi* are used to refer to sexual subjectivities that include same-sex relationships but do not exclude heterosexual families.[33] Massad describes Arab and Muslim countries where many men who engage in same-sex behaviors do not ascribe to a sexual identity, and those who penetrate remain part of the societal norm, though this system is threatened by essentialist discourses of global gay rights groups.[34] Studying sexualities in 1990s Guadalajara, Mexico, Héctor Carrillo observed a complex overlay between a Western sexual orientation–based system and a traditional sex-gender system. In the gender-based system, men identified as "hombres" or "normal" may penetrate men and still maintain their status as potential partners of women. By contrast, "maricones" are men who are penetrated and who maintain a feminized position. Yet among Carrillo's interview respondents, same-sex behavior may have been interpreted through either or both of these systems.[35] Other societies have been taken to illustrate the possibility of universal homosexual practices, yet the circumstances of these relationships call into question whether they truly apply to a model of universal sexual fluidity. For example, the "Sambia," a pseudonymously named tribe in Papua New Guinea, historically enacted a ritual in which adolescent males ingested semen of older men in order to attain "life force," though this is no longer practiced following international scrutiny.[36] Ancient Greece is also known for mentoring relationships between older men and adolescent males.[37]

While a gay/straight dichotomy is a dominant discourse for men in the United States, researchers have found much sexual fluidity despite it. A key finding of the largest sex survey ever conducted in the United

States was that sexual attraction, identity, and behavior do not always neatly line up for either men or women.[38] Some men on Internet hookup sites identify as heterosexual and seek sex with other men. In interviews, these men explained how sex with other men makes them "more heterosexual."[39] Furthermore, men working in the porn industry maintain their heterosexual identity by explaining that their "gay for pay" work is not based on their own sexual desire but rather is justified by being paid, and is still authentically heterosexual because they use straight porn on the set to stay aroused.[40] While these cases illustrate ways in which the straight/gay binary can be partially resisted, they also point to the reality that some men experience sexual fluidity. Yet, the resistance expressed toward male bisexuality by gay as well as straight men supports the fact that the gay/straight dichotomy remains a tremendously strong cultural force.[41]

With all of this variation in sexual categorization systems across the planet, how could it be that the identities of "gay," "lesbian," and "straight" are innate and immutable? Offering an alternative to the stale metaphors of eye color, on the one hand, and alcoholism, on the other, Tom Boellstorff provides a metaphor to explain how sexualities are learned yet still have a biological basis. Boellstorff notes that people can be said to have a biological predisposition to acquire language, but whether that language is English or Chinese depends on the cultural context.[42] Sexual subjectivities can be understood in the same way. Whether one grows up in a society where there is great sexual fluidity or distinct sexual binaries has a tremendous impact on how one develops sexually. Another alternative metaphor for thinking about how sexualities are learned is cuisines. Consider how many people in the United States shudder at the thought of eating insects, yet in many places in the world, insect consumption is commonplace and insects are even considered a delicacy. There may be a "basic mammalian capacity" to consume the larvae of insects and even adult scorpions. However, the revulsion that many feel to this idea is learned. Likewise, the revulsion that many gays and lesbians may feel about heterosexuality, or that straight people may feel about homosexuality, is learned.

What does the idea that sexualities are learned mean for how we should teach young people about sexuality? Sex education experts have promoted the idea of teaching kids that they may be gay, lesbian, bisexual, or heterosexual. In Uganda such efforts by UNICEF have been met with moral condemnation and accusations of "recruitment" of children. The introduction of the idea that there are people with fixed sexual orientations in the world, who identify as LGBT, is certainly a worthy undertaking for teaching cultural competency. But to tell young people that they have a predisposition toward an innate heterosexuality or homosexuality is to introduce looping effects that reify these binary constructions. It might be more prudent to tell them that they may or may not experience variation in their sexual desires and even their gender identification across a wide spectrum, and that in the end, sexuality and gender are mysterious but should be treated with respect, and these parts of life need not be based on adherence to coercive norms.

Bringing Sexual Rights into Dialogue

Life within a modern nation-state involves processes of "co-production";[43] that is, decisions about how we live and claims about our nature come into being simultaneously. The acceptance of gays and lesbians as healthy and maintaining subject positions worthy of full inclusion into the citizenry of the nation-state has been predicated on an understanding of sexual orientation as innate and immutable. Advancing protection from the state in the form of rights has involved delineating a population, and in this pursuit, the innate and immutable model has been useful. After all, the idea that homosexuality could be reoriented has been used to exclude gay and lesbian people from obtaining rights. In that instance, the idea that heterosexuality was the only "natural" expression of human sexuality had been co-produced along with laws against homosexuality. So it is understandable how this new formulation came about. If, however, the normativity of heterosexuality was a coercive regime, so is the regime of "the gay citizenry and the straight citizenry." If rights are predicated on being within a sexual orientation category for life, this precludes numerous ways of being in the world.

At the same time, rights of individuals, as delineated in the U.S. Constitution, have been conceptualized as being God-given and inalienable properties of human beings. They have been critically important for minority groups who might be oppressed by the tyranny of the majority. Moreover, when Hillary Clinton argued that "gay rights are human rights," she was appealing to a set of universal human rights chartered by the United Nations. Yet these modernist notions of rights, as prediscursive properties of individuals, are simultaneously emancipatory and regulating discourses. As long as rights are conceptualized as "universal," they will exist as top–down discourses that have regulatory functions.[44] We might move beyond the dualism of universalism and cultural relativism and instead promote cultural dialogue. This would require a realization that not all cultures have the same conceptualization of human dignity. We might, as Boaventura de Sousa Santos suggests, conceive of human rights as "mestiza" or hybrid. That is, rather than emerging out of universalism imposed from above, rights might be established and developed through dialogue. For example, the concept of dharma in Hindu cultures and the concept of human rights within Western international institutions are both concerns about human dignity but within very different frameworks, yet dialogue across these cultures could produce alternative understandings. Such a dialogue across the United States and Uganda might proceed on the basis of aligning "human rights" with *ubuntu*. This term, which translates to "humanness," was suggested by Makerere University Law professor Sylvia Tamale as a new basis for respecting the dignity of LGBT persons in Uganda. The concept of "human rights," which applies to individuals, may not fully correspond to another concept of human dignity, such as *ubuntu*, that aligns parts with a greater whole, yet, dialogue might aid in the production of "mestiza" rights that allow us to better envision human dignity, diversity, and possibility in ways we may not yet understand. In short, more dialogue could develop human rights on the basis of argument and justification rather than on appeals to universals.

In the United States, the model of freedom of religion might be a starting point for an alternative to immutability politics in gaining gay rights. Freedom of religion means that the state cannot require a person to change religion in order to obtain rights. This preserves rights for a trait that is widely seen as malleable, although it might be immutable for some. A person could change religion in theory, yet that person's religion might constitute such a deep part of her sense of self that if the state required the person to change, it would be a violation of her human dignity. If such a model were adopted for LGBT rights in the United States, it would involve the acknowledgment of sexual and gender fluidity that many people experience, and would sidestep the coercive politics of fixity, while still granting rights to people who experience their sexualities as fixed. Settling for a world in which gay and straight exist as separate species is settling for a world in which same-sex eroticism still maintains a degree of taboo, but is tolerated because some people just "can't help it." Rather than starting from the folk belief that same-sex sexual desire is genetic in origin, we might instead begin with the idea that consensual sexual behavior between members of any sex, including sex between men, is not inherently shameful.[45]

Returning to Spitzer's concept of "suboptimal" invites further reflection about why sexualities must be "optimal" as "natural variants" to be considered worthy of citizenship. In *The Queer Art of Failure*, Judith

(Jack) Halberstam explores how dominant notions of success in society may be unattainable and undesirable for queer people. Likewise, striving for biological optimality, achieving some kind of scientific ideal of biological evolutionary potential, may undermine other ways of creating justice and experiencing pleasure in the world.[46] Rooting "natural variation" in a biological determinism may also undermine struggles for justice in other ways. Eve Kosofsky Sedgwick has argued that once gay rights turns to the issue of causes of homosexuality, the debate is already lost because the search for causes already implies the devaluation of gay and lesbian lives.[47] Jonathan Ned Katz offers an alternative view: "The emotional quality, the aesthetic and ethical value, and the cultural and personal worth of any eros is independent of biology, and of its socially and individually constructed origins."[48] This perspective suggests that we might justify the value of different sexualities primarily for how they enhance human lives, rather than because they are parts of "nature" that cannot be helped.

Yet the more we develop our sexual natures in tandem with the modern nation-state, the more natural that the nation-state and fixed sexual orientations seem. Modern nation-states, predicated on universal rights, are not the only way of organizing human beings. Science, conceptualized as a transparent window onto nature, is not the only way of knowing, and has never been truly transparent. By unearthing the seeming naturalness of the gay/straight dichotomy as it has been conceptualized in science and as it has been developed in tandem with rights discourses, I join other queer scholars in the hopes of further opening the door to other ways of being and knowing perhaps not yet experienced. Within the cacophony of clashing experts all claiming to have the illusory objective truth of our sexual nature, it is worthwhile to consider cultivating sexual natures that are just and humane, developing concepts of sexual rights through dialogue, giving sexual minorities a seat at the table, and being respectful of people's claims about themselves regardless of the direction they are taking. This does not mean that "anything goes," but rather that we might come together to have discussions about the boundaries of human freedom and acceptable sexualities, without necessarily imposing strict binaries and universals, but making our justifications with substantive arguments. While this approach may not provide moral certainty, at least it "means that we will be cautious and deliberate in our sexual judgments."[49] These pursuits may help preserve the mystery and discovery that are part of living a sexual life complete with its own experiential evidence. In the end, we might learn to trust ourselves and each other.

ACKNOWLEDGMENTS

I am truly grateful to those who helped me to make this book possible. While my name stands in the place of the author, it is without a doubt the product of numerous productive conversations, great mentorship, and the generosity of many people. I would first like to thank the respondents from all sides of reorientation debates who participated in this research and provided insight and candor in interviews. People involved in polarized conflicts often feel many reasons to be wary of outsiders, and I am grateful for those who were willing to let me inside their social worlds. I am also grateful for the funding I received from the National Science Foundation in the form of a Dissertation Improvement Grant, which helped me travel within the United States to conduct interviews and attend conferences. The Science in Human Culture Program at Northwestern University funded my trip to Uganda through my postdoctoral fellowship, and I am thankful for that as well. The University of Minnesota Press has been wonderful to work with, and I thank Jason Weidemann for being such a supportive and enthusiastic editor, Mary Byers for her meticulous and tremendously helpful work in copyediting, two anonymous reviewers, and Laura Westlund, Ana Bichanich, Emily Hamilton, Alicia Gomez, and other staff at the Press for their very creative and inspiring work.

I would like to express deep appreciation to my many mentors who worked closely with me on this research over the years. Clearly, I stand on many shoulders. First, my graduate school adviser, Steven Epstein, helped me to conceptualize the project, saw me through the dissertation phase at University of California, San Diego, and supervised my postdoctoral fellowship at Northwestern University. The value of his mentorship and insight for this project is immeasurable. Julia Ericksen, whom I have the honor of succeeding at Temple University, worked with me on the development of the book manuscript, helping me write a text that can be read by a wider audience; I am grateful for these efforts. My committee members, including Mary Blair-Loy, Lisa Cartwright, Andrew Lakoff, and David Serlin, provided valuable feedback and support. Mary Blair-Loy has been immensely helpful for bridging the worlds of science studies and the sociology of culture. While faculty of the Northwestern

University sociology department and Science in Human Culture program were extremely supportive, I would like to acknowledge Héctor Carrillo, Wendy Griswold, Carol Heimer, Mary Pattillo, and Christian Ukaegbu, who helped with developing the transnational dimensions of this research. I would also like to express appreciation to Kearsley Stewart, who helped prepare me in so many ways for my trip to Uganda, as well as Kelly Moore, Rhys Williams, and Jane Lowicki-Zucca. I also thank Ken Alder and Wendy Espeland, who both have been inspirational in thinking about the cultural dimensions of knowledge production techniques. The UCSD Student Choice Speaker program allowed me to get direct feedback from Michelle Murphy and Sheila Jasanoff, which I truly appreciate. Additional inspiring mentors I worked with include Rick Biernacki, Rebecca Klatch, Lester Kurtz, Martha Lampland, Naomi Oreskes, Susan Leigh Star, Bob Westman, and Christine Williams.

I received useful feedback from audiences at meetings of the American Sociological Association, Society for the Social Studies of Science, UC San Diego Science Studies Colloquium, the Northwestern Science in Human Culture Program Klopsteg Lecture Series and Midwestern Regional Science and Technology Studies Conference, and the Temple University sociology department. Many useful conversations with colleagues informed this work; thanks go to Marissa Brandt, Karl Bryant, Ricardo Sánchez Cárdenas, Erin Cech, Natasha Dennison, Michael Evans, Clare Forstie, Joseph Guisti, Lyn Headley, April Huff, Katie Kenny, Jeff Kosbie, Eric Martin, Alka Menon, Jamie Morse, Kevin Moseby, Tanya Munz, Aaron Norton, Kellie Owens, Melissa Minor Peters, Margarita Rayzberg, Talia Shiff, and many others. Alka Menon helped tremendously as a research assistant while I was in Uganda, and I sincerely appreciate her support and advice on international travel.

I would like to thank members of the Temple University Department of Sociology faculty and staff for their support while I developed this manuscript. There are too many to mention everyone, but I especially thank my chair, Robert Kaufman, for his support, as well as colleagues Michelle Byng, Sherri Grasmuck, Dustin Kidd, Judith Levine, and Matt Wray.

Finally, I acknowledge and thank my mother and father and many friends, including café baristas, all of whom supported me during this research in their own ways.

METHODOLOGICAL APPENDIX

The methodological approach in this book is derived from that pioneered by Steven Epstein in *Impure Science: AIDS, Activism, and the Politics of Knowledge.*[1] Prior to that work, the field of science and technology studies was preoccupied with explaining the construction of scientific facts as produced by actors known as the "core set"—professionally accredited scientists only. Epstein, in his study of how AIDS activists shaped knowledge about HIV/AIDS and drug development, broadened this focus to take seriously the role of social movements in the construction of knowledge. In summarizing related scholarship that has emerged since this advance, Epstein outlined a research program in "patient groups and health movements," to which this book is intended as a contribution.[2] In particular, I examine the ways in which the dynamics of opposing social movements targeting science can be a contributing factor in knowledge production struggles that are culturally specific.

In order to examine the shifting credibility of measurement practices within the process of relegating sexual reorientation to the scientific fringe, the sources for this research were chosen to follow the key claimants through this scientific controversy, both within science and within public domains. Primary sources for this work include scientific research studies located through searches in the Web of Science database, and special journal issues. For example, the 2003 special issue of *Archives of Sexual Behavior* devoted to the Spitzer study and the 2004 special issue of *Counseling Psychologist* devoted to reconciling conflict were crucial. To elucidate which were the most important publications and claims and who were the most important claimants, I conducted participant observation at key conferences. These included the inaugural meeting of Beyond Ex-Gay in 2007 in Irvine, California; the 2007 annual meeting of the National Association for Research and Therapy of Homosexuality in Dallas, Texas; a regional conference of Exodus International in 2008 in Fresno, California; and the 2008 American Psychological Association Convention in Boston, Massachusetts. The APA meeting was important for observing the confrontation between NARTH and the APA during the deliberations of the APA task force. These meetings were also occasions to collect and analyze activist literature.

Within the constraints of travel possibilities and respondent availability, I selected key claimants for a total of thirty-five interviews.
These included leaders of Beyond Ex-Gay and Exodus International and
members of the APA Task Force. Other key U.S. public figures included
Dr. Robert Spitzer, interviewed in 2008 and in 2012; Clinton Anderson
of the APA Office of LGBT Concerns; psychologist Charles Silverstein of
the Gay Activist Alliance; and reorientation therapist Janelle Hallman.
In Uganda, interview respondents included Frank Mugisha, director
of Sexual Minorities Uganda; Brian Nkoyooyo, director of Icebreakers
Uganda; Member of Parliament David Bahati; and members of the Family
Life Network.

Archaeology, Genealogy, and Symmetry

In applying Epstein's method, my work involves juxtaposing claims made
over time through the scientific literature and by dissenters, looking
for key moments of rupture, consolidation, and discontinuity in shifting knowledge regimes. In this regard, it is loosely based on the work of
Michel Foucault. For Foucault, a work is archaeological if it unearths the
conditions that make different ways of thinking possible at a particular
historical moment.[3] A work is genealogical when it demonstrates those
moments of rupture, revealing that knowledge production is not a con-
tinuous process toward truth, but rather is wrought with discontinuous
twists and turns that do not follow a clear logic beyond the historical
conditions that produce them.[4] This process also requires identifying
elements within and across institutions that operate as elements of an
"intellectual opportunity structure," properties of knowledge-producing
institutions that enable or constrain social movements when trying to
shape knowledge claims. While the intellectual opportunity structure
constrains the kinds of official scientific facts that can be produced, it
does not necessarily delineate what can be thought. Although the theory
of intellectual opportunity structure utilized here was derived from this
case and built from prior sources, there may be additional elements of
this structure for future researchers to theorize.

In the sociology of scientific knowledge, a key principle of symmetry
requires withholding an assessment of the "truth" or "falsity" of claims
and, instead, tracing the process by which claims do or do not become
facts. Applying this approach, I attempted to bracket a number of questions.[5] This included first suspending judgment on whether or not "reorientation works." Second, I suspended judgment about the basis of "sexual

orientation" and the best way to measure it. As a second principle of symmetry, I also traced the coconstruction of measurement technologies and sexual subjectivities within credibility struggles over sexual reorientation. The role of physical bodies has been important in this process, because physiological processes have been yoked to these subjectivities through technologies such as phallometric testing.[6]

The Role of the Researcher

To adhere to the principles of symmetry as best as possible, I needed to be reflexive about my own role as a researcher and my own interests in producing this work. From NARTH's perspective, a study of scientific controversies over reorientation therapy might better be explained as a fifty-fifty "scientific debate" rather than a process of relegating reorientation to the scientific fringe. Yet this would be a misrepresentation, given that powerful scientific institutions and journals have weighed in on the matter, definitively rejecting reorientation research. NARTH provides a voice of dissent from the fringe, and this voice has been important for prompting mainstream scientific work. NARTH's charges that the members of the APA task force were predominantly gay or gay sympathizing could apply to this work as well. Indeed, as a member of the American Sociological Association, I too am bound by ethics that require that my research not contribute to discrimination on the basis of sexual orientation or gender. NARTH might charge that I, like members of the APA task force, am another "fox guarding the henhouse." Yet I have striven in my work to "bend over backwards," in Epstein's terms, to examine and understand all views and apply principles of symmetry. NARTH members, and other readers, might consider this work valuable insofar as it has examined all science through a constructionist lens.

My own background may lend credibility to the idea that I could be fair-minded about this research. Coming from the conservative North Texas town of Plano, I came out as gay in 1989 when I was nineteen years old, but soon after this I attempted to live a heterosexual life. I was unaware of any ex-gay groups at the time, and I returned to college and explored evangelical student groups. I left these ministries because of philosophical differences, and during the mid-1990s I reentered the gay world. People in my personal and public worlds know my identity as being "gay," yet my approach to this is decidedly queer, acknowledging its contingent nature and the problematic notions of sex/gender on which it is based. I have always remained somewhat ambivalent about mainstream gay activism for its use of essentialism and for its frequent inattention to other social justice concerns. Queer politics offers an alternative. While I identify as "gay," this is an open-ended identity that does not refer to an innate essence, and this identity may or may not change given changing cultural circumstances. Indeed, if taboos against same-sex eroticism were ever to be completely lifted, I might be just another person. Thus, although I am under the LGBTQ umbrella, I am also interested in acknowledging queer notions of sexual fluidity that exist on both sides of the reorientation debate, while at the same time challenging coercive regimes that impose unreasonable norms on human gender and sexual expression. Throughout all my participation observation and interviews, I maintained a position as "learner" and queerly withheld any assertion about my own identity. Only once was I asked about my own sexuality—by Robert Spitzer—and I explained to him my view of the concept of "queer."

My intellectual background spans the fields of sociology and science studies. As such, I am not committed to scientific positivism in this work. I do not treat scientific truths as "invisible windows" into reality, but rather I treat all knowledge production as contingent, situated, and subject to revision. My dual background in sociology and science studies came in particularly handy when I was working to build trust within the disparate social worlds I was studying. In evangelical organizations, presenting myself as a "science studies scholar" who examines science as a "human endeavor" resonated strongly with those who believe God is the ultimate knower of truth while humankind struggles with situated limitations. In more science-oriented worlds such as NARTH and the APA, emphasizing my sociology background was more helpful, as I might be seen as a fellow traveler developing objective knowledge.

In sociology, while it is imperative to consider risks to research participants, there are also risks to researchers to consider. Projects involving organizations labeled "hate groups," especially if one is a member of the group being "hated," require particular considerations before proceeding.[7] The benefits of this kind of work must be weighed against the potential risks to the researcher that might result from venturing into these spaces. While sociology as a field tends to operate with an imagined distance between the researcher and the object of study, this is not always possible, and, as this book argues, is always an illusion. Self-care is important for researchers in sociology, especially when our work delves into spaces filled with trauma and conflict, perhaps where our work is most needed.

The Ugandan State and Institutional Review Boards

On a final note, the research for this book conducted in the United States was approved by the UCSD Institutional Review Board (IRB) and Temple University IRB. For work in Uganda, the Northwestern University IRB approved the research protocol. Uganda has a government panel called the Uganda National Council for Science and Technology (UNCST), from which all foreign scientific researchers are required to obtain approval for research conducted in the country. This council's work is important, given the legacy of research that has been part of colonial and neocolonial domination in the country. After much thought, however, I decided not to alert the UNCST to my research because of the high degree of institutionalized violence against LGBT people in Uganda. During the time I was going to Uganda, the proposed Anti-Homosexuality Bill included the death penalty for "aggravated homosexuality." LGBT activists there were repeatedly harassed by police forces. The locations for headquarters of Sexual Minorities Uganda and Icebreakers Uganda were known only by word of mouth. Given the situation, it would have been unwise to alert the Ugandan authorities to my work, and I elected to pursue the research without approval from the UNCST to protect all research participants from harm. Given the dire situation for people identifying as LGBT in the country, my decision had to weigh the risk of harm to them against the Ugandan state's concern with overseeing research conducted within its borders by Western researchers. I take responsibility for that difficult decision.

NOTES

Introduction

1. Joseph Nicolosi's reparative therapy program is laid out in *Reparative Therapy of Male Homosexuality: A New Clinical Approach* (Northvale, N.J.: Jason Aronson, 1991) with case studies found in *Healing Homosexuality: Case Stories of Reparative Therapy* (Northvale, N.J.: Jason Aronson, 1993). More recent works include Joseph Nicolosi, *A Parent's Guide to Preventing Homosexuality* (Downers Grove, Ill.: InterVarsity Press, 2000), coauthored with Linda Nicolosi, and an update to the practice in Joseph Nicolosi, *Shame and Attachment Loss: The Practical Work of Reparative Therapy* (Downers Grove, Ill.: InterVarsity Press, 2009). Nicolosi's "reparative therapy" is named for its aim of healing a "reparative drive," a drive underlying same-sex desire that intends to heal lost attachments to same-sex peers and a same-sex parent. "Reparative therapy" is often understood as depicting a need to "repair" gays, but that is not the basis of the term.

2. "Thomas Aquinas Psychological Clinic," Joseph Nicolosi, accessed June 14, 2013, http://www.josephnicolosi.com.

3. David Pickup now runs a reparative therapy clinic in Dallas, Texas, and continues to serve as a board member for NARTH; "David Pickup," David Pickup, accessed September 1, 2014, http://www.davidpickuplmft.com.

4. David Pickup, interview by author, Encino, California, February 2009.

5. Erik Eckholm, "Rift Forms in Movement as Belief in Gay 'Cure' Is Renounced," *New York Times*, July 7, 2012, A9.

6. Melissa Steffan, "Alan Chambers Apologizes to Gay Community, Exodus International to Shut Down," *Christianity Today*, June 21, 2013, accessed June 22, 2014, http://www.christianitytoday.com/gleanings/2013/june/alan-chambers-apologizes-to-gay-community-exodus.html.

7. Some early proponents of ideas of homosexuality as "inversion" include Richard von Krafft-Ebing, *Psychopathia Sexualis: With Especial Reference to the Antipathic Sexual Instinct*, trans. F. S. Klaf (New York: Stein & Day, 1965); Magnus Hirschfeld, *Homosexuality of Men and Women*, trans. Michael A. Lombardi-Nash (New York: Prometheus Books, 2000); and Sigmund Freud, *Three Essays on the Theory of Sexuality*, trans. James Strachey (New York: Basic Books, 1962).

8. On medicalization struggles over "gender identity disorder," and transsexual and transgender persons, see Karl Bryant, "Making Gender Identity Disorder of Childhood: Historical Lessons for Contemporary Debates," *Sexuality Research and Social Policy* 3, 3 (2006): 23–39; Joanne Meyerowitz, *How Sex Changed: A History of Transsexuality in the United States* (Cambridge, Mass.: Harvard University Press, 2002). On struggles over the medicalization of intersex conditions, see Suzanne Kessler, *Lessons from the Intersexed* (New Brunswick,

263

N.J.: Rutgers University Press, 1998); Katrina Karkazis, *Fixing Sex: Intersex, Medical Authority, and Lived Experience* (Durham, N.C.: Duke University Press, 2008).

9. Nancy J. Knauer, "Science, Identity, and the Construction of the Gay Political Narrative," *Law and Sexuality* 12, 1 (2003): 1–86. Jeffrey Jones of Gallup observes, in the wake of growing acceptance of gay rights in polls, "A growing belief on the part of Americans that same-sex preference has innate causes is part of a larger trend in more positive views of gays and lesbians, and it may also help to promote even greater acceptance of gays and lesbians in the future"; Jeffrey M. Jones, "More Americans See Gay, Lesbian Orientation as Birth Factor," Gallup. May 16, 2013, accessed June 21, 2014, http://www.gallup.com/poll/162569/americans-gay-lesbian-orientation-birth-factor.aspx.

10. American Counseling Association, *Resolution Adopted by the Governing Council of the American Counseling Association: On Appropriate Counseling Responses to Sexual Orientation* (Alexandria, Va.: American Counseling Association, 1998); American Psychiatric Association, "Position Statement on Therapies Focused on Attempts to Change Sexual Orientation (Reparative or Conversion Therapies)," *American Journal of Psychiatry* 157 (2000): 1719–21; American Psychoanalytic Association, *Position Statement on Reparative Therapy* (New York: American Psychoanalytic Association, 1999); American Academy of Pediatrics, "Homosexuality and Adolescence," *Pediatrics* 92 (1993): 631–34; National Association of Social Workers, *Social Work Speaks: National Association of Social Workers Policy Statements*, 4th ed. (Washington, D.C.: NASW Press, 1997). In addition, the American Medical Association policy H-160.991, "Health Care Needs of the Homosexual Population," includes the statement that the AMA "opposes the use of 'reparative' or 'conversion' therapy that is based upon the assumption that homosexuality per se is a mental disorder or based upon the a priori assumption that the patient should change his/her homosexual orientation."

11. American Psychological Association, *Report of the Task Force on Appropriate Therapeutic Responses to Sexual Orientation* (Washington, D.C.: American Psychological Association, 2009).

12. "Survivor Collage," Daniel Gonzales, 2007, accessed June 21, 2014, http://www.beyondexgay.com/collage/dang.html. Also see Daniel Gonzales testimonial, Ex-gay Watch, "Ex-Gay Therapy Doesn't Work, I Tried It," 2006, accessed June 21, 2014, http://www.youtube.com/watch?v=PDn7cEgxvtg.

13. Jallen Rix, "The Ex-Gay Survivor's Survey Results," 2013, accessed June 21, 2014, http://www.beyondexgay.com/survey/results.html. See responses to question 10: "If you feel that you were harmed, please check the below boxes that describe the kinds of harm you experienced."

14. Peterson Toscano, interview with author, Frostburg, Md., 2009.

15. Sara Ahmed, *Queer Phenomenology: Orientations, Objects, Others* (Durham, N.C.: Duke University Press, 2006).

16. Ian Hacking, "Making Up People," in *Historical Ontology* (Cambridge, Mass.: Harvard University Press, 2002).

17. Anthony Giddens, *The Transformation of Intimacy: Sexuality, Love, and Eroticism in Modern Societies* (Cambridge: Polity Press, 1992).

18. Much of the sociological research on the ex-gay movement utilizes par-

ticipant observation within live-in ministries. Ponticelli studied ex-lesbian identity in "Wings," a pseudonymous ex-gay ministry, with eight months of participant observation, attendance at conferences, and interviews. She found that peer interaction played a crucial role in developing an ex-lesbian identity within the ministry; Christy Ponticelli, "Crafting Stories of Sexual Identity Reconstruction," *Social Psychological Quarterly* 62, 2 (1999): 157–72. Wolkomir studied the factors shaping decision making for people experiencing conflict between same-sex attraction and religious faith. Those who chose an ex-gay path tended to have found religion later in life, while those who chose to become gay Christians tended to have been raised in conservative churches; Michelle Wolkomir, *Be Not Deceived: The Sacred and Sexual Struggles of Gay and Ex-Gay Christian Men* (New Brunswick, N.J.: Rutgers University Press, 2006). Erzen conducted an eighteen-month participant observation study of "New Hope Ministries" and interviewed men undergoing conversion as well as ministry leaders. She found that ex-gay identity often involves a ghettoization, or exclusion from a wider evangelical Christian community and exclusion from the gay community. Ex-gays also exhibited what Erzen called "queer conversion," adopting a heterosexual identity while repeatedly experiencing "sexual falls"—homosexual experiences—followed by repentance; Tanya Erzen, *Straight to Jesus: Sexual and Christian Conversions in the Ex-Gay Movement* (Berkeley: University of California Press, 2006). Through participant observation and discourse analysis, Moon examined the uptake of expert discourse within an ex-gay ministry and a gay Christian church. She found that ex-gays foreclose the possibility of being simultaneously happy, healthy, and gay, while gay Christians foreclose the possibility of sexual fluidity; Dawne Moon, "Discourse, Interaction, and Testimony: The Making of Selves in the U.S. Protestant Dispute over Homosexuality," *Theory and Society* 34 (2005): 551–77. Using discourse analysis of reorientation expert literature, Robinson and Spivey found that these discourses promote male domination as an implicit assumption; Christine M. Robinson and Sue E. Spivey, "The Politics of Masculinity and the Ex-Gay Movement," *Gender and Society* 21, 5 (2007): 650–75. Also see Lynne Gerber, *Seeking the Straight and Narrow: Weight Loss and Sexual Reorientation in Evangelical America* (Chicago: University of Chicago Press, 2011); Bernadette Barton, *Pray the Gay Away: The Extraordinary Lives of Bible Belt Gays* (New York: New York University Press, 2012).

19. Sidney Tarrow, *Power in Movement: Social Movements and Contentious Politics,* 2nd ed. (Cambridge: Cambridge University Press, 1998), 4.

20. Taylor and Whittier theorized "collective identity" as "the shared definition of a group that derives from members' common interests, experiences, and solidarity" (105). The boundaries of collective identity are defined by "the social, psychological, and physical structures that establish differences between a challenging group and dominant groups" (105). Movements develop forms of consciousness as "the interpretive frameworks that emerge from a group's struggle to define and realize members' common interests in opposition to a dominant order" (111). Finally, collective identity includes negotiation strategies, "the symbols and everyday actions subordinate groups use to resist and restructure existing systems of domination" (111). See Verta Taylor and Nancy E. Whittier, "Collective Identity in Social Movement Communities:

Lesbian Feminist Mobilization," in *Frontiers in Social Movement Theory*, ed. Aldon D. Morris and Carol McClurg Mueller (New Haven: Yale University Press, 1992), 104–29. Bernstein has also noted that, while collective identity can be a mobilizing tool, it can also be an end in itself, as movements might seek to destigmatize an identity and achieve acceptance of personal expression. In her theory, "identity deployment" transforms the person into a terrain of conflict in order to achieve movement goals; Mary Bernstein, "Celebration and Suppression: The Strategic Uses of Identity by the Lesbian and Gay Movement," *American Journal of Sociology* 103, 3 (1997): 531–65.

21. Elizabeth A. Armstrong and Mary Bernstein, "Culture, Power, and Institutions: A Multi-Institutional Approach to Social Movements," *Sociological Theory* 26, 1 (2008): 74–99.

22. Nancy Whittier, *The Politics of Child Sexual Abuse: Emotion, Social Movements, and the State* (New York: Oxford University Press, 2009). For Whittier, "therapeutic politics" have emerged in response to the state, which has used therapeutic tactics as a form of social control at the level of feeling and subjectivity. This case shows how therapeutic politics can emerge in response to science, which may also shape and deny the existence of forms of feeling and subjectivity.

23. Wayne Besen, *Anything but Straight: Unmasking the Scandals and Lies Behind the Ex-Gay Myth* (Binghamton, N.Y.: Harrington Park Press, 2003), 138.

24. Steven Epstein, "Patient Groups and Health Movements," in *Handbook of Science and Technology Studies*, 3rd ed., ed. Edward J. Hackett et al. (Cambridge, Mass.: MIT Press, 2007), 499–539.

25. Verta Taylor, *Rock-a-by Baby: Feminism, Self-Help, and Post-Partum Depression* (New York: Routledge, 1996).

26. Ronald Bayer, *Homosexuality and American Psychiatry: The Politics of Diagnosis*, 2nd ed. (Princeton, N.J.: Princeton University Press, 1987).

27. Vololona Rabeharisoa, "The Struggle against Neuromuscular Diseases in France and the Emergence of the 'Partnership Model' of Patient Organization," *Social Science and Medicine* 57 (2003): 2127–36.

28. The "political process model" was developed to explore general external factors that might enable or constrain a movement's success in accomplishing its goals when targeting the state. A major concept developed in this perspective is the "political opportunity structure," which describes the conditions that shape movement efficacy when it is targeting a state, as a particular state regime might be more open or closed to movement ideas and tactics. In state-centered analyses, an opposing social movement is thus a facet of a movement's political opportunity structure, and vice versa. David S. Meyer and Suzanne Staggenborg, "Movements, Countermovements, and the Structure of Political Opportunity," *American Journal of Sociology* 101, 6 (1996): 1628–60. Earlier work in this area had theorized that social movements, typically on the left, led to "countermovements," typically on the right. That perspective was succeeded by Meyer and Staggenborg's "opposing social movement" approach, which applied a symmetrical analysis to political conflict.

29. Tina Fetner, *How the Religious Right Shaped Lesbian and Gay Activism* (Minneapolis: University of Minnesota Press, 2008).

30. Erving Goffman, *Frame Analysis: An Essay on the Organization of Experience* (New York: Harper and Row, 1994).

31. Robert Benford and David A. Snow, "Framing Processes and Social Movements: An Overview and Assessment," *Annual Review of Sociology* 26 (2000): 611–39.

32. Melinda S. Miceli, "Morality Politics vs. Identity Politics: Framing Processes and Competition among Christian Right and Gay Social Movement Organizations," *Sociological Forum* 20, 4 (2005): 589–612.

33. Anne W. Esacove, "Dialogic Framing: The Framing/Counterframing of 'Partial-Birth' Abortion," *Sociological Inquiry* 74, 1 (2004): 70–101.

34. Tina Fetner, "Working Anita Bryant: The Impact of Christian Anti-Gay Activism on Lesbian and Gay Movement Claims," *Social Problems* 48, 3 (2001): 411–28.

35. Robert L. Benford, "Frame Disputes within the Nuclear Disarmament Movement," *Social Forces* 71, 3 (1993): 677–701.

36. Tarrow, *Power in Movement*, 20–21.

37. David S. Meyer and Nancy Whittier, "Social Movement Spillover," *Social Problems* 41, 2 (1994): 277–98.

38. Fetner, *How the Religious Right Shaped Lesbian and Gay Activism*.

39. David Valentine, *Imagining Transgender: An Ethnography of a Category* (Durham, N.C.: Duke University Press: 2007).

40. Jane Ward, *Respectably Queer: Diversity Culture in LGBT Activist Organizations* (Nashville, Tenn.: Vanderbilt University Press, 2008).

41. Matthew Waites, "The Fixity of Sexual Identities in the Public Sphere: Biomedical Knowledge, Liberalism, and the Heterosexual/Homosexual Binary in Late Modernity," *Sexualities* 8, 5 (2005): 539–69.

42. Melissa Hackman, "Constructing the 'Ex-Gay' Subject: Cultural Convergences in Post-Apartheid South Africa," in *Sexual Diversity in Africa: Politics, Theory, Citizenship*, ed. S. N. Nyeck and Marc Epprecht (Montreal: McGill-Queens University Press, 2013), 109–28.

43. Annie Wilkinson, *"Sin sanidad, no hay santidad": Las prácticas reparativas en Ecuador* (Quito: FLASCO-Ecuador, 2013).

44. The term *homonormativity* describes the importation of heterosexual norms into LGBT politics, including gender normativity and consumerism, creating a hierarchy among queers. See Lisa Duggan, *The Twilight of Equality: Neoliberalism, Cultural Politics, and the Attack on Democracy* (Boston: Beacon Press, 2003). Warner asserts that gay marriage will lead to a "hierarchy of shame" among LGBT groups, with particularly pernicious effects on HIV prevention; see Michael Warner, *The Trouble with Normal: Sex, Politics, and the Ethics of Queer Life* (Cambridge, Mass.: Harvard University Press, 1999).

45. José Esteban Muñoz, *Cruising Utopia: The Then and There of Queer Futurity* (New York: New York University Press, 2009).

46. Michel Foucault, *History of Sexuality*, vol. 1, *An Introduction* (New York: Vintage Books, 1978), 43.

47. Ibid., 59–60.

48. Ibid., 54. Ann Stoler further explores the connections among *scientia sexualis*, racism, and colonialism in *Race and the Education of Desire: Foucault's History of Sexuality and the Colonial Order of Things* (Durham, N.C.: Duke University Press, 1995).

49. Foucault, *History of Sexuality*, 1:54

50. Ibid., 57–58.

51. Jonathan Ned Katz, *The Invention of Heterosexuality* (Chicago: University of Chicago Press, 1995).

52. Eve Kosofsky Sedgwick, *Epistemology of the Closet* (Berkeley: University of California Press, 1990).

53. Steven Seidman, *The Social Construction of Sexuality*, 3rd ed. (New York: Norton, 2014).

54. Ahmed, *Queer Phenomenology.*

55. Steven Epstein, "A Queer Encounter: Sociology and the Study of Sexuality," *Sociological Theory* 12, 1 (1994): 188–202.

56. John Gagnon and William Simon, *Sexual Conduct: The Social Sources of Human Sexuality*, 2nd ed. (New York: Aldine Transaction, 2005).

57. William Simon and John Gagnon, "Sexual Scripts: Permanence and Change," *Archives of Sexual Behavior* 15, 2 (1986): 97–120.

58. Sheila Jasanoff, *The Fifth Branch: Science Advisers as Policymakers* (Cambridge, Mass.: Harvard University Press, 1998).

59. Erzen, *Straight to Jesus.* In another case of mismatch between behavior and identity, Escoffier has examined the phenomenon of "gay for pay"—straight men who perform in gay pornography yet maintain a heterosexual identity. Using Gagnon and Simon's sexual scripts approach, Escoffier observes how these porn actors use particular rationalizations, such as a financial rather than sexual motivation, and particular actions, like insisting on heterosexual pornography playing on set, to maintain a heterosexual identity even while performing homosexual acts; Jeffrey Escoffier, "Gay for Pay: Straight Men and the Making of Gay Pornography," *Qualitative Sociology* 26, 4 (2003): 531–55.

60. Ashley Currier, *Out in Africa: LGBT Organizing in Namibia and South Africa* (Minneapolis: University of Minnesota Press, 2012).

61. Marc Epprecht, *Heterosexual Africa? The History of an Idea from the Age of Exploration to the Age of AIDS* (Athens: Ohio University Press, 2008).

62. Sokari Ekine and Hakima Abbas, eds., *Queer African Reader* (Cape Town: Pambazuka Press, 2013); Xavier Livermon, "Queer(y)ing Freedom: Black Queer Visibilities in Postapartheid South Africa," *GLQ* 18, 2–3 (2012): 297–323; Notisha Massaquoi, "The Continent as a Closet: The Making of an African Queer Theory," *Outliers* 1, 1 (2008): 50–60.

63. See Epprecht, *Heterosexual Africa?*, 6–26.

64. Although there is no one single definition of "science studies," this is one I use for purposes of this work. While many trace its origins to a blending of history and philosophy of science, evident in the work of Thomas Kuhn's *The Structure of Scientific Revolutions* (Chicago: University of Chicago Press, 1962), it has also been characterized as the work of scholars concerned with ecological and other social justice issues; see Brian Martin, "The Critique of Science Becomes Academic," *Science, Technology, and Human Values* 18, 2 (1993): 247–59.

65. Barry Barnes, *Scientific Knowledge and Sociological Theory* (New York: Routledge, 1974).

66. Thomas Gieryn, *Cultural Boundaries of Science: Credibility on the Line* (Chicago: University of Chicago Press, 1999).

67. Anne Cross, "The Flexibility of Scientific Rhetoric: A Case Study of UFO Researchers," *Qualitative Sociology* 27, 1 (2004): 3–34.

68. Steven Shapin, "Cordelia's Love: Credibility and the Social Studies of Science," *Perspectives on Science* 3, 3 (1995): 255–75.

69. Steven Epstein, *Impure Science: AIDS, Activism, and the Politics of Knowledge* (Berkeley: University of California Press, 1996), 3.

70. Susan Leigh Star, *Regions of the Mind: Brain Research and the Quest for Scientific Certainty* (Stanford, Calif.: Stanford University Press, 1989), 140–42.

71. Bruno Latour, *Science in Action: How to Follow Scientists and Engineers through Society* (Cambridge, Mass.: Harvard University Press, 1999), 2–3.

72. Anselm Strauss, "A Social World Perspective," *Studies in Symbolic Interaction* 1 (1978): 119–28. Also see Adele Clarke, "A Social Worlds Research Adventure: The Case of Reproductive Science," in *Theories of Science in Society*, ed. Susan Cozzens and Thomas Gieryn (Bloomington: Indiana University Press, 1990), 15–42.

73. Pierre Bourdieu, "The Specificity of the Scientific Field and the Social Conditions of the Progress of Reason," *Social Science Information* 14, 6 (1975): 19–47.

74. The author would like to thank Andrew Lakoff for suggesting this concept.

75. Tom J. Waidzunas, "Intellectual Opportunity Structures and Science-Targeted Activism: Influence of the Ex-Gay Movement on the Science of Sexual Orientation," *Mobilization: An International Journal* 18, 1 (2013): 1–18.

76. Scott Frickel and Neil Gross, "A General Theory of Scientific/Intellectual Movements," *American Sociological Review* 7, 2 (2005): 204–32.

77. Sociologists of social movements have theorized "political opportunity structure" in different ways. McAdam theorized a coherent political opportunity structure as the relative oppressiveness or openness of political regimes to political protest, the availability of resources for social movements, and various institutional rules; Doug McAdam, *Political Process and the Development of Black Insurgency, 1930–1970* (Chicago: University of Chicago Press, 1982). Tarrow theorized similar factors as "political opportunities" and "political constraints" depending on their relation to social movements; Tarrow, *Power in Movement.* Gamson and Meyer added cultural elements to the political opportunity structure, including aspects of a nation's political culture; William A. Gamson and David S. Meyer. "Framing Political Opportunity," in *Comparative Perspectives on Social Movements: Political Opportunities, Mobilizing Structures, and Cultural Framings*, ed. Doug McAdam, John D. McCarthy, and Mayer N. Zald (Cambridge: Cambridge University Press, 1999), 275–90. McAdam, Tarrow, and Tilly further theorized the concept as contingent on social movements recognizing the existence of opportunity, or the "attribution" of opportunity; Doug McAdam, Sidney Tarrow, and Charles Tilly, *Dynamics of Contention* (Cambridge: Cambridge University Press, 2001), 95.

78. Armstrong and Bernstein, "Culture, Power, and Institutions." Other "opportunity structures" theorized for institutions beyond the state include an "industry structure," developed by Schurman to analyze the anti-biotech movement in Europe and its successful efforts in banning genetically modified foods; Rachel Schurman, "Fighting 'Frankenfoods': Industry Opportunity Structures and the Efficacy of the Anti-Biotech Movement in Western Europe," *Social Problems* 51, 2 (2004): 243–68. Wahlström and Peterson developed "economic and corporate opportunity structure" to analyze the anti-fur movement's efforts to

stop fur production and consumption in Sweden. Mattias Wahlström and Abby Peterson, "Between the State and the Market: Expanding the Concept of 'Political Opportunity Structure,'" *Acta Sociologica* 49, 4 (2006): 363–77. Frickel and Gross theorized "intellectual opportunity structure" in terms of SIMs (scientific/intellectual movements) within the academy. SIMs consist of "collective efforts to pursue research programs or projects for thought in the face of resistance from others in the scientific or intellectual community" (206). For Frickel and Gross, an intellectual opportunity structure consists of the availability of resources and the capacity for SIMs to use them, including academic employment, communication channels, and funding; Scott Frickel and Neil Gross, "A General Theory of Scientific/Intellectual Movements," *American Sociological Review* 7, 2 (2005): 204–32.

79. Karin Knorr-Cetina, *Epistemic Cultures: How the Sciences Make Knowledge* (Cambridge, Mass.: Harvard University Press, 1999).

80. Kelly Moore, "Political Protest and Institutional Change: The Anti-Vietnam War Movement and American Science," in *How Social Movements Matter*, ed. Marco Giugni, Doug McAdam, and Charles Tilly (Minneapolis: University of Minnesota Press, 1999), 97–118.

81. Nicholas A. Cummings and William T. O'Donohue. "Psychology's Surrender to Political Correctness," in *Destructive Trends in Mental Health: The Well-Intentioned Path to Harm*, ed. Rogers H. Wright and Nicholas A. Cummings (New York: Taylor & Francis Group, 2005), 3–28.

82. Andrew Abbott, *The System of Professions: An Essay on the Division of Expert Labor* (Chicago: University of Chicago Press, 1988).

83. John Grundy and Miriam Smith, "Activist Knowledges in Queer Politics," *Economy and Society* 36, 2 (2007): 294–317. Porter argued that a propensity for trust in numbers in political debates in the United States emerged out of a fragmented culture, in which numbers are assumed to play an adjudicating role; Theodore Porter, *Trust in Numbers* (Princeton, N.J.: Princeton University Press, 1995). Jasanoff theorized "civic epistemology" to describe the kinds of evidence and expertise that political cultures find most credible in policy debates, comparing the political culture in the United States with that of Germany and the United Kingdom. In this research, Jasanoff also found a propensity for trust in numbers within U.S. political culture; Sheila Jasanoff, *Designs on Nature: Science and Democracy in Europe and the United States* (Princeton, N.J.: Princeton University Press, 2007).

84. Joshua Gamson, "Must Identity Movements Self-Destruct? A Queer Dilemma," *Social Problems* 42, 3 (1995): 390–407.

85. Steven Hilgartner, "The Dominant View of Popularization: Conceptual Problems, Political Uses," *Social Studies of Science* 20 (1990): 519–39.

86. Ann Swidler, *Talk of Love: How Culture Matters* (Chicago: University of Chicago Press, 2003).

87. Elizabeth Borland, "Cultural Opportunities and Tactical Choice in Argentine and Chilean Reproductive Rights Movements," *Mobilization: An International Journal* 9, 3 (2004): 327–39.

88. Ruud Koopmans and Susan Olzak, "Discursive Opportunities and the Evolution of Right-Wing Violence in Germany," *American Journal of Sociology* 110 (2004): 198–230; Myra Marx Ferree et al., *Shaping Abortion Discourse: De-*

mocracy and the Public Sphere in Germany and the United States (Cambridge: Cambridge University Press, 2002)

89. In science studies, Barad and Murphy have both developed theories of "materialization" built on the concept developed by Judith Butler in *Bodies That Matter.* For Butler, discursive practices make some matter more or less relevant than other matter, bringing it into being and rendering it intelligible; Judith Butler. *Bodies That Matter: On the Discursive Limits of "Sex"* (New York: Routledge, 1993). In her concept, Barad explicitly included the agency of matter itself, as it unfolds, in conversation with human discourse; Karen Barad, *Meeting the Universe Halfway: Quantum Physics and the Entanglement of Matter and Meaning* (Durham, N.C.: Duke University Press, 2007). Murphy also extends Butler's theory of materialization to include the agency of material objects; Michelle Murphy, *Sick Building Syndrome and the Problem of Uncertainty: Environmental Politics, Technoscience, and Women Workers* (Durham, N.C.: Duke University Press, 2006).

90. Murphy, *Sick Building Syndrome.* For more on materialization in relation to sexual physiological testing, see Tom Waidzunas and Steven Epstein, "'For Men Arousal Is Orientation': Bodily Truthing, Technosexual Scripts, and the Materialization of Sexualities through the Phallometric Test," *Social Studies of Science* 45, 2 (2015): 187–213.

91. Bringing the agency of bodies into the sociology of sexuality, Green has expanded on Gagnon and Simon's theory of what happens at the intrapsychic level in the development of sexual desire, as he claimed that people develop an "erotic habitus," a pattern of sexual attraction and behavior, which is deeply ingrained and produced in an interaction between biology and society; Adam Isaiah Green, "Erotic Habitus: Toward a Sociology of Desire," *Theory and Society* 37, 6 (2008): 597–626.

92. Epstein, *Impure Science,* 355–60.

93. Ibid., 357. Foucault's archaeological method, characteristic of his earlier work, is outlined in Michel Foucault, *The Archaeology of Knowledge and The Discourse on Language* (New York: Pantheon Books, 1972). Foucault's genealogical method, characteristic of his later work, is outlined in Michel Foucault, *Power/Knowledge: Selected Interviews and Other Writings, 1972–1977,* ed. Colin Gordon (New York: Pantheon Books, 1980).

1. The Reorientation Regime

1. Stephanie Coontz, *The Way We Never Were: American Families and the Nostalgia Trap* (New York: Basic Books, 1993).

2. Alfred Kinsey, Walter B. Pomeroy, and Clyde E. Martin, *Sexual Behavior in the Human Male* (Philadelphia: Saunders, 1948), 623.

3. Ibid., 659.

4. Julia Ericksen, "With Enough Cases, Why Do You Need Statistics? Revisiting Kinsey's Methodology," *Journal of Sex Research* 35, 2 (1988): 132–40.

5. Howard Hsueh-Hao Chiang, "Effecting Science, Affecting Medicine: Homosexuality, the Kinsey Reports, and the Contested Boundaries of Psychopathology in the United States, 1948–1965," *Journal of the History of the Behavioral Sciences* 44, 4 (2008): 300–18.

6. John D'Emilio, *Sexual Politics, Sexual Communities: The Making of a*

Homosexual Minority in the United States, 1940–1970 (Chicago: University of Chicago Press, 1983), 37.

7. Ibid., 42.

8. Ronald Bayer, *Homosexuality and American Psychiatry: The Politics of Diagnosis* (Princeton, N.J.: Princeton University Press, 1981); Eli Coleman, "Changing Approaches to the Treatment of Homosexuality," *American Behavioral Scientist* 25, 4 (1982): 397–406; Jack Drescher, "I'm Your Handyman: A History of Reparative Therapies," *Journal of Gay & Lesbian Psychotherapy* 5, 3/4 (2001): 5–24; Timothy F. Murphy, "Redirecting Sexual Orientation: Techniques and Justifications," *Journal of Sex Research* 29, 4 (1992): 501–23.

9. Jennifer Terry, *An American Obsession: Science, Medicine, and Homosexuality in Modern Society* (Chicago: University of Chicago Press, 1999), 75–76.

10. Foucault, *History of Sexuality*, 1:43.

11. Sigmund Freud, "Anonymous (Letter to an American Mother)," *The Letters of Sigmund Freud*, ed. E. Freud (New York: Basic Books, 1935), 423–24.

12. Terry, *American Obsession*, 42–43.

13. Henry L. Minton, *Departing from Deviance: A History of Homosexual Rights and Emancipatory Science in America* (Chicago: University of Chicago Press, 2002), 8–9.

14. Irving C. Rosse, "Sexual Hypochondriasis and Perversion of the Genetic Instinct," *Journal of Nervous and Mental Disease* 17, 11 (1892): 802.

15. Western European practices of scientifically classifying sexualities took shape amidst the politics of colonialism, distinguishing types of "superior" people who were suitable for being granted rights, and those regressed "inferior" people who were suitable for enslavement. Observed behaviors of "primitives" were understood as inextricably linked to the innate, biological status of their bodies. In Victorian society, the study of the female "primitive" served to create a means for domesticating white women, cast as "passionless" in contrast to lascivious women abroad. This produced a "natural" social hierarchy with white heterosexual men at the top. Homosexual men and lesbians were grouped with the lascivious, biologically "inferior." As deviants from the two-gender system, homosexuals first became known as "inverts" who possessed the worst characteristics of both sexes. Terry, *American Obsession*, 28–38. Also see Stoler, *Race and the Education of Desire*.

16. Terry, *American Obsession*, 77.

17. Stoler, *Race and the Education of Desire*. For an example of the construction of notions of sexual deviance within the context of U.S. settler colonialism, including the equation of homosexual practices with degeneracy, see Jean E. Balestrery, "Intersecting Discourses on Race and Sexuality: Compounded Colonization among LGBTQ American Indians/Alaska Natives," *Journal of Homosexuality* 59, 5 (2012): 633–55. For a Western anthropological text that was part of the construction of colonialist depictions of sexual deviance in Africa see J. Driberg, *The Lango: A Nilotic Tribe in Uganda* (London: Thorner Coryndon, 1923). Ironically work such as this has been useful to counter the notion that homosexuality did not exist in Africa prior to colonization (see chapter 5).

18. Terry, *American Obsession*, 81–83.

19. Ibid., 103–4.

20. Ibid., 107–10; Minton, *Departing from Deviance*, 55.

21. Terry, *American Obsession*, 178–219.

22. David Serlin, *Replaceable You: Engineering the Body in Postwar America* (Chicago: University of Chicago Press, 2004), 115–16.

23. Chandak Sengoopta, "Glandular Politics: Experimental Biology, Clinical Medicine, and Homosexual Emancipation in Fin-de-Siècle Central Europe," *Isis* 89, 3 (1998): 445–73.

24. Serlin, *Replaceable You*, 113–14.

25. H. S. Barahal, "Testosterone in Psychotic Male Homosexuals," *Psychiatric Quarterly* 14 (1940): 329.

26. See also S. J. Glass and R. H. Johnson, "Limitations and Complications of Organotherapy in Male Homosexuality," *Journal of Clinical Endocrinology* 11 (1944): 540–44.

27. William H. Masters and D. T. Magallon, "Androgen Administration in the Post-Menopausal Woman," *Journal of Clinical Endocrinology* 10 (1950): 348.

28. For example, Robert M. Foote, "Diethylstilbestrol in the Management of Psychopathological States in Males," *Journal of Nervous and Mental Disease* 99, 6 (1944): 928–35.

29. One notable exception, African American lesbian Gladys Bentley underwent estrogen treatment in the early 1950s and appeared in an article in *Ebony* magazine in 1952 telling her story of "cure." Bentley, an openly lesbian nightclub entertainer who often wore male attire, sought social respectability within increasingly conservative middle-class black culture. Through estrogen, she claimed to have overcome her lesbian lifestyle. The article featured several photographs of the newly "feminized" Bentley, posing as a housewife washing dishes, making a bed, and looking in the mirror holding jewelry. Even though psychoanalysis would rise to the forefront in the treatment of homosexuality in the United States in the post–WWII era, hormone treatments maintained cultural resonance in some circumstances, and in the context of their racialized history, potentially reinforced ideas about racial difference in their application. See Serlin, *Replaceable You*.

30. Sigmund Freud, "'A Child Is Being Beaten': A Contribution to the Study of the Origin of Sexual Perversions," in *The Standard Edition of the Complete Works of Sigmund Freud*, ed. James Strachey (London: Hogarth Press, 1955), 17:200–201.

31. Freud, "Anonymous (Letter to an American Mother)."

32. Sigmund Freud, "The Psychogenesis of a Case of Homosexuality in a Woman," in *The Standard Edition of the Complete Works of Sigmund Freud*, 19:145–72.

33. For example, Abram Kardiner, Aaron Karush, and Lionel Ovesey, "A Methodological Study of Freudian Theory: III. Narcissism, Bisexuality, and the Dual Instinct Theory," *Journal of Nervous and Mental Disease* 129 (1959): 207–21.

34. Sandor Rado, "Psychodynamics as a Basic Science," in *Psychoanalysis of Behavior: Collected Papers*, vol. 1, *1922–1956* (New York: Grune & Stratton, 1946), 169.

35. Rado claimed the concept of bisexuality entered science when biologists in the mid-nineteenth century discovered that the differentiated sex organs of

male and female organisms emerge from the same structure, leading scientists to believe erroneously that aspects of male and female remain within all people. When viewing this discovery, scientists such as Hirschfeld, Krafft-Ebing, and Freud tended to invoke an old Hindu myth that all human beings were really composed of both sexes. According to Rado, this myth was carried down through Plato's *Symposium* and had been imposed in scientific theory. Sandor Rado, "A Critical Examination of the Concept of Bisexuality," in *Psychoanalysis of Behavior*, 1:139–50. Ironically, this is the same myth Freud uses at the beginning of *The Three Essays* to characterize the view of those surprised by the pervasiveness of homosexual practices. In Freud's version, those who are shocked must be immersed in the myth from Plato's *Symposium*, in which humans were once composed of two sexes, but then broke in two, leading to ubiquitous heterosexual desire; Freud, *Three Essays*, 2.

36. Rado, "A Critical Examination of the Concept of Bisexuality," 143.

37. Newdigate M. Owensby, "Homosexuality and Lesbianism Treated with Metrazol," *Journal of Nervous and Mental Disease* 92 (1940): 65–66.

38. Ibid., 65.

39. Such was also the case with the transorbital lobotomy, or "ice pick lobotomy," developed by psychiatrist Dr. Walter Freeman of Washington, D.C., in the years following World War II. In this procedure an instrument was inserted through the eye socket to detach the frontal lobe of the brain from the hypothalamus, believed to be the source of irrationality. While such treatments were applied to homosexuals, they were by no means unique to this group, as this treatment was applied under a general theory of mental disorder. For a discussion of the rise and fall of the lobotomy in the United States, see Jack El-Hai, *The Lobotomist: A Maverick Medical Genius and His Tragic Quest to Rid the World of Mental Illness* (Hoboken, N.J.: Wiley and Sons, 2005).

40. Kenneth Lewes, *Psychoanalysis and Male Homosexuality* (Lanham, Md.: Jason Aronson, 2009), 83–88.

41. Edmund Bergler, "The Myth of a New National Disease: Homosexuality and the Kinsey Report," *Psychiatric Quarterly* 22 (Jan. 1948): 71.

42. Ibid., 71–72.

43. Abram Kardiner, Aaron Karush, and Lionel Ovesey, "A Methodological Study of Freudian Theory: I. Basic Concepts," *Journal of Nervous and Mental Disease* 129 (1959): 11–19; Abram Kardiner, Aaron Karush, and Lionel Ovesey, "A Methodological Study of Freudian Theory: IV. The Structural Hypothesis, the Problem of Anxiety, and Post-Freudian Ego Psychology," *Journal of Nervous and Mental Disease* 129 (1959): 341–56.

44. While Heinz Hartmann is often seen as a key figure in developing ego psychology in *Ego Psychology and the Problem of Adaptation* (1958), some U.S. psychoanalysts thought even Hartmann did not go far enough in his rejection of the instincts, and they called for a completely instinct-free theory; Kardiner, Karush, and Ovesey, "A Methodological Study of Freudian Theory: IV," 351–54.

45. Edmund Bergler, *Homosexuality: Disease or Way of Life?* (New York: Hill and Wang, 1956), 240.

46. Bergler, "The Myth of a New National Disease," 68–73.

47. Bergler also lamented the fact that impotent men would be suspected of

being homosexual by their wives. Bergler states, "Women have a simple formula: 'Impotent, ergo a fairy.' This, of course, is erroneous." Bergler, "The Myth of a New National Disease," 86.

48. Ibid., 87.

49. John S. Poe, "The Successful Treatment of a 40-year old Passive Homosexual Based on an Adaptational View of Sexual Behavior," *Psychoanalytic Review* 39 (1952): 23.

50. Ibid., 31.

51. Lionel Ovesey, *Homosexuality and Pseudohomosexuality* (New York: Science House, 1969), 130–31.

52. Nathan Hale Jr., *The Rise and Crisis of Psychoanalysis in the United States: Freud and the Americans, 1917–1985* (Oxford: Oxford University Press, 1995), 309–13.

53. Hans J. Eysenck, "The Effects of Psychotherapy: An Evaluation," *Journal of Consulting Psychology* 16, 5 (1952): 323.

54. Irving Bieber et al., *Homosexuality: A Psychoanalytic Study of Male Homosexuals* (New York: Vintage Books, 1962), 19–25.

55. Ibid., 295–96.

56. D'Emilio, *Sexual Politics, Sexual Communities*, 70–71.

57. Ibid., 75–84.

58. Donald Webster Cory, introduction to *Homosexuality: Its Causes and Cures*, by Albert Ellis (New York: Institute for Rational Living. 1965), 7.

59. Ellis, *Homosexuality*, 78.

60. "Award for Distinguished Contribution to Psychology in the Public Interest: Evelyn Hooker," *American Psychologist* 47, 4 (1992): 501–53.

61. Evelyn Hooker, "Reflections of a 40-Year Exploration: A Scientific View on Homosexuality," *American Psychologist* 48, 4 (1993): 450–53.

62. Evelyn Hooker, "A Preliminary Analysis of Group Behavior of Homosexuals," *Journal of Psychology* 42 (1956): 219.

63. Ibid., 223.

64. Evelyn Hooker, "The Adjustment of the Male Overt Homosexual," *Journal of Projective Techniques* 21 (1957): 18.

65. Ibid., 26.

66. Minton, *Departing from Deviance*, 243–45.

67. Quoted in D'Emilio, *Sexual Politics, Sexual Communities*, 163.

68. Quoted in ibid., 167.

69. Minton, *Departing from Deviance*, 252–53.

70. Ovesey, *Homosexuality and Pseudohomosexuality*, 117–18.

71. Quoted in D'Emilio, *Sexual Politics, Sexual Communities*, 216.

72. Charles Socarides, *The Overt Homosexual* (New York: Grune & Stratton, 1968), 8.

73. Ibid., 90.

74. John A. Mills, *Control: A History of Behavioral Psychology* (New York: New York University Press, 2000), 2–3.

75. The work of Russian psychologist Ivan Pavlov and U.S. psychologist B. F. Skinner led to the development of treatment technologies that would later be applied to humans in the treatment of homosexuality and a panoply of other

conditions. In Pavlov's "classical conditioning" learning method, a stimulus (the "unconditioned stimulus") that ordinarily evokes a response (the "unconditioned response") becomes associated with a neutral stimulus (the "conditioned stimulus") that usually has little effect. The effect of the association leads to a "conditioned response" to the neutral stimulus in the absence of the unconditioned stimulus. In Pavlov's famous experiments with dogs, he was able to condition dogs to salivate at the sound of a bell by associating the sound of the bell with the presentation of food. B. F. Skinner developed "operant conditioning" (also known as "instrumental conditioning") as a means to train voluntary responses in animals (such as pressing a lever to obtain food), through rewarding desired responses and punishing nonaction; see Mills, *Control*. Behavior therapists would remain divided as to which of these models was appropriate for the treatment of homosexuality; see M. P. Feldman and M. J. MacColluch, *Homosexual Behaviour: Therapy and Assessment* (Oxford: Pergamon Press, 1971).

76. Feldman and MacColluch, *Homosexual Behaviour*, 166–70.

77. In 1971 British behaviorists Feldman and MacColluch speculated about the nature of female homosexuality as distinct from male homosexuality. They noted lesbians often had poor relationships with their fathers as children, suggesting a need for further research. Female homosexuality involved a degree of aggression not seen in male homosexuals, because over time, these women had to fend off the advances of men and, consequently, developed aggressive personalities. They conjectured that the treatment of women would need to include extinguishing aggression. This research program would not come to pass, however, as the behavior therapy of homosexuality ended soon after. Feldman and MacColluch, *Homosexual Behaviour*, 186–87.

78. Mills, *Control*, 8.

79. Kurt Freund, "Some Problems in the Treatment of Homosexuality," in *Behaviour Therapy and the Neuroses*, ed. H. J. Eysenck (London: Pergamon, 1960), 312–26.

80. Stanley Rachman, "Sexual Disorders and Behavior Therapy," *American Journal of Psychiatry* 118 (1961): 235–40.

81. Basil James, "Case of Homosexuality Treated by Aversion Therapy," *British Medical Journal* 1 (1962): 769.

82. J. G. Thorpe, E. Schmidt, and D. Castell, "A Comparison of Positive and Negative (Aversive) Conditioning in the Treatment of the Homosexual," *Behaviour Research and Therapy* 1, 2–4 (1963): 357–62.

83. Kurt Freund, "Laboratory Differential Diagnosis of Homo- and Heterosexuality: An Experiment with Faking," *Review of Czechoslovak Medicine* 7 (1961): 20–31. For further history of the phallometric test, see Waidzunas and Epstein, "'For Men Arousal Is Orientation.'"

84. Kurt Freund, "A Laboratory Method for Diagnosing Predominance of Homo-Erotic or Hetero-Erotic Interest in the Male," *Behaviour Research and Therapy* 1, 1 (1963): 85–93; Kurt Freund, F. Sedlacek, and K. Knob, "A Simple Transducer for Mechanical Plethysmography of the Male Genital," *Journal of the Experimental Analysis of Behavior* 8, 3 (1965): 169–70.

85. John H. Bancroft, Gwynne Jones, and B. R. Pullan, "A Simple Transducer for Measuring Penile Erection with Comments on Its Use in Treatment of Sexual Disorders," *Behaviour Research and Therapy* 4, 3 (1966): 239–41.

86. Australian psychiatrist Nathaniel McConaghy developed a version of the vacuum air chamber plethysmograph that he claimed was less cumbersome in the lab, and applied it to the aversion therapy treatment of homosexuals. Nathaniel McConaghy, "Penile Volume Change to Moving Pictures of Male and Female Nudes in Heterosexual and Homosexual Males," *Behaviour Research and Therapy* 5 (1967): 43–48. McConaghy would later argue that the vacuum air chamber plethysmograph is superior to the strain gauge because during tumescence, the penis increases in length before it increases in girth. He demonstrated this phenomenon by conducting an experiment with subjects simultaneously hooked up to both devices. Nonetheless, the strain gauge became the most popular method in the United States. See Nathaniel McConaghy, "Unresolved Issues in Scientific Sexology," *Archives of Sexual Behavior* 28, 4 (1999): 285–318.

87. Thomas S. Szasz, "Behavior Therapy and Psychoanalysis," *Medical Opinion and Review* 2 (1967): 24–29.

88. Bayer, *Homosexuality and American Psychiatry*, 103.

89. Terry, *American Obsession*, 295–96.

90. David H. Barlow and W. Stewart Agras, "Fading to Increase Heterosexual Responsiveness in Homosexuals," *Journal of Applied Behavior Analysis* 6, 3 (1973): 355–66.

91. Gerald Davison, "Elimination of a Sadistic Fantasy by a Client-Controlled Counterconditioning Technique," *Journal of Abnormal Psychology* 73, 1 (1968): 84–90.

92. This more "humane" method was initially developed by British psychologists Feldman and MacColluch, and taken up by therapists in the United States. One notable exception to the continued use of aversion therapies in the United States was army psychiatrist Barry Maletzky, who held valeric acid under the noses of subjects to induce nausea when mental imagery alone failed to produce the desired outcome. Avoiding the controversial term *aversion therapy*, this study was published under the heading of "'assisted' covert sensitization"; Barry M. Maletzky, "'Assisted' Covert Sensitization: A Preliminary Report," *Behavior Therapy* 4 (1973): 117–19.

93. George Sintchak and James H. Geer, "A Vaginal Plethysmograph System," *Psychophysiology* 12, 1 (1975): 113–15.

94. For images of advertisements and news stories from this time period, compiled by Jamie Scot, program manager of the ONE National Gay & Lesbian Archives, see Jamie Scot, "Shock the Gay Away: Secrets of Early Gay Aversion Therapy Revealed," *Huffington Post,* June 28, 2013, accessed June 15, 2015, http://www.huffingtonpost.com/jamie-scot/shock-the-gay-away-secrets-of-early-gay-aversion-therapy-revealed_b_3497435.html. Also see the ONE Archives Foundation for information on a traveling exhibition, "Homosexuality: From Illness to Identity," available Fall 2015. ONE Archives Foundation, "Traveling LGBTQ History Exhibitions," accessed June 15, 2015, http://www.onearchives.org/traveling-history-exhibitions.

2. The Evolution of Dr. Robert Spitzer

1. For example, see Robert Spitzer and Jean Endicott, "DIAGNO: A Computer Program for Psychiatric Diagnosis Utilizing the Differential Diagnostic Procedure," *Archives of General Psychiatry* 18 (1968): 746–56.

2. Robert Spitzer, interview with author, Princeton, N.J., 2008.

3. Martin Duberman, *Cures: A Gay Man's Odyssey* (New York: Dutton, 1991), 268.

4. This scientific evidence included the research of Evelyn Hooker, Alfred Kinsey, Clellan Ford and Frank Beach, Judd Marmor, Richard Green, Martin Hoffman, Sigmund Freud, and Marcel Saghir and Eli Robins. Saghir and Robins's *Male and Female Homosexuality* (1973) was particularly influential for Spitzer. The authors studied a nonpatient population of homosexual male and female subjects, including correlating characteristics and behaviors, in comparison with heterosexual controls. The researchers did not consider homosexuality a priori to be a disorder or to be normal. The study found that "homosexuals are not *a priori* sick. Many of them present little or no psychopathology and those who do are rarely disabled by their disorder"; Marcel Saghir and Eli Robins, *Male and Female Homosexuality: A Comprehensive Investigation* (Baltimore, Md.: Williams and Wilkins, 1973), 317.

5. Charles Silverstein described the disorder classification as particularly stigmatizing and harmful to gay relationships: "We are told, from the time that we first recognize our homosexual feelings, that our love for other human beings is sick, childish and subject to 'cure.' We are told that we are emotional cripples forever condemned to an emotional status below that of the 'whole' people who run the world. The result of this in many cases is to contribute to a self-image that often lowers the sights we set for ourselves in life, and many of us asked ourselves, 'How could anybody love me?' or 'How can I love somebody who must be just as sick as I am?'" Quoted in Bayer, *Homosexuality and American Psychiatry,* 119.

6. Robert Spitzer, "A Proposal about Homosexuality and the APA Nomenclature: Homosexuality as an Irregular Form of Sexual Behavior and Sexual Orientation Disturbance as a Psychiatric Disorder," *American Journal of Psychiatry* 130, 11 (1973): 1215.

7. Ibid.

8. Ibid.

9. Bayer, *Homosexuality and American Psychiatry,* 136–37.

10. Spitzer, "A Proposal about Homosexuality and the APA Nomenclature," 1216.

11. Bayer, *Homosexuality and American Psychiatry,* 137.

12. Gerald Davison, interview with author, Los Angeles, 2009.

13. Gerald Davison, "Values and Constructionism in Clinical Assessment: Some Historical and Personal Perspectives on Behavior Therapy," in *A History of the Behavior Therapies: Founders' Personal Histories,* ed. William T. O'Donohue et al. (Reno, Nev.: Context Press, 2001).

14. Gerald Davison, "Homosexuality: The Ethical Challenge," *Journal of Consulting and Clinical Psychology* 44, 2 (1976): 161–62. Emphasis in the original.

15. Barry A. Tanner, "A Comparison of Automated Aversive Conditioning and a Waiting List Control in the Modification of Homosexual Behavior in Males," *Behavior Therapy* 5 (1974): 29–32; Barry A. Tanner, "Avoidance Training with and without Booster Sessions to Modify Homosexual Behavior in Males," *Behavior Therapy* 6 (1975): 649–53.

16. Nathaniel McConaghy, D. Proctor, and R. Barr, "Subjective and Penile

Plethysmography Responses to Aversion Therapy for Homosexuality: A Partial Replication," *Archives of Sexual Behavior* 2, 1 (1972): 73.

17. J. J. Conger, "Proceedings of the American Psychological Association, Incorporated, for the Year 1974: Minutes of the Annual Meeting of the Council of Representatives," *American Psychologist* 30, 6 (1975): 633.

18. Charles Silverstein, "Homosexuality and the Ethics of Behavioral Intervention. Paper 2," *Journal of Homosexuality* 2, 3 (1977): 206.

19. Robert Galbraith Heath, "Pleasure and Brain Activity in Man: Deep and Surface Electroencephalograms during Orgasm," *Journal of Nervous and Mental Disease* 154, 1 (1972): 3–18.

20. Silverstein, "Homosexuality and the Ethics of Behavioral Intervention," 208–9.

21. Henry E. Adams and Ellie T. Sturgis, "Status of Behavioral Reorientation Techniques in the Modification of Homosexuality: A Review," *Psychological Bulletin* 84, 6 (1977): 1171–88.

22. Fetner, *How the Religious Right Shaped Lesbian and Gay Activism*, 24.

23. Bayer, *Homosexuality and American Psychiatry*, 167; Harold Lief, "Sexual Survey #4: Current Thinking on Homosexuality," *Medical Aspects of Human Sexuality* 11 (1977): 110–11.

24. Bayer, *Homosexuality and American Psychiatry*, 168.

25. Quoted in ibid., 176, 177.

26. William Masters and Virginia Johnson, *Homosexuality in Perspective* (Boston: Little, Brown, 1979), 392.

27. Through interviews with Virginia Johnson and Richard Kolodny, research associate to Masters and Johnson, Maier exposes that much of the data in *Homosexuality in Perspective* was fabricated. Johnson felt very reluctant to publish this book, especially given the context of social transformations that had taken place regarding the social acceptance of homosexuality; Thomas Maier, *Masters of Sex: The Life and Times of William Masters and Virginia Johnson, the Couple Who Taught America How to Love* (New York: Basic Books, 2009), 281–98.

28. Quoted in Maier, *Masters of Sex*, 295–96.

29. Charles Socarides, *Beyond Sexual Freedom* (New York: Quadrangle/New York Times Book Co., 1975); Charles Socarides, *Homosexuality* (New York: Jason Aronson, 1978).

30. Fetner, *How the Religious Right Shaped Lesbian and Gay Activism*, 58–60.

31. Troy Perry, *The Lord Is My Shepherd and He Knows I'm Gay* (Los Angeles: Nash, 1972), 3.

32. Erzen, *Straight to Jesus*, 31–33.

33. Kent Philpott, *The Third Sex? Six Homosexuals Tell Their Stories* (Plainfield, N.J.: Logos International, 1975), 76–77.

34. Ibid, 171–72.

35. E. Mansell Pattison and Myrna Loy Pattison, "'Ex-Gays': Religiously Mediated Change in Homosexuals," *American Journal of Psychiatry* 137, 12 (1980): 1553.

36. Elizabeth Moberly, *Homosexuality: A New Christian Ethic* (Cambridge, Mass.: James Clarke, 1983), 6.

37. Joe Dallas, *Desires in Conflict: Hope for Men who Struggle with Homosexuality* (Eugene, Ore.: Harvest House, 1990), 17–18.

38. Ibid., 194.

39. Charles Silverstein, *Gays, Lesbians, and Their Therapists: Studies in Psychotherapy* (New York: Norton, 1991), 8.

40. Bayer, *Homosexuality and American Psychiatry*, 203–4; Peter Conrad, *The Medicalization of Society: On the Transformation of Human Conditions into Treatable Disorders* (Baltimore, Md.: The Johns Hopkins University Press, 2007), 104–9.

41. Fetner, *How the Religious Right Shaped Lesbian and Gay Activism*, 61–63.

42. Association of Gay and Lesbian Psychiatrists (AGLP), accessed June 22, 2014, http://www.aglp.org.

43. Robert Spitzer, "The Diagnostic Status of Homosexuality in DSM-III: A Reformulation of the Issues," *American Journal of Psychiatry* 138 (1981): 210–15.

44. Quoted in Bayer, *Homosexuality and American Psychiatry*, 215.

45. Ibid., 217.

46. Vivienne C. Cass, "Homosexual Identity Formation: A Theoretical Model," *Journal of Homosexuality* 4, 3 (1979): 219–35.

47. John Gonsiorek, "Introduction: Present and Future Directions in Gay/Lesbian Mental Health," in *Homosexuality and Psychotherapy: A Practitioner's Handbook of Affirmative Models,* ed. John Gonsiorek (New York: Haworth Press, 1982), 9.

48. John C. Gonsiorek and James D. Weinrich, "The Definition and Scope of Sexual Orientation," in *Homosexuality: Research Implications for Public Policy,* ed. J. Weinrich and J. Gonsiorek (Newbury Park, Calif.: Sage, 1991), 1–12.

49. Ibid., 1. See Michael G. Shively and John P. De Cecco, "Components of Sexual Identity," *Journal of Homosexuality* 3, 1 (1977): 41–48. Shively and De Cecco designed their model of sexual orientation in contrast to Kinsey's "bipolar" continuum from homosexual to heterosexual. Instead, their model includes four scales. Two scales are used to describe "physical preference": a heterosexual continuum ranges from "not at all heterosexual" to "very heterosexual," while a homosexual continuum ranges from "not at all homosexual" to "very homosexual." Two analogous scales are used to describe heterosexual and homosexual dimensions of "affectional preference." Unlike Kinsey's scale, which involves a trade-off between homosexual and heterosexual sexual behavior and desire, this model delinks affectional and physical desire, while also making homosexual and heterosexual attraction independent of one another.

50. Gonsiorek and Weinrich, "The Definition and Scope of Sexual Orientation," 2. In addition to citing Richard Green's essay for this claim ("The Immutability of [Homo]Sexual Orientation: Behavioral Science Implications for a Constitutional [Legal] Analysis," *Journal of Psychiatry and Law* 16, 537 [1988]: 555–68), the authors also pointed out the landmark study by Alan P. Bell, Martin S. Weinberg, and Sue Kiefer Hammersmith, *Sexual Preference: Its Development in Men and Women* (Bloomington: Indiana University Press, 1991), and John Money, *Gay Straight, and In-Between: The Sexology of Erotic Orientation* (New York: Oxford University Press, 1988).

51. Ibid., 5–6.

52. Doug Haldeman, "Sexual Orientation Conversion Therapy: A Scientific Examination," in Weinrich and Gonsiorek, *Homosexuality*, 149–60.

53. Ibid., 155.

54. Bayer, *Homosexuality and American Psychiatry*, 187.

55. Charles Socarides, *Preoedipal Origin and Psychoanalytic Therapy of Sexual Perversions* (Madison, Conn.: International Universities Press, 1988); Charles Socarides, *Homosexuality: Psychoanalytic Therapy* (New York: Jason Aronson, 1989).

56. Elaine V. Siegel, *Female Homosexuality: Choice without Volition* (Hillsdale, N.J.: Analytic Press, 1988).

57. Psychoanalysts began to question the pathologizing view. Judd Marmor provided an overview of available research on homosexuality, without pathologizing views; Judd Marmor, *Homosexual Behavior: A Modern Reappraisal* (New York: Basic Books, 1980). Richard Friedman expressed uncertainty about whether psychoanalysis can successfully reorient a client and called for better research. In addition, he pointed to prenatal hormone exposure as a likely candidate for the cause of homosexuality; Richard Friedman, *Male Homosexuality: A Contemporary Psychoanalytic Perspective* (New Haven, Conn.: Yale University Press, 1988). Significantly, gay psychoanalysts began publishing new theories. Richard Isay discussed homosexuality as rooted in biology, and provided a view of therapy that helped the client come to terms with societal biases and move toward self-acceptance; Richard Isay, *Being Homosexual: Gay Men and Their Development* (New York: Farrar, Straus and Giroux, 1989). Psychiatrist Jack Drescher provides a gay-affirmative therapeutic regimen to help men discover and accept their fixed same-sex sexual orientations; Jack Drescher, *Psychoanalytic Therapy and the Gay Man* (Hillsdale, N.J.: Analytic Press, 1998).

58. Knauer, "Science, Identity, and the Construction of the Gay Political Narrative."

59. Fetner, *How the Religious Right Shaped Lesbian and Gay Activism*, 102.

60. Simon LeVay's study on the hypothalamus was central to developing this perspective. Believing that the hypothalamus is important in heterosexual male activity, LeVay hypothesized that there would be a difference between homosexual and heterosexual men, and that homosexual men would show similarities to women. This is indeed the pattern he found when looking at the INAH3 region. When speculating on the cause of this correlation, LeVay stated that it was not known whether the difference he observed was the cause or consequence of sexual orientation, but he did note that the hypothalamus in rats could be modified by prenatal hormone exposure; Simon LeVay, "A Difference in Hypothalmic Structure between Heterosexual and Homosexual Men," *Science* 253, 5023 (1991): 1034–37. LeVay would later argue that Robert Spitzer's study on ex-gays should not be dismissed, commenting that neuroscience and psychology have taught us that the human brain is immensely plastic; Simon LeVay, "Can Gays Become Straight?," *New Scientist* 180, 2416 (2003): 19.

61. A significant study by lead author Dean Hamer claiming that homosexuality was correlated with the Xq28 marker on the X chromosome would soon reinforce this trend; Dean Hamer et al., "A Linkage between DNA Markers on the X Chromosome and Male Sexual Orientation," *Science* 261, 5119 (1993): 321–27.

Michael Bailey coauthored a study of twins that suggested a hereditary component of homosexuality. However, this research program has not definitively established that genes cause homosexuality; J. Michael Bailey and R. C. Pillard, "A Genetic Study of Male Sexual Orientation," *Archives of General Psychiatry* 48 (1991): 1089–96.

62. Valerie Richardson, "Homosexual 'Conversion' Has Psychiatrists in a Tiff," *Washington Times*, May 21, 1994, A1.

63. "A 20 Year History of NARTH," published January 22, 2013, NARTH, accessed June 22, 2014, http://www.youtube.com/watch?v=tb_mks65Gwg.

64. "Thomas Aquinas Psychological Clinic," 2009, accessed June 22, 2014, http://www.josephnicolosi.com; "National Association for Research and Therapy of Homosexuality," accessed June 22, 2014. Originally at http://www.narth.com/menus/history.html; now available at http://www.narth.org/menus/history.html.

65. Nicolosi, *Healing Homosexuality*, ix.

66. Ibid.

67. Ibid., viii.

68. Mel White, *Stranger at the Gate: To Be Gay and Christian in America* (New York: Plume, 1995).

69. Meyer and Staggenborg, "Movements, Countermovements, and the Structure of Political Opportunity," 1642.

70. "International Healing Foundation," segment on CNN, *Larry King Live*, 1994, accessed June 6, 2010.

71. Charles Socarides et al., "Don't Forsake Homosexuals Who Want Help," op-ed, *Wall Street Journal*, January 9, 1997, A12.

72. Douglas Haldeman, interview with author, Seattle, 2009.

73. Douglas Haldeman, "The Practice and Ethics of Sexual Orientation Conversion Therapy," *Journal of Consulting and Clinical Psychology* 62, 2 (1994): 221–27.

74. American Psychological Association, "Resolution on Appropriate Therapeutic Responses to Sexual Orientation," *American Psychologist* 53, 8 (1998): 934–35.

75. Ibid. Here the American Psychological Association referenced Gerald Davison, "Constructionism and Morality in Therapy for Homosexuality," in Weinrich and Gonsiorek, *Homosexuality: Research Implications for Public Policy*, 137–48; Haldeman, "The Practice and Ethics of Sexual Orientation Conversion Therapy"; and Letter to the Editor (1997, January 23), *Wall Street Journal*, A17.

76. Haldeman, interview with author, Seattle, 2009.

77. Fetner, *How the Religious Right Shaped Lesbian and Gay Activism*, 126.

78. PFOX, "What We Do," accessed October 1, 2014, http://www.pfox.org/about-us/what-we-do.

79. "Imagine . . . ," Joseph Nicolosi, 2009, accessed June 22, 2014, http://www.josephnicolosi.com/imagine.

80. Quoted in Julia Durin, "New Psychiatric Study Says Gays Can Alter Their Orientation; Conclusion Based on Study of 200 Ex-Homosexuals," *Washington Times*, May 9, 2001, A2.

81. Quoted in ibid. Challenging Spitzer's "transformation," Drescher claimed

that all along Spitzer believed gays could change, given his support for SOD and EDH: "In 1984, I heard Spitzer speak at a New York conference on homosexuality at which he defended the still extant EDH diagnosis, saying, 'If a guy comes to me and says he wants to change his homosexuality, I believe he should have the right to try and change'"; quoted in Jack Drescher, "The Spitzer Study and the Culture Wars," *Archives of Sexual Behavior* 32, 5 (2003): 431–32.

82. Besen, *Anything but Straight.*

83. Michael Schroeder and Ariel Shidlo, "Ethical Issues in Sexual Orientation Therapies: An Empirical Study of Consumers," in *Sexual Conversion Therapy*, ed. Ariel Shidlo, Michael Schroeder, and Jack Drescher (New York: Haworth Press, 2001), 152.

84. Ibid., 159.

85. "Psychiatric Association Schedules May 2000 Debate on Reorientation Therapy: Gay-Affirming Psychiatrists Refuse to Participate" NARTH, accessed July 19, 2010. Originally at http://www.narth.com/docs/debate.html; now available at http://www.narth.org/docs/debate.html.

86. "A 20 Year History of NARTH."

87. Additional criteria for inclusion in Spitzer's study included "(1) predominantly homosexual attraction for many years, and in the year before starting therapy, at least 60 on a scale of sexual attraction (where 0 = exclusively heterosexual and 100 = exclusively homosexual); (2) after therapy, a change of at least 10 points, lasting at least 5 years, toward the heterosexual end of the scale of sexual attraction"; Robert Spitzer, "Can Some Gay Men and Lesbians Change Their Sexual Orientation? 200 Participants Reporting a Change from Homosexual to Heterosexual Orientation," *Archives of Sexual Behavior* 32, 5 (2003): 405.

88. American Psychiatric Association, "Position Statement on Therapies Focused on Attempts to Change Sexual Orientation (Reparative or Conversion Therapies)."

89. Images of these protests are documented at NARTH, "Photos: Ex-Gays Picket the 2000 American Psychiatric Association Conference," accessed October 1, 2014, http://www.narth.org/docs/photos.html.

90. Malcolm Ritter, "Some Gays Can Go Straight, Study Suggests," Associated Press, May 8, 2001.

91. Erica Goode, "Study Says Gays Can Shift Orientation," *New York Times,* May 9, 2001, A24.

92. Rabeharisoa, "The Struggle against Neuromuscular Diseases."

93. Randy Thomas, quoted in "Media Spotlights," September 30, 2003, accessed December 28, 2009, http://www.exodusinternational.org/content/view/483/37.

94. Susan Leigh Star and James R. Griesemer, "Institutional Ecology, Translations, and Boundary Objects," *Social Studies of Science* 19, 3 (1989): 393.

95. Jack Drescher, interview with author, New York, 2010.

96. Quoted in Besen, *Anything but Straight*, 235.

97. Robert Spitzer, "Psychiatry and Homosexuality," *Wall Street Journal,* May 23, 2001, A26.

98. Ariel Shidlo and Michael Schroeder, "Changing Sexual Orientation: A Consumers' Report," *Professional Psychology: Research and Practice* 33, 3 (2002): 249–59.

99. A. Lee Beckstead, "The Process toward Self-Acceptance and Self-Identity

of Individuals Who Underwent Sexual Reorientation Therapy" (Ph.D. diss., University of Utah, 2001), 284.

100. Robert Spitzer, "Can Some Gay Men and Lesbians Change their Sexual Orientation?," 406–7.

101. Robert Spitzer, interview with author, Princeton, N.J., 2008.

102. Milton L. Wainberg et al., "Science and the Nuremberg Code: A Question of Ethics and Harm," *Archives of Sexual Behavior* 32, 5 (2003): 455–57.

103. John Bancroft, "Can Sexual Orientation Change? A Long-Running Saga," *Archives of Sexual Behavior* 32, 5 (2003): 421.

104. Ibid.; A. Lee Beckstead, "Understanding the Self-Reports of Reparative Therapy 'Successes,'" *Archives of Sexual Behavior* 32, 5 (2003): 421–23; Drescher, "The Spitzer Study and the Culture Wars," 432; Richard C. Friedman, "Sexual Orientation Change: A Study of Atypical Cases," *Archives of Sexual Behavior* 32, 5 (2003): 432–34; John H. Gagnon, "The Politics of Sexual Choices," *Archives of Sexual Behavior* 32, 5 (2003): 434–36; Gregory M. Herek, "Evaluating Interventions to Alter Sexual Orientation: Methodological and Ethical Considerations." *Archives of Sexual Behavior* 32, 5 (2003): 438–39; Wainberg et al., "Science and the Nuremberg Code," 456; Roger L. Worthington, "Heterosexual Identities: Sexual Reorientation Therapies, and Science," *Archives of Sexual Behavior* 32, 5 (2003): 460–61.

105. Kenneth M. Cohen and Ritch Savin-Williams, "Are Converts to Be Believed? Assessing Sexual Orientation 'Conversions,'" *Archives of Sexual Behavior* 32, 5 (2003): 427–29; see also Lisa M. Diamond, "Reconsidering 'Sexual Desire' in the Context of Reparative Therapy," *Archives of Sexual Behavior* 32, 5 (2003): 429–31; Wainberg et al., "Science and the Nuremberg Code," 455.

106. Beckstead, "Understanding the Self-Reports of Reparative Therapy 'Successes,'" 423; Craig A. Hill and Jeannie D. DiClementi, "Methodological Limitations Do Not Justify the Claim That Same-Sex Attraction Changed through 'Reparative Therapy,'" *Archives of Sexual Behavior* 32, 5 (2003): 440–42; Bruce Rind, "Sexual Orientation Change and Informed Consent in Reparative Therapy," *Archives of Sexual Behavior* 32, 5 (2003): 447–49; Donald S. Strassberg, "A Candle in the Wind: Spitzer's Study of Reparative Therapy," *Archives of Sexual Behavior* 32, 5 (2003): 451–52; Paul L. Vasey and Drew Rendall, "Sexual Diversity and Change along a Continuum of Bisexual Desire," *Archives of Sexual Behavior* 32, 5 (2003): 453–55.

107. Hill and DiClementi, "Methodological Limitations," 441.

108. Bancroft, "Can Sexual Orientation Change?," 420; Helena M. Carlson, "A Methodological Critique of Spitzer's Research on Reparative Therapy," *Archives of Sexual Behavior* 32, 5 (2003): 425–27; Cohen and Savin-Williams, "Are Converts to Be Believed?," 428; Herek, "Evaluating Interventions," 438; Hill and DiClementi, "Methodological Limitations," 441; Rind, "Sexual Orientation Change," 447–48; Wainberg et al., "Science and the Nuremberg Code," 456; Worthington, "Heterosexual Identities," 460–61.

109. Herek, "Evaluating Interventions," 438.

110. See "Peer Commentaries on Spitzer (2003)," *Archives of Sexual Behavior* 32, 5 (2003): 419–68.

111. Beckstead, "Understanding the Self-Reports," 422; Cohen and Savin-Williams, "Are Converts to Be Believed?," 428; Lawrence Hartmann, "Too Flawed:

Don't Publish," *Archives of Sexual Behavior* 32, 5 (2003): 436–38; Rind, "Sexual Orientation Change," 448–49; Worthington, "Heterosexual Identities," 460.

112. Rind, "Sexual Orientation Change," 448–49.

113. Gregory Herek, telephone interview with author, 2008.

114. Carlson, "A Methodological Critique," 426–27; Hartmann, "Too Flawed," 436; Hill and DiClementi, "Methodological Limitations," 441–42.

115. Diamond, "Reconsidering 'Sexual Desire,'" 429.

116. Paula Rodriguez Rust, "Reparative Science and Social Responsibility: The Concept of a Malleable Core as Theoretical Challenge and Psychological Comfort," *Archives of Sexual Behavior* 32, 5 (2003): 449–51.

117. Joseph Nicolosi, "Finally, Recognition of a Long-Neglected Population," *Archives of Sexual Behavior* 32, 5 (2003): 445–47.

118. Joseph Nicolosi, A. Dean Byrd, and Richard W. Potts, "Retrospective Self-Reports of Changes in Homosexual Orientation: A Consumer Survey of Conversion Therapy Clients," *Psychological Reports* 86, 3, pt. 2 (2000): 1071–88. Herek characterizes this journal as "pay to publish," and hence questions the scientific merit of the study as it was not properly peer-reviewed.

119. Robert Spitzer, "Reply: Study Results Should Not Be Dismissed and Justify Further Research on the Efficacy of Sexual Reorientation Therapy," *Archives of Sexual Behavior* 32, 5 (2003): 70.

120. Ibid., 472.

121. Besen, *Anything but Straight*, 241.

122. Jeffrey Satinover, "Testimony before Massachusetts Senate Committee Studying Gay Marriage," April 28, 2003. Accessed December 20, 2009. Originally at http://www.narth.com/docs/senatecommittee.html; now available at http://www.narth.org/docs/senatecommittee.html.

123. Olli Stållström and Jussi Nissinen, "The Spitzer Study and the Finnish Parliament," *Journal of Gay and Lesbian Psychotherapy* 7, 3 (2003): 83–95.

124. Quoted in ibid., 90–91.

125. "NARTH Sends Second Letter to AMA Appealing for Correction in Encyclopedia," Joseph Nicolosi, 2004, accessed December 20, 2009. Originally at http://www.narth.com/docs/correctionletter3.html; now available at http://www.narth.org/docs/correctionletter3.html.

126. "Can Homosexuality Be Treated and Prevented? Dr. Dobson Discusses Various Topics concerning Homosexuality," Focus on the Family, James Dobson, 2002, accessed December 20, 2009, http://www2.focusonthefamily.com/docstudy/newsletters/a000000264.cfm.

127. Latour, *Science in Action*, 259.

128. Robert Spitzer, interview with author, 2008.

129. See Benford, "Frame Disputes within the Nuclear Disarmament Movement."

3. Ex-Ex-Gays Match Testimony with Testimony

1. "Ex-Gay Featured in Video No Longer Part of Ex-Gay Movement," Ex-Gay Watch, Timothy Kincaid, January 8, 2007, accessed September 1, 2013, http://www.exgaywatch.com/2007/01/ex-gay-featured.

2. "I Do Exist FAQs," Warren Throckmorton, 2006, accessed September 1, 2013, http://wthrockmorton.com/i-do-exist-faqs.

3. Tom J. Waidzunas, "Standards as 'Weapons of Exclusion': Ex-Gays and

Materialization of the Male Body," in *Routledge Handbook of Science, Technology, and Society,* ed. Daniel Lee Kleinman and Kelly Moore (New York: Routledge, 2014).

4. Benford, "Frame Disputes within the Nuclear Disarmament Movement."

5. "Convergence" is a phenomenon seen in other cases of clashes between opposing social movements. For example, Klatch observed that the dialectical dynamics of the New Right and New Left gave rise to libertarianism as a form of conceptual convergence; Rebecca Klatch, *A Generation Divided: The New Left, the New Right, and the 1960s* (Berkeley: University of California Press, 1999). Esacove describes a "dialectical dance of meaning making" as pro-life and pro-choice activists converged on the existence of a phenomenon called "partial-birth abortion," even though they maintained different understandings of the phenomenon; Anne W. Esacove, "Dialogic Framing: The Framing/Counterframing of 'Partial-Birth' Abortion," *Sociological Inquiry* 74, 1 (2004): 70–101.

6. Suzanne Staggenborg, "Critical Events and the Mobilization of the Pro-Choice Movement," *Research in Political Sociology* 6 (1993): 319–45.

7. Human Rights Campaign Foundation, *Finally Free* (Washington, D.C.: HRC Foundation, 2000).

8. *This Is What Love in Action Looks Like,* directed by Morgan Jon Fox (Sawed-Off Collaboratory Productions, 2011).

9. *But I'm a Cheerleader,* directed by Jamie Babbit (Cheerleader LLC, 1999).

10. Fox, *This Is What Love in Action Looks Like.*

11. John Evans, quoted in "Love in Action Co-Founder: 'My Ministry Shatters Lives,'" Wayne Besen, July 24, 2005, accessed September 1, 2013, http://www.waynebesen.com/columns/2005_07_24_archive.html.

12. Fox, *This Is What Love in Action Looks Like.* According to the documentary, Zachary Stark went on to college, where he participated in LGBTQ organizations. Even Refuge program director John Smid eventually came out as gay, declaring that he had never seen a man successfully change from gay to straight.

13. Nicolosi and Nicolosi describe the "prehomosexual boy" in *A Parent's Guide to Preventing Homosexuality.* They claim that "little boys who have a fascination and preoccupation with feminine activities have at least a 75 percent chance of growing up to be homosexual, bisexual, or transsexual"; Nicolosi and Nicolosi, *A Parents' Guide to Preventing Homosexuality,* 33.

14. The authors cite Ariel Shidlo and Michael Schroeder, "Changing Sexual Orientation: A Consumer's Report," *Professional Psychology: Research and Practice* 33, 3 (2002): 249–59.

15. "Randy Thomas and Alan Chambers Invited to White House, Lobby for Marriage Amendment," Ex-Gay Watch, Daniel Gonzales, 2006, accessed September 1, 2013, http://www.exgaywatch.com/2006/06/randy-thomas-an.

16. Tanya Erzen. "Testimonial Politics: The Christian Right's Faith-Based Approach to Marriage and Imprisonment," *American Quarterly* 59, 3 (2007): 998.

17. Wayne Besen, interview with author, Brooklyn, N.Y., 2008.

18. "Truth Wins Out," Wayne Besen, 2013, accessed September 1, 2013, http://www.truthwinsout.org.

19. Jim Burroway founded *Box Turtle Bulletin* in response to conservative activism against gay marriage, but it would later become a key anti-reorientation blog, especially in following the activities of ex-gay leaders in Uganda. *Box*

Turtle Bulletin, Jim Burroway, 2006, accessed September 1, 2013, http://www
.boxturtlebulletin.com/About/AboutUs.htm.

20. Stephanie Simon, "'Ex-Gay' Group Draws Fire from Allies," *Los Angeles Times,* October 15, 2006.

21. Wayne Besen, interview with author, 2008.

22. "Stand Up for Scientific Integrity," Respect My Research, Truth Wins Out, 2007, accessed September 1, 2013, http://www.resepectmyresearch.org.

23. Quoted in "(Out of) Focus on the Family; Dr. Robert Spitzer," Truth Wins Out, 2007, accessed September 1, 2013, http://respectmyresearch.org/scientists/dr-robert-spitzer.

24. Quoted in ibid.

25. Wayne Besen, interview with author, 2008.

26. "Beyond ExGay: An online community for those who have survived ex-gay experiences," Beyond Ex-Gay, 2007, accessed September 1, 2013, http://www
.beyondexgay.com.

27. Peterson Toscano, interview with author, Frostburg, Md., 2009.

28. Peterson Toscano, *Doin' Time in the Homo No Mo' Halfway House: How I Survived the Ex-Gay Movement,* 2008, https://petersontoscano.com/portfolio/homo-no-mo-halfway-house.

29. Toscano, interview with author.

30. Stephen Fried, "They Tried to Cure Me of Being Gay," *Glamour,* April 1, 2007, accessed September 1, 2013, http://www.glamour.com/sex-love-life/2007/04/gay-therapy.

31. Christine Bakke, interview with author, Denver, 2010.

32. Fieldnotes, Beyond ExGay National Conference, Irvine, Calif., 2007.

33. Beyond ExGay, "Survivor Collage Gallery," 2007, accessed October 1, 2014. http://www.beyondexgay.com/resources/collages.html.

34. Toscano, interview with author.

35. Erzen, "Testimonial Politics," 991.

36. Arthur Frank, *The Wounded Storyteller: Body, Illness, and Ethics* (Chicago: University of Chicago Press, 1995), 153.

37. Meyer and Whittier, "Social Movement Spillover," 277.

38. Erzen, *Straight to Jesus.*

39. Christine Bakke observed that those who provide personal narratives in this movement tend to be primarily religious people who had been through ex-gay ministries.

40. Mark Yarhouse and Lori Burkett, *Sexual Identity: A Guide to Living in the Time Between the Times* (Lanham, Md.: University Press of America, 2003), 4.

41. Ibid.

42. Warren Throckmorton and Mark Yarhouse, "Sexual Identity Therapy: Practice Framework for Managing Sexual Identity Conflicts," 2006, accessed September 1, 2013, http://wthrockmorton.com/wp-content/uploads/2007/04/sexualidentitytherapyframeworkfinal.pdf, 4.

43. Ibid., 5.

44. Alan Chambers and the Leadership Team at Exodus International, *God's Grace and the Homosexual Next Door: Reaching the Heart of the Gay Men and Women in Your World* (Eugene, Ore.: Harvest House Publishers, 2006).

45. Erzen, *Straight to Jesus.*

46. Mike Goeke, "Is Change Possible?," in Chambers, *God's Grace and the Homosexual Next Door*, 68–69.

47. Ibid., 73.

48. Ibid., 73–74.

49. Alan Cooperman, "Church Leader Resigns after Gay Sex Claim: Evangelical Pastor in Colorado Denies Male Escort's Story of Repeated Trysts," *Washington Post*, November 3, 2006, A16.

50. Quoted in Tom Baldwin and Anna Stroman Washington, "Disgraced Christian Leader Is 'Cured of Being Gay,'" *Times* (London), February 8, 2007.

51. Quoted in Baldwin and Washington, "Church Leader Resigns."

52. Quoted in Stephanie Simon, "Approaching Agreement in Debate over Homosexuality," *Los Angeles Times*, June 18, 2007.

53. Ex-Gay Watch, "Ex-Gay Guru Richard Cohen," July 1, 2008, accessed October 1, 2014, http://www.youtube.com/watch?v=VtGouVqsmsg.

54. Sandra G. Boodman, "A Conversion Therapist's Unusual Odyssey," *Washington Post*, August 16, 2005, accessed October 1, 2014, http://www.washingtonpost.com/wp-dyn/content/article/2005/08/15/AR2005081501063.html.

55. Fieldnotes, Exodus International West Coast Regional Conference, Fresno, Calif., April 2008. These observations of gender nonconformity align with those made by Bernadette Barton at another Exodus International conference. See Barton, *Pray the Gay Away*.

56. Stanton Jones and Mark Yarhouse, *Ex-Gays? A Longitudinal Study of Religiously Mediated Change in Sexual Orientation* (Downers Grove, Ill.: InterVarsity Press, 2007), 250–61.

57. Ibid., 358.

58. Ibid., 368–70.

59. Ibid., 112–17.

60. Alder explains how the polygraph has been instrumental in extracting confessions in police work, and the threat of the polygraph has been deployed to invoke fear within the souls of government workers and company employees in the interests of maintaining loyalty; Ken Alder, *The Lie Detectors: A History of an American Obsession* (New York: Free Press, 2007).

61. Alan Chambers, interview with author, Orlando, Fla., 2008.

62. Fieldnotes, NARTH National Conference, Dallas, 2007.

63. Ibid.

64. Frank York, "President Koocher Says the APA Has No Disagreement with the Treatment of Unwanted Homosexual Attraction," *NARTH Bulletin* 14, 2 (2006): 1–2, 39.

65. Joseph Nicolosi, "Open Letter to APA President Koocher," August 11, 2006, accessed September 1, 2013. Originally at http://narth.com/docs/nicospeech.html; now available at http://www.narth.org/docs/nicospeech.html.

66. Ibid.

67. "NARTH's Governing Board Unanimously Accepts the Leona Tyler Principle," Linda Ames Nicolosi, February 8, 2007, accessed September 1, 2013. Originally at http://www.narth.com/docs/ltyler.html; now available at http://www.narth.org/docs/ltyler.html.

68. David Pickup, interview with author, Encino, Calif., 2009. Subsequent quotations from Pickup in this chapter are taken from this interview.

69. Stanton Jones developed his perspective by drawing on the work of Thomas Kuhn, who challenges the fact/value dichotomy in *The Structure of Scientific Revolutions;* Stanton Jones, "A Constructive Relationship for Religion with the Science and Profession of Psychology: Perhaps the Boldest Model Yet," *American Psychologist* 49, 3 (1994): 184–99.

70. I explained that I was there as a researcher to better understand the organization from their point of view, as they had been maligned in the media, and because I was interested in the formation of scientific community. While I had not planned to introduce myself publicly, I had the good fortune of being able to follow another sociologist, Karl Bryant, who was also at the conference conducting research and who provided a model answer.

71. During a break, I asked this life coach for clarification regarding what it meant to be "more than a therapist and less than a friend." To illustrate, he looked me in the eye and asked me in a seductive voice to think about what I wanted more than anything in the world at that moment, and to think about what was keeping me from getting what I wanted. He then asked me what I was thinking about. I said that I was thinking about my dissertation. Yet, in the context of reorientation coaching, the method, with its seductive questions and probe for self-revelation, seemed to encourage ex-gays to experience homoeroticism, but to learn to redirect or sublimate these feelings into alternative life goals.

72. Fieldnotes, NARTH conference, Dallas, 2007.

73. Susan L. Morrow et al., "Impossible Dreams, Impossible Choices, and Thoughts about Depolarizing the Debate," *Counseling Psychologist* 32, 5 (2004): 782.

74. Peterson Toscano, interview with author, Frostburg, Md., 2009.

75. Janelle Hallman, *The Heart of Female Same-Sex Attraction: A Comprehensive Counseling Resource* (Downers Grove, Ill.: InterVarsity Press, 2008), 24.

76. Ibid., 24–25.

77. Christine Bakke, interview with author, Denver, 2010.

78. Ibid.

79. Lisa Diamond, *Sexual Fluidity: Understanding Women's Love and Desire* (Cambridge, Mass.: Harvard University Press, 2008), 3.

80. Hallman, *Heart of Female Same-Sex Attraction,* 27. Emphases in the original.

81. "Respect my Research, Dr. Lisa Diamond," Wayne Besen, 2008, accessed November 1, 2013, http://respectmyresearch.org/scientists/dr-lisa-diamond.

82. Lisa Diamond, interview with author, Salt Lake City, 2010.

83. John Gonsiorek, "Reflections from the Conversion Therapy Battlefield," *Counseling Psychologist* 32, 5 (2004): 752.

84. Susan Morrow et al., "Impossible Dreams, Impossible Choices, and Thoughts about Depolarizing the Debate," 780.

85. Ibid., 782.

86. A. Lee Beckstead and Susan L. Morrow, "Mormon Clients' Experiences of Conversion Therapy: The Need for a New Treatment Approach," *Counseling Psychologist* 32, 5 (2004): 655.

87. A. Lee Beckstead, interview with author, Salt Lake City, 2009.

88. Quoted in Beckstead and Morrow, "Mormon Clients' Experiences," 680.

89. Beckstead and Morrow, "Mormon Clients' Experiences," 685.

90. Douglas C. Haldeman, "When Sexual and Religious Orientation Collide: Considerations in Working with Conflicted Same-Sex Attracted Male Clients," *Counseling Psychologist* 32, 5 (2004): 691–715.

91. Roger Worthington, "Sexual Identity, Sexual Orientation, Religious Identity, and Change: Is It Possible to Depolarize the Debate?," *Counseling Psychologist* 32, 5 (2004): 742.

92. Ibid., 743. In this quotation, Worthington cites Lisa Diamond, "Reconsidering 'Sexual Desire' in the Context of Reparative Therapy," *Archives of Sexual Behavior* 32, 5 (2003): 429–31; R. L. Worthington and R. L. Navarro, "Pathways to the Future: Analyzing the Contents of a Content Analysis," *Counseling Psychologist* 31, 1 (2003): 85–92.

93. Ibid.

94. Gonsiorek, "Reflections from the Conversion Therapy Battlefield," 758.

95. Erinn E. Tozer and Jeffrey A. Hayes, "Why Do Individuals Seek Conversion Therapy? The Role of Religiosity, Internalized Homonegativity, and Identity Development," *Counseling Psychologist* 32, 5 (2004): 716–40.

96. Alicia Salzer, *Abomination: Homosexuality and the Ex-Gay Movement* (San Francisco: Association of Gay and Lesbian Psychiatrists, 2006, Frameline [distributor]).

4. Reorientation's Last Stand

1. American Psychological Association Task Force on Appropriate Therapeutic Responses to Sexual Orientation, *Report of the American Psychological Association Task Force on Appropriate Therapeutic Responses to Sexual Orientation* (Washington, D.C.: American Psychological Association, 2009), 120.

2. Gieryn, *Cultural Boundaries of Science*, 4.

3. Ibid., 17–18.

4. This case has some parallels with the case of HIV dissenters and AIDS research in the late 1980s and early 1990s. At this time in the history of AIDS, dissenters had amassed so much popular credibility outside science that Robert Gallo and other proponents of the HIV hypothesis were forced to respond and provide further proof for their views. Epstein, *Impure Science*, 141.

5. American Psychological Association, "Resolution on Appropriate Therapeutic Responses to Sexual Orientation," *American Psychologist* 53, 8 (1998): 934–35.

6. Clinton Anderson, director of APA Office of LGBT Concerns, interview with author, Washington, D.C., 2008.

7. "Directorates," American Psychological Association, accessed June 22, 2014, http://www.apa.org/about/offices/directorates.

8. "About the Lesbian, Gay, Bisexual and Transgender Concerns Office," American Psychological Association, accessed June 15, 2015, http://www.apa.org/pi/lgbt/about/index.aspx.

9. Irwin offers his theory of "citizen science," including dialogue between citizens and scientists, as an alternative to "science-centered" views, which often see the public as irrational, and "critical" views, which often see science as an excessively rational force that is disenchanting the world; Alan Irwin, *Citizen Science: A Study of People, Expertise, and Sustainable Development* (New York: Routledge, 1995).

10. Clinton Anderson, interview with author, Washington, D.C., 2008.

11. Ron Schlittler, interview with author, Washington, D.C., 2008.

12. At the time of this writing, Schlittler had become program coordinator for the Office of LGBT Concerns.

13. Anderson, interview with author.

14. On "trials of strength" see Latour, *Science in Action,* 78.

15. Jack Drescher, interview with author, New York, 2010.

16. "New APA Task Force Lacks Reparative/Reorientation Therapists," Mike Hatfield, NARTH, 2007, accessed June 10, 2010. Originally at http://www.narth .com/docs/lacks.html; now available at http://www.narth.org/docs/lacks.html.

17. Anderson, interview with author.

18. Ibid.

19. Judith Glassgold, interview with author, Washington, D.C., 2010.

20. A. Lee Beckstead, interview with author, Salt Lake City, 2009.

21. Glassgold, interview with author.

22. The "anti-scientific" work to which Glassgold refers draws on the theory of Thomas Kuhn, *The Structure of Scientific Revolutions,* to argue that because science is always based on values, one can propose an Evangelical Christian-based science. See Jones, "A Constructive Relationship for Religion with the Science and Profession of Psychology."

23. Glassgold, interview with author.

24. Beckstead, interview with author. Beckstead has published articles drawn from his master's thesis and doctoral dissertation. A. Lee Beckstead, "Cures versus Choices: Agendas in Sexual Reorientation Therapy," *Journal of Gay & Lesbian Psychotherapy* 5, 3–4 (2001): 87–115; Beckstead and Morrow, "Mormon Clients' Experiences." This research examines people who have undergone reorientation therapies and who are now either "proponents" or "opponents" of the therapy. Proponents may not claim to be fully heterosexual, but they have been "converted" to a reorientation therapy ideology. Beckstead's research outlines the harms and benefits of reorientation therapies for both samples. He has provided commentary on the Spitzer study (Beckstead, "Understanding the Self-Reports") and commentary on reorientation therapies more broadly (Morrow et al., "Impossible Dreams, Impossible Choices"). In addition to more recent publications on sexual orientation, he was part of a research team that studied pedophilia using phallometric testing (James M. Cantor et al., "Intelligence, Memory, and Handedness in Pedophilia," *Neuropsychology* 18, 1 [2004]: 3–14).

25. In *Psychoanalytic Therapy and the Gay Man,* Drescher provided a relational theory of psychoanalysis that treats homosexuality as a normal variant of human sexuality. Drescher rejected any etiological theorizing as evidence of anti-gay bias, and discussed this type of theorizing among his clients as internalized homophobia. In addition, Drescher rejected all reorientation therapy as heterosexism. Additional publications by Drescher on reorientation therapy reject reorientation on ethical terms (for example, Drescher, "The Spitzer Study and the Culture Wars"). He is emeritus editor of the *Journal of Gay and Lesbian Mental Health.*

26. Drescher, interview with author.

27. Ibid.

28. Glassgold, interview with author. See Judith M. Glassgold, "Bridging the Divide: Integrating Lesbian Identity and Orthodox Judaism," *Women & Therapy*

31, 1 (2008): 59–72. See also Judith M. Glassgold & Suzanne Iasenza, eds., *Lesbians and Psychoanalysis: Revolutions in Theory and Practice* (New York: Free Press, 2000).

29. Among Greene's vast number of publications in psychology, she has coedited two volumes on lesbian and gay psychology: Beverly Greene and Gregory M. Herek, eds., *Psychological Perspectives on Lesbian and Gay Issues*, vol. 1, *Lesbian and Gay Psychology: Theory, Research, and Clinical Applications* (Thousand Oaks, Calif.: Sage, 1994); Beverly Greene and Gladys L. Croom, eds., *Psychological Perspectives on Lesbian and Gay Issues*, vol. 5, *Education, Research, and Practice in Lesbian, Gay, Bisexual, and Transgendered Psychology: A Resource Manual* (Thousand Oaks, Calif.: Sage, 2000). Her emphasis on multiple identities has included work on diversity among lesbians and gay men: Beverly Greene, ed., *Psychological Perspectives on Lesbian and Gay Issues*, vol. 3, *Ethnic and Cultural Diversity among Lesbians and Gay Men* (Thousand Oaks, Calif.: Sage, 1997); and African American lesbian and bisexual women: Beverly Greene, "African American Lesbian and Bisexual Women," *Journal of Social Issues* 56, 2 (2000): 239–49.

30. "Roger L. Worthington," University of Missouri, 2009, accessed June 20, 2010, http://education.missouri.edu/faculty/ESCP/Worthington_Roger.php.

31. Although Worthington has published widely on topics in educational psychology such as campus climate, he has also done extensive work on developing research methods for the study of sexual orientation. This work includes developing a Measure of Sexual Identity Exploration and Commitment (MOSIEC): Roger L. Worthington et al., "Development, Reliability, and Validity of the Measure of Sexual Identity Exploration and Commitment (MOSIEC)," *Developmental Psychology* 44, 1 (2008): 22–33; and using MOSIEC and other instruments to study identity subgroups within sexual orientation groups: Roger L. Worthington and Amy L. Reynolds, "Within-Group Differences in Sexual Orientation and Identity," *Journal of Counseling Psychology* 56, 1 (2009): 44–55. He has also studied heterosexual identity development: Roger L. Worthington and Jonathan Mohr, "Theorizing Heterosexual Identity Development," *Counseling Psychologist* 30, 4 (2002): 491–95. In the reorientation therapy debate, he has provided commentaries, including advocacy for "sexual orientation identity" as separate from sexual orientation: Worthington, "Heterosexual Identities"; Worthington, "Sexual Identity, Sexual Orientation."

32. Miller's work on HIV prevention has included evaluations of AIDS service organizations (Robin Lin Miller, "Organizational and Intervention Characteristics Affecting Program Adoption," *American Journal of Community Psychology* 29, 4 [2001]: 621–47), developing techniques to evaluate AIDS service groups (Robin Lin Miller and Brian J. Cassel, "Ongoing Evaluation in AIDS-Service Organizations: Building Meaningful Evaluation Activities," *Journal of Prevention and Intervention in the Community* 19, 1 [2000]: 21–39), and evaluating evidence-based practice in these organizations (Robin Lin Miller, "Adapting an Evidence-Based Intervention: Tales of the Hustler Project," *AIDS Education and Prevention* 15, Suppl. 1 [2003]: 127–38).

33. Quoted in "New APA Task Force Lacks Reparative/Reorientation Therapists."

34. Ibid.

35. "Press Release: American Psychological Association Appoints Political

Activists to New Committee," Joseph Nicolosi, June 20, 2007, accessed December 10, 2010. Originally at http://www.narth.com/docs/press15.html; now available at http://www.narth.org/docs/press15.html. Emphasis in the original.

36. Quoted in "New APA Task Force Lacks Reparative/Reorientation Therapists."

37. Cummings and O'Donohue, "Psychology's Surrender to Political Correctness," 9–10.

38. Fieldnotes, American Psychological Association Convention, Boston, 2008. Also quoted in "Convention of Mental Health Professionals Highlights Liberal Agenda," CitizenLink, August 28, 2008, http://www.youtube.com/watch?v=mJhs_UaZ4gw. Here Pickup employs a strategy that, in some ways, runs parallel to the GayPA strategies in the 1970s during the struggle to demedicalize homosexuality. In both cases mental health professionals used their own status as simultaneously being mental health professionals and marginalized to promote a viewpoint.

39. Fieldnotes, American Psychological Association Convention, Boston, 2008.

40. Ibid.

41. American Psychological Association Task Force, *Appropriate Therapeutic Responses*, 1.

42. Fieldnotes, American Psychological Association Convention, Boston, 2008; also quoted in "Convention of Mental Health Professionals Highlights Liberal Agenda."

43. Latour, *Science in Action*, 33–44.

44. James E. Phelan, Neil Whitehead, and Phillip M. Sutton, "What Research Shows: NARTH's Response to the APA Claims on Homosexuality," *Journal of Human Sexuality* 1 (2009): 9. Here Phelan et al. cite Alfred Kinsey, Walter B. Pomeroy, and Clyde E. Martin, *Sexual Behavior in the Human Male* (Philadelphia: Saunders, 1948); Fritz Klein, *The Bisexual Option: A Concept of One Hundred Percent Intimacy* (New York: Harrington Park Press, 1978); Randall L. Sell, "Defining and Measuring Sexual Orientation: A Review," *Archives of Sexual Behavior* 26, 6 (1997): 643–58. While Kinsey developed the bipolar "Kinsey scale" ranging from homosexual to heterosexual, Klein, a bisexuality activist, proposed a tabular measure of sexual orientation across seven variables (attraction, behavior, fantasy, emotional preference, social preference, identity, and lifestyle) that could be rated for past, present, and future. Sell's review summarizes dichotomous measures in addition to the scales of Kinsey, Klein, and Shively and De Cecco. He argues that none of these measures are satisfactory.

45. Ibid., 20.

46. Fieldnotes, NARTH conference, Dallas, 2007.

47. Phelan et al. aggregate data from Joseph Nicolosi, A. Dean Byrd, and Richard W. Potts, "Retrospective Self-Reports of Changes in Homosexual Orientation: A Consumer Survey of Conversion Therapy Clients," *Psychological Reports* 86, 3, pt. 2 (2000): 1071–88; Ariel Shidlo and Michael Schroeder, "Changing Sexual Orientation: A Consumers' Report," *Professional Psychology: Research and Practice* 33, 3 (2002): 249–59; Robert Spitzer, "Can Some Gay Men and Lesbians Change their Sexual Orientation? 200 Participants Reporting a Change from Homosexual to Heterosexual Orientation," *Archives of Sexual Behavior* 32, 5 (2003): 403–17.

48. Phelan et al. cite an interview with Cummings from the NARTH website, "Former APA President Dr. Nicholas Cummings Describes his Work with SSA Clients," accessed June 15, 2015, http://www.narth.org/docs/cummings.html.

49. Phelan, Whitehead, and Sutton, "What Research Shows," 18.

50. Ibid., 10.

51. Phelan and coauthors do not explain why believing that homosexuality is "innate" is an indicator of favorable attitudes toward homosexuality. However, they do suggest in the conclusion of the essay that this belief means homosexuals cannot be blamed for their condition; Phelan, Whitehead, and Sutton, "What Research Shows," 51. This indicates the strength of the idea operating in this social world that belief in innateness means support for gay rights, which is not a necessary linkage by any means, if the prospect of genetic screening is considered.

52. While many of these types of dubious claims have been associated with Family Research Institute cofounder Paul Cameron, Cameron's name is conspicuously absent from the document.

53. Phelan, Whitehead, and Sutton, "What Research Shows," 68. It is unclear how this claim about the nonexistence of anilingus among heterosexuals can be made based on a citation of David McWhirter and Andrew Mattison, *The Male Couple: How Relationships Develop* (Englewood Cliffs, N.J.: Prentice-Hall, 1984). The book is an interview study of gay male couples only and contains no data on the sexual practices of heterosexuals.

54. Beckstead, interview with author.

55. Ibid.

56. American Psychological Association Task Force, *Appropriate Therapeutic Responses*, 26.

57. Ibid., 27.

58. Ibid., 31.

59. Ibid., 30.

60. Ibid.

61. Ibid., 31.

62. Glassgold, interview with author.

63. Beckstead, interview with author.

64. Drescher, interview with author.

65. American Psychological Association Task Force, *Appropriate Therapeutic Responses*, 120.

66. These discursive evocations of phallometry by task force members amount to what Michelle Murphy has called "materializations," practices by which material objects are "granted or not granted existence" (Murphy, *Sick Building Syndrome*, 7). By citing phallometric studies employing physical measures of genital arousal in men during the 1970s, material bodies were brought into being to speak on behalf of the fixity of sexual orientation, located in the physiological process of arousal to visual stimuli. In SOCE research, this discourse effectively reconfigures what Michelle Murphy has called the "regime of perceptibility." Murphy defines this term as "the regular and sedimented contours of perception and imperceptions produced within a disciplinary or epistemological tradition"; Murphy, *Sick Building Syndrome*, 24. In this newly established regime, for a sub-

ject's sexual orientation to be perceived, the discursively materialized physical body must speak. Subjects' own perceptions can no longer be the sole source of knowledge for research to be considered scientific.

67. American Psychological Association Task Force, Appropriate Therapeutic Responses, 41.

68. Ibid., 41–42.

69. Here the task force utilized harm data from Ariel Shidlo and Michael Schroeder, "Changing Sexual Orientation: A Consumers' Report," *Professional Psychology: Research and Practice* 33, 3 (2002): 249–59; A. Lee Beckstead and Susan L. Morrow, "Mormon Clients' Experiences of Conversion Therapy: The Need for a New Treatment Approach," *Counseling Psychologist* 32, 5 (2004): 651–90. While it was not discussed in the task force report in terms of harm, in an interview, Beckstead discussed the Jones and Yarhouse study offered by NARTH as the "most methodologically rigorous" study that demonstrated efficacy and safety of therapy. Beckstead noted that the measures of harm used by Jones and Yarhouse, a depression symptoms checklist, would not capture the specific harms measured in his research; Beckstead, interview with author. In addition, Jones and Yarhouse had a significant dropout rate from their study and they did not investigate what happened with these subjects. Instead they declared that there was no evidence of harm; Jones and Yarhouse, *Ex-Gays?*

70. EBPP is a less stringent alternative to "empirically supported treatments" (EST), defined as "interventions for individuals with specific disorders that have been demonstrated as effective through rigorously controlled trials," American Psychological Association Task Force, *Appropriate Therapeutic Responses*, 14.

71. Beckstead, interview with author.

72. Quoted in American Psychological Association Task Force, *Appropriate Therapeutic Responses*, 19

73. American Psychological Association, "Resolution on Religious, Religion-Related, and/or Religion-Derived Prejudice," *American Psychologist* 63 (2008): 431–34.

74. Indirectly, the maintenance of a strict boundary between the philosophical bases of science and religion in these two resolutions presents a challenge to Stanton Jones's proposed "Evangelical science" in his 1994 article, "A Constructive Relationship for Religion with the Science and Profession of Psychology." Kuhn's views notwithstanding, the APA implies that to base a scientific research program on the value that homosexuality is sin is to problematically blend two distinct methodological, epistemological, historical, theoretical, and philosophical domains.

75. Glassgold, interview with author.

76. American Psychological Association Task Force, *Appropriate Therapeutic Responses*, 18.

77. Ibid., 4.

78. For a news feature on this development, see Mimi Swartz, "Living the Good Lie," *New York Times*, June 19, 2011, MM30.

79. American Psychological Association Task Force, *Appropriate Therapeutic Responses*, 68–69.

80. Brandon K. Thorpe and Penn Bullock, "How George Alan Rekers and His

Rent Boy Got Busted by New Times." *Miami New Times News,* May 13, 2010, accessed October 1, 2014, http://www.miaminewtimes.com/2010–05–13/news/how-george-alan-rekers-and-his-rent-boy-got-busted-by-new-times.

81. Gabriel Arana, "My So-Called Ex-Gay Life," *American Prospect,* 2012, accessed June 22, 2014, http://prospect.org/article/my-so-called-ex-gay-life.

82. Benedict Carey, "Psychiatry Giant Sorry for Backing Gay 'Cure,'" *New York Times,* May 18, 2012, accessed December 1, 2014, http://www.nytimes.com/2012/05/19/health/dr-robert-l-spitzer-noted-psychiatrist-apologizes-for-study-on-gay-cure.html.

83. Robert Spitzer, "Spitzer Reassesses His 2003 Study of Reparative Therapy of Homosexuality," *Archives of Sexual Behavior* 41 (2012): 757.

84. Arana, "My So-Called Ex-Gay Life."

85. Wayne Besen, "TWO Exclusive Video: Interview with Dr. Robert Spitzer Who Discusses Retracting His Infamous 'Ex-Gay' Study," May 30, 2012, accessed June 22, 2014, https://www.truthwinsout.org/blog/2012/05/25725.

86. Christopher Rosik, "Spitzer's 'Retraction' of His Sexual Orientation Change Study: What Does It Really Mean?," May 31, 2012, accessed June 22, 2014, http://www.lifesitenews.com/news/spitzers-retraction-of-his-sexual-orientation-change-study-what-does-it-rea.

87. Alice Dreger, "How to Ex an 'Ex-Gay' Study," Fetishes I Don't Get, *Psychology Today,* April 11, 2012, accessed June 22, 2014, http://www.psychologytoday.com/blog/fetishes-i-dont-get/201204/how-ex-ex-gay-study.

88. Rosik, "Spitzer's 'Retraction' of His Sexual Orientation Change Study."

89. Robert Spitzer, interview with author, Princeton, N.J., 2013.

90. Ibid.

91. Erik Eckholm, "Rift Forms in Movement as Belief in Gay 'Cure' Is Renounced," *New York Times,* July 7, 2012, A9.

92. "SB-1172 Sexual Orientation Change Efforts," California Legislative Information, 2011–12, accessed June 22, 2014, https://leginfo.legislature.ca.gov/faces/billNavClient.xhtml?bill_id=201120120SB1172. Additional professional associations cited in the Senate Bill 1172 include the American Psychiatric Association, American School Counselors Association, American Academy of Pediatrics, American Medical Association Council on Scientific Affairs, National Association of Social Work, American Counseling Association Governing Council, American Psychoanalytic Association, American Academy of Child and Adolescent Psychiatry, and the Pan American Health Organization.

93. Melissa Steffan, "Alan Chambers Apologizes to Gay Community, Exodus International to Shut Down," *Christianity Today,* June 21, 2013, accessed June 22, 2014, http://www.christianitytoday.com/gleanings/2013/june/alan-chambers-apologizes-to-gay-community-exodus.html.

94. "Alan Chambers, Exodus International President, Talks Homosexuality and Organization's Closure," *Huffington Post,* June 20, 2013, accessed June 24, 2014, http://www.huffingtonpost.com/2013/06/20/exodus-international-homosexuality-_n_3474460.html.

95. See S. J. Creek, "'Not Getting Any Because of Jesus': The Centrality of Desire Management to the Identity Work of Gay, Celibate Christians," *Symbolic Interaction* 36, 2 (2013): 119–36.

96. Mel White, "Warning: Exodus Is Finished but the Ex-Gay Movement Has

Just Begun," *Huffington Post,* June 25, 2013, accessed June 22, 2014, http://www
.huffingtonpost.com/rev-mel-white/warning-exodus-is-finishe_b_3488200
.html.

97. "NARTH statement on Exodus," June 2013, accessed January 15, 2014.
Originally at http://www.narth.com/2013/06/narth-statement-on-exodus; now
available at http://www.narth.org/2013/06/narth-statement-on-exoduss.

98. Alliance for Therapeutic Choice and Scientific Integrity, 2015. Accessed
June 15, 2015. http://www.therapeuticchoice.com. The "NARTH Institute" comprises two of the five divisions of the Alliance for Therapeutic Choice and Scientific Integrity: The "Clinical Division" and the "Research Division." Additional
divisions include "Public Education & Client Rights," "Ethics, Family & Faith,"
and "Medical." These divisions are all under the leadership of an Alliance board
of directors, executive committee, and executive director.

99. Beckstead, interview with author.

100. For a discussion of "pumping" and other methodological concerns with
phallometric testing, see Kurt Freund, Robin Watson, and Douglas Rienzo, "Signs
of Feigning in the Phallometric Test," *Behaviour Research and Therapy* 26, 2
(1988): 105–12; Waidzunas and Epstein, "'For Men Arousal Is Orientation.'"

101. Olga Khazan, "Can Sexuality Be Changed?," *Atlantic,* June 3, 2015,
accessed June 15, 2015, http://www.theatlantic.com/health/archive/2015/06/
can-sexuality-be-changed/394490.

5. A National Movement against "Homos"

1. Rebecca Hodes, "Uganda Throws a Party to Celebrate Passing of Anti-Gay
Law," *Guardian,* April 2, 2014, accessed June 12, 2014, http://www.theguardian
.com/world/2014/apr/02/uganda-celebrates-anti-gay-law.

2. Abby Ohlheiser, "Ugandan Lawmakers Promise to Revive Their Anti-Gay
Law, Just Days after the Country's Constitutional Court Struck It Down," *Washington Post,* August 5, 2014.

3. Scott Lively and Kevin Abrams, *The Pink Swastika: Homosexuality in the
Nazi Party* (Keiser, Ore.: Founders Publishing Company, 1995).

4. UN Secretary-General Ban Ki-moon, "Remarks to Special Event on 'Leadership in the Fight against Homophobia,'" United Nations, December 10, 2012,
accessed January 28, 2014, http://www.un.org/sg/statements/index.asp?nid=6504.
Hillary Rodham Clinton, "Clinton's Human Rights Day Speech on Gay Rights,"
U.S. Department of State, December 6, 2011, accessed January 28, 2014, http://
www.monitor.co.ug/News/World/-/688340/1286050/-/11l4a0i/-/index.html.

5. Reuters, "Obama Condemns Uganda Anti-Gay Bill as 'Odious,'" February 4,
2010, accessed January 28, 2014, http://www.reuters.com/article/2010/02/04/
us-uganda-gays-obama-idUSTRE6134EZ20100204. BBC News, "Uganda Fury at
David Cameron Aid Threat over Gay Rights," October 31, 2011, accessed January 28, 2014, http://www.bbc.co.uk/news/world-africa-15524013.

6. Frank Jordans, "U.N. Protection Resolution Passes, Hailed as a 'Historic
Moment,'" *Huffington Post,* June 17, 2011, accessed January 29, 2014, http://www
.huffingtonpost.com/2011/06/17/un-gay-rights-protection-resolution-passes
-_n_879032.html.

7. Patrick Strudwick, "Dinesh Bhugra: Psychiatry Needs a Broader Focus,"

Guardian, November 26, 2013, accessed January 28, 2014, http://www.theguardian
.com/society/2013/nov/27/dinesh-bhugra-psychiatry-mental-illness.

8. Psychological Society of South Africa, "An Open Statement from the Psychological Society of South Africa to the People and Leaders of Uganda concerning the Anti-Homosexuality Bill 2009," 2010, accessed January 28, 2014, http://
www.psyssa.com/documents/Open%20Statement%20from%20PsySSA%2023
-02-10.pdf.

9. Psychological Society of South Africa, "Sexuality and Gender Interest Group," accessed January 3, 2014, http://www.psyssa.com/documents/Sexuality
%20and%20Gender%20Interest%20Group.pdf. The PsySSA is part of the International Network on Lesbian, Gay, and Bisexual Concerns and Transgender Issues in Psychology, based at the Lesbian, Gay, Bisexual and Transgender Concerns Office of the American Psychological Association.

10. Daniel Howden, "Kenyan Writer Binyavanga Wainaina Declares 'I Am Homosexual,'" *Guardian,* January 21, 2014, accessed February 8, 2014, http://
www.theguardian.com/world/2014/jan/21/kenyan-writer-binyavanga-wainaina
-declares-homosexuality.

11. Laura Trevelyan, "UN Split over Homosexuality Laws," *BBC News,* December 19, 2008, accessed January 29, 2014, http://news.bbc.co.uk/2/hi/europe/
7791063.stm.

12. Gardiner Harris, "India's Supreme Court Restores an 1861 Law Banning Gay Sex," *New York Times,* December 12, 2013, A6. A lower court had declared the law unconstitutional in 2009.

13. David M. Herszenhorn, "Gays in Russia Find No Haven, Despite Support from the West," *New York Times,* August 12, 2013, A1.

14. Al Jazeera, "Nigeria Passes Law against Gay Relationships," January 13, 2014, accessed January 25, 2014, http://www.aljazeera.com/news/africa/2014/01/
nigeria-passes-law-banning-gay-marriage-2014113151626685617.html.

15. Charles Sakala, "Zambia: New Zambian Constitution to Ban Homosexuality," *Zambia Reports,* April 15, 2013, accessed January 26, 2014, http://allafrica
.com/stories/201304161240.html.

16. Daniel Politi, "Zimbabwe President Robert Mugabe Vows to Behead Gays," slate.com, July 28, 2013, accessed January 28, 2014, http://www.slate.com/
blogs/the_slatest/2013/07/28/zimbabwe_president_robert_mugabe_vows_to
_behead_gays.html.

17. Trevelyan, "UN Split over Homosexuality Laws."

18. The question of how science travels has been posed in the science studies literature on transnational negotiations in technoscience. Analysts have observed cases where science travels from the West to a location with fewer resources and less government regulation. Petryna examined "how experiments travel" in clinical drug trials to nations with fewer regulations. Scientists from funding nations may take advantage of these conditions. Adriana Petryna, *When Experiments Travel: Clinical Trials and the Global Search for Human Subjects* (Princeton, N.J.: Princeton University Press, 2009). Sleeboom-Faulkner and Patra examined how entrepreneurs trained in the West go to developing countries with fewer regulations to set up "bionetworks" for experimenting with controversial procedures like stem cell research; Margaret Sleeboom-Faulkner and Prasanna

Kumar Patra, "Experimental Stem Cell Therapy: Biohierarchies and Bionetworking in Japan and India," *Social Studies of Science* 41, 4 (2011): 645–96. Rajan theorized "biocapital," examining global inequalities in relation to the development of biotechnologies across the United States and India; Kaushik Sunder Rajan, *Biocapital: The Constitution of Postgenomic Life* (Durham, N.C.: Duke University Press, 2006). Finally, Crane examined how researchers in Uganda studying ways in which HIV/AIDS medications may prevent mother-to-child transmission of the virus advocated for lower research standards for pragmatic purposes, walking a tightrope between agreement and disagreement with the Global North to maintain their legitimacy as scientists; Johanna Taylor Crane, *Scrambling for Africa: AIDS, Expertise, and the Rise of American Global Health Science* (Ithaca, N.Y.: Cornell University Press, 2013). Like Crane, this chapter examines how practitioners must walk a tightrope across communities, but in this case, the social conditions involve *more* government regulation rather than less.

19. Joseph Massad, "Re-Orienting Desire: The Gay International and the Arab World," *Public Culture* 14, 2 (2002): 361–85; Joseph Massad, *Desiring Arabs* (Chicago: University of Chicago Press, 2007).

20. Jeff Sharlet, *The Family: The Secret Fundamentalism at the Heart of American Power* (New York: HarperPerennial, 2008); Jeff Sharlet, *C Street: The Fundamentalist Threat to American Democracy* (New York: Little, Brown, 2011).

21. *"Vanguard": Missionaries of Hate*, Jim Fraenkel, director (Current TV, 2010); *God Loves Uganda*, Roger Ross Williams, director (Variance Films, 2013).

22. "Russia's Anti-Gay Law Is One of my 'Proudest Achievements,' Claims Pastor Scott Lively," *Huffington Post*, September 24, 2013, accessed January 8, 2014, http://www.huffingtonpost.com/2013/09/24/russia-scott-lively-_n_3982608 .html.

23. *"Vanguard": Missionaries of Hate*.

24. Member of Parliament David Bahati, interview with author, Parliament Building, Kampala, Uganda, 2011.

25. Sylvia Tamale, dean of Faculty of Law, interview with author, Makerere University, Kampala, Uganda, 2011.

26. Margaret Keck and Kathryn Sikkink, *Activists beyond Borders: Advocacy Networks in International Politics* (Ithaca, N.Y.: Cornell University Press, 1998), 2.

27. Ibid., 9.

28. Sidney Tarrow, *The New Transnational Activism* (Cambridge: Cambridge University Press, 2006).

29. Peter A. Jackson, *Queer Bangkok: 21st Century Markets, Media, and Rights* (Hong Kong: Hong Kong University Press, 2011).

30. Aili Mari Tripp, *Museveni's Uganda: Paradoxes of Power in a Hybrid Regime* (Boulder, Colo.: Lynne Rienner Publishers, 2010).

31. Giles Fraser, "Given Uganda's Homophobia, Why Does It Lead the Way in Googling Gay Porn?," *Guardian*, January 10, 2014, accessed June 24, 2014, http://www.theguardian.com/commentisfree/belief/2014/jan/10/uganda-homophobic -googling-gay-porn.

32. Rev. Dr. Alex Ojacor, "Uganda: Biwempe and the Cult of Pastors," *New Vision*, November 4, 2006, accessed February 8, 2014, http://allafrica.com/ stories/200611060589.html.

33. Alessandro Gusman, "HIV/AIDS, Pentecostal Churches, and the 'Joseph Generation' in Uganda," *Africa Today* 56, 1 (2009): 66–86.

34. Rev. Kapya Kaoma, *Globalizing the Culture Wars: U.S. Conservatives, African Churches, & Homophobia* (Boston, Mass.: Political Research Associates, 2009).

35. Ibid., 9–10.

36. Edward C. Green et al., "Uganda's HIV Prevention Success: The Role of Sexual Behavior Change and the National Response," *AIDS and Behavior* 10, 4 (2006): 335–46.

37. Dennis Muhumuza, "Janet Museveni's Dream for Ugandan Youth," accessed October 1, 2014, http://janetmuseveni.org/newsroom/youth.php.

38. Josh Kron, "In Uganda, an AIDS Success Story Comes Undone," *New York Times,* August 3, 2012, A5.

39. Frank Mugisha, director, Sexual Minorities Uganda, interview with author, undisclosed location, Uganda, 2011.

40. Seggane Musisi, interview with author, Kampala, Uganda, 2011.

41. Massad, "Re-Orienting Desire," 383–84.

42. Kopano Ratele, "Male Sexualities and Masculinities," in *African Sexualities: A Reader,* ed. Sylvia Tamale (Oxford: Pambazuka Press, 2011).

43. "Demonstration in Jinja, Uganda in support of Anti-Gay Bill," *Box Turtle Bulletin,* February 15, 2010, accessed June 24, 2014, http://www.youtube.com/watch?v=fCgjtgmBMmU. Subsequent quotations in this paragraph are transcribed from this YouTube footage.

44. Susan Muyiyi, "UNICEF Book Supports Teen Homosexuality," April 5, 2009, accessed February 8, 2014, http://www.newvision.co.ug/D/8/12/676939.

45. See *Call Me Kuchu,* Malika Zouhali-Worrall and Katherine Fairfax Wright, directors (Cinedigm Entertainment Group, 2012).

46. Before converting to evangelical Christianity, Martin Ssempa witnessed the death of his brother and sister from AIDS and blamed sexual promiscuity. After attending Makerere University he obtained a counseling degree from Philadelphia Biblical Seminary (now Cairn University) in Langhorne, Pennsylvania. Arthur Baguma, "Martin Ssempa Turned Saturday Night at MUK into Prime Time," *New Vision,* June 23, 2008, accessed June 23, 2014, http://www.newvision.co.ug/D/9/657/631662.

47. *"Vanguard": Missionaries of Hate.*

48. Martin Ssempa, "Uganda Response Letter to Rick Warren 1," December 28, 2009, accessed June 23, 2014, http://www.youtube.com/watch?v=3YqEw6rq-V8.

49. Family Life Network, group interview (five members) with author, Kampala, Uganda, 2011.

50. Scott Lively, "Witness to Revival in Africa: A Report of the Ministry of Scott and Anne Lively in Uganda, Kenya, and Egypt, June 12–25, 2002," Abiding Truth Ministries, accessed June 24, 2014, http://www.defendthefamily.com/_docs/resources/3038513.pdf.

51. "Uganda Response Letter to Rick Warren 1." A similar controversy over the virgin myth erupted in South Africa in 2002. While many argued that there really was no risk of people committing "aggravated defilement," some believed that it happens because of insufficient access to treatments for HIV/AIDS;

IRIN News, "SOUTH AFRICA: Focus on the Virgin Myth and HIV/AIDS," April 25, 2002, accessed January 29, 2014, http://www.irinnews.org/report/39838/south-africa-focus-on-the-virgin-myth-and-hiv-aids.

52. IRIN News, "UGANDA: Death Penalty for HIV-Positive Child Sex Offenders," April 19, 2007, accessed June 23, 2014, http://www.irinnews.org/report/71713/uganda-death-penalty-for-hiv-positive-child-sex-offenders.

53. *"Vanguard": Missionaries of Hate.*

54. "Interview with George Oundo of Uganda on His Homophobic Campaign," TheMasterloader, May 3, 2009, accessed February 8, 2014, http://www.youtube.com/watch?v=gb_u0SsSV24.

55. Martin Ssempa, "A Prayer for George Oundo—Determined to Leave Sodomy for Salvation," Martin Ssempa, PhD, March 12, 2010, accessed January 11, 2014, http://martinssempa.blogspot.com/2010/03/prayer-for-george-oundo-determined-to.html.

56. Brian Nkoyooyo, director, Icebreakers Uganda, interview with author, undisclosed location, Uganda, 2011.

57. Famly Life Network, group interview with author, Kampala, Uganda, 2011.

58. Ibid.

59. MP David Bahati, interview with author, Kampala, Uganda, 2011.

60. Charles Tuhaise, president of NASWU, interview with author, Ugandan Parliament Building, Kampala, Uganda, 2011.

61. Isadora Hare, "Defining Social Work for the 21st Century: The International Federation of Social Workers' Revised Definition of Social Work," *International Social Work* 47, 3 (2004): 407–24.

62. NASWU, "National Association of Social Workers of Uganda," 2011, accessed December 15, 2011, http://www.naswu.org.

63. "Charles Tuhaise, Principal Research Officer for Uganda's Parliament," *Mother Jones*, March 10, 2014, accessed June 23, 2014, http://www.youtube.com/watch?v=-hDK31T1CiU.

64. Tuhaise, interview with author, 2011.

65. NASWU, "Statement on Anti-Homosexuality Bill 2009," 2010, accessed January 15, 2011, http://www.naswu.org; also see Warren Throckmorton, "Uganda Social Work Association Calls for Prohibition on Homosexuality," March 26, 2010, accessed June 23, 2014, http://www.patheos.com/blogs/warrenthrockmorton/2010/03/26/uganda-social-work-association-calls-for-prohibition-on-homosexuality.

66. Tuhaise, interview with author, 2011.

67. Ibid.

68. Ibid.

69. NASWU, "Statement on Anti-Homosexuality Bill 2009."

70. Tuhaise, interview with author, 2011.

71. Ibid.

72. NASWU, "Statement on Anti-Homosexuality Bill 2009."

73. Tuhaise, interview with author, 2011.

74. "IFSW Statement on Anti-Homosexuality Bill," IFSW, President David N. Jones, 2010, accessed July 1, 2011, http://www.ifsw.org/p38002016.html.

75. Gary Bailey, president of IFSW, "Letter to President Museveni, Ugandan

Parliament," December 20, 2013, accessed January 13, 2014, http://cdn.ifsw.org/assets/ifsw_104716–6.pdf.

76. Alexis Okeowo, "Gay and Proud in Uganda," *New Yorker*, blog entry, August 6, 2012, accessed June 23, 2014, http://www.newyorker.com/online/blogs/newsdesk/2012/08/gay-and-proud-in-uganda.html.

77. Val Kalende, "Gay Ugandans, Loud and Proud," in *Africa Perspectives* (IGLHRC, 2012), accessed January 12, 2014, https://iglhrc.org/sites/default/files/AfricaPerspectivesFinal.pdf.

78. Sylvia Tamale, "Out of the Closet: Unveiling Sexuality Discourses in Africa," *Feminist Africa* 2 (2012), accessed February 8, 2014, http://agi.ac.za/sites/agi.ac.za/files/fa_2_standpoint_3.pdf.

79. Frank Mugisha, SMUG, interview with author, undisclosed location, Uganda, 2011.

80. Leonard Okello, Action AIDS, interview with author, Kampala, Uganda, 2011.

81. Frederick Nzwili, "Ugandans Don't Understand Homosexuality, Says Christopher Ssenyonjo, former Anglican Bishop," *Huffington Post*, December 20, 2013, accessed February 8, 2014, http://www.huffingtonpost.com/2013/12/20/ugandan-homosexuality-bishop_n_4481437.html.

82. Nkoyooyo, interview with author, 2011.

83. *Kuchus of Uganda*, Mathilda Piehl, director (RFSL, 2008).

84. Nkoyooyo, interview with author.

85. "2011: Frank Mugisha, Uganda," Robert F. Kennedy Center for Justice and Human Rights, 2011, accessed January 29, 2014, http://rfkcenter.org/2011-frank-mugisha.

86. "Sexual Minorities Uganda vs. Scott Lively," Center for Constitutional Rights, 2012, accessed January 29, 2014, http://ccrjustice.org/LGBTUganda.

87. In a strong sense, this activist work aligns with Keck and Sikkink's notion of the "boomerang pattern" in transnational advocacy network strategy. When faced with blocked access to rights or resources, as in the situation experienced by SMUG, local activists may reach out to allies abroad to put pressure on the oppressive state. While SMUG is constrained in the kinds of activism it can conduct in the country, transnational activism may be able to apply other kinds of pressure. In a postcolonial context, however, pressure from abroad faces the criticism of "Western influence," making locality a key asset for SMUG members. Keck and Sikkink, *Activists beyond Borders*.

88. Joshua Gamson, "Messages of Exclusion: Gender, Movements, and Symbolic Boundaries." *Gender and Society* 11, 2 (1997): 178–99.

89. ILGA, "ILGA's Public Stance against Paedophilia and Commitment to the Protection of Children," 2006, accessed January 6, 2014, http://ilga.org/ilga/en/article/861.

90. ILGA, "Call to Action: International Protest against Child Abuse in front of the Vatican Embassies," 2010, accessed January 6, 2014, http://ilga.org/ilga/en/article/mnWP2Sg1t3.

91. Sylvia Tamale, interview with author, Kampala, Uganda, 2011.

92. Susan Dicklitch and Doreen Lwanga, "The Politics of Being Non-Political: Human Rights Organizations and the Creation of a Positive Human Rights Culture in Uganda," *Human Rights Quarterly* 25, 2 (2003): 482–509.

93. Sexual Minorities Uganda, "From Torment to Tyranny: Enhanced Persecution in Uganda Following the Passage of the Anti-Homosexuality Act 2014," 2014, accessed June 23, 2014, http://www.sexualminoritiesuganda.com/Torment%20to%20Tyranny%2009–05–2014%20FINAL.pdf.

94. Tabu Butagira, Agatha Ayebazibwe, and Stephen Otage, "Ugandans Lose Jobs as US Cuts Funding," March 13, 2014, accessed June 23, 2014, http://www.africareview.com/News/Ugandans-lose-jobs-as-US-cuts-funding/-/979180/2242010/-/10tst4xz/-/index.html.

95. Tamale, interview with author.

96. Mugisha, interview with author, 2011.

97. Center for Constitutional Rights, "Sexual Minorities Uganda v. Scott Lively," accessed October 1, 2014, http://ccrjustice.org/LGBTUganda.

98. Laurie Goodstein, "Ugandan Gay Rights Group Sues U.S. Evangelist," *New York Times*, March 15, 2012, A20. This coffeehouse, which offers free coffee to teenagers in exchange for conversation and religious fellowship, had been a site of controversy the year before when truant students were congregating at the store during school hours. Soon afterward, the manager, who lived in an apartment above the store, was arrested for not registering as a sex offender, though Lively denied knowledge of this. Peter Goonan, "Police Arrest Manager of Holy Grounds Coffee House—Operated by Anti-Gay Pastor Scott Lively—as Unregistered Sex Offender," Masslive.com, January 13, 2011, accessed October 1, 2014, http://www.masslive.com/news/index.ssf/2011/01/springfield_police_arrested_ho.html.

99. Conor Berry, "Anti-Gay Activist Scott Lively's Crimes-against-Humanity Case to Proceed after Federal Court Denies His Petition to Dismiss Lawsuit," MassLive, December 5, 2014, accessed June 15, 2015, http://www.masslive.com/news/index.ssf/2014/12/scott_lively.html.

100. Interview with anonymous therapist, undisclosed location, Uganda, 2011.

101. Tamale, "Out of the Closet." In this passage, Tamale cites S. Murray and W. Roscoe, *Boy-Wives and Female Husbands: Studies of African Homosexualities* (New York: St. Martin's Press: 1998); Feminist Review, ed., *Sexuality: A Reader* (London, Virago Press, 1987); J. Driberg, *The Lango: A Nilotic Tribe in Uganda* (London: Thorner Coryndon, 1923); J. Laurance, *The Iteso: Fifty Years of Change in a Nilo-Hamitic Tribe of Uganda* (Oxford: Oxford University Press, 1957); M. Mushanga, "The Nkole of Southwestern Uganda," in *Cultural Sources Materials for Population Planning in East Africa: Beliefs and Practices*, ed. A. Molnos (Nairobi: East African Publishing House, 1973); R. Needham, "Right and Left in Nyoro Symbolic Classification," in *Right and Left: Essays on Dual Classification* (Chicago: University of Chicago Press, 1973); M. Southwold, "The Baganda of Central Uganda," in Molnos, *Cultural Source Materials for Population Planning in East Africa;* J. Faupel, *African Holocaust: The Story of the Uganda Martyrs* (New York: P. J. Kennedy, 1962).

102. According to Driberg, *mudoko dako* males were deemed "impotent," adopted the dress and social roles of women, and could marry men. Driberg, *The Lango*. In a gender and sexual orientation system such as that associated with white gay and transgender rights advocates in the United States, such an arrangement might evoke the identity of "heterosexual transwoman" rather than "homosexual."

103. Uganda Health and Science Press Association, *Gay Love in Pre-colonial Africa: The Untold Story of Ugandan Martyrs* (Kampala: UHSPA Uganda, 2012).

104. Tamale, interview with author.

105. Leonard Okello, interview with author.

106. See Seggane Musisi and Eugene Kinyanda, eds., *Psychiatric Problems of HIV/AIDS and Their Management in Africa* (Kampala, Uganda: Fountain Publishers, 2009).

107. Musisi, interview with author.

108. Anonymous psychiatrist, interview with author, Kampala, Uganda, 2011.

109. Paul Nyende, interview with author, Makere University, Kampala, Uganda, 2011.

110. Ibid.

111. Musisi, interview with author.

112. Ibid.

113. Nyende, interview with author.

114. Paul Bangirana, interview with author, Makerere University, Kampala, Uganda, 2011.

115. Ibid.

116. A press release from the National Resistance Movement Caucus listed the original members of the eleven-member Ministry of Health panel who presented the report to President Museveni and the NRM Caucus: Dr. Jane Ruth Aceng, director general of health services; Dr. Isaac Ezati, director of planning and development at the Ministry of Health; Dr. Jacinto Amandua, commissioner clinical services; Dr. Sheila Ndyanabangi, head, mental health desk; Prof. Seggane Musisi, professor of psychiatry at Makerere; Assoc. Prof. Eugene Kinyanda, senior research scientist, Medical Research Council; Dr. David Basangwa, director, Butabika Hospital; Dr. Sylvester Onzivua, senior pathologist, Mulago Hospital; Dr, Misaki Wayengera, geneticist, Makerere; Dr. Paul Bangirana, clinical psychologist, Makere; Prof. Wilson Byarugaba, retired professor and former head of human and molecular genetics, Department of Pathology, Makerere. Vision Reporter, "Uganda Scientists Turn Homosexuality Debate Around," *New Vision*, February 15, 2014, accessed June 15, 2015, http://www.newvision.co.ug/news/652594-uganda-scientists-turn-homosexuality-debate-around.html.

117. Ministry of Health, Republic of Uganda. Scientific Statement on Homosexuality, February 10, 2014, 6, accessed June 15, 2015, http://www.boxturtlebulletin.com/btb/wpcontent/uploads/2014/02/UgandaScientificReportOnHomosexuality.pdf. Emphasis in the original.

118. Ibid., 7–8.

119. Vision Reporter, "Uganda Scientists Turn Homosexuality Debate Around." On February 23, 2014, the day before Museveni signed the Anti-Homosexuality Bill into law, the Ministry of Health issued a second report, intended to be the final version. Its release was publicly overshadowed by the signing of the bill. Musisi and Kinyanda do not appear as members of the panel in the final report. Replacing them are Assoc. Prof. Charles Ibingira, dean/surgeon/anatomist, School of Biomedical Sciences, Makerere University College of Health Sciences; and Dr. Hannington Kasozi, lecturer in neuropsychiatry, Department of Medical Physiology, School of Biomedical Sciences, Makerere University College of Health Sciences. This version drops all discussion of whether homosexuality should be regulated, and instead focuses exclusively on whether homosexuality is caused by "nature" or "nurture." It includes a more extensive literature

review of scientific studies on this question. The report concludes, "Nature (genes) and nurture (environment) interact to yield homosexuality. Nurture appears to play a greater role, however, as the heritability coefficient of homosexuality is evidently low." Ministry of Health, Republic of Uganda, *Scientific Evidence on Homosexuality*, February 23, 2014, 11, accessed June 15, 2015, http:// wp.patheos.com.s3.amazonaws.com/blogs/warrenthrockmorton/files/2014/02/ FINAL24th-Feb-2014.pdf.

120. Amy Lind, "Introduction: Development, Global Governance, and Sexual Subjectivities," in *Development, Sexual Rights, and Global Governance* (New York: Routledge, 2010), 1–20.

Conclusion

1. Shapin, "Cordelia's Love."

2. A. Lee Beckstead, interview with author, Salt Lake City, 2009.

3. Star and Griesemer, "Institutional Ecology, Translations, and Boundary Objects."

4. Epstein, *Impure Science*, 333.

5. Steven Epstein, "Activism, Drug Regulation, and the Politics of Therapeutic Evaluation in the AIDS Era: A Case Study of ddC and the 'Surrogate Markers' Debate," *Social Studies of Science* 27, 5 (1997): 716.

6. Evelleen Richards, "The Politics of Therapeutic Evaluation: The Vitamin C and Cancer Controversy," *Social Studies of Science* 18, 4 (1988): 686.

7. If we acknowledge that objects have agency as well, then politics becomes an even more complicated affair. See Bruno Latour, *Reassembling the Social: An Introduction to Actor-Network Theory* (New York: Oxford University Press, 2005).

8. Sedgwick, *Epistemology of the Closet*.

9. Ibid., 26.

10. Dawne Moone has observed an analogous dynamic within the domain of religion. In conflicts over homosexuality, church members claimed that "our" theology is pure while "their" theology was corrupted by politics. Yet, no theology is free of human mediation and social construction. Dawne Moone, *God, Sex, and Politics: Homosexuality and Everyday Theologies* (Chicago: University of Chicago Press, 2004).

11. On enrollment of allies and trials of strength, see Bruno Latour, *Science in Action*.

12. For example, during the pedophile priest scandal in the Catholic Church, gay priests were targeted for firing because many of the victims were boys. Stephen Clark, "Gay Priests and Other Bogeymen," *Journal of Homosexuality* 51, 4 (2006): 1–13.

13. Alix Spigel, "Can Therapy Help Change Sexual Orientation?," NPR, August 1, 2011, accessed October 1, 2014, http://www.npr.org/blogs/health/2011/08/01/138820526/can-therapy-help-change-sexual-orientation.

14. Amin Ghaziani, "Post-Gay Collective Identity Construction," *Social Problems* 58, 1 (2011): 99–125.

15. Suzanna Danuta Walters, *The Tolerance Trap: How God, Genes, and Good Intentions Are Sabotaging Gay Equality* (New York: New York University Press, 2014).

16. Rebecca Jordan-Young has argued that while there is much hype about brain organization theory in the media today, little of the theory has been proved, primarily because research conducted is quasi experimental, and outcome research is largely inconclusive due to shifting gender meanings in society. Sexual orientation research is often confounded by inconsistencies with regard to whether gay men are supposed to be like heterosexual women or like lesbians, and whether lesbians are supposed to be like heterosexual or gay men. See Rebecca Jordan-Young, *Brainstorm: The Flaws in the Science of Sex Differences* (Cambridge, Mass.: Harvard University Press, 2011).

17. LGBTscience.org, "Dr. Simon LeVay," accessed October 1, 2014, http:// www.lgbtscience.org/simon-levay.

18. LGBTscience.org, "Dr. Milton Diamond," accessed October 1, 2014, http:// www.lgbtscience.org/milton-diamond.

19. Kate O'Riordan, "The Life of the Gay Gene: From Hypothetical Genetic Marker to Social Reality," *Journal of Sex Research* 49, 4 (2012): 362–68.

20. The origins of the gender/sex binary have been traced to the theories of John Money and Anke Ehrhardt, who created a theory of gender in work with intersex infants. See Joanne Meyerowitz, *How Sex Changed: A History of Transsexuality in the United States* (Cambridge, Mass.: Harvard University Press, 2004).

21. See Suzanne Kessler, *Lessons from the Intersexed* (New Brunswick, N.J.: Rutgers University Press, 1998); Anne Fausto-Sterling, *Sexing the Body: Gender Politics and the Construction of Sexuality* (New York: Basic Books, 2000); Katrina Karkazis, *Fixing Sex: Intersex, Medical Authority, and Lived Experience* (Durham, N.C.: Duke University Press, 2008).

22. Diamond, *Sexual Fluidity.*

23. Diamond, "Reconsidering 'Sexual Desire' in the Context of Reparative Therapy," 430.

24. Cavan Sieczkowski, "'Ex-Gay' Group Erects Billboard Saying 'Nobody Is Born Gay,'" *Huffington Post*, December 10, 2014, accessed December 12, 2014, http://www.huffingtonpost.com/2014/12/10/ex-gay-billboard-virginia_n _6301334.html.

25. Gagnon and Simon, *Sexual Conduct.*

26. Ken Plummer, *Telling Sexual Stories: Power, Change, and Social Worlds* (New York: Routledge, 1994).

27. Giddens, *Transformation of Intimacy.*

28. Foucault, *History of Sexuality,* vol. 1.

29. John H. Gagnon and William Simon, *Sexual Conduct: The Social Sources of Human Sexuality,* 2nd ed. (New Brunswick, N.J.: Aldine Transaction, 2005), 2.

30. See Steven Epstein, "Sexuality and Identity: The Contribution of Object Relations Theory to Constructionist Sociology," *Theory and Society* 20, 6 (1991): 825–73.

31. See Elizabeth Wilson, *Psychosomatic: Feminism and the Neurological Body* (Durham, N.C.: Duke University Press, 2004).

32. Hacking, "Making Up People."

33. Tom Boellstorff, *The Gay Archipelago: Sexuality and Nation in Indonesia* (Princeton, N.J.: Princeton University Press, 2005).

34. Massad, "Reorienting Desire."

35. Héctor Carrillo, *The Night Is Young: Sexuality in Mexico in the Time of AIDS* (Chicago: University of Chicago Press, 2002).

36. Gilbert Herdt, *The Sambia: Ritual and Gender in New Guinea* (New York: Holt, Reinhart, and Winston, 1987).

37. Michel Foucault, *History of Sexuality*, vol. 3, *The Care of the Self* (New York: Vintage Books, 1984).

38. Edward O. Laumann et al., *The Social Organization of Sexuality: Sexual Practices in the United States* (Chicago: University of Chicago Press, 1994).

39. Jane Ward, "Dude Sex: White Masculinities and 'Authentic' Heterosexuality among Dudes Who Have Sex with Dudes," *Sexualities* 11, 4 (2008): 414–34; Jane Ward, *Not Gay: Sex Between Straight White Men* (New York: New York University Press, 2015).

40. Escoffier, "Gay for Pay."

41. Kenji Yoshino, "The Epistemic Contract of Bisexual Erasure," *Stanford Law Review* 52, 2 (2000): 353–461.

42. Boellstorff, *The Gay Archipelago*, 10–11.

43. Jasanoff, "The Idiom of Co-Production."

44. Boaventura de Sousa Santos, "Toward a Multicultural Conception of Human Rights," in *Moral Imperialism: A Critical Anthology*, ed. Berta Hernández-Truyol (New York: New York University Press, 2002).

45. The position that challenges the marginalization of a sexual expression with the phrase "not inherently shameful" is, in part, inspired by Hoang's assertion in her ethnography of sex workers in Vietnam: "I do not believe that having sex for pay is shameful." Kimberly Kay Hoang, *Dealing in Desire: Asian Ascendancy, Western Decline, and the Hidden Currencies of Global Sex Work* (Berkeley: University of California Press, 2015), 21.

46. Judith Halberstam, *Queer Art of Failure* (Durham, N.C.: Duke University Press, 2011).

47. Eve Kosofsky Sedgwick, "How to Bring Your Kids Up Gay," *Social Text* 29 (1991): 18–27.

48. Katz, *Invention of Heterosexuality*, 17.

49. Seidman, *The Social Construction of Sexuality*, xiv.

Methodological Appendix

1. Epstein, *Impure Science.*

2. Epstein, "Patient Groups and Health Movements."

3. Foucault, *Archaeology of Knowledge.*

4. Foucault, *Power/Knowledge.*

5. On principles of symmetry from the sociology of scientific knowledge, see David Bloor, *Knowledge and Social Imagery* (New York: Henley, 1976).

6. For more on the process of "technosexual scripting" in the processes of coconstructing technologies and sexual subjectivities, see Tom Waidzunas and Steven Epstein, "'For Men Arousal Is Orientation': Bodily Truthing, Technosexual Scripts, and the Materialization of Sexualities through the Phallometric Test," *Social Studies of Science* 45, 2 (2015): 187–213.

7. For example, see Kathleen Blee, *Inside Organized Racism: Women in the Hate Movement* (Berkeley: University of California Press, 2003).

INDEX

adaptational school of psychoanalysis, 42–45, 47. *See also* Rado, Sandor
aggravated defilement, 200, 300n51
Ahmed, Sara, 19. *See also* queer theory
AIDS (acquired immune deficiency syndrome), 82, 85, 91, 290n4; in Uganda, 193. *See also* HIV/AIDS prevention in Uganda
AIDS activism, 85; in Uganda, 219
Alder, Ken, 131, 288n60. *See also* polygraph
American Academy of Pediatrics (AAP): position statements on homosexuality, 7, 88–90
American Counseling Association (ACA), 130; position statement on homosexuality, 7, 88–90
American Medical Association (AMA): position statements on homosexuality, 88–90, 107–8, 264n10
American Psychiatric Association (APA), 7, 86; position statements on homosexuality, 72, 88–90, 93, 96; resolution against Anti-Homosexuality Bill, 187
American Psychiatric Association Nomenclature Committee, 71–73. *See also* Silverstein, Charles; Spitzer, Robert
American Psychoanalytic Association (APA): position statements on homosexuality, 85, 88–90
American Psychological Association (APA): affirmative policy on diversity, 156, 175–77; Code of Ethics, 133–34, 155–57, 173–75; Division 44, 82; governance structure, 26–27, 162; position statements

on homosexuality, 74–75, 88–90, 92–93, 98, 109, 146, 151–54, 163; President's Town Hall Meeting, 162–64; Public Interest Directorate, 152–54; public policy advocacy, 6–7; resolutions on religion and psychology, 174–75, 295n74
American Psychological Association Task Force on Appropriate Therapeutic Responses to Sexual Orientation (APA Task Force), 150–63; charge, 163; members, 157–60; NARTH critique of composition, 160–63; NARTH nominees, 154–57. *See also* Beckstead, A. Lee; Drescher, Jack; Glassgold, Judith; Greene, Beverly; Miller, Robin Lin; Worthington, Roger
Anderson, Clinton, 151–54, 163. *See also* American Psychological Association: Public Interest Directorate; citizen science; Office of Lesbian, Gay, Bisexual, and Transgender Concerns
Anti-Homosexuality Act (Uganda), 185; celebration in Kampala, 185; repeal, 185
Anti-Homosexuality Bill (Uganda), 33, 177, 200; as pressure to overcome homosexuality, 202; provision against pro-gay advocacy, 222–23
anti-homosexuality movement (Uganda), 195–209, 228; Jinja march, 195; waves, 196. *See also* Bahati, David; Family Life Network; National Association of Social Workers of Uganda; Ssempa, Martin; Tuhaise, Charles

anti-reorientation activism. *See*
Besen, Wayne; Beyond Ex-Gay;
Box Turtle Bulletin; Burroway, Jim;
Ex-Gay Watch; Soulforce; Truth
Wins Out
*Appropriate Therapeutic Responses to
Sexual Orientation* (APA report,
2009), 4, 7, 149–51, 168–77; appeal
to studies with phallometric test,
169–72; elevating measures of
harm, 172–73, 295n69; resource
for laws banning reorientation for
minors, 180–81; review of reori-
entation literature, 168–73; sexual
orientation identity exploration,
176; telic and organismic congru-
ence, 175–76
Arana, Gabriel, 178–79. *See also* ex-
ex-gay; Spitzer, Robert
Association for the Advancement of
Behavior Therapy (AABT), 61–62,
70. *See also* behavior therapy
Association of Gay and Lesbian
Psychiatrists (AGLP), 82, 146–47;
Abomination, 146–47
Association of Gay Psychologists, 74.
See also American Psychological
Association: Division 44
autonomy (APA Code of Ethics),
2, 133–34, 238; within APA
Task Force report, 176–77.
See also informed consent;
self-determination
aversion therapy, 7, 61–63, 166,
277n94; hostility toward, within
United States, 63. *See also* penile
plethysmograph; phallometric test

Bahati, David, 31, 190, 202. *See also*
anti-homosexuality movement
Bailey, Michael, 182, 281n61. *See also*
brain scanning; phallometric test
Bakke, Christine, 122–24, 139–40.
See also Beyond Ex-Gay
Bancroft, John, 62, 102
Bangirana, Paul, 222, 225–26. *See
also* Ugandan psychology

Barad, Karen, 271n89
Barahal, Hyman, 42
Beck, Aaron T., 224
Beckstead, A. Lee, 33, 100, 291n24;
elephant metaphor for reorientation controversy, 231–32; ex-gay /
ex-ex-gay study, 100–101, 142–44;
experience in Kurt Freund
Phallometric Laboratory, 100,
171; horizons of understanding
approach, 142–43; on Jones and
Yarhouse study, 295n69; meeting
and disagreement with Spitzer,
100–101; on NARTH nominees to
APA Task Force, 156; on NARTH's
"What Research Shows," 168; on
phallometric test, 171, 183; on
psychology of religion, 174; role
on APA Task Force, 157–58
behavior therapy, 59–64, 73–75,
235, 275n75; critique of psychoanalysis, 51, 65; consciousness
as epiphenomenal, 60; treatment
failures, 74; treatment of lesbianism, 276n77. *See also individual
behavior therapies*
Bergler, Edmund, 46–47, 165; confrontational therapeutic style, 47;
critique of Kinsey studies, 48
Bernstein, Mary, 265n20
Besen, Wayne, 94, 106, 116, 119–22;
Anything but Straight, 106; letter
to Spitzer, 94. *See also* Truth Wins
Out
Beyond Ex-Gay, 7, 28, 31, 122–26. *See
also* Bakke, Christine; ex-ex-gay;
Toscano, Peterson
Bieber, Irving, 51–53, 70
binaries: critique, 244–46; homo-
sexual/heterosexual, 18–19; male/
female, 19; sex/gender, 244–45;
sexual orientation / sexual orientation identity, 32, 145, 170, 176,
244–46
black boxing of facts, 24. *See also*
Latour, Bruno
Boellstorff, Tom, 250

NARTH (National Association for
Research and Therapy of Homosexuality), 1–6, 31, 86–92, 96,
106–8, 119–21, 132–38, 154–57,
160–69, 232; Alliance for Therapeutic Choice and Scientific Integrity, 182, 237, 297n98; conference,
132–33, 136–38, 165, 289n70,
289n71; division of labor with ex-
gay ministries, 11–12; founding of
organization, 86–87; International
Federation for Therapeutic Choice,
200; *Journal of Human Sexuality*,
164, 237; promoted in Uganda,
186; public policy advocacy, 6, 106;
rift with ex-gay ministries, 12,
137–38, 180–82; "What Research
Shows," 164–68, 293n44, 294n51,
294n52, 294n53. *See also* ex-gay
movement; Nicolosi, Joseph;
Pickup, David; Rekers, George
Alan; Socarides, Charles
National Association of Social Workers (NASW), 7; position statements on homosexuality, 88–90
National Association of Social Workers of Uganda (NASWU), 188,
203–9; statement supporting
Anti-Homosexuality Bill, 204–9,
228; use of NARTH documents
in statement, 206, 209, 228; use
of theology in statement, 206. *See
also* Family Life Network
National Gay and Lesbian Task Force:
Youth in the Crosshairs, 118
naturalist view of homosexuality, 28
Nicolosi, Joseph, 1–2, 263n1; commentary supporting Spitzer
study, 104–5; criticism of APA
Task Force membership, 160–63;
founding of NARTH, 1, 86–88;
letter to American Medical Association, 107–8; letter to APA
president Gerald Koocher, 133–34;
NARTH nominee to APA task
Force, 155–56; presentation of
"What Research Shows" to Kazdin,
163–64; reparative therapy, 1, 87,

263n1; on science and politics rela-
tionship, 87–88. *See also* NARTH
Nicolosi, Linda, 263n1
Nkoyooyo, Brian, 213–14. *See also*
Icebreakers Uganda; SMUG
North American Conference of Ho-
mophile Organizations (NACHO),
57. *See also* homophile movement
Nyende, Paul, 222–25. *See also* Ugan-
dan psychology

Obama, Barack, 186; as target of
Ugandan anti-homosexuality
movement, 195–96, 198–99
Office of Lesbian, Gay, Bisexual, and
Transgender Concerns (APA),
151–54. *See also* American Psychological Association; citizen
science
Okello, Leonard, 211, 219. *See also*
AIDS activism
opposing movement dynamics,
12–14; convergence, 113–16, 147,
239, 286n5; critical event, 13,
116–19; dialogical framing, 13–14;
targeting science, 236–40; targeting state, 12–13, 266n28. *See also*
social movements
oral stage etiology of male homosexuality, 46–47, 52–53. *See also*
Socarides, Charles
orgasmic reconditioning ("Playboy
therapy"), 63. *See also* Davison,
Gerald
Oundo, George/Georgina, 201, 208.
See also ex-ex-gay
Ovesey, Lionel, 50–51; response to
homosexual identity, 57
Owensby, Newdigate, 44–45

Pan American Health Organization
(PAHO): position statement on
homosexuality, 181
Parents and Friends of Ex-Gays
(PFOX), 93–94, 180, 247
Parents and Friends of Lesbians and
Gays (PFLAG), 93, 153
Pattison, Mansell, 79–80

TOM WAIDZUNAS is assistant professor of sociology at Temple University. His work brings together sexuality and gender studies, science studies, and sociology of social movements.

Made in the USA
Columbia, SC
18 January 2025

52106142R00200